AF650297

MOGUL INDIA
1653—1708
OR
STORIA DO MOGOR

Aurangzeb in old age

Frontispiece

MOGUL INDIA
1653–1708

OR

STORIA DO MOGOR

Volume 4

Translated with Introduction and Notes
WILLIAM IRVINE

NICCOLAO MANUCCI

ATLANTIC
PUBLISHERS & DISTRIBUTORS (P) LTD

ATLANTIC
PUBLISHERS & DISTRIBUTORS (P) LTD
7/22, Ansari Road, Darya Ganj, New Delhi
Tel.: +91-11-4077 5252, 2327 3880
E-mail: orders@atlanticbooks.com
Web: www.atlanticbooks.com

This edition published in 2025 by Atlantic Publishers & Distributors (P) Ltd.
Reprint 2022, 2025

Copyright © Atlantic Publishers & Distributors (P) Ltd., 2025, 1989

All rights reserved. No part of this publication may be reproduced, stored in a retrieval system, transmitted or utilized in any form or by any means, electronic, mechanical, photocopying, recording or otherwise, without the prior permission of the copyright owner. Application for such permission should be addressed to the publisher.

Trademark Notice
Product or copyright names may be trademarks or registered trademarks and are used only for identification and explanation without any intent to infringe or defame.

Disclaimer

The author and the publisher have made every effort, to the best of their skill, expertise, and knowledge, to provide correct material in the book. However, if any mistakes persist in the content of the book, the publisher does not take responsibility for them. The publisher shall have no liability to any person or entity with respect to any loss or damage caused, or alleged to have been caused, directly or indirectly, by the information contained in this book.

The author has made every effort to follow copyright law. However, if any work is found to be similar, it is unintentional, and the same should not be used as defamatory or to file a legal suit against the author.

If readers find any mistakes, we would be grateful if they would point them out to us so that they can be corrected in the next edition.

All disputes are subject to the jurisdiction of the Delhi courts only.

Printed & bound in India by Atlantic Print Services

CONTENTS

PART IV. (*Continued*)

PAGE

PART V.

ILLUSTRATIONS TO VOL. IV.

HISTORY OF THE MOGUL

FOURTH PART—*Continued*

[165][1] Relation of what happened in madraspatao from the arrival of the most illustrious and most reverend lord, charles thomas de tournon, patriarch of antioch and apostolic visitor of china, with the powers of legate *a latere, et cetera,* until his departure from this coast of choromandal for the philippine isles.

PREFATORY NOTE ON CHARLES MAILLARD DE TOURNON, PATRIARCH OF ANTIOCH.

[The practice of conceding certain points to the prejudices of high caste Hindus, when they became converts to Christianity, began in India with the mission of the Jesuit Roberto de' Nobili to the so-called Pescaria coast in 1606. The earliest objections to the practice were disposed of by an order from Pope Gregory XV., dated January 31, 1623, 'Romanæ Sedis Antistes.' Another prohibition (in respect to a parallel difficulty in China) was issued by Innocent X. on September 12, 1645, and modified by Alexander VIII. on March 23, 1656. Similar orders were passed from time to time by other Popes. But murmurs on the subject were still heard from the earlier established non-Jesuit missions in China and India. Influenced by the growing importance of these questions, Pope Clement XI., who had received the tiara in November, 1700, resolved to send a legate to India and China with authority to enquire into and dispose of the matters in dispute.

The Pope's choice fell on one of his domestic chaplains, Charles Maillard de Tournon, belonging to a good Savoyard family, and born at Turin on December 21, 1668. On December 21, 1701, the Feast of St. Thomas the Apostle, Tournon was created Patriarch of Antioch, having already been empowered

1. From this point the manuscript ceases to be in French, and is continued in Portuguese.

by a brief dated December 9, 1701, to enquire into and regulate the practices of the missionaries in India and China. He was made Apostolic visitor with the powers of a legate a *latere*, and left Rome on July 4, 1702, taking with him several zealous missionary recruits, and made his way to Spain. While waiting there for some means of transport to the East, he received from the King of France the offer of a passage to India. He therefore left Cadiz on February 9, 1703, and joined the French man-of-war *Maurepas* (Denis de Fontaine, captain) at the Canary Islands, whence they set sail on May 3, 1703.

Clement XI. had already announced the patriarch's deputation to the Archbishop of Goa and the Bishop of San Thome of Meliapur by letters dated June 20, 1702. The legate's instructions were contained in a brief dated July 2, 1702, 'Speculatores Domus Israel.'

On November 4, 1703, the ships were off Madras, and on the 5th close to Pondicherry. The party landed on the evening of November 6 (1703), and proceeded to the house of the Jesuits. Compelled to wait for a means of reaching China, his ultimate destination, the patriarch devoted the nine months of his sojourn at Pondicherry to an enquiry into the differences in India between the Jesuits and the other missionaries. His original intention had been to reserve these questions until his return from China. His principal evidence was drawn from the mouths of two Jesuits, Jean Venant Bouchet, Superior of the Karnatik mission, and Carlo Michaele Berteldi, missionary in Madura. He had interrogated them after having hidden in the room two of his own secretaries, who overheard and were thus able to prove all that was said.

Satisfied that he had arrived at an exhaustive knowledge of the points in dispute, the patriarch drew up a decree dated June 23, 1704. It dealt with the following topics: (1) The omission of saliva, salt, and insufflation at baptism; (2) the imposition of names at baptism other than those in the Roman martyrology; (3) names of holy things and of the sainfs were to be strictly adhered to in translating them, but the Latin form to be retained if possible; (4) baptism of infants not to be unduly postponed; (5) marriages by the *tali* at six or seven years of age were prohibited; (6) no tali was to be worn unless it bore a cross or the image of our Lord; (7) the cord suspending the *tali* round a bride's neck must not have 108 threads, nor be of saffron colour;

Veritable Portrait
du
Cardinal de Tournon Legat aux Indes & a la
Chine en 1702 decedé en 1710 dans sa prison a
Macao

(8) superstitious ceremonies at weddings were prohibited, including any use of an *aresciomaram* (*araśu or* pipal-tree) branch: the number of dishes of food provided and their contents must be altered, and the use of the yellow dishes in which the food was placed must be abandoned, while the use of crowns, supposed to drive off demons, was prohibited; (9) coco-nuts must not be used publicly at weddings, because of the heathen belief in omens obtained by breaking them; (10) no one must be excluded from the church or the confessional, not even women when in a state of impurity; (11) no public feast on a girl's arrival at puberty to be tolerated; (12) the pariahs to be treated as on an equality with every one else—they must be visited during illness, and no differences should be made in the administration of extreme unction; (13) prohibition against Christian musicians attending at Hindu temples; (14) bathing, as allowed by Gregory XV., must be confined to physical cleanliness, and such baths taken at times different from the Hindu usage; (15) the use of ashes of cowdung was prohibited, whether on forehead, chest, or other part of the body, the employment of ashes being only permissible on Ash Wednesday; (16) books of Hindu fable were prohibited, subject to the permission of the missionaries. This decree was published on the 8th, and publicly promulgated on July 11, 1704, the day that the patriarch embarked for Manila.

The Jesuits pressed the legate to suspend the operation of the above decree, chiefly on the ground that such sudden changes would be disastrous. Affected by their appeals, he yielded so far as to grant a suspension for three years, pending orders from Rome, in regard to all the prohibitions except that in the paragraph *ferre partum non possumus*—that is, the heading referring to the pariahs, to which I have given the number 12 in the abstract above entered. At the reiterated instances of the Jesuits he finally included this article also in his order of suspension, as is stated in his letter to the Holy Office of July 9, 1704.

The Jesuits sent two deputies to Rome, Francesco Laynez and Jean Venant Bouchet. On arrival there they found that Pope Clement XI. had already approved the patriarch's decree, as set forth in a decree of the Inquisition dated January 7, 1706, 'until the Holy See should otherwise decide.' The preparation of a summary of the obnoxious rites was ordered, in which were to be included those prohibited by Gregory XV. on January 31, 1623, as well as any other observances of the same kind not specified by the Patriarch of Antioch. The question of the pariahs was to be taken up separately.

The Jesuit appellants began by producing a 'Defence of the Madura Missions,' prepared by Father Laynez. Before it reached the Pope's hands via Portugal Father Laynez had left for India (1708) as successor to the Bishop of Meliapur. The steps taken in India to hinder the execution of the patriarch's decree are sufficiently disclosed in Manucci's text and my notes thereon.

The Patriarch of Antioch reached Manila in 1704, and Macao on April 2, 1705. He was received in audience by the Emperor of China at Pekin on December 31, 1705. In 1707 he was sent back to Macao by the Chinese on the instigation of the Jesuits. There the Portuguese Captain-General threw him into prison, where he died on June 8, 1710. On August 1, 1707, he had been raised to the dignity of Cardinal by Clement XI][1]

Ordinarily the common herd are very simple; thus it is not to be wondered at if they make bold to judge things according to their own rash caprice, resting the apology for their error solely on the subterfuge of a 'Thus they say.' Without getting at the substance of the business, and not having of it more evidence than is furnished to sight or is represented by imagination; disregarding the truth that the latter can never yield a certainty, and not remembering that the former ofttimes produces deception, they are led away by the fact that our intellects cannot endure uncertainty. Thus they constantly come to conclusions differing from reality. This is shown in the tribulation which fell upon the Capuchins of Madras after the arrival of the Lord Patriarch of Antioch at Pudicheri (Pondicherry). It lasted over six months, and disturbed the whole coast of Choromandal. For most people, not to say almost all (I speak of what the common people did), understood that the poor fellows' disgrace arose from two sources, which were in reality only accidents. But they held that he who designs the end must have contrived the plot.

They connected one of these causes, which we will call the first, with five thousand *pagodas* which a Dominican father, an

1. 'Nouvelle Biographie Générale' (Didot), xlv, 546; Norbert, 'Mémoires Historiques' (1747), i. 76, 77, 111, 116, 140, 141, 145; ii. 622; Cristofori, 'Storia dei Cardinali' (Roma, 1888), p. 270.

Armenian by race, had collected by begging during twelve years that he had wandered about for this purpose in these regions by the authority of his superiors and under their written orders. He died at Fort St. George on December 6, 1703, and committed the money to the Capuchins and others[1] with directions to remit it to Bengal and Persia, finally to be delivered over to his convent.

The other matter to which they attributed the Capuchin disgrace was their neglect to go to Pondicherry when summoned by his Excellency (the title of the Lord Patriarch). Yet they were unable to go, being stopped by the gentlemen of the government in the country where they dwelt.

When proceedings were taken against the Capuchins with the excessive rigour that is notorious, the above is what was said, and still to this day is declared; which means, without denying that the common people are very simple-minded, that in this matter their inattention was not to blame for their mistake. Only very wise men could have discovered and judged rightly the proposals which my readers will see stated further on. Let those, then, who wish to have true information on the causes and to know the facts of the case, go on reading this narrative, and they will acquire not only something to divert their minds, but will learn the true story and be profited accordingly.

Be it known, then, in the first place (for it is a certainty), that the Abbé François de St. George,[2] when he arrived at Madras, allowed it to be understood by his manner that his first and chief object (apart from his visitation) was the search for

---

1. This bequest is referred to again in Part V., fols, 69 and 280.
2. Of the twelve persons, including himself, who formed Cardinal de Tournon's party, one was the missionary Abate Francesco San Giorgio di Biandrā, of Turin (see Fatinelli, 'Relazione del Viaggio dall' Isola di Teneriff . . .,' p. 3, a log-book of the voyage out; Roma, 1704, 25 pages). The Abbé's name also appears twice in G. Borghesi, 'Littera Scritta da Pondeceri, February 10, 1704,' translated from the Latin by G. M. de' Crescimbeni, Roma, 1705. Borghesi was the Cardinal's physician. The Abbé is referred to again on fol. 196, and in Part V., fol. 173 (Manila). He is, no doubt, the 'Padre' of 'Fort St. George Public Consultations,' November 16, 1703, who 'came into Town with a complement from the Patriarch to the Governor with a present of Jacob's oyle and wine.' In another place in the Records he is referred to as the 'Abbot.' His name appears in the accounts of Cardinal de Tournon's stay in China, and he was deported from Pekin to Macao between 1706 and 1710 (Norbert, "Mémoires Historiques,' Lisbon edition, vi. 168, 366).

means of opening a negotiation for some places on the coast of Choromandal at which to establish a new company of certain Italian merchants. These men desired to navigate the Indian seas and trade within the territories of the Mogul. The first step to be taken for this design was to secure a capable person of good position, who could solicit this urgent business at the court and obtain a *farman* from the king. Furnished with this document, the new Italian company would be able to trade and deal freely throughout that king's widely-spread and equally admirable empire. Above all was this help wanted in Gulkandah, in which place there are mines of precious diamonds, or to which the stones are easily brought by merchants, it being very near those mines.

He had recourse to me because I spoke the Persian and Hindustan languages perfectly, and had great influence among the Mahomedans coupled with long experience of them. I excused myself on account of old age, and because at present [166] I had little intercourse with the king's court. Thus the Abate addressed himself to certain other persons. But as these affairs can only be prosecuted with exceeding slowness, and cannot be carried out except by the power of money, time (to which I now leave the question) will show hereafter the success of this first object, as to which up to the present nothing more is known.

The second matter, or what in the second place appeared essential to the Abate in order to give a happy start to his project, was to eject the Capuchins from Madras, and the Reverend Father Paulo de Saa from Cuddalore.[1] The latter priest administered the two churches at that place as priest of the parish. He (Abate di San Giorgio) desired to substitute for these ecclesiastics other priests from Italy, who could gradually, quietly, and without scandal, set everything—or, at any rate, a good many things—in the position required for his trading venture. In this way, when the gentlemen—that is, the officials and directors of the new company—should arrive, they would find the bed ready made for them, and everything prepared for an immediate commencement of their trade. Having the assistance of

1. Strictly transliterated, the name is Kudalur or Gudalur. I retain the official spelling. Mr. Philipps says the French use the form Goudelour (see 'Vingt ans dans l'Inde,' 1886, by M. J. Baulez, a Pondicherry missionary).

the Italian fathers at the places designated, they would not fail in receiving reports and information about everything with greater ease; and things being thus arranged, it was to be hoped that, with the good management that was assured, they would obtain from their dealings profits equivalent to their labours.

But, compared to the first object, the Abate conceived this second one to be much more difficult. How could he hope to succeed in moving out the fathers from Madras and Cuddalore and replacing them by Italians? In this he did not deceive himself, for their churches lie within the territory of the English, who claim the right and have the power of nominating as parish priests whoever seems to them best and most serviceable to their government.

Hesitating at these considerations, quite confused and perplexed, the Abate was unable to discover or decide on the best means to adopt for securing the end he sought. This end was to turn out the Capuchins from Madras and Father Paulo de Saa from Cuddalore without any disgrace or blemish attaching to him; for in dealing with the said fathers he thought it likely that they would make no difficulties, and if he granted them all they wished, they would carry out his proposals. The Abate then lighted upon a certain person, his countryman, a man to whom nothing appeared difficult, one who believed that everything had its remedy. Aware of his knowledge of the country, the Abate imparted to this man his ideas. When he had heard them, the honest compatriot raised not the slightest objection. He seized by the forelock this occasion that fortune had brought to his door; for he could desire nothing better than to pull out the sardine by use of the cat's paw, and thus succeed in the depraved intention that consumed him. This the reader will see from the price at which he sold his advice. He promised that if the pledge he demanded was given to him he would help the affair, as it is his habit to do. He told the Abate that to obtain what he wanted and to carry through his purpose nothing more was needed than to prepare one petition against the Capuchins in Madras and another against Father Paulo de Saa at Cuddalore. For these he drew up a good draft, turning the affair to his own profit as the "desuctar"[1] in the matter, *et cetera*. The condition was (as one

1. On this puzzling word Mr. J. Kennedy writes: '*Desugo* is Late Latin, "to suck out"; participle, *desuctus*. From this we might coin a word

foresaw) that the parish of Madras must become his, and that of Cuddalore fall to another man, his companion, who had been waiting here on the watch for two years. The Abate saw that by means of these fathers, they being well known and experienced in the country, he could hope in the future greater things towards the fulfilment of his designs than from the Italians he had brought with him. He accepted the proposal, and the compact was agreed to.

We have the theatre ready, or, to speak with more propriety, the amphitheatre; let us next see how the bulls fight. Now, without any mercy the Abate began to contend with the unhappy Capuchins over the money of the deceased Dominican, as I have said. He asserted that they were under obligation to make over to him the five thousand *pagodas* of the defunct. At that time he was carrying out a visitation in Madras under his authority as Commissary of the Lord Patriach of Antioch. He declared the money to belong entirely to the Holy Apostolic See. To this the Capuchins replied that the money was no longer in their power, but in that of the Armenians; but they would make every effort to collect it, and when received, they would make it over with great pleasure.

Who could have supposed that the Abate would not be satisfied with this reply, and that all the other matters would not be set at rest? But of a certainty it did not happen thus. How can I describe the disagreeables, report the molestations, and set forth the worries that arose from this money, and how the miserable Capuchins suffered for a space of two months and more? If I began I should never get to the end; suffice it to say here as follows [161]:

The Abate found it impossible to obtain the money from the Armenians; for in spite of all the pressure he put upon them, they would never agree to pay. He saw also that under this head he could never, without a great scandal and some damage to himself, squeeze the Capuchins any farther; for he knew quite well that on this question they were altogether without fault. He must work up a new intrigue, invent another cabal, and totally change his devices. This was necessary before he could totally

---

desuctor for (? romance) *desuctar*, "blood-sucker," the person obtaining improperly all the benefit. But I have not seen the word.' Littre, when giving the derivation of sneer, suggests a form *suctiare*, from which we might get *desuctor*, 'the sucker' Mr. Ferguson suggests reading 'director'.

ruin them, and obtain his own cherished object and the depraved design of him who advised him.

Consultations were held every night in the convent of these same Capuchins from nine to twelve o'clock between the Abate and his compatriot. It was decided to convey to the [Capuchin] superior an order to go to Pondicherry to render an account to the Lord Nuncio of his person and proceedings. Let it be remarked at this point that the Abate had already ended his visitation at Madras, during which the [Capuchin] superior had given *in rigore juris* [as required by strict law] an account of his mission, of his doings, and of his person. The direction above referred to was given because they well knew he would be detained by order of the [Madras] governor in connection with this same Abate, for reasons which can be seen elsewhere.

The ambush could not have been better planned in any other manner; for whichever way he turned himself, it was impossible for the unhappy friar not to tumble over the precipice. Astute subtlety! Diabolical invention! Exceptional malice! They included in this artful plot all possible contingencies, after having meditated on the case with the extremist care, not to say maliciousness. They argued in the following manner:

'If the friar should be detained by order of the governor (and of this there can be no doubt), then, when he prays for leave to go [to Pondicherry], he will not obtain it. If he goes without it, the English will never pardon him for absconding at such a time as this, and the least they will do will be to expel all the Capuchins from English territory; for in a case like this they could no longer consider them friends. The expulsion would be done on the pretext and under colour of their being untrustworthy, looking to the little loyalty displayed towards their political superiors in taking to flight during war time and joining the enemy [the French], who are of the same nation as themselves. The situation will thus put on a very good outward semblance, and we shall avoid raising any sort of evil presumption. Things being in this state, all will be smooth for our purpose, since the Theatines can then easily take their (the Capuchins') place. Very few will know [of our plot]. Should the friar ask leave from the English, it is certain he will be refused. Obviously it is unfitting in a time of war, as this is, to allow a man who has long lived in your country 10 quit it for that of the enemy, especially when he is of the same nation as that enemy.

'In this case we have the easy resource at hand of fulminating censures against him [from Pondicherry] in such a way that he will be unable to exercise his ecclesiastical functions. In this manner, should the friar by great exertions deliver himself from the Scylla of the English Government, it will not be easy for him to escape from the Charybdis of the Church's censures, and the other burthens with which it can overwhelm him. Even if he is freed from both, still, he will not be delivered from us, who already hold him like a fish in a net; and it will not be difficult for us to plunge the lancet behind his ear.

'This being admitted, in the execution of the project haste will have the larger share in our success. But for the present let us go to bed, for it is already very late; and from now onwards be sure that "Mon Pére" will not sleep so much to his taste in the bed that we have prepared for him as he has been doing hitherto.'

It is well to take a little rest when one has been awake so much. But it hardly seemed worth while when the designs which they had discussed had made them forget the time, nor did they wait for the day to dawn to make a commencement.

The reader must be told their progress in executing their plot—how they were not neglectful in perpetrating the evil deed that they had just agreed to. Thus, on the first of February, 1704, at half-past six in the evening, they communicated to the superior an order to start within three days for Pondicherry. God help us! Why could they not intimate the order before sunset, or leave it to be done the following day? Stupid doubt ! Indiscreet question! For was it not as is usual in such cases? Who knows not that ill-will, wishing for greater security to inflict hurt, flees from the brightness of day and seeks the obscurity of night? To postpone the attempt until the next day would be to lose time. That is not right. 'We are Christians; we must also prove we are Catholics. To-morrow is the Day of Purification [*i.e.,* the 2nd of February]. What we have to do is an evil thing, thus let it not wait for the morrow; now, now, and at night so much the better.'

At this blow, as may be easily understood, the poor friar was as much stunned as perturbed. He could not fail to perceive, by reason of the troubles he had already undergone, that they would succeed in totally ruining him. He considered himself lost inevitably; for it was certain they would not aim such a blow at him without they had him first of all well caught, as they had. In firing point-blank the bullet is never wasted. He was anxious, through a feeling of honour, to shield his reputation and that of his religion rather than evade damage to his own person. Thus he resolved on the instant to quit the convent at once, and employ all he had of influence in Madras, as he did through himself and his friends, in order to implore from the gentlemen of the government permission for his going to Pondicherry. But no result came of it, nor were his efforts rewarded, for they absolutely refused consent orally in the presence of the Abate [di San Giorgio], and also in writing, as is proved.[1]

On this order followed immediately a censure, as planned in the agreement made [168] between the Abate and his compatriot. Thereupon, disconsolate at the rebuff from the gentlemen of the government, and afraid of the thunderbolt of a censure with which his own superiors threatened him, hardly had the wretched friar reached his convent when there followed him into his cell the secretary of the Abate. He was sent with a written order of suspension from divine functions. Yet it was not then twenty-four hours since the order to proceed to Pondicherry within three days was communicated to him. What an extraordinary action!

At this suspension the friar felt more than suspense—he felt outraged, this being the [natural] effect of an injury thus inflicted. But, curbing his passion, he returned to himself, and became like a lamb. He considered that obedience was obligatory in all cases, except the impossible. Casting up his eyes to Heaven, he implored aid from our Lord in such an obvious danger. Then, with the written order in his hand, he thought of a means of redress. He determined to appeal from the interdict on the ground of the impossibility in which he found himself of putting into execution the order of his Excellency; for on that very second of February

1. The Madras Records have the following entries:
'*January* 22, 1704.—Refusal of leave to Padre Michael Angelo to go to Pondicherry in obedience to a summons by the Patriarch of Antioch.
'*January* 24, 1704.—A Petition received from the Padre.
'*January* 24, 1704.—Copy of Petition in French.
'*January* 24, 1704.—Governor and Council's answer in French' ('Ancient Records of Fort St. George,' Press List, No. 7, p. 193).
January 22, Old Style, corresponds to February 2, New Style.

when the gentlemen of the government refused permission they ordered him to be formally detained, whereas before he had only been forbidden to leave. He also alleged [in his petition] that the term set to him of three days was not yet completed, not even the half of it. These two important facts, according to the teaching of the learned and the directions of the Canon Law, of themselves annulled the interdict and made it of no effect. This he proved at large in a manifesto which he drew up.

No doubt the reader will weigh how they continued to carry everything into execution in conformity with the dispositions arrived at in their consultations, and how they made every effort to put them into force. So that he may have exact reasons for his judgment, let the reader attend carefully to what follows.

The appeal was of no avail; however just its allegations might be, how could the Abate accept them, for how could he admit them if they did not accord with his designs? Here comes in with effect the common proverb, 'Laws are weak where the king insists'; but I say, looking at all that we behold, that we must read here, 'where the clergy insist.' For king and law wrong no one.

Let us turn now to the wretched friar, who was perturbed, thunderstruck, and overwhelmed, as was to be expected, at finding himself in such a horrible position and subjected to such unheard- of doings. During the same night he left his convent and went to the house of an Englishman. There he continued to seek some means for obtaining leave to go to Pondicherry.

While he was at this friend's the advice-giving compatriot appeared once more. He had come to pay him a visit—not to help or console him, but to advise him to place himself, as before, in the noose which they had made ready for him. This is apparent from the pausing talk which he went on uttering. At first he showed himself all compassion, and almost wept. This is the substance of what he said: 'Father, there is no other preferable course, nor can your reverence find anything else in this very great affliction than to escape this very night disguised in the clothes of a Malabar' (*i.e.*, a Tamil). He spoke with such great demonstrations of true friendship that the owner of the house they were in, though he did not understand the words, paid great attention to the gestures. The good friar, as one who much desired the thing, though with some apprehension of being misled, was on the point of accepting the advice.

After he had given it the man went out by the door, and who can have a doubt that this deceiving counsellor was laughing over having carried through such a good piece of work? Thereupon came an opening to the house-owner to enquire from the friar the object of all those exaggerations and the cause of so many grimaces. He asked this as one who felt infinitely for his friend's troubles, as one who would in every way help him to redress. He urged this request regardless of the efforts of the friar to prevaricate and not disclose the facts. But the more he evaded telling him, the more the householder pressed the priest to speak out. He had already begun to show great resentment at the father's declining to communicate the circumstances to him; for it seemed to him that the conversation had reference to the disagreeables his visitor was already suffering under.

Seeing himself already pledged to the man of the house by having sought his aid, and yielding to so much insistence (thanks be to Heaven!), the friar was forced to disclose the secret, begging his friend to say how his flight was to be managed. But the said person, as soon as he heard the story, became quite disconcerted, and for a short time cast his eyes to the ground. After this pause, turning them on the friar, he broke the embarrassing silence in this form of words: 'My father, he who gave your reverence that idea is not your friend, and does not wish you well. On the contrary, he is your mortal enemy, and will destroy you. For to that end alone can that counsel serve; because there are very stringent orders at the gates (as I know) about the person of your reverence and your not leaving. I hold it to be impossible for you to get away without capture. Having seized you, they will without fail send you on board the ship about to set sail for England. Such a disaster would be a great disgrace both for you and your religion. They will catch your reverence in disguise taking flight for Pondicherry in time of war, and that after you have lived here so many years and been so well treated by all the English, especially by the government. Certainly it will not fail to appear a very abominable thing, an act unworthy of the personal character and conduct of your reverence. Not even among your own people will you be able to save your reputation; even when they learn that this attempted flight was not due to treason, they will not refrain from declaring that your reverence behaved very imprudently in attempting such an absurdity. If you fancy that you will be highly honoured for your zeal in obeying, you are much mistaken, for there is no one who is ignorant of the fact that obedience does not include such impossibilities, and among us such an act would never be done. In confidence I warn your reverence in these words; but you must decide as you please. As to this move, I do not advise you to make it. I conclude by saying that such a project proceeding solely from yourself might, under some conditions, be prudently accepted [169]; but coming from a third party it would in no way be prudent to acquiesce in it, much less to carry it out.'

It will easily be seen that he who discoursed in this wise did it with a disinterested mind and a feeling heart for the harm that he feared and was attempting to obviate. Even although he opposed what the father desired to do, it would certainly be a great piece of imprudence not to value his advice. The friar was aware that he who repeated all these things to him knew extremely well the English customs (they being his own), and that in what he had advised he had given proof of the great love he bore him, such as he had always experienced from him. The friar's judgment being, let it be supposed, a little affected, still he had not, by the pressure of events, lost it altogether. He weighed with care the Englishman's reasons, and attaching to all of them full weight, he accepted them. At the same time he acquired this piece of wisdom—namely, not to pay, for the future, any heed to the counsels of his loving counsellor, the priest. With this he took leave of the person in whose house he was, giving the requisite thanks, and returned to his convent, commending himself to God and giving to His Divine Majesty due thanks for the special favour vouchsafed to him at that hour, in permitting that the venom brought to him for his destruction should be turned into an antidote, by knowledge of which he could ever counteract the poison, as from that day forth he did. He implored the protection of the Virgin, to whom with insistence he prayed for help. For to console him in these great dangers he could not find anyone on earth, the great majority of men being tyrannous and false.

Leaving him at this stage, let us turn to the other piece of artillery that, during Lent, quite at the end of it, they loaded against him. It was one of pretty large caliber The Most Reverend Father Friar Lourenço,[1] head and superior of the

1. As the Father was a Frenchman, he is often styled Laurent.

Capuchins in India, was then present in Pondicherry. He craved leave from the Lord Patriarch to proceed to Madras for the consolation of his brethren under the affliction they were in during these earthquakes. The first application the Lord Patriarch refused. But he wrote to the Abate di San Giorgio, then at San Thome, asking him if there was any drawback in conceding leave to the said father. The Abate replied that he knew no reason for refusing his request; on the contrary, he thought that such an arrival would be of use in what he was attempting.

Upon receipt of this reply the leave to the Reverend Father Friar Lourenço was given. Let the reader here pay attention. The object of the Abate was to drive the superior of Madras into a corner, and he argued thus: 'If Friar Lourenço enters Madras, then the superior of Madras can go to Pondicherry. Whatever difficulty applies to the one applies to the other case. Thus the interdict which had been fulminated was properly launched.' Nor did he talk badly, since unjust acts, done out of place, cannot remain otherwise than committed, even if only executed in part. Let us, however, see the conclusion. 'If Friar Lourenço cannot get in, we can always try conclusions with the superior of Madras. In that case (at the very worst) we shall proceed against him as disobedient to his ecclesiastical superiors.' Let not the reader imagine that there is in this the slightest exaggeration—there is nothing but the purest truth. For thus spoke the Abate publicly at San Thome.

The Reverend Father Friar Lourenço[1] came with a letter of recommendation from Monsieur Martin, governor of Pondicherry, addressed to the Lord Governor of Madras. By its means, and assisted by an English friend, who took much trouble in this matter, he got into the Fort, where he was very well received by the Lord Governor. He came then to the convent, and all the time he remained he performed there the office of parish priest, to the content of all, whereby the Christians were relieved.

---

1. 'FORT ST. GEORGE, *September* 15, 1704.—Minutes of Consultation approving of a general letter to the Company reporting the permission given to the Capuchin Padre Laurenso (Lorenzo) to enter into Town, and there exercise his functions in the Portuguese Church in spite of the interdiction laid upon the Capuchins by the Patriarch and [the] Bishop of St. Thoma, to prevent any ill-consequences that may accrue from passing over it unnoticed' ('Public Consultations,' vol. xxxiii, p. 200; Press List, No. 7, p. 219).

This gladness, however, became a hardship to them, because the Abate found that the superior [Michel Ange] never appeared in all this business, nor allowed himself any entry into it. The Abate sent to ask urgently for the issue of an order from his Excellency [the Patriarch] directing the Reverend Father Friar Lourenço to quit Madras and return to Pondicherry. This was carried out at once, and the father left. This manoeuvre surprised the English very much, and it was felt intimately by the Catholics. All were upset—those on one side discouraged, and those on the other incensed. But no one discovered at whom this shot was directed. It was only Time, the index of all craftinesses, that demonstrated its object, as the reader shall briefly learn.

Hardly had the Reverend Father Lourenço arrived at Pondicherry, when the Lord Patriarch sent off the Reverend Father Friar Spirito (Esprit)[1] for Madras. They hoped he would find the same facilities for an entrance as obtained by Father Friar Lourenço. In the hope of obtaining success in the business, they neglected not to obtain for him a letter from Monsieur Martin to the Lord Governor [170] of Madras. Be it noted that these Italian gentlemen could not bear the sight of Father Friar Esprit because he opposed with all his power a sentence they wanted to pronounce against him, touching a complaint then actually pending at Rome. A decision was expected thence every day. But what was to be done?

They ordered him to Madras, where he would be overthrown irreparably like the others. They sent him off with a sealed bundle of letters and documents, and gave him an order that it must not be opened until after his entry into Madras. Who could have guessed that Father Esprit carried his own halter with him? Behold the trick which was afterwards unmasked! Inside the bundle he carried were two interdicts to be served on the two Capuchins then present in the convent, along with an order to them to appear *em atribos*[2] personally in Pondicherry in the presence of His Excellency, *subpoena suspensionis a divinis* [under penalty of suspension from divine functions].

1. He was a Frenchman, and in the French form his name is 'Esprit,' usually styled 'of Tours.' The dispute alluded to in the next sentence was, no doubt, the transfer, in 1699, of the native parish in Pondicherry from the Capuchins to the Jesuits.
2. I have found no satisfactory suggestion for a rendering of *em atribos*, but the context seems to require 'without fail.'

This command the poor creatures could not comply with, for they found themselves in the same inability as their superior, being forbidden by the gentlemen of the government to leave Madras. The piece had not been badly aimed, since with one discharge they demolished three priests—two of Madras, by prohibiting the exercise of their holy functions and the administration of the sacraments, and Father Friar Esprit by making him go to Madras. When he had got entry there, he must inevitably intimate the orders he brought from his Excellency. These orders having been communicated to them, the English gentlemen would never pardon him for doing it, and the very least they would do would be to kick him out of Madras. Should he neglect to communicate the interdicts, he could be made subject to an interdict himself. It would be seen whether the wretched man could escape some such blow if he once got into the town.

But Our Lord, the protector of the innocent, would not permit that such great evil should prevail on this occasion. For when the father reached the gates the sentries stopped him from entering until they had reported his arrival to the Lord Governor. This gentleman, as they told Father Esprit, fell into a great rage, wanting to know what was the use of so many priests who did nothing but come and go. They told him he bore a letter from Monsieur Martin for his Lordship (as the father had told them). The governor sent for the letter, but would never consent to allow Father Esprit to come in. By this rebuff the father was forced to turn back to Pondicherry.

When he was at San Thome he (Esprit) wrote a letter to Friar Euzebio, Capuchin, lately arrived from Surat, in which he warned him on behalf of his Excellency that he must secure an exit from Madras if he wished to be spared the threatened deluge of interdicts, which was on the point of overwhelming that unfortunate mission. As soon as Father Friar Euzebio received this letter, without delay or loss of time, he proceeded to the Fort to bid farewell to the Lord Governor before he went off to join Father Friar Esprit, when both would go together to Pondicherry. But on no consideration would the Lord Governor consent to his departure; on the contrary, he ordered him to take care that he remained in Madras.

Upon learning this, the three companions in misery were as much perturbed as confused at such extraordinary procedure being used against them. They recognised the target at which the arrows of so many misadventures were shot, attempting totally to ruin them. They felt acutely their inability to avoid the injury with which they were threatened, and the not having anyone to whom they could apply for help in the great calamity they dreaded, for their destruction was imminent. In this deliberation they wasted a little time, debating the best method to be adopted.

Not hitting upon anything calculated to deliver them from such an intricate labyrinth, they resolved to put in force what the Church, as a loving mother, concedes to her oppressed sons in alleviation of their sufferings. They decided to appeal to Rome against all that was being done against them. In putting this into execution their hearts were dilated for a moment or so. Instantly they drew up a petition of appeal in proper form, and craved as a favour that one of their friends would start at once with it for Pondicherry to lay it before his Excellency.

This was carried out properly on April 14, 1704, in the presence of witnesses of great weight. The Lord Nuncio took the petition, and after reading the first lines, refused it twice over, making no account of it. But afterwards he learnt that at the foot was appended an attestation of a number of persons; and when it was presented again, he glanced at the signatures of the witnesses, who were present and all of them persons of great weight there. He felt so angry with the Capuchins that he could neither repress nor conceal his passion; he let loose on them a deluge of benisons.

The storm having blown over, the sea became tranquil again. Having relieved his mind, he sifted the matter and gave better consideration to it. His Excellency failed not to acquire the conviction that the document was of juridical force, that it had been presented with all the formalities, and that by it his hands were tied. Concealing what he had in his mind, he entered on a search for all the paths and roads possible for hindering the Capuchins from doing a thing that hurt him so much at heart, and for inducing them to beg pardon for such great overboldness. This was the name that his Excellency gave to their appeal to the Holy Apostolic See, converting it into a crime of high treason in the highest degree.

But the Capuchins were now accustomed to thunders and lightnings from this quarter. In addition, they had in their minds the expectation, not to say the certainty, that all this talk was mere stratagem and invention for the object of getting from them the original documents [171] they held in their justification, and afterwards still making them have recourse to Rome—and it would not be 'for the King of France,'[1] as we say commonly. They replied with all modesty and submission that their consciences did not accuse them of having done a single thing to offend his Excellency; therefore they felt no obligation to ask his pardon, nor to disavow in public a boldness which had never entered into their imaginations. They would thereby confess themselves culpable, and constitute themselves criminals (which it did not suit them to do) before the tribunal of the Holy Apostolic See, to which they had appealed. As this was a thing so obvious, there was no need to say more about it; but if the Lord Patriarch made the request in order to get them to withdraw the petition of appeal, let him send to ask it. And his Excellency having adjusted all the things lying within his power, and put them in the state they were in before his arrival, they promised and agreed to burn all the documents they held connected with this affair in the presence of whatever witnesses he chose to appoint.

As this reply was not to the taste of the Lord Patriarch, nor in conformity with his designs, it was not well received by his Excellency, but he learnt by it the firmness with which the Capuchins meant to sustain and carry on their appeal. Thus it was necessary to seek some other by-path, and employ the weapons of the Vatican to overawe them, and drag them by force to the point he desired. For this purpose he then dispatched a servant named Lazaro, a negro born in India, making over to him two letters, one for the Father Friar Reynato,[2] and the other for the Father Friar Euzebio, both Capuchins, present in the convent at Madras. The servant arrived there on the 18th of May. Meeting Father Friar René in the street at seven o'clock at night, he made over to him both letters. As it was dark the father took them and carried them to the convent. There, each one opening his own, they found that instead of letters they were orders to

1. I can find no evidence that such a saying was common; perhaps it suggested Voltaire's more celebrated 'travailler pour le roi de Prusse' —in other words, to work without reward. Manucci's saying evidently means the same thing.
2. In the French form 'René,' usually styled 'of Angoulême.' Euzebio (Eusebius) was 'of Bourges.'

proceed to Pondicherry within five days, under pain of suspension a *divinis*.

One had been made out on the 5th, and the other on the 24th of April. They were the two documents that the Reverend Father Friar Esprit had brought, with directions to serve them in case he obtained entry into Madras. Each man wrote his reply at the foot of the document, to the effect that it was well known, in fact notorious, that they were unable to leave Madras. They had appealed to the Holy Apostolic See, and recognised no other judge in their cause than the Supreme Pontiff, Clement XI. Then they sent the documents back to Pondicherry, whence the servant had brought them, as has been said.

The Reverend Father René had already received an order not to celebrate Mass, although he was a third party; and this without any juridical formality, without his knowing up to this time the reason or cause thereof. Still, he did not fail in observance of the order, for reasons that will be described in their proper place and time. The Reverend Father Friar Euzebio, for other reasons already set forth, considered himself under obligation to continue his functions without being hindered by the suspension with which he was threatened; he did, in fact, go on with them. His Excellency, on hearing this by the spies that he kept or by messages sent to him—for he never desisted from doing to them in everything some harm or other—caused to be nailed on the gates of Madras, San Thome, and Pondicherry documents by which he declared the three Capuchins at Madras to be suspended *a divinis* (from divine functions). In this declaration made so publicly he inserted no reason beyond these three words, *Justis de causis* (for sufficient reasons). *Nunquam sic locutus est Summus Pontifex.*[1]

Imagining that by this coup he had entirely destroyed the Capuchins and brought them to the ground, and their mission along with them, he planned an attack upon those of Cuddalore. While we are talking of that place, we leave the wretched Capuchins of Madras to draw a little breath, a thing most necessary for them, for neither rest nor peace had been conceded to them at this time in the midst of such perilous attacks.

The Reverend Father Paulo de Saa at Cuddalore, parish priest of the two churches there, was now cited to appear person-

1. 'Never did the Supreme Pontiff speak thus.'

ally within three days at Pondicherry, *subpoena suspensionis a divinis* (*et cetera*).

This poor priest found himself under the same disabilities and in the same condition as the wretched Capuchins of Madras. He was under an embargo from the gentlemen of the government, and was unable to quit Cuddalore. He feared an interdict much more than he did thunder and lightning. He fell into such grief and deep melancholy that he did nothing but weep day and night over his sad fate, for in such a terrible conflict he had no one to whom he could unbosom himself, none whom he could consult as to what should be done to deliver this Christian congregation from this great pertubation, and avert from himself the violent storm that he saw was about to discharge itself upon his head.

But Divine Providence is always nearest the afflicted when they have the most need. In the midst of all this affliction, and at the moment of this lamentable blow which had fallen upon the poor priest, it permitted the entry at his door of a charitable Theatine. He was a Portuguese by race, and called D. Simao da Costa.[1] At sight of him, as we may suppose, some vigour returned, but Father Paulo was unable entirely to conceal his dejection. He was also stimulated by finding that the good priest did not fail to take notice of the circumstances in his hospice, for they were quite worthy of the deepest reflection in such a crisis as he was involved in.

'Priest of Divine Providence, Simao da Costa!' he exclaimed, as one in delirium. Owing to the bitter anxiety that consumed him, he repeated many times consecutively, 'Simao da Costa! Simao da Costa!' He assumed, no doubt, that he was another man of Cyrene come to relieve him of the cross of tribulation that he had to bear.

Nor was he deceived, as events will show, and the reader will be able to consider them [before he passes judgment]. I take upon myself to notify him thereof at the proper time. At present, not to lose our way, let us go on to recount [172] what passed between the poor priest and the loving Theatine. Seeing the other so sad, Simao was moved to compassion, and began to cheer up

1. Simao da Costa, Theatine, is mentioned again on fol. 189. He was still alive in 1710, and was then petitioning for reappointment to Cuddalore (see Penny, Church in Madras, quoting from the Consultation of January 13, 1710).

and console him in the best way he could. As a conclusion, after other words fitting for such an occasion, he told him he must have patience.

There can be no doubt that in all he said (let us give everyone his due) he spoke well; but the afflicted priest was not content with words of consolation only, and wanted some redress for his wrongs. He wanted some preservative against the thunder that threatened to fall on his head and consume his body. Seeing that the loving Theatine supplied him with none, his sorrow was redoubled, and his heart-bruises were greatly intensified, because, if so far the wretched priest had hit upon no comfort for himself, it is to be presumed, from his being to such an extent upset, that his thinking powers had fled. Ordinarily when a man is in trouble, if his dear ones desert him, his friends forsake him, those under obligations excuse themselves, his own wits equally abandon him; nor is he content, being unhappy, to have them restored easily. But, seeing that such a doctor [as the Theatine] was unable to prescribe, he was convinced that no other apothecary could prepare him anything.

Finding himself thus cast down, he resorted like a good Christian to the restorative of giving thanks to God, who ever encourages, alleviates, and consoles. But love, which is ingenious and always sympathetic, failed not to be of use on this occasion —one of the direst necessity. For if it did not take action earlier, it was not so much to see how best to kick the priest a little out of his nest, but rather to become more acceptable to him and more esteemed; for the discreet are aware that the greater the necessity the greater the value of a thing, it being then far more esteemed. As a prudent and charitable person, he must look out for himself, for is it not there that a well-ordered charity begins? Thus love failed not to inspire the charitable Theatine with the remedy so anxiously desired by the disconsolate priest, being also the one most favourable to himself. He influenced him (Father de Saa), in addition to the grace of persuasion, by circumstances favourable to the physician. This was in case the patient should refuse to swallow the pill or potion, though in this instance it was not very necessary that the prescription should be so very discreetly worded.

For from anxiety the wretched priest was so thirsty that if you presented to him the most poisonous drink in the most disgusting vessel, if it had only some similitude to a medicine, it would appear to him like the most delicious nectar contained in the most crystalline of cups. Nor is this to be wondered at; when a man so anxiously demands a thing, any sort of appearance of it deceives and satisfies him. This, as the reader will see, happened here between this afflicted priest and the charitable Theatine. The latter opened his case in some such words as these:

'Reverend Father Paulo de Saa, I will not deceive your honour, and after having weighed the matter, I think your case a troublesome one and the remedy for it not an easy one to accept, though it is the only suitable one, and there is no other course. Believe me, my reverend father, for the love of God, it is thus only that Our Father may help you and deliver you from similar torments for the future.' 'How will he assist me?' replied the poor priest timorously. 'What may be this remedy, and what must be done to obtain it?' To this answered the sympathizing messenger: 'Give up one of the two churches to the Theatines, and I pledge you my word you shall be left in peace, saved from these embarrassments, made whiter than snow before the Lord Nuncio, and restored to his favour.' I forewarned the reader that I bargained he would see by what was promised whether the priest (de Saa) deceived himself in thinking that this visitor was a second man of Cyrene come to deliver him from the cross of tribulations he was then suffering from, for Father da Costa told him clearly that he wanted for himself one of the two churches. But Father de Saa was not repelled, nor was there any reason for being so, for was it not love, moderate, well-arranged, better aimed, and still better concocted?

It seemed to the good Father Paulo de Saa that the Theatine who was speaking to him on this occasion was not a man, but an angel sent from on high (*de cima*), All the same, in making this assumption he did not altogether deceive himself; for, if I do not make a mistake, one's own land and the land adjoining are called in Portugal *terras de cima*. But what he knew for a certainty was that he came from below to his cost (*costa*)—I mean for his consolation.[1] Thus, from being half dead, those words quite

1. The author is evidently trying to pun by ringing the changes on *Simao* (the priest's Christian name), *cima* (above), and *terras de cima* (literally, 'lands just above'—that is, 'adjoining'). Again, there is the pun between *custo* (price or cost) and *Costa* (the priest's surname).

restored him to life. Strange remedy! Noteworthy influence! Wonderful force! Who could have anticipated it? Such a happy thought! Such a great success on the part of the physician! Such great good luck to the patient! Such a wonderful recovery (God being the greater part in it) in the case of one who was almost at the point of death. Once more the storm was appeased, almost at the point when the roaring thunder and the gleaming lightning were ready to burst over him so fiercely that out of mere fright he would be consumed. Rising from his seat, the poor priest took pen in hand, and forthwith wrote a letter to the Lord Nuncio, affirming that, so far as it depended on him, he resigned to the Theatines not one, but both the churches he administered; and he counted himself happy if, by so doing [173], he was restored to the favour of his Excellency. This surrender was the effect of fear, and Father de Saa's action should not cause surprise.

In good time Father de Saa's letter arrived, and was by the Lord Patriarch accepted and read—a fortune which others did not obtain; but there was nothing in those cases to be gained like this, which brought with it a thing that his Excellency so much desired. It is not easy to set forth here the joy with which it was greeted and the rejoicings made in its honour—feasts at Pondicherry, feasts in Cuddalore, feasts in Madras. But in no way was any time lost, because at once they prepared an attested copy, which was lodged among his Excellency's records. The original was sent at the same time to the Lord Governor of Cuddalore—'When they give thee the little pig,' *et cetera*.[1] They believed that at once, on view thereof, he would accept the resignation of Father Paulo de Saa, and make over at least one of the churches to the Theatines. But the Lord Governor of Cuddalore, as an experienced man who deals with cases deliberately, also having had in this affair long notice, was at once aware that Father Paulo de Saa had not written the letter on any other ground than the fear of an interdict. He kept the letter, and waited till he saw some other move in the game.

Meanwhile, until this is disclosed, let us go back once more to the poor Capuchins of Madras, for it was not thought right

1. Mr. M. Longworth Dames has kindly traced this for me. It is in full: 'Quando te derem o porquinho acode-lhe com o baracinho' (When they give you the pig, lead it away by the cord); in other words, 'Strike while the iron is hot.'

to leave them in tranquility in any way. For the better understanding of this the reader is informed that, at the time when the Lord Nuncio sent an order by which he declared the suspension *a divinis* of these unfortunate men, he sent to the Reverend Father Dom Guilhermo della Valle, a Theatine friar, a patent as parochial priest of Madras,[1] drawn up in Pondicherry on June 14 in the current year [1704]. With it was an order that, instead of making the suspension [of the Capuchins] public, he should seek rather some device by which he should obtain quiet entry into the Capuchin convent, and exercise the office of parish priest with the approbation of their superior; but he was to insist on the Reverend Father Friar Euzebio observing the state of suspension in which he had been placed, by not celebrating or exercising any sort of ecclesiastical function.

The Reverend Father Dom Guilhermo, to whom in this business all warning was needless and all instructions superfluous, failed in no particular that suited and helped forward his purpose. To better secure his object, in addition to clothing himself in the lamb's skin, he shielded himself, a still better disguise, under the best friend that the Capuchins had in India. Soliciting him to be his protector and mediator in respect to what he claimed, he communicated to him in the greatest secrecy what he designed to do. His project was that, after the Capuchins of Madras had given him a cell in their convent, and allowed him to perform all the functions of parish priest, they should abstain from any exercise of their ministry; while he undertook to act in such a way that things should continue in that condition, and the Capuchins remain under suspension from the divine office. They must consent not to prosecute their appeal any further, and if they desisted they would not be persecuted any more. But I say that the joke was not half a bad one—'to ask for a riding-saddle and carry off a pack-saddle.'[2]

He said, further, that he had in his possession a patent as

1. Gulielmus a Valle first appears in the English records in 1694, when President Higginson appointed him to Cuddalore (Wheeler, i. 276). In its Portuguese form his first name is Guilhermo; his surname was Della Valle, he being apparently an Italian.
2. The text is: 'Pedir cella [sella] pera enquaxar [encaixar] albarda.' I am indebted to Mr. Batalha-Reis and to Mr. Dames for the explanation of this proverbial saying. It is like our 'When given an inch to take an ell.' Manucci also puns upon *cella* (a cell) and *sella* (a saddle).

parish priest of Madras, but he did not wish to make use of it. Here it seems as if he wanted to make himself out an innocent, thereby better to cover up his sagacity. Feint of a discreet man! invention of a politic person! For he gave as his reason the great obligation he was under to the Capuchins for the kindness received from them (a finely-gilded pill!) in the period of three years and more they had kept him with them in their convent:

'Por la mano lheva el hombre
A su casa con que llore.'[1]

They had lived like brothers, without the least difference in treatment (we ought to say it was public on the part of the Capuchins, while secret on his, for they to-day are testing it, and Time publishes it). Therein he hoped to recompense those favours, if he could on this occasion help them (considering that the annihilation of the Capuchins was a small matter). If it cost him the blood from his veins, he meant to do it with a high heart. I believe him, and everyone may believe as he pleases or as it appears to him. For Time will disenchant us all, he being a pilgrim capable of dissimulations.

Who would not allow himself to be paid in such soft speeches and such honied arguments? But it pleased God that the friend to whom he confided those ideas knew very well how to count three, and though he was not so literate as the Theatine, was not a bit less wily, and thus allowed it to be supposed that he entered into his intentions. For, by refraining from arguing with him, he left it to be assumed that he had understood; or equally, it might seem that he left discussion over for a better opportunity. This did not hinder him, however, from seeing at once, and that quite plainly, that all this discoursing was directed by the father to his own introduction into the convent, and to deceiving the Capuchins, as if they were so many infants, anointing their lips with honey, and compelling them, through pleasant words and plausible reasoning, to give up their church of their own accord. After that their good relations with the English gentlemen would be at an end. These would never forgive a thing so much to their injury as giving up possession without first getting their consent. For were they not owners of the place, and entitled

1. Mr. Batalha-Reis says this is a Spanish proverb: 'Man himself leads home what makes him weep'; that is, we bring our misfortunes on ourselves.

to appoint at their own pleasure? Thus the friend imparted the facts to the Capuchins, and these, remembering the advice, *Non credos inimico tuo in eternum* (Eccles. xii.)[1] would not admit the father to their convent, and at once replied that the nomination of a parish priest for the Madras church did not concern them, but the English gentlemen; nor could the Reverend Father Friar Euzebio desist from continuing his ecclesiastical functions.

This reply was at once sent to the Lord Nuncio, who fully perceived that the Capuchins were aware of the trap, and had avoided falling into it. We must assume that he knew equally well the difficulty there was in cajoling them, yet, none the less, he continued to pursue them, it seeming to him that they must, in the end, give in from mere weariness. He next decided on the dispatch to Madras of the negro already mentioned[2] bearing two letters—one to the Reverend Friar Dom Guilhermo, and the other to the Reverend Father Friar Euzebio. The latter paper was a citation sent off, as the superscription purported, from San Thome, but inside without year, month, or day, nor the least indication of where it was issued. In it the friar was summoned to appear at Pondicherry in three days to give reasons for not having observed his order of suspension. This citation was flung down by the servant with studied carelessness in the street in front of the Capuchin convent [174] on June 24 [1704] during a very dark night. It was picked up by a palanquin 'boy,' who the next day brought it to the convent.

The citation having been received and read, the Reverend Father Friar Euzebio wrote at once a letter to his Excellency, in which he set forth that, being a prisoner by command of the government, it was impossible for him to leave in order to appear personally at Pondicherry. From this default he apprehended no ill consequence, feeling in conscience that he was in no way guilty; nor ought his Excellency to hold him to be so, for he had only lately arrived, as was notorious in those parts, where he had not caused any scandal by his acts. For this reason he did not observe the censure launched against him, looking on it as null and void. He proved its nullity by canonical law and by authors

1. 'Never trust thine enemy: [for like as iron rusteth, so is his wickedness]' (Eccles. xii. 10).
2. His name was Lazaro (*see ante*, fol. 171).

whom he quoted in the said letter. Above all, having appealed to the Holy Apostolic See, he no longer recognised his Excellency as his judge. The letter was carried to the Lord Nuncio by the Reverend Father Friar Thomas of Poictiers,[1] a Capuchin present in Pondicherry. The Nuncio declined to receive or look at the letter; on the contrary, he was much enraged, and used menaces to that father [Thomas] for having presented it to him.

On June 29 [1704], by order of his Excellency, there was fixed up on the gates of Pondicherry a small piece of paper, a palm in length and four fingers in breadth, bearing on it four lines of thick letters, without month, without year, without day or place whence such writing was issued, without the signature or seal of his Excellency, and, finally, having no sort of form. In it was a declaration excommunicating the Reverend Father Friar Euzebio. Not only so, for the same paper was published the following Sunday, reckoned as July 6, at San Thome, and affixed during the night at two different places in Madras. Where was there ever seen so strange a procedure as that of this prelate? The pen might extend itself greatly on this matter, but let us leave to the judgment of the reader what might be said about it. I pass on, not insisting on this beyond a mere mention, to recount other steps taken, at which there will be no less cause of wonderment.

At the same time the Reverend Father Dom Guilhermo della Valle received a letter from his Excellency by the hand of the same negro, Lazaro. This man was known in Madras as infamous according to the civil laws, and anathematized by Holy Mother Church, by reason of an office which he had held here and exercised publicly. If I do not name it on this paper, it is that I may not deprave my style; neither does modesty allow it to be spoken of. Nor would this reference to it be introduced, except that it is appropriate to call attention to the instruments made use of by the Lord Nuncio to send notices to ecclesiastics and convey to them his orders. Nevertheless, in the case of the reverend fathers of the Society of Jesus he did it in a better and more decent style.

Thus, it was notified to the Very Reverend Father Provincial

1. This is probably the Father Thomas, Capuchin, who succeeded Father Reynato (René) at Madras sometime before 1721. He died in April, 1734 (Penny, 'Church in Madras,' 238, 239). His name appears frequently in Norbert, 'Mémoires Historiques.'

of Madura that he must appear at Pondicherry before his Excellency. But the notification was *in forma juris*, and worded with the urbanity customary between ordained persons. The Provincial did not comply, nor to this moment is it known with certainty what reasons he alleged about his not going. Only it is talked of that the said Reverend Father Provincial replied in writing to the notification, saying that he had orders from the Lord Primate [*i.e.*, of Goa] not to obey his Excellency until the powers he brought from his Holiness as Visitor-General of India were made patent and public; and it had been proved that they were registered in the Chancery of His Majesty the King of Portugal, in accordance with the privileges conceded by different Supreme Pontiffs to that crown.

Be that as it may, it is certain that the said Reverend Father Provincial, though able to go, failed to appear. Yet the Lord Patriarch did not proceed against him as he did against the unhappy Capuchins of Madras. The latter, detained by the gentlemen of the government there, were unable to execute the order they received to present themselves in person at Pondicherry; but in their case he chastised the fault in a way for which there is no comparison to be found, nor has anything similar ever been seen. He loaded them with interdicts, disregarding the harm that would ensue therefrom to the whole of the population, exceeding nine thousand souls, that they tended, or to their Church—a procedure of which the evil results are to-day visible.

But, leaving this with God, who alone can remedy it, since there is no one here below to sympathize, let us turn to the abovenamed letter received by the Reverend Father Dom Guilhermo della Valle, in which he was enjoined to show to the Lord Governor of Madras his patent as parish priest. He did as ordered without delay, presenting it on June 29 [1704], the festival of St. Peter and St. Paul, which of a truth was not ill chosen. But, still, it did not turn out well for him: the governor would not agree. Here it has to be pointed out, and should be noted for the future, that the Capuchins are the legitimate parish priests of Madras. For the Reverend Father Ephraim (whom God have in His keeping), when he came to the coast of Choromandal, did not mean to stop there, but was going on to Pegu, conformably to the requirements of his patent. While he was staying in Madras the Christians there entreated him to remain.[1]

1. These facts are given in Tavernier (edition Ball), i. 220, and

But before they obtained his consent they wrote to San Thome, praying for a padre to be sent to take charge of them. At San Thome they declined to concede this request, but, on the contrary, answered with much scorn, saying: 'What thing is this Madras that we should send a priest there?' After this rebuff they decided on a petition to the Madras Council for their consent to Father Ephraim's appointment. At the instance of these Christians, and to aid them in the necessity he saw them to be in, he decided to remain, with the consent of the government. The latter always held him in high esteem, treating him in the way that is well known.

Whence it cannot fail to be seen what a monstrous injustice it is to take from the Capuchins this charge and place it in the hands of others! For they had to serve their church four priests working in the parish, and appointed under different orders—namely, two friars and two secular priests—without reckoning the other claimants, who only awaited the moment when the Capuchins should fail to make good their own pretensions. As to the reply that the lord governor gave to the Reverend Father Dom Guilhermo when he produced his patent of appointment, I say nothing here. I leave it to the judgment of the reader, who will, no doubt, decide wisely, as I trust he will do also in the following case, not merely rare, but actually unheard of.

There chanced to come a Frenchman of Pondicherry to be married at Madras, and he was in fact married there. The ceremony took place in the Capuchins' church on June 25 of the current year [1704]. It was the Reverend Father Friar Euzebio who officiated at the wedding. A few days after the marriage they went back to Pondicherry, arriving there on July 4. The next day [175] the Lord Patriarch sent for the husband, and ordered him to live apart from his wife, saying he was not properly married, and it was necessary to issue fresh banns and be married over again. The Frenchman was astonished at such a novel ruling, and went off in great haste, not to say at the run, to the convent of the Capuchins there, and finding the Reverend Father Thomas of Poitiers, related to him what had occurred. The father declined to believe an absurdity of that sort, but the Frenchman assured him it was so. The astonished father defen-

---

Norbert, 'Mémoires Utiles et Nécessaires,' 93-96. The order to build a church for Father Ephraim at Madras is dated June 8, 1642, and is signed by Andrew Cogan, Thomas Vintner, and Henry Greenhill.

XXXXIX. Chandol, a kind of litter

ded the case vigorously and the validity of the marriage, proving it from many authors of weight, whose names he gave in writing to the Frenchman. He told him to carry the paper to his Excellency.

As soon as he looked at the paper the Patriarch became angry with him, and at once gave an order to fetch Father Friar Thomas. On his appearing he was asked in a great passion whether it was he who defended such a marriage as valid, and in such a way. The father replied in the affirmative, and at once pointed out (in a folio he had taken with him for this purpose) that by the Council of Trent, and by six other councils, as proved by innumerable authors, a marriage was valid at which the parish priest was present, although he might be a non-tolerated, excommunicated person.[1] On hearing this the Lord Nuncio sent at once for a father of the Society of Jesus to examine into the case.

The result was in accordance with the Capuchin's assertions. The marriage was valid, although the Reverend Father Friar Euzebio might be excommunicated. How much more so when he was not? as was also abundantly proved.[2] Notwithstanding this report, his Excellency resolved to pursue his own course, closing eyes and ears to everything. I hardly know if my pen dare to write here what I saw elsewhere written—namely, that great men's errors are proportionate: 'The greater the man, so much the greater the error.' It is not I who say it.

On the same day he gave an order to the Reverend Father Friar Laurent to proceed at night to the Frenchman's house with two witnesses, and *januis clausis* (with closed doors) remarry them both, the husband and the wife. The Reverend Father Friar

1. There are three kinds of censure: (1) Excommunication, (2) suspension, (3) interdiction. By the major excommunication a Christian is deprived of the communion of the faithful in things sacred and civil. This is the 'non-tolerated excommunicated person' of the text (see V. Todcschi, 'Manuel du Droit Canonique,' pp. 602 and 603; Paris, 1880) (W.R.P.).
2. 'A marriage is equally valid when celebrated before an irregular curé, or one fallen under censure, or one expressly forbidden by the Ordinary to be present; on condition, however, that he has not been deprived of his office for any length of time' (V. Todeschi, work cited, p. 405) (W. R. P.). To the same general effect, see 'Dict. Enc. de la Théologie Catholique' (a French translation of Wetzer and Welte), vol. xiv., pp. 229 and 237; but the presence or sanction of the *curé* appears to be indispensable (Waterworth, 'Council of Trent,' p. 198).

Laurent knew very well in his conscience that he could not so act, it being obvious to him that by the Council of Trent and the other councils, as previously set forth, the marriage was already duly performed and therefore valid. However, out of fear of an interdict, which without fail would fall on him in case of disobedience, he obeyed. Demanding an order from his Excellency, as he was bound to do in a case as rare as it was peculiar, the priest went about eight o'clock at night to the house of the married couple. With him went two witnesses, one a Tonquinese, the other an Armenian, men expressly selected by his Excellency. Having closed the doors, he robed himself in a surplice and a black stole, then married them over again.

At this point the reader may agree to weigh in silence and ponder over the mysterious surroundings of this second marriage. Although to me it seems this would be discreet and wise, yet there cannot fail to be those (including all the common people) who will ask: 'Why marry persons that were already married, and well married? Why at night and not in the day? Why clandestinely and not in the face of the congregation? Why in a house instead of in a consecrated edifice? Why Armenians and Tonquinese, who do not know the language of the contracting parties, instead of French or Portuguese, understanding it? Why, finally, in a black stole and not a white one? *Mysterium vobis dico* ['Behold, I show you a mystery' (1 Cor. xv. 51)].

Finally, the Lord Patriarch embarked on July 11, 1704,[1] considerably grieved and angered at departing without having succeeded in carrying out his purposes. He wanted to appoint Italian fathers to Cuddalore in the place of Father Paulo de Saa, and to Madras in that of the Capuchins; but the English gentlemen refused their consent. Assuming that the Patriarch would surely leave distinct orders to carry out without fail the one and the other project after his departure, the Reverend Father Paulo de Saa, some days before his Excellency's embarkation, quitted Cuddalore one night without the knowledge of the gentlemen of the government. This he could easily do by disguising himself so as not to be recognised, he being a native of India. The distance was only three leagues, and, after all, not being a Frenchman, he did not at that time run much risk.

1. This date is confirmed by the extracts from the Cardinal's journal printed in Norbert, 'Mémoires Historiques' (Besançon, 1747), i. 176.

The father proceeded to Pondicherry in order to throw himself at the Patriarch's feet and demand pardon, and submit himself in all respects to his will. He persisted for three days, which he passed concealed in the College of the fathers of the Society of Jesus, never once appearing outside. But the more he insisted, the less he succeeded in obtaining his desires. It was too late, and the sentence against him had already been sent to the Reverend Father Dom Guilhermo della Valle to be put into execution. By the said sentence Father Paulo de Saa was compelled to abandon the two churches of Cuddalore and Tevana-patam.[1] He was directed to place them in the hands of the Theatine Fathers, and forbidden to administer the Sacraments within them. Failing the execution of this decree, there was an order to proceed against him in legal form. He was also directed to render an account of three years' income from both churches, and to make effective delivery thereof.

Up to this time this sentence has never been carried out, but Father Paulo de Saa has remained at Cuddalore in the capacity of parish priest as before, celebrating daily Mass, but without administering the Sacraments. The Lord Bishop of Meliapur (Mailapur) sent a priest to supply this deficiency. With regard to the Capuchins of Madras, the Lord Patriarch left them under suspension, and nominated as parish priest the Very Reverend Father Dom Guilhermo della Valle, as already stated. The Lord Bishop, on his part, selected another priest. Each of them held an order of appointment, but neither could exercise the functions, because the gentlemen of the government declined to recognise them, not even so far as to allow them inside the fortress.

Seeing this, and the lamentable condition into which this congregation of Madras had fallen, without parish priest, without ordained minister, without anyone who could administer the Sacraments, the superior of the Capuchins went on July 19 [1704] the San Thome to fling himself at the feet of the Lord Bishop of Mailapur. He made clear to him the necessity and misery of the wretched Christians who lived in Madras. He supplicated that he would be pleased to recall his order of suspension at any rate, until a decision on the case arrived from Rome. The Lord Bishop declined to listen to him on any terms, and in reply the superior asked him if the Reverend Father Paulo de Saa was

1. Tevanapatanam is the native village adjacent to Fort St. David.

to continue suspended [176] from the office of parish priest and from the administration of the Sacraments in accordance with the Lord Patriarch's decree. His lordship replied in the negative, and said that he would soon write to him, and on the first opportunity, that he might exercise all the functions of parish priest, and might administer the Sacraments.

The superior interrupted him by saying: 'What, my lord! are we not in the same case? If your lordship can remove the suspension of Father Paulo de Saa, can you not equally cancel ours, seeing that they were both promulgated by one and the same Lord Patriarch?' The Bishop replied that Father Paulo de Saa was a secular priest, while they were regulars. On receiving this reply the superior returned to Madras, whence he urged his demand by a petition and two protests, the one after the other, in which he inquired what were his faults. He proved by invincible arguments that not only his lordship could, but must, remove the suspension, in order not to allow so populous a Christian community to perish in abandonment, deprived of the Sacraments and of every sort of spiritual consolation. Nothing was of any avail, nor did his lordship deign to show himself benignant in any particular. The people themselves, as might be expected in such a terrible conjuncture and under such excessive rigour, made one or two appeals to the Lord Bishop, begging him to be so good as to assist them for the love of God in a case of such urgent necessity, and send them some father who could say Mass and administer the Sacraments.

The answer received was that Father Friar Miguel Anjo [Michel Ange] might nominate an ordained person, either a friar or a secular priest, who should exercise his functions as parochial priest in his place. To that the Christians replied that the gentlemen of the Government would not agree to admit any priest other than the Capuchins already present in Madras, and in addition threatened to expel from their territory all the other fathers then present there that they could lay hands on, as in fact they did. All of this was not enough to make the Lord Bishop feel any pain for that poor community, or apply any remedy. On the contrary, he remained as inexorable as ever, and would not consent to annul the suspension of the Capuchins. All he said was that he had not the power to do it; at the same time he did not neglect to set aside that of Father Paulo de Saa by sending to him an order that he might exercise the functions of parish priest in the two churches of Cuddalore and Tevanapatam. Accordingly, he entered on their exercise. The Capuchins of Madras remained under suspension as before, and the Christians there were deprived of Mass, Sacraments, and a priest capable of aiding them in their spiritual necessities. *Deus omnipotent provideat*! (Let Almighty God provide).

Without a doubt, after having seen and thoroughly considered all herein reported, the reader will enter into an understanding of the gross error in which the common people persist, attributing the disgrace of the wretched Capuchins to the two causes which I set out by specifying (IV. 165). They believed these misadventures to be directed to some other particular end. They were all the more convinced of this because the Lord Patriarch also claimed the right to eject the Capuchins of Pondicherry from that place, meaning to substitute Italian fathers. He insisted on this as much as ever he could with Monsieur Martin, hoping to get his consent; but that gentleman always gave him the answer that he could not permit it without express orders from the king and the Company. Thus were those unhappy friars [of Pondicherry] delivered from this and similar tribulations, and that design of the Lord Patriarch was entirely frustrated. From this it might seem that the above tragedy arose more from some hidden agreement, or from a secret aversion to the whole of a religious order, than from the motives made public and obvious to the simple-minded. In considering this matter there can be nobody who on good grounds can blame the poor Capuchins for the way they acted, for it is ever hard to bear an injury, although it may be a disguised one; how much the harder, then, was it to cope with all those wiles, as can today be easily recognised. May our Lord of His goodness have compassion on the unhappy priests, and permit them the rest which they and the whole congregation require for His greater glory and the good of souls! Amen.

Equally does it seem to me requisite to give here a brief and succinct account of another tragedy, that of the unfortunate brothers of the confraternity of the Rosary at Madras. It was founded many years ago with the licence and consent of the Most Reverend the Vicar-General of the Dominicans in Goa, and ratified by a patent recently come from the Most Reverend Father the Master of the Order at Rome, confirming and approving the said confraternity. In spite of all this it remains at this day suppressed by the order of the Lord Patriarch at the instance of the Reverend Father Friar Diogo do Sacramento, Dominican, living at San Thome, in charge of the Church of San Domingo.[1] There he has started a new confraternity of the Rosary, under whose name he began a contest with that of Madras about some wrought silver of the ancient confraternity of San Thome. If I were to report here the disagreeables and disputes that broke out on this matter it would be an unending business; therefore, as the shortest way, I rely upon a manifesto drawn up by the brothers of Madras and submitted to the Lord Patriarch when cited by the said Reverend Father Friar Diogo do Sacramento before the tribunal of his Excellency. Its terms are as follows [177]:

Most Exalted Lord,

We, the president, *et cetera*, officers of the ancient confraternity of Our Lady of the Rosary at San Thome, at present transferred to this church of Madras, where we are its unworthy members, obeying the command of your Excellency as humble servants and obedient sheep of the Catholic flock, produce the information you ask from us about the said confraternity. We rely upon your Excellency's benignity to pardon us for the faults of style which we are sure to commit before your tribunal, not only in our own remarks, but in the use of judicial terms. Thus, though unlearned, we shall obtain from your Excellency's benevolence special excuse for our admitted ignorance, being in our intentions humble, sincere, and obedient. We set forth as follows:

The legitimate and veritable title of our confraternity is the same as that of the ancient city of San Thome. It was founded with all the necessary requirements, and the permission of the Very Reverend the Vicar-General of Goa. After the loss of the

1. The Church of St. Domingo appears on the plan of Madras in Pharaoh's Map of Southern India, 1855, and is marked on Plate XLI. of Constable's 'Hand Atlas'; it is to the west of San Thome Cathedral. But Mr. Philipps says it does not appear in the 'Madras Catholic Directory,' 1885, or in the 'Annuario' of Goa, 1885, already cited; but it is probably the 'Rosary Church' of the one, and the 'N. Senhora do Rosario' of the other.

above city[1] it was transferred to that of Madras, whither all, or at any rate the majority of the brothers, removed, and there settled. Some of those, by grace of the Virgin, are still alive. With a view to their general consolation, they prayed the Reverend Father Friar Ephraim of Nevers, vicar of this [Madras] church at that time, to draw up a petition to the said Vicar-General for the issue of his license. This we obtained, and still hold, as is proved by the said petition and the order of the Vicar-General of Goa, which we produce along with it. Thereby your Excellency will see that we are still the same confraternity of San Thome.

The Reverend Father Friar Diogo do Sacramento, out of caprice, has founded a confraternity at his own church. Granted that this is at the place which was formerly the city of San Thome, still, it is not the [same] city of that name. To this confraternity he gave the name of the Rosary [of San Thome]. He should not have acted thus, since his church is not at a convenient distance, as provided by the statutes.[2] Simply from this one fact it ought not to receive the name of a confraternity. But to secure his object the said reverend father collected some of our brothers who happened to be dwellers there, men who were lovers of novelty. By various promises he started the said confraternity and began to dispute with ours, endeavouring to extinguish it by threats of interdicts. He disparaged it by the use of names so ignominious that modesty compels us not to report them here to your Excellency.

Seeing these things, we had recourse to the tribunal of the Lord Bishop for a decision as to what might be just. The said reverend father [Diogo] declined to submit himself to him, giving him out for suspected. Thus we were forced to have recourse to the judgment-table of the Sacred Congregation and the tribunal of his Holiness, where at this moment the case is pending. We hope it will be decided in our favour, for on the same occasion we wrote to the Most Reverend the Master of the Order of Preachers [*i.e.*, the Dominicans] at Rome, praying him to

1. San Thome was taken by the Gulkandah king in 1662 (see *ante*, IV., fol. 22). Madras was founded in 1639. Father Ephraim was Vicar of Madras from 1642 until his death in 1694.
2. 'Apparently this means that, being at San Thome, it was at too great a distance from Madras, where most of the members lived' (W.R.P.).

deliver us from the scruples and doubts propounded to us by the Reverend Father Friar Diogo do Sacramento. This dignitary was good enough to do us the kindness of sending us a patent of which a copy is hereto appended. From it your Excellency will see that he approved our devotion and admitted our confraternity to be that same ancient one of San Thome, subject to the condition that when there shall be in this place [Madras] a church of San Domingo, we shall transfer ourselves thereto. In this there never will be on our part any objection, whenever our Lord shall so permit.

As for the property demanded by the inhabitants of San Thome, jointly with the Reverend Father Friar Diogo do Sacramento, we are ignorant of the right by which they make this claim. For, besides being legally ours, created by the efforts and devotion of our predecessors, it was a second time redeemed, after the loss of San Thome city, from the hands of Jacomo Cardozo Barreto, into whose possession it was pledged by the vicar, who at that time was of our confraternity, the Father Friar Luis Fragozo, who also disposed surreptitiously of various jewels and ornaments, as may be seen from the affidavits of witnesses, which we also present herewith. All these things were lost by our confraternity, we not knowing to whom they were sold. As for the pledging of the remainder, which came to our notice, those things were bought back at our instance by a devout lady, who afterwards was made a sister and our manager. This embezzlement was one of the motives which caused our predecessors to submit the above-mentioned petition to Goa by the intermediary of the Reverend Father Ephraim, and was the chief reason for securing at Goa that order in our favour with the indulgences and privileges we still enjoy, for our consolation, as will appear from the said document itself.

As for the requisition in which they claim the return of this remainder of things to the confraternity of San Thome, on the pretext that it was founded in that place, there is no reason by which it can prevail against us. We are ourselves the ancient confraternity, as proved by the petition, together with the order thereon of the Vicar-General of Goa, and the patent from the Most Reverend Father the Master of the Order of Preachers at Rome, as we said above. Although the said claimants cannot sue us under the pretext of place—for in this respect there is wanting to them *now* all the chief circumstances of *then*—we make no attempt to dispute on that head (since, for the security of our confraternity the papers we possess are sufficient), and we beg to be excused from entering into it. Here we will solely point out a few details, from which your Excellency can obtain evidence of the small reason with which they are perturbing and molesting us.

Anciently the city of San Thome belonged to the King of Portugal, who governed it by his officials absolutely without the slightest dependence on anyone. The churches and inhabitants enjoyed rents and privileges, which were all lost through various faults when the Mahomedans took the country, which to this day has not been restored, those now living there no longer enjoying that ancient freedom [178]. On the contrary, they are subject to the government of the Mahomedans, being continually troubled and molested by them. For this reason we contend that there is no one who can compel us to forsake this place of safety, where we execute in the Virgin's service all that our strength can accomplish without the least trouble, molestation, or hindrance; or force us to go elsewhere and involve ourselves in that labyrinth, thereby laying ourselves open to a thousand disagreeables.

Finally, we make known to your Excellency that the Reverend Father Friar Diogo do Sacramento, not having succeeded in his designs by means of our brothers, who had returned to live at San Thome as already stated, has expelled all of them as unworthy, and has admitted Portuguese gentlemen into his confraternity. This is contrary to the directions of the ordinances, bulls, *et cetera*, all of which set forth that the confraternity of the Rosary must be constituted out of natives of the soil, a phrase known and customary throughout India. This is inevitably one of the principal reasons for asserting that the confraternity of the Reverend Father Friar Diogo is not, and cannot be, the ancient one of San Thome, for it differs from it as black from white. By all this your Excellency will perceive the great reason we have on our side, and the little with which we are molested and disturbed.

With this we take shelter under the protection of your Excellency, from whom with all submissiveness we entreat, for the love of God and for the increase of His kingdom whose cause this is, that we be defended for His greater glory. For what those of the other party demand is to be inferred as evidence of their wish to diminish that glory, without regard to the scandal they are causing throughout this congregation and the stimulus they are giving to the adversaries of our religion. Therefore, since we continue assured of your Excellency's zeal, we wait for justice.

Madras, this 28th of April, 1704

With the above petition and all the papers in its support the brothers of Madras sent one of their number to Pondicherry, becoming sureties for his expenses. He was to plead their cause there. As his protector and their procurator, they elected the Very Reverend Father Joao Baptista Sidotte,[1] a person among those who accompanied his Excellency, and one of much influence. He worked fairly well in the negotiation, and had almost succeeded in it, according to the advices received from Pondicherry. He proposed an amicable compromise between the two confraternities for the greater praise of the Virgin and contentment of the brethren. But where self-will reigns reason has no esteem.

After agreeing to the compromise, the Reverend Father Friar Diogo do Sacramento disavowed it, and went off to San Thome, leaving the matter undecided, as afterwards appeared. Thereupon the brother who had been deputed from Madras decided also to withdraw. On going to kiss the Lord Patriarch's hand and ask for his documents, he had difficulty in obtaining a vague reply to the effect that, having been once presented, they must remain in the chancery of his Excellency. With that he came away without the Lord Patriarch saying a single word to him about the dispute. As to it, all he said to his auditor, Salinos Marianos,[2] when the brother asked for his documents, was that,

1. Giovanni Battista Sidotti, Palermitano, appears on p. 3 of Fatinelli's 'Relazione' (Rome, 1704) as one of the eleven persons in the Cardinal's entourage. In Part V., fol. 173, we are told that he settled at Manila.
2. This name appears in Fatinelli's 'Relazione' (Rome, 1704), p. 3, as Sabino Mariani, of Bari, one of the eleven persons in the Cardinal's suite. His name also crops up in the China proceedings, he having been expelled from Pekin and sent to Macao between 1706 and 1710 (Norbert, 'Mémoires Historiques,' Lisbon edition, vi. 264, 294, 365, where he is called 'auditor' of the Cardinal).

in order to avoid further differences between the confraternities, he would not give them back.

When their deputy reached Madras, it was understood by all that on hearing the report of their appeal to Rome, as testified in their manifesto, his Excellency had declined to decide the complaint, one of the parties being dissatisfied [with the tribunal]. In this they were greatly misled, for at the time of his departure (and there were not wanting those who suspected he would do this) he deliberately, to the end that the brothers should not be able to reply to or appeal from his sentence, sent his final order upon the affair. It was entirely in favour of the Reverend Father Friar Diogo do Sacramento, and imposed the severest rigours of an interdict in case the brothers of Madras failed to carry it into execution, even in the least particular.

Upon this arose not only great murmuring, but there were not wanting those who said that this decision was a gratification or reward for the merits acquired by the said Father Friar Diogo by giving informal advice on every point known to him to the Abate San Giorgio at the time when he was in San Thome. But it would not be lawful for me to speak here on these matters, nor do I desire to say about them one single word. Confining myself to the subject of the wretched brothers of Madras, I continue.

After there had been great discussions with the Reverend Father Friar Diogo do Sacramento about the silver, the Very Reverend the Vicar-General of the Bishop of Mailapur sent a Portuguese called Joao Coelho Colembro to say on his behalf to the Reverend Father Friar Michel Ange[1] that as a friend he advised him to take no part in the dispute over the silver plate of the brothers of the Rosary. If he did, he, the Vicar-General, would be compelled to include him in the declaration that he was on the point of publishing against the said brothers.

This notice very much astonished the Father Friar Michel Ange, for it gave him clearly to understand that at San Thome it was talked of or was presumed, that in the future he meant

1. The text has 'Miguel Anjo'; but, as he was a Frenchman, I revert to the French form. He is the Michael Angelo of the English records.

to defend the silver. But from the very first, when the Lord Abate had sent the Very Reverend Friar Laurent from San Thome to speak to him about it, he being then in Madras, he had told the brothers that it concerned them to defend their plate if they so pleased. But neither he nor his colleagues [179] would do so in any shape, nor was it fitting for them to interfere. After that answer, the brothers from that time sent persons to inform the Lord Abate about the facts of the case, and they commenced their suit at Pondicherry. In all this the brothers of Madras never involved the Father Friar Michel Ange in any way.

At once, on the very same day, the father sent for the president and some of the other brothers, and made over to them the key of the chest which held the said plate, declaring at the same time that he resigned office as Vicar of the Confraternity. He repeated to them afresh that he had nothing to do with the said plate, nor would have from that day forth. They might dispose of it according as to them seemed appropriate. They accepted the key, and as they left the church they ran against some other brothers in the street. To these men they gave the information that they had received the said key from the hand of the Reverend Father Friar Michel Ange, who, on making it over, had resigned his vicariate of the confraternity. Discussing these matters, some approving and some disapproving the receipt of the key, they arrived finally almost to raising their hands against each other. Such a great disturbance did they create that it was necessary to call in the watch to separate them. As the incident arose close to the gate, the corporal on guard there reported to the captain, and the latter to the Lord Governor, as was his duty and happens usually after any extraordinary quarrel or tumult.

When this strife was over, the president [of the Rosary] went back to Father Friar Michel Ange, and requested him most urgently to be pleased to take back once more the key he had delivered to him. For if he did not, he (the president) ran a risk of receiving a good beating from the other brothers, who took it ill, and were much irritated that he had accepted it outside of a board meeting, and without the consent of all the members. Moved by compassion, the father took the key so as to pacify him for the time, and to avoid the scandal likely to arise among them if he refused.

But two days afterwards, being the 18th of the same month [August, 1704],[1] the brothers having met in consultation, he sent them the key of the silver, and made it over to them in the presence of three witnesses. They accepted it, and as to what then passed there is full certainty through those who were present. After that they went together, and drew up an inventory of all that belonged to their confraternity, whether gold, silver, or ornaments. After shutting up the whole in a chest, they carried the key to the house of the president. When that was accomplished, Father Friar Michel Ange sent for them to his cell, and asked them if they were in possession of the key, and whether it had been removed from his control to theirs, so that they could deal with it in whatever way they wished, being its owners and masters. They all replied in the affirmative.

'Then,' resumed the father, 'hand me over a certificate.' They drew it up at once, and in it the president and other officers of the board declared that they had entered into possession of all the articles of gold, silver, *et cetera,* belonging to their confraternity, kept formerly at their desire by the Father Friar Michel Ange in his control. At this present time, to avoid molestation, he had made over to them everything, at the same time divesting himself of every interest connected with their confraternity. Whereas they had lived under his protection, and the above statements were the truth, they executed this affidavit by swearing on the Holy Gospels, and they also signed at the foot.

As soon as the certificate was completed it was sent to the Very Reverend Vicar-General, who replied to the writing forwarded to him in this form of words: 'I have seen what you write; it agrees with what he said, which makes it certain that he was not negligent' (he spoke here of the Father Friar Michel Ange), 'for there is no reason for not making over the silver, *et cetera.*' On the Saturday following, which comes to the 23rd of the same month [August, 1704], the Lord Governor of Madras sent for the president, and reading to him a document sent to him from San Thome, said to him he must explain how they came into possession of the silver, and ordered him forthwith to bring

1. The month is not named, but it is fixed by the mention of September 3 on fol. 180. The Patriarch sailed from Pondicherry on July 11, 1704.

the key of it. This was done without delay, for the president brought it and made it over to the governor. It was not right, nor was it possible, to make the slightest resistance to such a mighty lord.

Next day, Sunday, the 24th of the same month [August, 1704], there was read in the church of San Domingo and in that of Mae de Deus in San Thome a proclamation whereby the president, the officers of the board, the outside procurator, and all the other brothers were declared to have incurred the major excommunication, and were therefore to be shunned. Their crime was the non-delivery of the plate. On the excommunication having been read, some students came out at once to eject publicly the brothers of Madras from the church of Mae de Deus,[1] they having gone there to attend the service. This project was forthwith put into execution to the causing of great scandal.

Upon the news reaching Madras there arose such great tribulation among the Catholics that none consented to speak to another, most of them being brothers [of the confraternity]. These men went in troops for three whole days to get themselves absolved. There was such a concourse of people that the Vicar-General grew worried about giving absolution, and to deliver himself from so many troubles declared those only to be affected who had signed the certificate. By this means the people were pacified, and those only who had signed applied for absolution.

To this intent, on the 28th of the month [? August, 1704], they all went in a body to throw themselves at the feet of the Reverend Vicar-General, begging as a favour that he would absolve them. After having examined them and found them without fault, he sent the whole of them to the house of the secretary to the Lord Bishop to take an oath that they were not the cause of the non-delivery of the silver. They were then to return to be absolved. They all came out much relieved, and went at once to take the oath. While they were there [180] ready to take it, the Reverend Father Friar Diogo do Sacramento appeared with a protest, in which it was asserted that the certificate they drew up was forced upon them; for this reason he prayed and protested that they must delay the absolution until that doubt

1. Mae de Deus Church still exists in Madras (see Constable's 'Hand Atlas,' Plate XLI.; the 'Madras Catholic Directory,' 1906, p. 289; and the 'Annuario' of Goa, 1885, already cited).

was investigated. The Reverend Vicar-General postponed it, and sent the wretched brothers to the house of the Dominican, being that of the complaining party.

They obeyed at once, and went to throw themselves at the feet of the Reverend Father Friar Diogo do Sacramento, praying him as a favour to have compassion upon them in the piteous state they were in. The decision they obtained from his mouth was that there was no other means of delivering themselves from the excommunication than the drawing up of a document, showing how Father Friar Michel Ange compelled them forcibly to prepare the certificate about the delivery into their custody of the silver and the key pertaining thereto.

To this they all replied with one voice that they could not in their consciences raise up so great a falsehood against Father Friar Michel Ange, and as little could they swear that the said certificate was drawn up under compulsion. For they had drawn it up of their own accord, as was reasonable, without any objection or constraint, things which were not necessary, seeing that Father Friar Michel Ange did not thereby ask them any favour, nor had they done him any. Moreover, to ask an acknowledgment of what has been delivered seems no more than what is just, and to deny what you have received can never fail to be an act of bad faith; they were not in the custom of employing such subterfuges in such matters. To receive the things and not admit it, even if they wished to act thus, would produce no result, for they could always be placed under compulsion. For the document which his paternity wished them to execute would not do the slightest harm to Father Friar Michel Ange; but it would bring evils on them, poor creatures! for having published falsehoods under constraint from the said Father Friar Diogo do Sacramento.

Who is there that could be persuaded that such dreadful proceedings, an absurdity so dreadful, would be resorted to by the Reverend Father Friar Diogo do Sacramento, a regular cleric, so aged, so able, of such authority? There can be no doubt of it, since the thing really happened, and it was spoken of by all the brothers present at the time. They came forth much cast down at the act of the said Reverend Father Friar Diogo do Sacramento. Things continued thus, and they stopped for three days more preparing papers, and more papers, without doing themselves the slightest good. They endured great privations.

For in San Thome there was not one man who would give them as much as a glass of water, and all persons there thrust them aside as excommunicated. It was a sorrow to see the poor creatures wandering from door to door among the Hindu Malabaris asking for a mouthful of rice and some water. They received these in the palms of their hands, and out of them they ate. The rice and the water were dropped into them from a height by the Hindus, it not being their habit to come into contact with Christians, or to touch them in any matter of eating or drinking. Then for sleeping the poor things had no other accommodation than the hard stone benches at those Hindus' street-doors, on which they passed the nights. These Hindus still showed some humanity, but the Christians were without compassion. But why wonder at the Christians not succouring them, when the Church (I mean those who governed it there) showed no commiseration for them, although they appealed for it by making themselves out culprits (simply to show their obedience) about a thing wherein they were in nowise guilty.

Unable to endure any longer, they appointed an attorney, who in their absence might plead for their absolution. They then returned to their houses in Madras. Within a very few days one man died and another began to spit blood, while one old man fell very ill from the hardships suffered by first walking all day long in the sun, which at that season in these regions is very powerful, then by passing the whole night in the chilly open air. Nearly all of them were men advanced in years, afflicted with misery and poverty to such a degree that they could hardly feed themselves in their own homes. In those homes it was not a less but a much greater grief to behold the clamour with which the poor wives and daughters implored Heaven, praying from God the help and remedy which they did not receive from His ministers upon earth, after having prostrated themselves at their feet so many times.

Four days afterwards, being September 3 [1704], they went back to throw themselves at the feet of the Very Reverend the Vicar-General, praying to be absolved by him. His answer was that he would be very pleased to grant absolution, but it was also necessary to satisfy the complaining party; that done, he would absolve them at once.

On getting this reply, they went on to the house of the Dominican. As soon as he saw them he dropped on his knees before them and, almost weeping, said to them: 'Gentlemen and brothers, for the love of God and the Most Holy Virgin of the Rosary, will you not do me the pleasure of handing to me the silver?' To this they all replied that they would so do with all their heart, if the silver were only in their control. His paternity knew very well that it was no longer in their hands; yet on hearing these words the father rose in a great rage, and in a loud voice, growing louder as he went on, he said: 'Brothers, either the silver or its money value; there is no middle term.' In this he did not speak badly, for, as is herein to be seen, in all that he did about this wearisome silver there appeared naught but extremes, and his acts concerning it passed from one extreme to another. He continued: 'Unless one [181] or the other is delivered, there is no way for you to get absolution.'

The brothers gave once more the same answer. Then the father went on: 'I will show you a good expedient. Go, all of you, and fall at the feet of the Reverend Father Friar Michel Ange, and beg him for the love of God and His Most Holy Mother to solicit the return of the silver, and then all your troubles will be ended.' 'Reverend father,' retorted the brothers, 'we know very well that it is not from the hands of Father Friar Michel Ange that we should solicit the return of the silver, for if he could have done it we should not have had to wear ourselves out thus and anger your reverence.' Then, giving up this effort, he thrust them out of his house, saying as they left: 'You will have to stop as you are, excommunicated.'

Vexed and cast down at the great inhumanity they found in the Reverend Father Friar Diogo do Sacramento, they sought out the Most Illustrious the Lord Bishop, and, dissolving into tears, they prostrated themselves at his lordship's feet, and supplicated his compassion on their misery and his aid in the difficulty overwhelming them; for they knew not what fresh steps to take, nor had they anyone else they could have recourse to. Beholding this, the Lord Bishop was moved to pity, and asked them if they had instigated the Lord Governor of Madras to take away the key, so that the plate might not be delivered. All asseverated that this was not the case, and they spoke with such force that the Lord Bishop acquired the clear conviction that they were innocent in the case. He accorded them his blessing and sent them home, saying three times, as reported by several brothers, that none of them was under ban any longer.

Happy in an extreme degree, the poor things rose from the ground; but as this verbal order would not be enough to satisfy the common crowd, they asked the Lord Bishop to be pleased to give them a writing, so as to convince the populace, who were treating them as excommunicated persons. His lordship directed them to draw up a petition, and send it to him in the morning. The brothers did so, and left it in the secretary's office to be dealt with as promised by his lordship. This done, they went home.

On the next day, the fourth of the same month [September, 1704], the Lord Bishop, while wishing to carry out his word, was anxious also to please the other party. To this intent he went in person to visit the Reverend Father Friar Diogo do Sacramento, whose house was close to his, his object being to acquaint him with the facts and explain how the wretched brothers were not under a ban. As soon as his lordship reached the father's house the latter issued from it and received him with a wordy protest against the result. When they began to discuss the question, the Bishop was so little satisfied with the answers of the Dominican that, unable longer to listen to his prolixities, he rose at once and set out for his own house, the interview having lasted only long enough to say the *Credo*.

During the same day the attorney of the brothers went to the Bishop's house to press for an order on the petition already referred to. His lordship told him he was unable to issue such an order without first of all the other side being satisfied as to their protest. Thereupon the attorney of the brothers went off to interview Father Friar Diogo. After much argumentation, he found only one way to deliver the brothers of Madras from the excommunication, in spite of the Lord Bishop having said repeatedly that they were not under interdict. That way was to execute a document by which they should all confess that the silver in dispute belonged under a decree of the Patriarch to the confraternity of San Thome.

Here it was that the poor men had to endure more than ever. A very hot controversy arose among them as to whether they should or should not sign such a document. The greater number, eager to be relieved from that fantastic excommunication, were of the opinion that they ought to sign. Others, more wary, were against signing it on any terms, foreseeing that by so doing they risked a great danger. The dispute lasted some twenty days, during which a thousand atrocities were perpetrated upon them;

for the attorney whom they had called in to defend them turned against them, and became the worst weapon they encountered at San Thome. He there affronted them several times in the most opprobrious terms, without regard to the fact that the poor fellows, having confided in him, had put themselves entirely in his hands. Nor did he remember the fact that he had counselled all they had done, both in the defence of the plate and of their confraternity, helping them in the preparation of several documents and petitions on the subject.

But I believe the reader is hardly likely to wonder at such procedure, seeing how this man behaved to the Capuchins. He ate with them and, for over three years, lived with them as a brother. After that, what is there to be surprised at in this other instance? How much less amazement can it cause, it being in comparison as a single point in a huge circumference! Moreover, if the Capuchins were taken in by him, in spite of being enlightened by such a long period passed together, how much more likely is it for these poor brothers to be deceived by his fine speeches! By these he hoped to win them to be his friends, in order to make use of them should there arise any objection or opposition on the part of the people to his introduction as vicar, as he aspired to be.[1]

When all his hopes were frustrated, and, as he asserted, all his efforts insufficiently rewarded [182], he planned to get something out of the brothers which, in the future, might be of use in his projects against the Capuchins. But, finding that he could not secure this from the brothers, he was totally undeceived (that is if he had ever been deceived), and, altogether renouncing them, threw them over and openly stamped upon them, until the miserable beings, like so many asses, were reduced to signing the document that had been prepared for them. By this alone were they able to secure and obtain on September 24 [1704] an absolution for that of which they were not guilty.

As in giving this absolution there was a strange and mysterious circumstance, it is not well to pass it over here in silence. The case stood thus: The Lord Bishop ordered the *curé* of the cathedral to absolve them *ad cautelam* while he carried it out *in forma juris*.[2] What could be said upon this I leave to the pene-

1. The allusion here, I presume, is to Guilhermo della Valle, Theatine.
2. V. Todeschi, 'Manuel du Droit Canonique,' p. 604. A censure

tration of the reader, for it is not always seemly to say what might be said, even if some might be pleased to hear it. But all I will say is that one of the brothers noticed the circumstance that in his order the Lord Bishop said they were to be absolved *ad cautelam*, while the cure's certificate said that he absolved them *in forma juris*. Seeing that the two statements did not agree, this man went to a certain person and asked him what was meant by these words '*in forma juris*.' He construed it finely, for he told the man it was just the same as if the *curé* had tickled their ribs (*as costas*), as in effect he had done. 'Then, sir,' rejoined the poor man, 'keep it secret.' When he had been warmly thanked, his interlocutor offered his congratulations: 'And may it profit you much.' Therewith the story of the wretched brothers, which began as a tragedy, ends with a hearty laugh from those who wished to see them chastised, as they had been.

As to the troubles of the poor Capuchins, we know not yet how they will end. May God help them and all their congregation! What is certain is that if the Lord Patriarch had not been so harsh on his side, nor the Lord Governor of Madras on his, the poor Capuchins would not have been so much ground down, nor the Christians here so much troubled and upset by the want of spiritual consolations, which condition continues to this moment. May our Lord in His mercy ameliorate this in the future, and liberate the souls of the faithful from unjust claims, which, if on rare occasions they enrich, more commonly bring ruin! As it seems to me, there will not fail to be some faithful Christian, a lover of the truth, who will transmit to Rome some narrative like the above. But it appears to me he will give fuller details, for I cannot adduce many of the circumstances like any of the Capuchins could do.

Already the inquiring reader will have seen from the above narrative the reasons which rendered it necessary for the Reverend Father Friar Michel and the other friars resident in Madras to have recourse to the Lord Archbishop of Goa. In reply his Grace sent him a letter, of which a translated copy follows:[1]

---

may be removed (1) absolutely, (2) conditionally, (3) *ad cautelam*, where, for instance, there is a doubt whether the censure exists (W.R.P.).

1. A Latin letter to the same effect as that in the text was addressed by the Archbishop Primate to Pope Clement XI., who replied by a Brief of January 1, and a Declaration of January 4, 1707, setting aside the Primate's Mandate, and ruling that the Patriarch's powers had

MOST REVEREND FATHER MAITRE FRIAR MIGUEL ANJO,

With cordial interest I feel the troubles of your Reverence, and the scandals caused by Lord Dom Carlos Thomas. But his lordship's temerity is excused by his want of experience. He could have carried this thing out by giving me, as Primate in India, information of his delegation; and on his authority being recognised, the whole jurisdiction in the East could have been brought under control at pleasure, and with the greatest ease. But, like the sun behind clouds, so was this prelate obscured by his advisers, who, as is to be supposed by inference from their acts, were not the most circumspect of men. Further, he alienated reasonable persons, owing to the breaking out of these disputes, which scandalize these new plantations of Christianity in the East, and this, too, in the midst of infidels, a thing reproved by St. Paul, *et hoc inter infideles*.[1] But let us leave on one side past mistakes, and deal solely with a remedy for the difficulties at present existing.

The first thing is to consider what your reverence and your friars have declared to me. In truth, I could not believe in such temerities, were not those attesting them such veracious men. For it is an unbroken rule in God's Church that no one can constitute himself a delegate of the Apostolic See [183] without a general promulgation of the Bulls he holds. It is a fundamental doctrine, and as such upheld in the 'Directorium Inquisitorum,' chap. i.:[2] *'Ubi Penna* (? Peña) *in versu "poterit"*: *quia nemo creditur delegatus nisi probet delegationem*. [Where Peña says in the paragraph 'Poterif: 'Since no man is accepted as a delegate

---

been sufficiently published by their communication to the Bishop of San Thome (Norbert, 'Mémoires Historiques' 1747, i. 153-171).

1. Probably intended for '[Sed frater cum fratre judicis contendit:] et hoc apud infideles' (Vulgate, 1 Cor. vi. 6) (W. R. P.)—'But brother goeth to law with brother, and that before the unbelievers.'
2. I am indebted to the learned author of the 'History of the Inquisition,' H. C. Lea, L.L.D., of Philadelphia, for the identification of this work. It is by a fourteenth-century writer, Nicholas Eymerich, printed by Francisco Peña, with a copious commentary ('Venetis, apud Marcum Antonium Zalterium,' 1595, in folio). The passage quoted is in Peña's notes (Commentario I. of third part, fol. 392, paragraph 'Poterit,' in Venice edition of 1607). It is an utterance of Innocent III. in 1208, embodied in the 'Corpus Juris Canonici,' Extra or Decr., Gregorii IX., lib. i. tit. xxix., cap. 31: 'Non creditur quis delegatus nisi delegationem probet' (see edition of E. L. Richter, Leipzig, 1839, part ii., col. 169).

unless he prove his delegation' (credentials)]. Since the Lord Dom Carlos Thomas did not publish his Bulls within the primacy to which they referred, or, at the least, within the bishopric of San Thome, in no way was obedience due to him, nor could he be reputed the delegate of the Apostolic See. Much less need his interdicts be respected, or reckoned as such. There is an express passage in the chapter: '*Cum in jure de officio delegati*:' '*Ibi sic non ligat censuras quando datur copia dc delegationis'*— (*tenet* Connachis Brumus, in Tract. 'de Legati.,' lib. i., cap. 8). ['When a question of the office of delegate arises in course of a trial: ' 'there he does not make his censures so binding when opportunity is given to question (the authority) of the delegation. So holds Connachis Brunus.']

Nor even did it suffice for the Lord Dom Carlos Thomas to promulgate his powers without delivering them in writing to any party who demanded it. See the gloss in the chapter: *Porto extra.*[1] *'De privilegiis'*[2] *verbo 'ex inspectione': Ibi et est argumentum quod judex debeat facere copiam rescripti partibus ad inspiciendum; nec sufficit sola recitatio rescripti, quia falsitas potest ibi esse quae ex sola lectione deprehendi non possit: tenet* Filinus Castrensis, Cons, viii., n. 3.[3] [And there you will find a

1. Conradus Brunus (Braun), an Augustinian Canonist, died 1563 (see H. Hurter, 'Nomenclator,' i. 10, note, 'Opera Tria Nunc Primum Edita—De Legationibus Libri Quinque....,' folio, 1548, B.M., 521, m. 2). The titles referred to are: Book i., 'De Personis eorum qui mittent Legatos deque mandatis et rebus legationum'; cap. 8, 'De Mandatis Legatorum' (see pp. 17-19). The exact words quoted in the text do not appear. The whole passage in Peña reads: 'Quia nemo creditur delegatus, nisi probet delegationem, cap. "cum in iure de offic. delegati." ......de quo vide quae eleganter et copiose tradit Conradus Brunus, lib. i., "de legationibus," cap. 8.' As this is part of Peña's commentary, it is most probable that the word 'penna' in the text is meant for him, and not for the word 'poena' (penalty).
2. The heading is corrupt, and Mr. Kennedy would amend by reading, 'Portio extra "De Privilegiis" verbo "Ex Inspectione," ' and would translate thus: '[Additional matter on the words "Ex Inspectione" in the chapter "De Privilegiis"].'
3. I can find a Felinus Ferrariensis and a Franciscus Castrensis, but no Filinus Castrensis. I have looked at 'Consilia seu Responsa' of Felinus Maria Sandaeus, Ferrariensis, auditor of the Roman Rota (Venice, 1574), and his 'De Officio et Potestate Judicis Delegati' (72 pages, folio, no date or imprint); also at the 'Constitutçoes Synodaes do Bispado da Guarda,' 1621, by Bishop Francisco de Castro (Franciscus Castrensis). In

reason why the judge should give the parties an opportunity of inspecting the rescript; nor is the mere reading out of the rescript sufficient, because it may contain some flaw, which cannot be detected from the mere recitation. So holds Filinus Castrensis.]

The reason of the Catholic Church for this rule is justifiable and evident. It does not wish that any delegate should hold himself out as such until he has first presented his Bulls *in extenso*. By this piece of sincerity it cuts short the ambition leading some men to force themselves on God's flock, not as pastors, but as robbers, entering otherwise than by the door. This has already happened in Portugal, as is related by Savedra[1] of a legate who, entirely without authority, introduced himself into the kingdom, and, exercising a jurisdiction which he did not possess, set up a tribunal of the Inquisition. If experience can show us this in Europe, so near to Rome, what might not happen in Asia if legates were acknowledged without minute examination of their Bulls and the powers they have brought!

Neither your reverence nor the other friars, ecclesiastical persons, and secular priests could in any way obey without an explicit display of the Pontifical Bulls, such being the order of the Supreme Pontiff, Boniface, and in the 'Clementinia':[2] *'Iniunctae nobis' sane 'de electione' inter communes: ibi 'sane, 'quam periculosum existat quod aliquis in officio, dignitate, vel gradu fore se asserat et pro tali etiam habeatur, nisi prius ipse quod asserit, legitimis ostenderit documentis, tam ex civilibus quam ex canonicis institutis, colligitur evidenter; asserenti namque*

none of these have I found the passage sought for. The only other identification I can suggest is Alphonsus a Castro Zamorensis (1495-1558) an Observantist, but I cannot find any work of his on procedure.

1. Juan Perez de Saavedra, known as the 'False Nuncio of Portugal.' was a Spaniard of good family, born at Cordova. He was a marvellously expert forger. Having fabricated a Papal Bull, he entered Portugal in 1540, and, although not even a priest, passed himself off as a Cardinal and Legate a *latere* sent to establish the tribunal of the Inquisition. In January, 1541, he was arrested by the Spanish authorities; in 1544 he was condemned to ten years in the galleys, and was not released until 1562. In 1567 he wrote his story; and it has also formed the subject of a comedy—see Juan Antonio Llorente, 'Histoire Critique de l'Inquisition d'Espagne,' translated from the Spanish by Alexis Pellier (4 vols., Paris, 1818), vol. ii., pp. 88-103; and H. C. Lea, 'History of the Inquisition of Spain,' vol. iii., p. 243, note.
2. Compare with fol. 228, Part IV., which shows that Pope Boniface VIII. (1294-1303) is intended.

cum mandatis principis se venisse, credendum non est, nisi hoc scriptis probaverit, nec similiter creditur se asserenti legatum. Numquam enim apostolicae sedis moris fuit absque signatis apicibus unumcumque legationem suscipere; sed nec dicenti se delegatum sedis ejusdem creditur vel intenditur, nisi de mandato apostolico fide doceat oculata.'[1] [It is easy to see what a danger it would be, should anyone assert his claim to some office, dignity, or rank, and be admitted for such, unless he have first proved his claim by legal documents, whether according to the civil law or the canonical institutes. For no credence is to be given to one who claims to come with the orders of the prince, unless he prove it by written documents. In like manner no faith is to be placed in the word of one who asserts himself to be a (Papal) legate, for never was it the practice of the Apostolic See to entrust anyone with a legation of any sort without rescripts signed and sealed; nor if even anyone should say that he is a delegate of the same See can we believe in and hearken to him, unless he produce secret proofs for believing in the Apostolic mandate he brings.]

After enumerating all the dignitaries of the Church, the 'Clementina' concludes that in no way shall they be received or obeyed without having previously shown the letters and powers they have brought: *ibique nulli eos absque dictarum literarum ostensions recipiant, aut eis pareant vel intendant.* [And that without the production of the said letters none may receive them or obey or give ear to them][2] By these terms I do not consider that your reverence need have had any scruples, but rather owed the promptest obedience to these detailed precepts, on the condition that the Lord Dom Carlos Thomas declined to promulgate his Bulls. As for myself, I shall ever promulgate only the consuming eagerness I have for the peace of this Church in the East,

1. The title is 'De Electione,' and the chapter begins: 'Iniunctae nobis ......' (see the 'Decretales Extravagantes que emanaverunt post Sextum,' following the 'Constitutiones dementis Pape Quintuna cum Apparatu Dominis Ioannis Andree,' Venetis, Nic. Jenson, 1479, on fol. H_1 *recto*); or the edition of the 'Corpus Juris Canonici,' by J. H. Boehmer and E. L. Richter (Leipzig, 1839), col. 1,152, lines 4 to 14, book i., tit. iii., 'De Electione,' chap. i., beginning 'Iniunctae nobis,' a ruling issued by Boniface VIII.
2. See the same work as in the preceding note, 'Decretales Extravagantes ....," the same edition, and on the same page, or the edition of 1839, col. 1,153, lines 21, 22.

encircled by the heathen and oppressed by their might, shedding my blood even to the last drop in its defence and in submission to the Church Catholic and Roman. In this vow I have to include your reverence by praying you that as my reward you breathe in my behalf some sighs to God, to whose keeping I commend your reverence.

Goa, on the 1st September of 1704,

Your servant,

THE ARCHBISHOP PRIMATE.[1]

[184] Being now old and with little strength left, the king (Aurangzeb) was very desirous of returning to the city of Dihli, repenting of not having listened to the advice of his sister, Begam Sahib. But he could not wisely do this, or leave someone in his place. For to those who know the force and energy of Shiva Ji [*i.e., the Mahrattahs*], to act as he proposed would lead to the loss of all the above-named kingdoms [*i.e.*, the Dakhin], in addition to some other portions of his empire. Resigning himself to the necessity of protecting his conquests as well as he could, he has continued up to the present time in the kingdom of Bijapur, occupying himself in different directions with the reduction of some fortresses of the said Shiva Ji, expending much time, much money, and many lives. Nor does he desist from issuing orders, which no one obeys.

In the month of August of the year above named [1704] he ordered Da,ud Khan to take up the additional post of governor over the territory of Adoni. While Da,ud Khan was on his march the army of Shiva Ji surrounded him, and made every effort to destroy him. In this they did not succeed, for the said Da,ud Khan entrenched himself beneath a fortress called Darmavarao (Dharmavaram[2]) and defended himself valiantly. The Mahrattahs, finding that they could not overcome him, and were losing time better devoted to other enterprises, contented themselves with

1. Frei Agostinho da Annunciaçao, of the Order of Christ, consecrated 1690, arrived 1691. He was a zealous defender of the Portuguese Crown's right of patronage. He died July 6, 1713 (Müllbauer, p. 365; Fonseca, 'Goa,' p. 73; and a list in *O Anglo-Lusitano* of Bombay, November 18, 1886).
2. Dharmavaram, now a village, the headquarters of a *talook* in the Anantapur district, 200 miles north-west of Madras. The walls of the fort have been demolished ('Madras Manual of Administration,' iii. 273). It is eighty or ninety miles south of Adoni.

accepting again seven hundred thousand rupees, which Da,ud Khan gave them as a present.

Aurangzeb had in his army an officer called Xemxir Can (Shamsher Khan)—that is, The Great Sword'—a Pathan by race, and a man of great courage. The king, having noticed that this officer's nephew had gone to join the rebel prince, Akbar, who up to the present time is in Persia;[1] ordered him at the public audience to send for this man and produce him. The uncouth, peasant-like Pathan, paying the king no respect, replied to him: 'My nephew will never obey me; he treats me just as Prince Akbar behaved to your majesty.' Aurangzeb, on hearing these words, withdrew, much disturbed by the answer. When Shamsher Khan drew near his tent, there came an order from the king demanding his sword. The bold Pathan, recognising that if he ceded it he would have to die, gave as his reply that the sword borne by him at his waist went with his honour. Rather than make over his sword he would die with it. He then made ready with his small retinue to die resolutely. The king's displeasure was intensified by these words, and he ordered twelve thousand men, the best he had in his bodyguard, to go and bring back the man's head, killing everybody who resisted. Seeing this force approaching, the Pathan sallied out, followed by five hundred soldiers, who were his relations and friends. They threw them selves on the opposing force and slew the principal men who were to the front, and threw the whole body into confusion. The king's men retired, but returned to the attack several times, until they succeeded in putting the Pathan to death. In the royal army there were seven hundred and fifty-two men killed. Their commanding officer was more than annoyed, for the whole army scoffed at him for having retreated before so few [185] men, and to ease their passion they began to say that he, too, ought to be executed as a traitor to the crown.

The courteous reader will have seen in Part IV. (fol. 152)

1. Akbar died in Persia on the 17th Zi, 1 Hijjah, 1117 H. (March 31, 1706). The last two lines of an elegy inscribed on his tomb at Mashhad are:

   'Az jafae-charkh wa zi be-mihri-i-Aurangzeb,
   Burd akhir arzuemand ra Akbar ba khak.'

   (Through the spheres' ill-will and Aurangzeb's disfavour,
   His unfulfilled desire Akbar carried to the grave.)

   'Tarikh-i-Muhammadi' and 'Miftah-ut-tawarikh,' p. 295).

what happened at the port of Surat, and how King Aurangzeb ordered his officials to return the property they had taken from the Europeans at that seaport. He conceded to them the privileges they had in the time of King Shahjahan. But this order was a deception intended to make those men [the Europeans] collect more riches. A few months had passed since this first order, when the king issued instructions for the seizure of all Europeans and whatever Christians might be found in the town, together with a great number of rich Armenian merchants. He directed nineteen (19) millions of rupees to be requisitioned from them, in addition to what had been already taken, in compensation for the loss suffered by the Mahomedan merchants through what the pirates had carried off. They must also ratify the surety bond for the safety of ships leaving the port. At the present time they are in prison. They are under rigorous confinement, are deprived of enough to eat and drink, suffering both abuse and affronts. Four Capuchin fathers were also arrested, and were detained for a month in prison, enduring much; they were then released on the condition that they should appear when sent for. They found as their bail Monsieur de Pilavan (Pillavoine[1]), the director, a Frenchman of that port, and himself a prisoner.

About the time of the issue of the above orders there came two ships of war of Great Britain to the port of Surat, demanding the delivery of the English general, who had then been a prisoner for some years. They also asked for the money taken from him. In case of refusal they were to set fire to whatever they could find. The Mahomedans paid little heed to them, and following these requests, the prisoners were treated more rigorously than before, and at the present moment things are in the condition I have stated.[2]

1. Pillavoine was of the Surat Council from 1674. He is also named in 1680 (H. Weber, 'La Compagnie Française des Indes,' p. 208, note 1, and p. 209, note 3). After a visit to France, he returned to Surat towards the end of 1700 (J. Sottas, 'Histoire,' 386, 393, 409, 413). His name appears again in Part V., fol. 24.
2. Two ships of war—the *Severn* (Captain Richards) and the *Scarborough* (Captain Fowles)—were ordered to the East Indies in 1703 for the suppression of pirates and protection of trade (Bombay General Letter, June 16, 1703, 'Letter Book,' No. 12, p. 165). On the voyage out Richards died, and was succeeded by Robert Harland. The ships reached Bombay May 27, 1704, then proceeded to Surat, and in December, 1704, returned to Bombay. There is correspondence between Harland

I shall take the liberty of saying what I believe and have learnt by experience as to the mode of finishing these negotiations, which for so many years have caused the Europeans in this empire to be ill-treated and affronted, in addition to having whatever was possible taken from them, and all arguments of humanity ignored. The plan would be to assemble three thousand Europeans, who would be quite enough for this enterprise, and sack the city of Surat, putting everyone to the edge of the sword, being Mahomedans, sparing no living creature among them. On departing, let them burn all that is there. By acting in this manner the Mahomedans would be forced to concede all European demands. I have seen this done in various parts of this empire. Employing force against them [186] brings them to reason, though it be against their will. Seeing they are dissimulators, I should adopt the same course in the ports of Bengal, whereby they will recognise that Europeans are not accustomed to be insulted and tyrannized over, as they do to their Hindu princes and vassals.

In the month of September, 1704, there arrived at the said port (Surat) three ships from Mecca very richly freighted. In one of them was a personage held by King Aurangzeb to be a great saint.[1] He had gone from India to Mecca to make his pilgrimage, and on the return voyage he and others were captured

---

and the Surat Governor in 'Factory Records, Surat,' vol. viii., and in 'Original Correspondence,' vol. vi. The only reference to the seizure of Europeans is in a letter from Surat of July 28, 1704, referring to 'the Mogul's order just given to continue the imprisonment of Sir John Gayer and Council.'

1. Press Lists of 'Fort St. George Records,' No. 7, p. 219, entry No. 1626. A letter from Surat of September 13, 1704, mentions the detention by the Dutch of Nurall Hock (Nur-ul-haqq), 'a favourite of the king.' The matter is further noticed on October 24, entry No. 1665, p. 223, and No. 1670, p. 224, same date: 'Renewal of troubles at Surat.' Entry No. 1682 of November 14 mentions 'breach by Europeans at Surat.' Entry No. 1719 of December 3, a letter from Masulipatam: 'They have heard of an accommodation of affairs between the Dutch and Moors at Surat, and the supersession of Rustam Dil by a new *faujdar*.' No record can be traced of the Dutch and English fighting their way to freedom and taking to their ships. Nothing can be found except a note that the Dutch demanded Rs. 100,000 for the treatment they had received, and on a refusal quitted Swally, and 'went on board ship' (General Letter from Surat, February 24, 1705, paragraph 6, 'Abstracts of Letters received from Bombay,' vol. i.).

XL. 'IMARI, or closed elephant litter

by the Dutch. Without ill-treating them, the captors sent a message to the governor of Surat calling on him to repay the money he had taken from them by force. On being paid, they would without fail restore the ships. If not, they must levy what had been taken from them, and they threatened to take other measures. The governor reported this to the court.

The English and the Dutch who were prisoners in their houses, having first consulted together and come to a resolve, issued from prison with some arms. They killed the sentinels and guards, and making an effort, united and released the English general, who had been so long a prisoner. Full of heart, they went bravely marching on, killing all who came against them; and leaving by the gate on the river bank, they embarked in vessels which had arrived for the purpose during the night, through a signal they had given. After bombarding the city they set sail, disregarding the shots fired from the castle, and without receiving any damage they left the river, and going on board ship, they were free.

After the above had happened an order was sent from court to the governor of Gulkandah to seize the Dutch factor and the rest of his staff. The order was executed at once.[1] The Europeans who lived on the coasts of Choromandal and Gergelim (Gingerli), becoming apprehensive of war, began to make preparations. In the province of Bengal they did the same, withdrawing all the factors occupying various posts in the interior of the country [187].

In the year and month already named [September, 1704] there arrived in the town of San Thome from Goa a new chief captain, called Nuno Silvestro Frade, superseding the man who then ruled over the Portuguese quarter, one Matheus Carvalho da Silva whose daughter he offered to marry. Already several days had passed without his visiting the Mahomedan governor at the same town, whose name was Mir 'Usman. I know not if it was carelessness, bad advice, or some suspicion. However, at once, without leave of the said governor, and without paying

1. The Dutch agent's letters from Gulkandah of December 6 and 31, 1704, say nothing of this incident, neither does the General Letter from Batavia to the Dutch Company. But Fort St. George Press List, No. 7, entry 1678, November 10, 1704, records a letter from Masulipatam, in which 'the money demanded by the Moors from the Dutch Resident at Gulcondah' is referred to.

him a visit, he ordered the preparation of 100 *candis* of powder and the erection of walls for *gudoms* (*godowns*, or ware-houses). The new captain marched about under an umbrella, with drums beating, giving himself the air of master of the country. Although aggrieved by these doings, showing they meant to ignore him, the Mahomedan governor kept his counsel, and noting how the heedless fellow had overpassed all limits, waited for some days an occasion to injure him.

This came on October 5 in the above-named year [1704], when the procession of the Most Holy Rosary was held.[1] Many Mahomedans mingled in or followed this procession, making many insolent remarks and taking the candles out of the hands of the Christians, paying respect to neither man nor woman, interfering with the *charolas*[2] and flags, uttering scoffs and abuse. These interferences had occurred at every festival, and no one would listen to my advice to conduct such devotions more quietly, with the doors of the church closed. This would have hindered the entry of the Mahomedans, and prevented them sitting on the altar-steps, smoking tobacco, laughing, and gazing at the women during the saying of Mass and the delivery of the sermon. They might find an excuse in all this pomposity and vain display paid for by the alms raised from the devout of Madras and other places, with no regard to the fact of these San Thome Christians being Mahomedan subjects, a thing contrary to our holy religion.

The Portuguese, unable longer to bear these insults, broke

1. The English records bear out Manucci's account otherwise, but they place the riot correctly on a Sunday—September 24, 1704 (October 4, New Style)—and give the name of the man killed as John Rebeiro. Senhor Matthias Cavallo is mentioned as one of the fugitives to Madras (Wheeler, 'Madras,' ii. 39, and Press List, No. 7, p. 221, entry No. 1641 of September 21, 1704). Mir 'Usman, the *faujdar*, is mentioned elsewhere in the Madras records (see, for instance, Press List, No. 7, entry No. 1448, March 16, 1704, for his letter threatening to oust the English, and Governor Pitt's reply). Mr. Philipps says the Feast of the Rosary is held on the first Sunday in October. It was first sanctioned for all the churches which had an altar of the Rosary in 1573; then extended to all churches throughout Spain, 1671; and finally to the whole Latin Church, 1716 Nilles, 'Kalendarium,' i. 527).
2. *Charola* or *cheirola* (in French *cherolle*): there seems no exact English equivalent for this old Portuguese word. It is a sort of hand barrow, bearing a niche or shrine, in which an image is carried in procession. Non-Christian use similar things for carrying their idols (W.R.P.)

the head of a Mahomedan. His companions, feeling incensed, collected and bared their weapons, whereby great confusion arose in the procession, and it scattered in all directions. The vicar, Father Friar Diogo do Sacramento, Dominican [188], and Simao de Loyolo,[1] who bore the pyx in the procession, by great efforts secured shelter in the church, where they intended to celebrate first Mass. But both Mass and sermon were stopped, and the Portuguese had to retire, each one to his house.

Seizing the occasion, Mir 'Usman jumped on his horse, followed by a considerable number of soldiers. He proceeded to the house of the new chief captain, who, learning of his approach, came out to greet him at the street-door, imagining that it was a friendly visit paid to him. Mir 'Usman seized him by the collar violently and made him over to his soldiers, and drawing his sword, ordered them to carry the Portuguese officer away a prisoner. At this moment there arrived a Portuguese gentleman called Joao Rebello, he being president of the Rosary, who fired his musket and killed the man who was removing the chief captain. As Mir 'Usman lifted his sword to slay him (the captain), there ran up at once a French trader called Monsieur Guelly,[2] and placing himself in front of him, prayed that the life of the Portuguese officer might be spared. During this interval the Mahomedans slew Joao Rebello. Then some more Portuguese arrived, and they killed another Mahomedan. During this diversion the chief captain found time to escape, but bearing a small wound in his right side. Frightened by the fighting, the Mahomedans fled, and with them Mir 'Usman.

The chief captain, on trying to re-enter the house he had come from, discovered the door was barred, a proclamation to that effect having been issued on that day. There was not a soul in the street to help him; all had shut themselves up in their houses. He sought out the Lord Bishop's, but all in vain: he declined to open his door. A Portuguese widow who lived near took him in, and at night conducted him to his father-in-law's house. Mir 'Usman posted sentries at the gates of the Portuguese quarter and stopped the entry of supplies. On the next day,

1. Simon di Loyola was a priest and writer in the Bishop of Mailapur's office (see his attestation at foot of the excommunication of Father Esprit, dated November 27, 1706, Part V., fol. 247).
2. Monsieur Guelly or Guety, the French merchant, turns up again in the disputes of 1706 (see Part V., fols. 241, 242, 244, 261, 284).

seeing how they suffered, I went to him and begged he would release them from this trouble. He conceded my demand and sent orders to withdraw the sentries. The Portuguese being frightened, arid considering themselves insecure, came out at night with their families and went away as best they could, taking with them the wounded chief captain.

Of these I will specify: (1) Nuno Silvestro Frade, the chief captain; (2) Matheus Carvalho da Silva, his predecessor;[1] (3) Manoel de Sanche, nominated magistrate on behalf of his [Portuguese] majesty. Of the four councillors, the first and second—that is to say, Gaspar de Motta and de Brito [189],— contented themselves with a removal to Madras. Pedro de Torres de Oliveira, manager of his majesty's plantations, receiver of taxes and collector of the money taken from each house from time to time for payment to the Mahomedans, for permission to be left to live in peace; Luis da Fonseca Varjao, judge of the orphans; Antonio Tullimao, public notary; Francisco George, assistant—these were the other principal officials.

The principal inhabitants who left along with these officials are the following: Manoel Roiz, Antonio Cassella do Valle, Alvaro Cassella do Valle, Francisco Lopez do Figueredo, Luis Carvalho da Silva, Joao de Moroes Mexias, Joao da Fonsequa Varjao, Joseph de Fonsequa Varjao, Antonio Gonzalves de Amerim, Joao Ribiero de Coullo. They were accompanied by some sons of the soil and some *topazes*.[2] The following are the friars and priests: Dom Simao, Dom Joao Milton, Theatines;[3] Friar Manoel de Nevis, Augustinian; and the clerics, Manoel da Silva da Menezes, Lucas Luy de Oliveira, Estevao Roiz, Manoel Roiz, Antonio de Figueredo, Manoel Pinto. These came to Madras and applied to the Lord Governor, Thomas Pitt, who received them kindly.

Those who remained in San Thome with the Lord Bishop were the following: the Father Nicolao Roiz, of the Society of

1. The 'Matthias Cavallo' of the Madras records.
2. *Topaz*, dark-skinned or half-caste claimants of Portuguese descent and Christian profession (Yule, 933).
3. Dom Simao must be the Simon da Costa, Theatine, who wheedled P. de Sax out of his cure at Cuddalore (see *ante*, IV. 171). Joao Milton, Theatine was an Englishman, as to whom see Penny, 'Church in Madras,' pp. 229-232. He died in 1714 at Bencoolen in Sumatra.

Jesus, first counsellor and a native of Macao, who looked after His Most Illustriousness (the Bishop); secondly, the vicar-general, an African, and a man of learning; thirdly, the secretary, Alleixo Barretto,[1] fourthly, the *curé*, Pascoal Pinheiro, a white man; fifthly, Joseph Carvalho; sixthly, Simao de Loyola; seventhly, Bartholomeo de Abreo; eightly, Belchior Dias, who held charge of the seal, and collected the proper amounts; besides some small people, students dependent on the Lord Bishop.

Other friars and priests who remained were: Friar Diogo do Sacramento, Dominican; Friar Pedro de Silveyra, Augustinian; Friar Francisco Baylao, Capuchin; Friar Joao da Ascensao, commissary of the Holy Office; Friar Francesco do Purificacao, Franciscans; Friar Joao de Sao Jasinto, Capuchin; also two friars recently come from Goa, whose names I do not know; the rector, Joseph Roiz, and the vicar, Silvestro de Souza, Jesuits; Dom Guilhermo della Valle, Theatine; the priests, Lourenço Pereira da Cunha, Diogo de Siquiera Peixotto, white men; Father Lazaro de Sao Boaventura, Pascoal de Lima, Pascoal Pereira da Cunha [190], Thome Correa de Brito, white men; Xavier Lopez, Clemente Pereira, Thome Tullimao, white men; Francisco Borges, Manoel de Rozario.

Those of the counsellors who remained were: Francisco Mendes Pereira, Joao Costa de Saâ, and Joao Bautista Munis. These last two have been long in India; they were at Goa at the time when the Paulists[2] sent out the green donkey, as will have been already seen in my Third Part (III. 219). Antonio de Almeida de Amaral; Manoel de Naves; Manoel Carvalho, procurator for the city; Antonio Gonçalves de Abreo—these being very old, almost unable to see, decided to stop, from inability to travel.

The following are the churches in the town (San Thome): The cathedral church and Sao Domingo[3] were in the Portuguese

1. A. Baretto, writer, of the Episcopal Chancery of Meliapur. He attested a document on July 18, 1699 (Norbert, 'Mémoires Utiles...,' p. 127).
2. 'Paulists,' a common name for the Jesuits in India (Yule, 688). The affair of the 'green donkey' occurred about 1653-55 (see Part III., fol. 219).
3. For St. Domingo Church, see note 29 to fol. 176; for Madras (or Mae) de Deus, see fol. 179; and for N.-S. da Luz, see fol. 142. San Lazaro is given in the 'Madras Catholic Directory for 1906,' p. 289, as a chapel affiliated to the Church of Mae de Deus in Mailapur; it is

quarter. In the suburbs, where the Mahomedans lived, were the churches of Sao Lazaro, controlled by secular clergy; Madre de Deus, N.-S. do Descanço, of the Jesuits; N.-S. da Luz, of the Franciscans; and a hospice, with its sister-hood, of the Augustinians. Besides these churches there were between Great Mount and Sao Thome two churches, also controlled by the Jesuits, dedicated to N.-S. da Saude[1] and to the Holy Cross. On Great Mount was a church, as I have already mentioned in another place (III. 191). At the foot of the said Mount there belong to that church four small chapels, dedicated to N.-S. da Conceiçao., N.-S. do Rozario, N.-S. da Lembrança, and Sao Lazaro. Thus there are a number of churches and clergy, but few of the former are frequented.

After some days Mir 'Usman sent to invite back the Portuguese, who had retired to Madras. He forwarded a document pledging himself not to interfere with them and to forget the past. The refugees did not feel this promise was enough, and they wrote to Da,ud Khan telling him what had happened, demanding justice and forwarding a small present. The answer he gave them was to go back to their houses, adding that he had written already to Mir 'Usman forbidding him to touch them. With this reply they were not fully satisfied, and they dissembled [191]. Mir 'Usman continued to invite them with polite speeches. Finally, becoming aware that they did not intend to return, he sent to say that if they did not come at once and reoccupy their houses he must knock down their flagstaff and destroy their houses along with the churches.

This message threw them into a great fright. On going to bid farewell to the governor of this place (Madras), they received from him fifty soldiers as an escort half-way on their road. There they found the said Mir 'Usman, who had come thus far to receive them. Having done them this honour, he carried them to his

close to that church, but nearer the sea. Perhaps N.-S. do Descanço is now represented by the chapel of Our Lady of Health on the Coopum, subordinate to the Cathedral, or by Our Lady of the Visitation, subordinate to the Luz Church. In 1885 the Goa 'Annuario' called it Nossa Senhora da Visitaçao in Paria Parcheria, half a mile from Mae de Deus (W. R. P.).

1. This must be the Church of Our Lady of Health at the Little Mount, Saidapet (see 'Madras Catholic Directory,' 1906, p. 290). 'N.-S. da Conceiçao' may be 'N.-S. do Descanço'—*i.e.*, 'B.V. a Quiete' (W. R. P.).

house, where he gave them betel-leaf and rose-water. He threw over the chief captain a *xalla* (shawl) worth ten *patacas* (Rs. 20), and another over his father-in-law. After many friendly speeches he sent them home.

Two days afterwards the said Mir 'Usman came to visit them, accompanied by various officials, and he was received with much courtesy. They gave to him some pieces of cloth worth one hundred *patacas*, a tribute which he got out of them, and after this they were somewhat reassured. But those Portuguese I have named never had been in unison, and now they are at cross purposes. They are divided into various camps, each claiming the right to govern. It is for this and similar reasons that they lost their territories in India, as I shall recount farther on.[1]

It is now eighteen years ago (? 1686) that there was in this San Thome a captain called Antonio Ferreira da Silva, who claimed control over the Mahomedans and declined to pay fifty *patacas* due to the *diwan*. A eunuch who was then governor sent to him several times asking him to pay what he owed. He gave very little heed to these words; finally he used threats of chastisement. The eunuch who ruled the country felt aggrieved, and went out against him with his soldiers. He sent a message that he must arrange to pay at once, and desist from interfering in matters of government, it being Mogul territory. He should behave himself as a trader, and not talk of chastising people. The message did not please the chief captain, and he made signs of resistance by force of arms, being thus the cause of his own death; for the eunuch surrounded his house, killed him together with others in his company, and collected the money due.

On the day following the killing of the men [see *ante*, fol. 187]—that is, October 6 [192] of the already cited year [1704]—the Dominican Father, Friar Diogo do Sacramento, sent very early to convene the Portuguese Brothers of the Rosary for the election of new officials. They replied that they were unable to attend, being busy with the burial of their defunct president. Would he postpone the election to another day? Incensed at this answer, the Dominican sent word that if they did not come at once he should call in the women and put them in the place of the men. The men, being seated sad and mournful behind their barred doors, and in fear of some fresh attack, put him off. In their

1. The subject of San Thome and its government is resumed in Part V., fol. 50.

default the devout and energetic father, without any concern for the dead or for the existing confusion, attempted to collect the women. These replied through their closed doors that the father must be mad; let him devote himself to praying for the soul of the defunct and imploring God to deliver them from the peril they were in.

I have read in the Lusitanian Chronicles about the early times of their conquest in India, where it is noted that the ships of that nation visited many places. It happened that one of their ships was lost on the coast of China, but all of the crew were saved and some of their property. It is the custom of that country to report minutely to the court everything that occurs. When the emperor heard of the shipwreck he felt compassion, and ordered the viceroy who ruled those territories to assign the men a place near the sea for them to dwell in, and give them ground to cultivate. He conferred on them many other favours. They began to trade, and the population increased. In time they became rich, when they began to think of ruling over lands which were not theirs, collecting thieves, escaped criminals and fugitive debtors, abducting the daughters of other men, and angering the governors. They ignored the benefits they had received, and showed no want of the pride which always develops in the Portuguese when prosperous as those men were.

There came to the country a ship in which was a Portuguese. To display their grandeur and indulge their vanity the settlers erected a street of arches from the town to the seashore. It was fully adorned with mirrors, cloth of gold, and other fabrics of gold and silver thread [193], while the ground was entirely carpeted with rich cloth stuffs. Then the greatest men in the settlement went to meet the new arrival, and as he disembarked they prostrated themselves at his feet, making him profound obeisances. Then they seated him in a gilt litter, and they followed him on foot. In front were carried golden censers, with which he was incensed, accompanied by many women musicians playing on various instruments. At the corner of every arch stood a beautiful lady between two women servants, who carried trays of varied flowers. All along the route the ladies threw these flowers upon the litter. In this way they conducted their visitor into the town, and treated him like some great prince.

Seeing this surprising novelty, the Chinese asked the Portuguese what personage this was who had newly arrived. With all the signs of dread they said he was the son of a very great man. For his father held the office of farrier for the horses of His Lusitanian Majesty, whom God preserve. Thereby they insinuated that the King of Portugal was greater than the Emperor of China. The governor of the place, who was unfavourable to these people, wrote the whole story in detail to the court. Remembering the care that the had always bestowed on them, and fearing they might raise an insurrection in his country, the emperor ordered them all to be put to the edge of the sword, not sparing one of them. The order was forthwith carried out: three thousand human beings were beheaded, and the town was ruined. From this anecdote will appear their (the Portuguese) pride and their unreasonable conduct.

For years past many friars and priests have claimed, as they still claim, the charge of the Church in Madras, wishing to expel from it the French Capuchins. Among these assailants the principal is His Lordship the Bishop, Dom Gaspar Affonço. He made considerable efforts to exclude them after the departure of the Lord Patriarch for Manila, which took place on July 11 of the afore-cited year [1704]. He sent an excommunication against the said fathers at the time when the said Dominican father[1] excommunicated the brothers of the confraternity in Madras. Thence arose great confusion in many thousand souls deprived of sacraments for a period of twelve months.

The said friars, finding themselves always persecuted and unjustly injured, made violent [194] efforts several times to abandon the mission and return to Europe, and live there in their own convents. But the governor and the rest of the council of the said town of Madras would never consent to give them their dismissal. The English said the Capuchins were the founders of the Church, that they were of benefit to the Catholic population among their subjects, and if they quitted their post consent would never he given to admit the fathers of any other order. Such were the instructions they had received from Europe.[2] If they went away the church would be demolished, and warehouses built upon the site (as I have myself heard the governor say many times). If this happened the congregation would be destroyed.

1. For Friar Diogo do Sacramento's agitation against the Madras Confraternity, see *ante*, Part IV., fols. 176-182.
2. Orders of a similar tenor were reiterated by the Court of Directors in 1716 (Penny, 'Church in Madras,' 233).

At this time there arrived a letter from the Lord Archbishop, Primate of Goa, wherein he held for null and void the acts of the said Lord Patriarch.[1] This will have been gathered from the letter, a copy of which has already been given (IV. 182, 183). Upon seeing this letter the Lord Bishop sent men to remove the documents of excommunication that had been affixed on the doors of the cathedral church, and the population, hearing of the letter aforesaid, were joyful and consoled, and began to frequent the church with great eagerness. Only a few days afterwards, although they had seen the letter of the Lord Primate, the Bishop once more caused to be fixed up the very document that he had withdrawn. But no one paid any heed, holding so many changes to be unjust, and attendance at church went on as before.

The Reverend Father Dom Guilhermo della Valle, Theatine, with his two companions—who were, like him, pretended travellers—saw that his hidden efforts with the Abate di San Giorgio and the Lord Patriarch, as well as with the Lord Bishop, made in reliance on several friends and devout persons, had not succeeded as he had hoped. Thereupon, out of his own absolute power, he excommunicated afresh the Madras fathers at the church of Sao Domingo [in San Thome]. He fixed up this decree on the inside of the door of that church, without any recourse to the Lord Bishop, thus declaring himself to be a head of the Church.

This is how Dom Guilhermo repaid the Madras fathers for having taken him into their convent for three and a half years. They had treated him with every courtesy and respect, and allowed him to want for nothing. The whole population was by this time disabused through seeing so many changes. They recognised the ill-will of the other priests against these virtuous and innocent [Capuchin] fathers; they remembered what had been done to Father Friar Ephraim of Nevers, as already seen in his narrative (IV. 125-147).

At this time there started from Madras for Pondicherry a Capuchin missionary who had arrived not long before from Surat [195]. His name was Friar Euzebio of Bourges, and he wished to travel to France by the first opportunity arising. On his arrival the Jesuits made inquiries, and learnt this fact. Father Dolu and the others, to prevent his journey, spread a story throughout the

1. For the terms of the Archbishop's Pastoral, dated December 22, 1704, see farther on, fol. 226.

town, going from house to house and notifying to all men the arrival of such-and-such a person, who had been excommunicated. Whoever spoke to him would inevitably incur the same penalty. Father Euzebio went out to pay some visits, but noticed that all people fled from him, shutting their doors and avoiding any speech with him. The humiliated priest was forced to withdraw, and return to [Madras] whence he had come.[1]

Further, I will say that the Jesuits in Pondicherry also for years claimed the church there. But they employed other arts;[2] as the proverb says, they 'drew out the sardine by the cat's paw.' They had recourse to the Lord Patriarch in the end, and many times applied humbly and with presents to the lords of that territory [the French] to be given possession. But as the said gentlemen much distrusted those reverend fathers, they sent them about their business, saying, 'From the Jesuits *libera nos, Domine!*'

I will relate two trivial instances that happened at the College of these same Jesuits at Pondicherry, when the Lord Patriarch was actually living in it.[3] The governor, Monsieur Martin, sent him a leg of veal. On its being brought to him, he ordered his cook to roast half and prepare another dish with the rest. While the cook was at this work there entered to him in his kitchen Brother Rupia, who was astonished at the spectacle. Seizing the spit and the pot containing the stew, he carried them off with violence out of the house to a marsh close by and threw them into it, saying in a passion, for the benefit of the Hindus and the new Christians, that 'the Jesuit fathers were not *pariahs* and low caste; they did not eat cow's flesh' [196].[4] Thus the meat did not appear at his Excellency's luncheon, and on his asking the reason

1. Apparently Father Euzebius (Euzebio) was on his way to Rome with the Capuchin appeal. He did finally succeed in leaving India, for it was he who brought home the Venice Codex of Parts I.-IV. of Manucci's work; but I can find out nothing farther about him. In Part V. he is referred to as having spent twelve years in India.
2. The author means other arts than the violence used by Father Guilhermo della Valle, Theatine, at Madras.
3. That is, between November, 1703, and July 11, 1704.
4. The point of the story is that the Jesuits, following the practice of Roberto de' Nobili, gave themselves out as 'White Brahmans,' and observed the rules of Indian caste. They were also known as *Romapuri*, or the Roman ascetics. Mr. Philipps tells me that abstinence from beef is still practised by the missionaries of the Paris seminary now at Pondicherry.

for there being no veal, they told him the facts. He concealed his feelings, and said not one word.

The second affair is as follows: The Jesuits introduced a fresh ceremonial, taken from the Hindus, which up to this time had not been performed. It prevails among a race of Hindus called Genovar (? Shanar).[1] Its signification is the first creation of human kind; but they carry it out with other details, both men and women, though human modesty constrains me not to explain minutely these enormities.

These reverend fathers are accustomed to begin the saying of Mass one hour before daybreak, and continue until ten o'clock. Within these hours all the Europeans and *topazes*, with their families, attend and hear Mass. But one Mass, which is postponed until eleven o'clock, is celebrated on account of the native Christian converts. It happened that three soldiers who had been detained on duty came to this last Mass. They were met by the Reverend Father Tropen,[2] who, with honied words, sent them away, telling them that the Mass and sermon were postponed until midday, and they would not be able to get to their midday meal [if they waited]. On hearing these words they made a motion as if to go out, and the father retired into the sacristy.

Those three worshippers turned and re-entered the church. They saw the said father had come to the foot of the high altar in surplice and stole, and bearing a maniple on his arm. There he lay on the ground at full length on his side, with his feet stretched out towards the congregation. All those present were already standing, men and women; then, advancing one by one, before reaching the father they fell on their knees and made obeisance, inclining the head three times. The fourth time, bending still lower, they kissed the great finger of the father with much reverence. This ended, he made them a short speech, standing, in the Tamil language, which none but the Malabaris (natives) present could understand [197]. Finally he put on his vestments and said Mass.

1. Dr. Barnett suggests Shanar, the cultivators of the Toddy palm, so numerous in Tinnevelly district (see 'Madras Manual of Administration,' iii. 814). But I have not traced the rites to which Manucci refers. R. Caldwell ('The Tinnevelly Shanars,' Madras, 1849) speaks of their devil-dances and bloody sacrifices, but says nothing about any obscene rites.
2. Most probably meant for Father Turpin, a Jesuit priest, whose name will be found in Part V. under the year 1706.

As the soldiers referred to had never seen such a ceremonial in the Roman Church, they were visited with scruples, and went to inform the Father Friar Spirito,[1] Capuchin, chaplain of the Fort church. They gave him a minute description of all that had taken place. The father took the soldiers as witnesses before some of the principal officials of the Compagnie Royale, so that they might learn the truth and write to France an account of the thing. The officials answered him that they were traders, that they had to conduct the business of the Compagnie Royale, that they had no desire to mix themselves up in the Jesuits' affairs. If they were to write such things, orders would come from France expelling them from the service, they would lose their credit, and be persecuted for the rest of their lives.

I may give as an example what happened in Bengal a few months ago [1704] to seven gentlemen, the chief officials of the said Compagnie Royale of France. Their fault was not to have acted as they [the Jesuits] wished, and complaints against them were sent to France. These were listened to, the Jesuits having the greatest people at court under their control. The gentlemen were: (1) Monsieur Regnault, the second, next to Monsieur Dulivier, the director; he was a merchant and in the council. As a councillor he declined to agree to what Father Queren, Jesuit,[2] wanted, holding it to be prejudicial to the said company. By this refusal the father became his enemy (as is their custom when anyone refuses to do their will). (2) Monsieur Soulaz, merchant, and second councillor, who refused to communicate to the said father the news received from various places, whereby he considered himself aggrieved. (3) Monsieur Chesenault, manager of the domains. It would take me too long to tell the story of the reasons that turned the father against this gentleman, but he publicly threatened him that he would take his revenge. The other four officials were all friends who had united for the benefit of the said company, and declined to submit to what the said father demanded. They were dismissed in a body from the service, without any regard for their being married or their having served so many years faithfully, and their earning [198] profits for the

---

1. This is the Portuguese and Italian form; as a Frenchman, his name was really Father Esprit (of Tours).
2. This Father Queren or Quenin seems to be the person spoken of in Part V. fols. 9 and 181, where see father about him. Father Van Meurs, S. J., says the name is properly Quencin.

company. Men of all nations were much distressed at this act, knowing well that the persons involved were men of merit. The said father ruled over and interfered in things that it is not convenient for me to speak of.[1]

1. *Dulivier.*—Pierre Dulivier was second at Hugli under A. Boureau Deslandes, and succeeded him in 1701; he was transferred to Pondicherry, on the death of F. Martin, in December, 1706. Deslandes wrote: 'He works hard, is well-behaved, and of the temper required in India; he is quite fit to be chief' (Ministére des Colonies, 'Corres pondance Génerate de 1699, 1700,' C^2 II., 65, fol. 138). There are indications that, instead of opposing, he was too complaisant to the Jesuits. Hébert writes on February 12, 1709 (C^2 II., 68, fols. 252 and 253), that, since F. Martin's death, Dulivier had postponed everything, and had not farmed out the Pondicherry lands because Pére Tachard, S.J., wished to prevent some native Christians from losing their posts as rent-collectors. Other complaints are added, ending with the statement that Dulivier was led by the officials and the Jesuits, as he had been in Bengal by the Pére Quencin, and he continued to be, as before, harsh and haughty, sowing discord everywhere. To wind up with (fol. 262, verso), his wife 'est assez jolie, elle ne manque pas de beaux habits, mais la plus salope que je connoisse. Elle est née en Angleterre; son mary y a demeuré longtemps et leurs inclinations sont trop angloises pour estre à la teste des affaires des François.' In March, 1713, Dulivier sailed again for India, and relieved Hébert in September of that year. There are several letters from him, one of ten folios of February 14, 1714 (C^2 II., 69, fols. 71-82).
Régnault is the fourth on the same Hugli list of 1699. Robert Regnaut (*sic*), merchant, is described as somewhat advanced in years. Since his arrival ten years before he had had charge of the warehouses at Hugli, and now wished to be relieved of the office. He had done well, and was thoroughly acquainted with the classes of goods. He meant to return home in three years, but might stay if some mark of distinction was conferred. He was fit to control a subordinate, factory. On December 24, 1703. Dulivier, then chief, writes that Regnault had been placed at the head of a board for the decision of cases (C^3 II., 67, fol. 104). On the same day he reports that he did not consider Regnault fit to be the head of a factory, as he had confined himself to the goods department, which he controlled well; besides this, his advanced age would force him to return to France by the next vessels, or, at the latest, in two years' time (the same letter, fols. 106 and 107). Perhaps he is identical with the Regnault who was an under-merchant at Swally (near Surat) in 1680 (see H. Weber, 'Histoire,' p. 210).
Soulaz.—Deslandes (C^2 II., 65, fol. 138, verso) writes that Alexandre Soular (*sic*), under-merchant, had been cashier for six years, and had long asked to be relieved. This had now been done. If he would only apply himself, he could do well. He was offered promotion if he

We have to point out that the Lord Patriarch had been sent to visit China, where he was to make an inquiry and draw up a true report. During some years there has been talk that the Jesuits offer up sacrifices and use ceremonial copied from the Chinese. As to this question, I have my doubts if the Lord Patriarch will be able to introduce any remedy for these disorders. He will need to put into use the greatest discretion.

But I did not meet with any signs of such; for when the Abate di San Giorgio arrived here at Madras, he at once displayed a desire for information as to the lives of the Christian priests and the customs of this country, and also wanted particulars of the Hindu religion. He came across many deviations which gave him little satisfaction. He was then advised that I could give him information. He suspected I might be a friend of or sent by the Jesuits, seeing that such emissaries were very necessary to them in this anxious occasion; and he was aware that they would not speak themselves, in order not to be held at Rome for idolaters.

I paid a visit to the said Abate di San Giorgio,[1] and addressed to him these words: 'Sir, may it please you to do me the favour of telling me, before we converse, if your honour is a Jesuit or their representative.' This question threw him into confusion; his colour fled, but he answered me mildly: 'I am a missionary priest, sent to find out the truth.' After that opening

---

stayed, but he says he intends to return to France in one year. In 1703 he was made second member of the board for trying cases, already referred to. Dulivier, in his letter of December 24, 1703, said he was a good man at outdoor work, and had done very well for a long time as cashier. But for two years he had idled, and his conduct had been outrageous. This had not been reported before, though he had tried to bring Dulivier into contempt, to intrigue against him, and to thwart him in everything. It was only from pity for an infant he had, and on account of the 10,000 rupees he owed, that he had not been sent home. Possibly this animosity to Soulaz was inspired by the Jesuit Quenin, to whom Dulivier was submissive. He and his wife (Eléonore Totain) had a son on June 17, 1703, who on the 21st was baptized François Alexandre, in the factory chapel, by the curé of Notre Dame (Chandarnagar); the godfather was the Chevalier François Martin, represented by Robert Regnault, and the godmother Dame Françoise Moisy, wife of Pierre Dulivier (Bibliothéque Nationale, Nouvelles Acquisitions Françaises, MS. No. 935[2], fol. 24, extracts of the Etat Civil made by P. Margry).

1. See *ante*, note 4 to fol. 165; he was the Abate Francesco San Giorgio di Biandrà.

we had a long conversation. We came to talk with great intimacy and freedom, until at last I said to him: 'Here is the Fourth Part of my book, and with it the account of the Hindu religion, which your honour can read and consider, or you can send them on to his Excellency. In them you will find much besides what we have spoken of. You can remove these evils if you choose, and you can make inquiry at Pondicherry as to my truthfulness. If there is anything wrong in what I allege, here is my head as a guarantee.' After [199] having read my Fourth Part, he gave it back to me, saying that God had permitted these things to be thus. He would neither listen to my advice nor believe the interested parties.

A few days having passed, I went to Pondicherry to interview the Lord Patriarch and try to obtain freedom for the people of Madras, and for the fathers along with them, from further persecution. Upon this subject I had a long talk with the said Lord. Finally, he said to me he had already written to Europe; at the same time he showed resentment against the Governor of Madras for replying to his letter of civility without giving him the titles he enjoyed, and other details; also for not receiving the Abate as he ought to have been received. The latter was a man of high quality and of noble family, who had filled posts of distinction. I observed from this talk that the Patriarch esteemed more the vanities of this world than success in maintaining and augmenting Christianity. He paid no attention to the ceremonial adopted by the said Jesuits in Pondicherry, and he went to live in their college. Yet he had given a promise to Monsieur Tixer,[1] missionary, that he would go to live at his convent. I know not the reason, although it was a place better fitted up than the other.

At his departure the said Lord Patriarch enjoined on the Jesuits that they must follow the ceremonial of the Roman Church, and none other. But they go on ever as before, just as they please. When about to go on board, accompanied by various friars and secular priests, he showed some emotion, and said:

1. Mr. Philipps suggests that by the missionary Tixer is meant Jacques du Quarelai Tessier, nominated titular Bishop of Rosalia. Norbert ('Mémoires Historiques,' ii. 26; Bensançon, 1747) gives a petition from him to the Council of Pondicherry, dated November 20, 1718. On p. 24 of the same volume Tessier is described as being, in 1707, the Procurator of the French 'Missions Etrangéres' at Pondicherry.

'God pardon those who are the ruin of the Christian congregation of Madras,' and, tears falling from his eyes, he embarked.[1]

I have found that a judge who has an interest can never do real justice. As an example, I refer to Portugal, where there was a judge upright and impartial. An old woman presented him with four ripe figs out of season. Without thinking, he took them and ate them. When he came to pay the old woman, she declined to be paid, and begged him to have compassion upon her and her son, then in prison. The judge repented him of having eaten the figs, and being angry, and although he had received a gratification [200], said he could do nothing to the prisoner except as the law prescribed, nor would he favour him.

Another order of judges I have also seen, who left criminals to suffer for years, continually giving them hopes of deliverance, and dragging money from them. When the culprits had nothing more to give, they passed on them sentence of death. Thus the man's family was left ruined. Yet these judges had forgotten that there was still a Creditor to whom they have to render an account for not obeying the commandments, and for paying no heed to the warnings and lessons that He gives us. Let us go back to speak of the Portuguese.

I have noticed with this race that if anyone gives them good advice, they are suspicious, and betray their feeling that there was no necessity for it. Sometimes they do the very contrary to what has been suggested, in order not to admit that advice has been received. Of this I shall give some instances from what happened to them in the year 1639.

The Portuguese were then masters of the fortress of Malacca, and possessed considerable power both by sea and land. The Dutch determined to take the place, and appeared off it with six ships, all well armed, under command of a general called Collumbo.[2] On their arrival near the port, the Portuguese sallied

1. Expressions to very much the same effect will be found in the Capuchin Superior's (? Father Laurent's) letter of January 11, 1708, to Father Timothée de la Fléche, secretary to the Procurator-General of the Order at Rome (Norbert, 'Mémoires Historiques,' third edition, 1747, p. 143).
2. The Dutch investment of Malacca began in 1639, and the Portuguese surrendered it on January 14, 1641 (Dubois, 'Vies des Gouverneurs-Généraux,' 126-128; Danvers, ii. 269, 279). Neither I nor Mr. D. Ferguson can find any name with a resemblance to 'Collumbo.'

out to meet them with six ships, well equipped. There was a stout fight, and the Dutch were defeated. The victors, returning to port elevated by their success, believed there were no more difficulties to encounter. Some old and experienced men advised them to pursue and seize the opportunity of annihilating the enemy. Such counsel was not in accord with their sense of honour; they chose to be offended, and retorted that the advice of those who stayed on land was not required. They took to feasting and passing the time in games. The Dutch without loss of time reformed their fleet, and next year (1640-41) came against them in greater strength. Renewing their exertions, they came out victorious, destroyed the Portuguese fleet, and invested the fortress. Finally, owing to the quarrels in the garrison, it was forced to surrender.

The Dutch made ready for a new enterprise [201], and resolved to become masters of the city of Ceilao (Ceylon). On receiving this information, the Portuguese prepared thirty vessels, laden with provisions and materials of war, and sent them to relieve the place under convoy of five large ships of war (*galliçoens*), all of which had three tiers of heavy guns and a numerous crew of fighting men. On drawing near the port, they discovered there five Dutch ships.

These Dutch ships were attacked by two galleons, one the *Bom Jesus*, commanded by Antonio Nunes Barretto. Two of the enemy came against this galleon, but it so damaged them by its heavy guns that they were forced to draw off, and to avoid the loss of all their lives they ran their ships ashore. The Dutch admiral then engaged the galleon, hoping to overcome it; but it did not turn out as he expected. For the Portuguese drew alongside when the combat grew fierce, and they (the Dutch) had almost surrendered to the enemy. Then the admiral's galleon, *N. S. de Graça,* commanded by Francisco Machado, came to his companion vessel's support. He had already damaged the two other ships, one of which was forced to run ashore like the others.

As Machado's ship came close, Antonio Nunes Barretto shouted to him to stand off and not rob him of his glory. These words threw the fighters into some disorder, when the Dutch admiral seized the chance and got away, continuing his voyage as

Mr. Ferguson thinks it possible some such encounter may have taken place, as a Dutch fleet, under Jacob Coper, passed through the Malacca Strait on its way to blockade Goa.

best he could in company of the others. The Portuguese remained victors.

The other three ships of war (*galleons*) reached their destination with the supplies they had convoyed. The captains quarrelled, and the crews set to killing each other, each man taking the part of his captain. The general in command of the fortress, Antonio de Souza Coutinho,[1] of whom I have already spoken in my Third Part (III, 230), annoyed by this outbreak, transposed the commands, making the admiral a captain, and the captain the admiral. He made the same changes in the other galleons. Upon this interference these officers considered themselves insulted, and, declining to obey any order, each became his own lord and master. They set sail for Goa one by one, just as they took it into their heads [202].

These facts could not be concealed from the Dutch, and the next year (? 1655) they blockaded the place (? Colombo) with twelve ships. They disembarked six thousand Europeans, of whom the majority were Frenchmen. On learning of this landing the general sent a message to Gaspar de Aranjo,[2] who commanded in the field, asking why he had permitted the disembakation when he could have prevented it.

This commander, being over-confident in his valour, without making use of prudence and occasion, replied that he had let them land and would take care to make them re-embark; if not, it would cost them their lives. But just the contrary happened, for when battle was delivered, the said Gaspar de Aranjo was routed with great loss of men. The Dutch invested the fortress and took it. This was on the 18th of May, 1656.[3] They were

1. Antonio de Souza Coutinho arrived at Colombo in August, 1655. He had originally eight frigates and 500 soldiers, but two vessels were captured by the Dutch and two driven ashore (Danvers, ii. 311). Mr. Ferguson thinks that if these events happened they must belong to 1654, and yet Manucci introduces the name of a commander who did not arrive until 1655.
2. Mr. Ferguson notes that this account of the Dutch proceedings in 1655 is very unreliable. Manucci has confused Gaspar de Araujo Pereira, who in 1653-54 was *capitao mór do campo* (chief field commander), with Gaspar Figuiera de Carpe, who was the man sent to oppose the Dutch landing (compare Baldaeus; Churchill, 'Voyages edition 1745, vol. iii., pp. 645, 681). The Portuguese General is recorded to have said that G. Figuiera 'deserved to be hanged.'
3. The battles fought by Gaspar Figueira were on October 17 and 18, 1655. The Dutch General Hulft began the siege on November 9,

aided by the King of Candia (Kandy), who brought forty thousand men. He carried off to his court over three thousand souls, including whole families, priests, servants, Caffres, Chinese, Japanese, and men of several other nations. Their descendants are to this day subjects of the King of Kandy, and have never been released.

After this conquest the Dutch proceeded to take the fortress of Jafanapatao in '58 [1658].[1] It was then in charge of Urbano Fialho. He might have saved his life, but refused to do so, uttering insults against the conquerors, and, declining to surrender, he was killed.

Hie inhabitants of Negapatao (Negapatam) had been invested by the ruler of the country, who was the prince of Tanjor. It was not long before the Dutch appeared. They invited the inhabitants to make over the place to them on condition of being left at liberty and retaining all their property.[2]

The victors went next against the city of Cochim (Cochin). They invested it, and after nine months occupied the fortress, with assistance from the rulers of the country; for, being disaffected [to the Portuguese], they all rushed to join the Dutch.[3]

When they had fortified all these new conquests, the Dutch conceived the idea of seizing the city of Goa. This was in the year 1660. They came with nine ships and a dispatch-boat,

---

1655; he was killed April 10, 1656; Colombo surrendered on May 12, 1656 (see Dubois, 187, and Danvers, ii. 314-318).

1. Jafnapatam, then commanded by Antonio do Amiral e Meneses, was taken June 22, 1658, by Admiral Rykloff van Goens (see Dubois, 187). The incident of Urbano Fialho Ferreira seems to belong to the capture of Cranangore in 1662 by the same Dutch Admiral (*ibid.*, 197). Mr. Ferguson remarks that the references to this Portuguese commander are slanderous, even the Dutch paying a tribute to his courage (see Wouter Schouten, 'Oost Indische Voyagie,' 1676, ii., chap. ix., pp. 206, 207, 210).
2. Negapatam fell to Major Van der Laan in August, 1658 (Dubois, 187).
3. After several unsuccessful attempts, beginning in February, 1662, Cochin was forced to surrender to the Dutch, January 7, 1663 (Dubois, 203). There was a blockade of Goa lasting from October, 1660, to August, 1661 (see 'Dagh Register, Anno 1661,' edited by J. D. Van der Chijs, pp. 93, 95, 190, 222, 255; The Hague, 1889). The blockading fleet consisted of eight ships and two yachts, under, first, Rothaes, and then Adriaen van Leenen. Luiz de Mendoçza Furtado, Dom Joan Manuel, and Antonio Mello de Castro (Governor of Mozambique), are mentioned; but the sea fight and other details are not corroborated.

blockading the mouth of the river, but lying out of the range of the shore cannon. No one was allowed out or in, and no one could catch them.

At this period, owing to this blockade, a disaster fell upon the Jesuits. They tried to send off a dispatch-boat (*pataxo*) destined for China in company of another vessel starting for Portugal. To avoid being seen they left at night, and crossed the river bar. The vessel for Portugal went on its way during the night and escaped in safety [203]. The other, taking a southern course, was seen by the Dutch as day broke. They pursued.

The fugitive ship was manned—captain, pilot, and sailors—by those of the Society. It was a sight to see the efforts they made, coming and going in their black gowns. The Dutch, observing that the vessel was lightly laden, and that they could not overhaul it, fired their guns at the prow. To the misfortune of the Jesuits a heavy shot struck them near the helm, which had been blessed with holy water. This shot caused their vessel to go to the bottom, without any profit from it to the Dutch. One Jesuit escaped on a plank, and the Dutch ship picked him up. Not having had any dealings with men of that nation, he was angry, shouting out curses, and using other such misplaced terms. The whole ship's company lost their temper at such insults, and bound the man, who was thereby still more enraged and shouted the worst curses you can imagine. The captain issued an order to emasculate him, which was done accordingly. He said that was how they dealt in his country with a stallion that was unmanageable.

Seeing themselves thus invested, the Portuguese prepared nine *galleons* and a dispatch-boat, all thoroughly armed, and came out to seek the Dutch. The latter, seeing that these ships sailed in good order, began to retire, discharging a few guns. The Portuguese followed, until, finding the Dutch declined to accept battle, they retired in the same way, while the Dutch turned again and anchored where they had been at first.

The next day the Portuguese resumed the same tactics and the Dutch acted as before. The same thing was done for three days, and still the Dutch declined to fight *galleons* being very large and powerful, and thus they could not hope to come out of it well. Foreseeing that the prudence of these people (the

Portuguese) would come to an end, they bided their time, in order to carry out their plan more safely.

The fourth time the Portuguese advanced to the attack their commander's ship sailed slowly, while the galleon *Sao Thome* forged ahead. Senhor Luis de Mendouça Furtado[1] considered himself aggrieved and drew in sail. Seeing the opening they had been waiting for, the Dutch attacked. The galleon *Sao Thome* [204] fought with great valour, believing that the other galleons would do likewise, but instead of that they hung back and hesitated. At this critical moment the galleon flew the admiral's flag as a signal to Senhor Luiz de Mendouça Furtado to put on all sail, also for the others to follow him. The Portuguese fleet was puzzled, not knowing whom to obey, and they dispersed in all directions.

Upon this the captain of the galleon *Sao Thome*, seeing that he was lost for want of support, set fire to his powder magazine, so that no one escaped alive. The Dutch hastened in pursuit of the others, who withdrew, firing a shot from time to time to persuade themselves they were winning, and then came to an anchor in the waters of Marmagao under cover of their forts. Thereupon the Dutch let go their anchors in their usual place.

During the following night there came a boat from the Dutch and set fire to a galleon lying under cover of the guns of Marmagao. There was not a living creature on board; all had gone on shore. Then came news of the peace between Portugal and Holland, and the ships of the latter nation then sailed away from the river-mouth at Goa, and the Portuguese were delivered from them.

But to this day the Portuguese are interfered with by the Arabs of Masqat, as will have been seen already in my statements (IV. 154). They go in great fear of them, as I have myself experienced. Coming from the town of Damao (Daman) in a ship of war on my way to Goa,[2] during the voyage a sail was seen. At once they all exclaimed that it must be an Arab ship, began to commend themselves to God, and hugged the shore, with the idea that if any ship made for them they could run for

1. Luiz de Mendoça Furtado was one of two Commissioners who held the government from June 14, 1661, to December 14, 1662 (Danvers,, ii. 324).
2. This must have been in 1682 or 1683 (see Part II. fol. 205).

the land and save their lives. But God was pleased to bring us safely to port without anyone having hailed or overhauled us.

The isle of Goa is supplied by provisions brought from territories in the province of Canara.[1] For this purpose a number of small vessels were sent once under the convoy of a 34-gun frigate, they being afraid of the Malabar pirates. It is the practice, when the vessels have arrived in safety at their destination, for the frigate to anchor near the shore in some arm of the sea.

On the following day a Dutch ship appeared which was on a voyage [205], but, detained by contrary winds, it had been forced to anchor near the frigate referred to. The Portuguese, believing it must be an Arab ship, said to the soldiers, 'Turn about, by God!'[2] They threw their arms into the sea, and, getting into their boats, escaped to the shore, first setting fire to the ship. The Dutch, who were close by, hurried to the spot in their boats, hoping to rescue some of the people. They found there was not a soul on board. On getting closer to shore they asked from the vessels lying there what was the cause of all the disturbance. They replied it was because an Arab flying the Dutch flag wanted to deceive the Portuguese ship and take it. This is the way these gentlemen behave.

In the year 1638[3] the King of Persia invested the fortress of Ormuz, a strong place belonging to the Portuguese; but he was unable to reduce it, as it was relieved from the direction of the sea. He then called in the English, who sent a strong fleet. The governor of the fort heard that they meant to disembark at a difficult place. The council pointed out to him that he ought to bar their passage, a movement he could undertake without danger. He declined to do it, saying that if they persisted in a disembarkation, he took it upon himself to make them prisoners.

The English disembarked and at once entrenched themselves, and placed field-pieces in position. The said governor did not put a high value on such people, but he sent all his soldiery, giving orders to their captains to capture the men who had landed; should they decline to submit, they must be exterminated.

1. An Anglo-Indian name for that part of the west coast, which lies below the Ghauts, from Mount Delly northward to Goa territory ('Madras Manual of Administration,' iii. 122).
2. The words in the text are *Vira ley de Does* ('Turn! God's law!').
3. The year 1638 must be wrong; it ought to be 1622 (Danvers, ii. 211).

The Portuguese marched and assaulted the trenches, where the English received them by a discharge of artillery with great noise, following it by musketry, whereby many were mown down. Losing not a moment, the English fell upon the survivors, aided by the Persians. Unable to resist this onslaught, the Portuguese took to flight and made for the fortress. The enemy followed, and the governor, seeing his routed troops approaching, opened the gates to receive them.

The English and Persians crowded in along with the fugitives [206] and overpowered the garrison. At this day the place belongs to the King of Persia. He owed money for the expenses of the English fleet; and it will have already been seen in my Fourth [read *First*] Part what efforts to recover this money were made by their ambassador, in whose suite I found myself. The fortress of Ormuz has an inscribed stone over the principal gate, which says: 'Open trenches, then lie down to sleep.' The noble Portuguese who commanded the place was liberated, and went to live in Goa city. Several gentlemen visited him there, and asked him why he did not 'open the trench,' as the stone directed. To save words, he replied to everyone that there was no place to throw the earth.[1]

The fortress of Mascatte (Masqat) was taken by the Arabs in 1644,[2] and the governor was the cause of its loss. He aggrieved one of his servants who acted as interpreter—a Jew by race—by ordering him to receive a shoe-beating, whereupon the angry victim vowed vengeance. He suggested to the Arabs that they should conceal the food-supplies throughout their country, and

1. There is a plate of Ormuz in Danvers, ii. 211; his details of the fighting do not agree with Manucci's. The English arrived before Ormuz on January 22, 1622. Mr. Ferguson has directed my attention to Luciano Cordeiro's 'Como se perdeu Ormuz' (Lisbon, 1896), where (p. 108), in a letter of February, 1622, to Simao de Mello, Captain or Ormuz, Ruy Freire de Andrada refers to the words as being cut on a shield at the foot of Albuquerque's statue:

   'Se inimigo da Europa n'esta barra vires surgir
   Abre a cava e deita te a dormir.'

   There is an allusion to this inscription in 'Commentaries of Dalboqueraue' Hakluyt Society edition, iv. 231.
2. Masqat was besieged by the Arabs from August 16, 1648 (Danvers, ii. 296). It capitulated October 31, 1648, and was finally ceded entirely—the fort on January 23, and the town on January 26, 1649 (*ibid.*, 298).

thus raise prices. He would then manage to obtain their entry into the place under the pretext of buying food. As soon as they saw themselves in sufficient numbers inside they could raise a disturbance and overpower the garrison.[1]

This was the very thing the Arabs longed for, and they entered into the plot. Now, the injured servant was aware that the governor relied on the advice of one of his women slaves called Luiza. This is customary enough among these nobles, who, being born in India, have lived from childhood among these people. The servant, then, advised the negro woman to speak to her master, saying he ought to sell his stored grain at a high price to the Arabs. An opportunity had arisen to gain a great deal of money, nor would it be long before more supplies arrived from Goa. The governor, impelled by greed, accepted the counsel, selling his stores at such high prices as to gain ten times the cost.

By reason of this fictitious famine many Arabs found entry into the place, and when they saw they were numerous enough they had recourse to their weapons [207], and slew every Portuguese they encountered. As soon as the Portuguese were aware of the treachery within the town they quitted their houses and assembled. There were many killed on both sides. Finally the Arabs were driven back till they took shelter inside a church, and here they were surrounded.

At this time an old man advised the commander of a fort upon a height to fire his guns and knock down the church, whereby some of the Arabs would be killed, while the rest would be slain by those who were in wait for them outside it. But as it is their habit to act contrary to any good advice given them, the captain declined, expressing his scruples about injuring a church. Just then another body of Arabs who were waiting

1. The origin of the quarrel and the other details are differently stated by different writers. Mr. Ferguson has called my attention to Captain A. W. Stiffe's article on Masqat in the *Geographical Journal*, 1897, x. 608-618. That writer's authorities are Dr. Badger's 'Imams of Oman' (Hakluyt Society, vol. xliv.), pp. xxv, xxvii, 81, 87; Captain A. Hamilton. 'New Account.' 1727. ii. 59-62: 'Commentaries of the Great Alfonso Dalboquerque,' ed. W. de G. Birch (Hakluyt Society, 1874-84), i. 80, 81, 83; Colonel Miles in 'Selections from Records of Government of India, Foreign Department' (Calcutta, 1885): and Colonel E. C. Ross, 'Annals of Oman' (Calcutta, 1874). Dellon ('Voyage to the East Indies,' 1698, part ii., chap. xv., p. 175) gives the same particulars as Manucci.

outside the walls became aware of the commotion within the city. Laying hold of their swords, they entered. Those who were watching at the church forsook their post and ran to bar the way to the new assailants. In the interval those inside the church sallied forth and attacked them in the rear. Hence the Postuguese soldiers were caught between two bodies of Arabs, and were all killed, and the place lost.

It happened that there was in this fortress a Portuguese prisoner, a criminal, who had relations, and many friars were his friends. All these made frantic efforts to obtain an order for his deliverance from the governor. He refused. Seeing no other course open, they all assembled, the friars carrying crucifixes, and entreated him for the love of God to pardon the man's life. This, too, was without effect. They then had recourse to the slave woman Luiza, who by a few words obtained the pardon. Nothing less than such disaster could be expected from such a governor and his government.

The first time that I arrived in Goa I met an old Portuguese gentleman, rich and wise, who had seen most parts of Europe. His name was Manoel Saraiva. He spoke Italian very well, and was a great friend of mine. On the first occasion of my seeing him he told me I had come among a nation out of whom I should have no satisfaction. As he expressed it, [208] the Portuguese nation 'sono poci matty y mal arrivatty' [they are a small number of madmen and troublesome fellows].[1] As it seems to me, he was largely right, as I have seen from my intercourse with them and from their actions.

I will conclude my remarks about the Portuguese by relating a little affair that happened in the town of Sao Thome. There was a Polish knight named Dom Theodoro de Sao Lucas who had been to Portugal and returned in one of their ships to India. Last year [? 1703] he was in Tramgambar (Tranquebar), belonging to the Dinamarcas (Danes). He was known to every one along these coasts.

To amuse his friends in Madras he sent a made-up letter to an old Portuguese friend of his, the Chief Captain Senhor Lucas

1. My copyist wrote the last word 'arraciatty'; but Dr. Cóggiola, who has looked at the original twice, says it is plainly 'arrivatty,' His French translation is: 'Ils sont un petit nombre de fous et de fâcheux.' I follow his reading.

Luiz de Oliveira,[1] who was a Sebastianist. In it he congratulated him on the good news received from Portugal, whence his friends had written that the King Dom Sebastiao[2] had now appeared. The said Senhor Lucas Luiz de Oliveira, on receipt of such joyful tidings, so ardently desired during so many years, was full of glee.

He made ready at once a great banquet, to which he invited the members of his council, the principal officers of justice, and the other nobles living in the town, also the parish priests and other friars. When the banquet was over, during which quite enough had been drunk, Senhor Lucas Luiz de Oliveira showed the letter in question to all the other gentlemen, who (at any rate, the majority) believed that what it stated was true. To do the news greater honour, and to announce it to everybody, they decided on a night masquerade. Collecting horses and borrowing costumes, they paraded the streets, carrying many torches, letting off fireworks, serving out bottles of wine on all sides, and shouting through the town, 'Long life, long life, to the newcome king!' As dawn approached they retired to their houses, some with broken arms, others with sore feet, others with heads split open, others well bruised and beaten. All this provoked the laughter of the neighbours at the sight of so much folly, and at finding [209] in such company priests and friars.

But I was not astonished, for I know them. Let me do no more than remark that there was a friar, both theologian and philosopher, a man of great learning, very pleasant of speech, who professed himself my great friend. On the day after the above outburst I met him. After talking together for some time, he fell into thought, threw his eyes up to heaven, stamped on the ground with one foot, and said: 'If it be true that King Dom Sebastian has appeared, there can be no other true religion in the world than that of Jesus Christ!' Thereupon I was troubled at hearing such talk and withdrew, never again caring for intercourse with such a fellow.

1. This Chief Captain is mentioned in the Bishop of San Thome's protest of February 22, 1702, as being then dead (see *ante*, fol. 103).
2. *Sebastianista,* one who believed that Dom Sebastian, King of Portugal (born January 20, 1554; died August 5, 1578), would some day return alive from Africa ('Nouvelle Biographie Générale,' Didot, xliii, 667).

Meanwhile, until I have further occasion to speak of King Aurangzeb, let me relate some things that happened to those who feign to be virtuous and holy, yet, moved by self-interest, deceive the rest of the world through their pretences. In addition to what I have said of the false holy men found in the Mogul country, I met in Bengal with the case of a married trader. His wife, finding her husband would not trust his money into her hands, pretended to be devout, wore nothing but the plainest clothes, and divested herself of all jewels. Every day she went off to church, always held her beads in her hand, and displayed great piety. Sometimes the husband would have liked to interfere, but did not dare to stop her prayer-going. As a further assurance to her husband of her virtue, she dressed in a *Beata*[1] costume. The husband, seeing all this ostentatious virtue, made over his money to her. Then came the season for entering into contracts, and he asked his wife for some money. She refused, and told him he was mad, and styled him a Jew for trying to withdraw her from her devotions. Such a name is among these people much disapproved. The husband's efforts were of no avail, and being persecuted by everybody on account of that name, he was forced to disappear, and the wife enjoyed a fine time of it.

In the days when Sultan 'Abdullah[2] reigned in the city [210] of Gulkandah there lived a Mahomedan who was venerated as a saint owing to his exceeding scrupulousness not to offend anyone, but to speak always good of everybody. Whenever he came out all the people followed, reciting his praises because he had never harmed anyone. He lived on good terms with his wives, and taught his sons well. He had also the habit of considering carefully where he placed his foot, to avoid hurting any ants or other insects. By this course of life he acquired a great reputation.

In his service were robbers by whom traders were brought to his house, with their precious stones, valuable stuffs, and such-like, on the pretext of his buying from them. Once they had entered they never left again; he beheaded them, and robbed

1. *Beata,* a sort of nun who goes about in the world, and is not secluded in a nunnery.
2. 'Abdullah, Qutb Shah, reigned 1611-72 (S. L. Poole, 'Mohammadan Dynasties,' p. 321).

XLI. PALKI or Litter for a Harem lady

them of all they carried. By this means he led a prosperous life, but in the course of time he was unmasked. The king then sent to have him privily strangled, to avoid a commotion among the people.

[Omitted, a similar story about a holy man in Babylon, in the city of 'Aspao,' pp. 211, 212, 213.]

[213] The judicious King of Bijapur, Sultan Muhammad 'Adil Shah,[1] as will have been seen earlier (III. 218), managed once by his cleverness to recover a precious stone out of the hands of the Jesuits. In his reign there was a Portuguese who showed much zeal for the Mahomedan religion, hoping thereby to obtain a certain woman of that faith. To secure his desires he had recourse to his Majesty in person, saying he wished to become a Mahomedan. To find out by experiment whether this proceeded from any interested motive or was said in good [214] faith, the king ordered a pot to be opened, and directed the man to extract the contents. When he placed his hand inside, there suddenly darted out a fierce cobra. In terror he gave a jump, and exclaimed, 'Jesus, my Mediator!' By this means the king discovered that he was moved by interest, not by faith, and turned him out of the city.

When the sixth King of Gulkandah, Sultan 'Abdullah Qutb Shah, was on the throne [1611-72], he had serving in his artillery men of four European nations. As these great rulers delight in acquainting themselves with persons' characters through the actions they perform, he tried an experiment.

He sent word for the slaughter of a stag, and it was divided into joints. He then ordered the distribution of the pieces, one to each nation. The Englishman, without waiting until they handed it to him, laid hold on the biggest piece there was, and carried it off. From this the king said this nation loves to take things at its own risk. The Dutchman held out a hand humbly, and accepted the share offered to him. From this it was inferred that this nation is one of merchants who through their humility have become rich.

The Portuguese refused his portion, telling his servant he might take it. At this the king said that this nation was over-

---

Muhammad, 'Adil Shah, reigned 1626-60 (S. L. Poole, 'Mohammadan Dynasties,' p. 321).

proud, and would rather die of hunger than abandon its dignity. The Frenchman, without waiting for orders, laid hold of his sword, stuck it into two pieces, and throwing out his chest, marched off. Judging from this, the king said this nation was a valorous one, most generous, and fond of good living. He ordered the Frenchman to be appointed the captain over his artillery.

Whatever remained over of the venison he ordered to be divided among his suite. These men, with the greatest respect and homage, took each a piece, making demonstrations as if they thought it a holy relic, and saying, 'May God increase the days and the wealth of his Majesty.' Of them he said: 'These people are flatterers [215] and hypocrites, saying pleasant things to me in my presence.'

I speak once more of the Jesuits, and with this I make an end. I will relate what they laid claim to and asked me to do in certain matters, where I would not act for them, it not suiting me to offend the princes without benefiting them (the Jesuits). Discovering that I did not accord them their desires, they set to work to ruin me entirely. Finding I was not in a position where they could satisfy their unreasoning passion, they wrote to their friends some letters containing remarks about my personality. This caused surprise, but their arts did not prevail. The careful rulers in the government examined into it, and recognised my innocence.[1] Thus were their intentions frustrated. In spite of this triumph, I cannot live in peace, for as the proverb says, 'He who has enemies never sleeps.' I know not if my vigilance will protect me.

I do not entertain a doubt that the judicious reader will, without fail, ponder the nature of my words about these and other similar individuals, uttered with all the freedom to which my conscience constrains me. I dwelt many years at the court of the Mogul Emperor, and often had disputes with one or other of the nobles or men learned in the Mahomedan law, discussions to which they had themselves invited me. I have now said fare-

1. This must be a veiled allusion to the objections raised in 1704 to the renewal of Manucci's lease for his house at Madras. A priest at Negapatam had sent a letter denouncing him as a traitor to the English ('Factory Records, Fort St. George,' vol. xiii., fol. 203).

well to all interests in this world, but am still a lover of my holy Roman faith, and willing to give my life for it, though it has not happened as I desired—namely, that I should be allowed to yield my life a sacrifice. But though I was not granted that privilege, I have ever remained a friend of truthful speaking [216]. Thus, as I am aware that I cannot live many years, I leave a reminder to those who rule over these individuals in order that they may redress the evils if they so desire. To do this will be of profit for the million,[1] and adversaries of our holy religion will then have nothing to bring up against us. Those who are involved in the affairs of this world are obliged to dissemble, and thus fail to do what God ordains. As I have seen, such persons are wedded to their own interests, disregard all murmurings, and mislead the world by deceit, paying no heed to the evil and scandal that they leave behind.

I can give as an example the King Jahangir, who, though a Mahomedan, yet showed spontaneously that he was not entirely engrossed by the world. For in this direction he always showed affliction at finding himself entangled in those cares of government which so many long to undertake. I spoke of this king in my First Part (I. 100-118).

One day he was passing through Lahor city when he saw a number of little children playing in the street. He descended from his elephant, sat himself down on the ground in their midst, and distributed sweets, flowers, clothes, gold and silver coin. After embracing and kissing them, he said tearfully: 'Better were it for me to die or to be a little one like you, not to be as I am to-day, with my conscience entangled in the affairs of this weary world.' At these words he took his departure with a salutation, the tears streaming from his eyes. From these and other like acts the people judged that this king feared God, and desired to live without causing harm to his vassals.

[217] Before this time the inquiring reader will have seen my four volumes,[2] and learnt the hope in which I sent them.

1. The words are *os mihoes*, and Mr. Dames prefers to read *os mehoes*—that is, *os meaos*, The middle class or gentry.' *Milhoen*, from 'million,' is quite modern. But I do not think 'middle class' suits the context.
2. *Four*, if we include the volume of paintings sent to Europe with Parts I.-III.

It is impossible for the inquiring reader to avoid remarking on the variety and inequality to be seen in the said work. The reason was that time permitted nothing else; I went on writing in the order that things happened. I continued thus, and the inquiring reader must be content to accept that work as it is. If God gives me longer life I shall go on with a fifth volume. I am already sixty-eight years of age,[1] and am in fear that my labours will come to an end without ever appearing before the world; and this fear was my reason for sending the volumes off. In addition. I am aware that Death gives warning to no one, nor waits for the affairs of those who have anything left unfinished, but takes a man quite against his will. Therefore, foreseeing that this must happen to me, I leave not my writings under the control of attorneys, being warned by the experience that I have had. I have seen a great number of such executors disregard the orders of the testator. Thus what I can finish in my life-time I decline to abandon to the pleasure of such people. For this reason I send the manuscript by this opportunity. Subsequently we will discuss the end, which must soon arrive, to the reign and the life of the present king, Aurangzeb, who is already eighty-nine years of age; and I will take measures to have this conclusion sent off.

Madraspatam, on the 5th of January, 1705.

(Signed) NICOLAO MANUCI.

[Here the manuscript breaks off, and resumes abruptly at the top of the next folio—*viz.*, 218. A leaf must be missing or misplaced. The fragments which follow consist most probably of detached passages which were to be worked up into Part V., in which some of them do appear.]

... [218] in my presence.

Aurangzeb feels forced to continue the war against Shiva Ji (*i.e.*, the Mahrattahs), and he has from the first had the ambition of conquering the countries of others, be it by treachery or force of arms. In the execution of these designs there have died in his armies over a hundred thousand souls yearly, and of animals, horses, pack-oxen, camels, elephants, *et cetera*, over

1. This passage, written in 1705, points to the author's birth having taken place in 1637; his age at landing in India (1656) would thus have been eighteen.

three hundred thousand. In spite of the greatness of the empire, by reason of which supplies of these necessaries always used to be forthcoming in abundance, the great nobles and the famed generals and captains have nowadays to go without them. Their families are in distress, and to such a state have their wives and daughters come that throughout the empire they are forced by their sufferings to ask alms in the streets. It is noteworthy that the wives of commanders of some consideration, through the distress they are in, move from door to door with nothing but a plain white sheet over their head.

In the Dakhin provinces there was no rain from 1702 to 1704, but instead plague prevailed. In these two years there expired over two millions of souls; fathers, compelled by hunger, offering to sell their children for a quarter to half a rupee, and yet forced to go without food, finding no one to buy them.

It is now twenty-five years since Aurangzeb came in person to the Dakhin to begin this war, as I have already stated (II. 200). Let the careful reader reflect on the enormous expenditure incurred, the unnumbered deaths during this time. Yet never did he (Aurangzeb) betray any sign of emotion. During any great peril or hardship that arrived he would say to the few generals with him that his great ancestor, Taimur-i-lang, gained his great fame as a conqueror precisely because similar contretemps had happened to him [219].

This king took a good many forts in the Cunçao (Konkan) belonging to the Mahrattahs. These forts were situated at the foot of lofty mountains near the sea, which stretch from the vicinity of Goa up to the neighbourhood of Chaul (Chanwal). But there were very heavy expenses, great losses both of men and animals, and great dearness from want of supplies. Sometimes it happened that the officers were forced to go in person to the baker's and carry a little flour to be made into a loaf—for this they paid him two rupees; while the few servants who stayed on subsisted on leaves and roots.

Finding himself in this desperate condition the king was forced to retreat, taking up a position under protection of Amadanaguer (Ahmadnagar) and its fortress. During this march the princes, his daughter, and the other queens made petition to his majesty, stating that it was now thirty years nearly since they left the court of Dihli, and all that time they had been on the march, and had suffered many hardships; they were now old women, and his majesty should concede to them before he died permission to retire into the fortress of Agrah. Thereby they would be saved from being made prisoners and insulted after his death. His answer was that on this point he had taken the requisite measures to place them in security two years before his death.

Da,ud Khan, after making an agreement with the Mahrattahs, withdrew, and took up his abode in Arkat, leaving the enemy present in the direction of Adoni and Sira.[1] The king sent him various orders, appointing him governor of that country, and telling him to make exertions to eject the enemy therefrom. In addition, he made him governor of the kingdom of Gulkandah, and he received instructions to expel the enemy from that region also. They had invested the fortress of Badanagar (? Bhagnagar)[2]by an army of thirty thousand horse.

Da,ud Khan replied that [220] the force he had under his command was much too small to make a campaign against, and fight with, so many enemies. He requested that someone else might be sent in his place, otherwise the enemy would inevitably occupy the whole Karnatik. At the same time, be instructed his representatives at court to make every effort, and not to leave the king without obtaining an advance of a million of rupees. Further on I will recount what has happened (IV. 233).

Without troubling himself about the increasing ruin to his empire due to the Mahrattahs, this king now plans the renewal of war against the Hindu prince of Maisur, or Saranpattan (Srirangapatanam). His ambition is to capture the great treasure possessed by this prince. This territory lies near the region of Malabar, and the prince possesses one hundred thousand matchlockmen and ten thousand cavalry. His revenue, after paying expenses, is every year eleven *carois* (*krors*) of rupees—that is, thirty-five millions.[3] He is lord over a large territory defended by over one hundred fortresses and many forests.

1. Adoni is 261 miles north-west of Madras, and Sira is in the north of the Nanddrug district in Maisur (see Plate XXXIV. in Constable's 'Hand Atlas,' and note 260, Vol. III., Part IV., fol. 160).
2. Bhagnagar is the original name of Haidarabad (Dakhin).
3. Apparently 35,000,000 of some coin not named, worth 3 1/7 rupees each; probably the *pagoda*. Eleven *krors* of rupees equals about £11,000,000. The figures must be grossly exaggerated.

This prince has a Brahman as his chief counsellor, named Duduhaja Daluahia (Duduhaja Dalwae), a man of sound judgment. The reigning prince is a nephew of the late ruler, and is deaf.[1] For this reason King Aurangzeb protests that this prince is not a legitimate successor, and claims the right to take possession. Thus he is making ready for a campaign, and has sent out orders to the princes of Tanjor, the princess of Trichinopoly, and other neighbouring rulers who are his feudatories. They must be prepared to invade Maisur; and should they refuse compliance they will, he says, be chastised.

The King of Gulkandah, Shah 'Abdullah Qutb Shah [1611-72] several times [221] made war against this monarch [*i.e.*, of Maisur], hoping to obtain his treasures and territory. But he had no success, the said prince defending himself valiantly; and the punishment he inflicted on his adversaries was to release them after cutting off their noses.

They say that the inhabitants of this country (Maisur) are so active that when horsemen are passing through their forests, they come out rapidly, and, placing their hands on the horse's quarters, spring up behind, and cut off the rider's nose with a sort of half-moon in iron that they carry. By this feat so much fear was established in the (Mogul) army that no one was so bold as to advance until the musketeers had fired. No one can enter or leave the Maisur ruler's territories without a passport.

The officials in charge of the diamond mines reported to his majesty (Aurangzeb) that they had obtained there a large diamond

---

1. 'Dalwae' is the title of the commander-in-chief; Wilks (i. 225) gives his name as Kanthi Raj, and that of his son as Basu Raj. 'Duduhaja' may be an epithet or nickname. For the succession of Maisur rulers, see the table on p. 16 of L. Bowring's 'Haidar Ali' ('Rulers of India'), 1893.

Chikka Deva Raj (that is, the younger),
1671-1704-5.
|
Kanthi Rae, the Dumb Rajah (a son),
1704-5—1716.
|
Dodda Krishna Raj (or the elder),
1716—1733.

Thornton ('Gazetteer,' 663) says that in 1699 Chikka Deva Raj sent an envoy to Aurangzeb at Ahmadnagar, and obtained the title of Jagat Raj. Wilks (i. 211, 224, 226) gives the dates somewhat differently from Bowring.

weighing two ounces and two eighths. He ordered it to be sent to the Presence; but it never reached him, the Mahrattahs having carried it off while it was on its way.

This old king (Aurangzeb) still shows his eagerness for war by the gestures he uses on the march. While seated in his palanquin, he unsheathes his sword, makes cuts in the air, first [222] one way, then the other, and, smiling all the while, polishes it with a cloth, then returns it to its scabbard. He does the same with his bow, to show that he can still let fly an arrow. But most of the time he sits doubled up, his head drooping so much that his beard lies on his chest, and it looks to you as if it grew out of his throat. When his officers submit any petition, or make report to him of any occurrence, he gently raises his head and straightens his back. He gives them such an answer as to leave no opening for reply, and still looks after his army in the minutest particulars.

But those who are at a distance pay very little attention to his orders. They make excuses, they raise difficulties; and under cover of these pretexts, and by giving large sums to the officials at court, they do just as they like. If he would only abandon his mock saint-hood, and behead a few of those in his empire, there would not be so much disorder, and he would be better obeyed. It is from this cause that they countermine him by working on his various scruples.

As an example I will give a case in Bengal. There is a province there which in the time of Shahjahan yielded seventeen *lakhs* of rupees. The king noticed that during his time It was bringing in no more than five *lakhs*. He asked the grand *wazir* the cause of the falling off. The *wazir* replied hypocritically that the government of Shahjahan was tyrannical and the people oppressed; whereas that of his majesty was compassionate and holy, leaving the people to live in peace and happiness. These words satisfied his majesty, and this is the method by which the officials succeed in doing as they please. Nowadays most of the old ones are dead, and those appointed in their places are wanting in experience; they also draw much less pay, and thus are discontented. With the Hindu princes it is just the same. One of them, having a grievance against the son-in-law of Mahamed

Amican (Muhammad Amin Khan),[1] deserted to the enemy [223] with two thousand horsemen, and on the march looted the royal baggage train.

Let us now talk about the Indian Ocean, and what happened there on November 7, 1704 (the 5th in Part V., fol. 30).[2] There appeared in the latitude of Chaul (Chanwal) four French ships: The flag-ship of 60 guns *L'Agréable*, commanded by Monsieur le Baron de Palhier (de Palliéres); the second-in-command, of 60 guns, called *La Muttiner* (La Mutine) under Monsieur Dudregne (Du Dresnay). These were two royal ships. The other two belonged to the Compagnie Royale. One of them carried 54 guns and the other 50 guns; one was *L'Aurore*, commanded by Monsieur Houssaby (Houssaye), and the other the *St. Louis*, commanded by Monsieur Martin. These ships steered for the port of Surat, and opposite the island of Bombahim (Bombay) overhauled a bark flying the English flag,[3] and the property of a Hindu in the service of the governor of that place. From it they learnt that in Surat port there were ten ships of war, seven Dutch and three English.

Thereupon Monsieur le Baron [de Palliéres] saw that the sides were too unequal, and, turning away, made for Pondicherry, although it was the monsoon. In the latitude of Vingorla,[4] near

1. This must be the Muhammad Amin Khan, Chin, cousin of the first Nizam-ul-Mulk, Asaf Jah, and not the noble with the same title mentioned in the earlier years of the reign. The first-named became Muhammad Shah's *wazir* in 1721, and died the same year.
2. These events arose out of the Triple Alliance of England, Holland, and the Emperor (Portugal joining afterwards) directed against France. The treaty was signed on September 7, 1701: Portugal withdrew in 1707; and the war ended with the signing of the Peace of Utrecht March 31, 1710 (Lecky, 'History,' i. 29, 102, 122). Robeck, Baron de Palliéres, *capitaine de vasseau*, became a midshipman February 1, 1666, and died June 28, 1717. His fleet included *L'Agréable*, fifty-two guns, commanded by himself; La Mutine, forty guns, Monsieur du Dresnay; L'*Aurore*, forty-four guns, Captain Houssaye; *Le Saint Louis*, forty guns, Captain Martin. The ships left Port Louis (Mauritius) on April 22, 1704 (Jules Sottas, 'Histoire,' 1905, p. 428). De Pallieres reached France again in October, 1705 (*ibid.*, p. 432).
3. The *Adventure*, eighty tons, bound for Calicut (Sottas, p. 428).
4. Vingorla, lat. 15° 50′, long. 73° 41′. There are some rocks, about two miles from the mainland, which are the 'Burnt Islands' referred

the Queimados Islands (Burnt Islands), twelve leagues from Goa, they encountered two Portuguese frigates, one of 28 guns, commanded by Senhor Salvador de Mello, and the other of 24 guns, commanded by Senhor Hieronimo de Mello.[1] Not wishing to fight them, he (the Baron) sent his boat with a message to Senhor Salvador de Mello, who was flying the commander's pennant, calling on him to surrender, when he should receive favourable treatment.

Salvador de Mello, touched on the point of honour, sent his answer by some volleys of cannon and musketry, which wounded an officer. Upon this [224] Monsieur le Baron (de Palliéres) ordered Monsieur Martin to force a surrender. The order was executed, and on approaching Senhor Salvador de Mello's ship a broadside was delivered which dismasted it and killed many of the crew. The commander, finding his frigate disabled, hauled down his flag. His companion at once did the same;[2] [the French boarded at once, when five officers from the chief ship were attacked by the Portuguese soldiers, and although they made a brave defence, some were killed and some wounded. The latter would also have been killed had not the officer highest in rank forced himself into De Mello's cabin, and, pointing his sword at his breast, obliged him to order his men to disarm. Following this, the leading frigate surrendered without a fight. Baron de Palliéres was extremely angry at De Mello's conduct, and wanted to punish him. But the latter pleaded in excuse that he had been born in India, and thus was not acquainted with the usages of war. Accordingly he was pardoned], and placing the wounded

---

to (see 'Handbook to the Ports on the Coast of India,' by H. S. Brown, Lieutenant R.N.R., Mangalore, 1897, p. 177, and in the map in D. Lopes's 'Historia dos Portugucses no Malabar,' copied from Bittner and Tomaschek's 'Die Topographischen Capitel des Indischen Seespiegels Mohit'). I am indebted to Mr. D. Ferguson for these references. In the map of Baldaeus's 'Coromandel,' 1672 (Churchill's 'Voyages,' edition 1744, vol. iii.), they appear as 'De brande Islanden.'

1. Two guard-ships—the *San gaetano,* twenty-eight guns, and Nossa *Dama de Misèricordia,* eighty-four guns—fitted out at Goa. The date was November 6, 1704 (Sottas, p. 428). Perhaps, in the above, for 'eighty-four' we ought to read 'twenty-four' guns.
2. This narrative is also given in Part V., fols. 28-33, with additions and variations. So far as these are important, I insert them in square brackets.

men in the second captured frigate, it was ordered to proceed to Goa. In it sailed a Jesuit, who on arrival in Goa was put in prison, as they said he was a spy. They found on him seventy thousand *patacas*, which he said he had brought for trading in diamonds. Upon the first opportunity he was deported to Lisbon.

The Viceroy Gaittano de Mello[1] advised Monsieur Martin [governor of Pondicherry] of this capture, and also sent word that he was fitting out five ships to take his revenge for the captured frigates.

Having dismantled it [the other frigate], they [the French] set it on fire, carrying off with them fifty Portuguese volunteers. [They released a Persian merchant vessel, which the said Portuguese frigate had captured, on the ground that it was not carrying a Portuguese passport;] and on arriving at the latitude of Calicut they came across another ship, an English one, which they took and burnt, [after taking out the best of her contents. This was on December 13, 1704.]

They arrived opposite Porto Novo, a place ten leagues from Pondicherry, and there found a Dutch ship of 54 guns flying a commander's pennant; it was called the *Fenix*.[2] Monsieur le Baron [de Palliéres] went up to it, and discharged a broadside into it, which killed the captain, the supercargo and ten other persons, besides wounding twenty-five. In spite of this the *Fenix* defended herself by three broadsides, but this did her little good. The *St. Lxuis* came up on the other quarter ready to give her another broadside, and they were not willing to try further conclusions, in spite of their having 240 Europeans on board, in addition to 160 men of India. They gave in at once. In this ship was captured the commissary for this coast (Choromandal), who had come from Batavia, and was on his way to Negapatam. [225] His name was Bernard Foucen (Phoosen), and he was removed to Pondicherry along with the ship, which was very valuable, estimated at fifty thousand *patacas*, there being in it two chests of gold coins of Japan, and 5,900 [4,900] chests

1. No. 69, Gaetano dc Mello de Castro, Viceroy, 1703-1707 (Danvers, ii. 489).
2. Sottas (p. 428) names it in French as the *Phénix d'Or*, or *Phénix Doré*, and it was on a voyage from Bengal. The commissary he calls Bernard Phoosen, which is the correct form.

of copper, each one [four] weighing a *candil*,[1] in addition to other merchandise, such as opium, white cloth of Bengal, *et cetera*. [The ships finally reached Pondicherry on January 18, 1705.[2]]

When the Dutch at Negapatam heard of this they came to see the said commissary at Pondicherry. He was set at liberty [after fifteen days], and a truce was entered into for two years that neither side should interfere with the other. It was to have effect from Ceylon as far as Bengal.[3] He (the commissary) and all his suite embarked in a small vessel called the *Marchand des Indes*, under the command of Monsieur Bono (Bouynot).

On July 11, 1704, the said French vessel [*i.e., Marchand des Indes*], carrying 14 guns, had arrived at Pondicherry under the command of Monsieur Bono (Bouynot).[4] He brought the news that four vessels (those already spoken of) were to follow him and go to Surat. In the month of October of the same year [1704] he set sail to avoid the severity of the monsoon on that coast. When in the latitude of the Malabar coast he captured

1. A *candy* is, roughly, 500 pounds. The Portuguese write this word *candil* (Yule, 155).
2. The captured Dutch ship was adjudged lawful prize at Pondicherry on January 25, 1705. It had 216,000 *livres* in gold pieces and some copper. The total cargo and the ship were valued at 97, 285 Pagodas 6 *fānams* 20 cash (1 pagoda equalled 3½ rupees, or 5 *livres* 5 *sols*). Thus the total valuewas about 527,000 *livres*, or £25,000 ('Archives de la Marine, Campagnes,' Register B^4 26, fol. 493). De Palliéres took the gold and the copper, and left the *Phénix* at Pondicherry (letter of Dr. Scottas, June 27, 1906: the figures are his).
3. 'Le commissaire hollandais fut rendu a Negapatam moyennant une tréve qui sauvegardit l'indépendance de Pondicherry pendant la guerre' (Sottas, p. 429; but see note to Part V., fol. 34, for a summary of this negotiation from the Dutch archives). Phoosen went by land, but the crew were sent by sea.
4. In December (1703?) the *Marchand dcs Indes* had set sail from France for Pondicherry as a dispatch-boat (J. Sottas, 'Histoire,' p. 427). Fort St. David writes to Fort St. George on October 13, 1704, about 'the departure of the French ship' (Press List, No. 7, entry No.' 1657). Bouynot was the commander's name, as is clear from the letter of Governor Martin and Council, dated October 2, 1704 ('Archives du Ministére des Colonies,' C^2 67, fol. 128). It was decided to send the *Marchand des Indes* round to Calicut to find out something about the four ships from France, of which nothing had been heard (*ibid.*, fols. 129 and 130). 'She sails well, and her captain, the Sieur Bouynot, is a man of experience.'

an English sloop from Madras, having as captain Mr. Welly.[1] The captain and his sloop were released, after taking from it half the cargo, with an acknowledgment to be paid at the said place (Madras), which was done accordingly, the amount being 7,000 *patacas*. This favour was done him by Mr. Bono (Bouynot) because the said captain (Wooley) had married an English Roman Catholic.

Wishing to return to Pondicherry, he (Bouynot) encountered two large Dutch ships, which attacked him. He defended himself bravely, and killed the captain of one of those ships and a number of the crew.[2] He then arrived safely in company of the four [French] ships referred to above, which had overtaken him on the voyage. The [English] sloop and the above-named captain, Mr. Welly (Wooley), were captured a second time by the four ships, but on his showing the passport given him by Monsieur Bono (Bouynot) they received him kindly. Monsieur le Baron [de Palliéres] wrote out a second passport [226], and sent him off with great civility and offers of service.

Already the careful reader will have beheld in my Fourth Part (IV. 166, 173) the confusion into which the Christians of Madras had been thrown by interested parties who unjustly claimed to take possession of and destroy that congregation. Grieving over these calumnies, I wrote to the Lord Archbishop

1. 'Welly' I take to be meant for Commander George Wooley. Apparently he was captured more than once. On November 25, 1703, Fort St. George heard from Anjengo, a factory in Travancore (Yule, 30), that there were four 'pyrats' on the coast of India, and they enclosed a copy of Wooley's letter giving an account of his seizure on March 10, 1703. He then commanded the *Pembroke* (Press List, No. 7, Fort St. George, entries Nos. 1352 and 1353). Entries Nos. 1357-1359 are also concerned with these pirates, and an account of the capture by E. Fenwick, the supercargo, is printed in Wheeler, ii. 22-27 (Factory Records, vol. xiii., p. 92). The only mention of the second capture found by me is in entry No. 1677—another letter from Anjengo, dated November 9, 1704, about 'the movements of the French ship that took Captain Woolly prisoner at Zeilon [? Ceylon].
2. We have, no doubt, a reference to this encounter in entry No. 1677, Anjengo, November 9, 1704 (Press List, Fort St. George, No. 7): 'Arrival of Captains Hamet and Chamberlain at Calicut, and of two Dutch ships that attacked the French ship there.'

Primate of Goa, informing him thereof in detail, in the hope of his introducing some cure for these disorders. From him I received a reply, dated on the 22nd of January in this present year, 1705,[1] and it is as follows:

Senhor Nicolao Manuchy,

The reputation of Your Honour is so well recognised in these regions that the trouble you take to acquaint me therewith is superfluous, for there survive abundantly in this Portuguese nation's memory the honours with which your exertions were rewarded in the time of the Most Excellent Senhor, the Count of Albor [Alvora]. I am extremely pleased to received your information and the documents you transmit, and I have had the greatest joy in reading your discreet narration. Yet the subject caused me great grief, being aware of the perturbation aroused in that Christian community by the intrigues of those who are soliciting its favours, and by the private interests which are trying to persuade it. I grieve equally over the small attention paid in the matter to the Canonical Law and the rights of the royal Patronage and of the Primate of the East. They thought that in the submission of the Bishop, who confesses his error, consisted the legalization of their rights, disregarding the fact that the Lord Bishop could do on prejudice to the Primatial rights, and much less to those of the King. [227] When persons act in a form that prejudices these, the Primate has the law on his side if he repels at once any such encroachment made on his suffragan and on the Primacy. I write to the Lord Bishop, and transmit to him a Pastoral, by which I forbid the Patriarch to interfere in this Diocese and this Primacy, or in the patronage rights of the King. God permitting, they will come in time to understand in this country the laws of the Church and the rights pertaining to each jurisdiction. Offering myself at the same time to serve Your Honour with the promptest goodwill, I pray that God may have you in His keeping.

Goa, 23rd of December of 1704.

Of Your Honour, etc.

(Signed) ARCHBISHOP PRIMATE.

1. This must be an oversight; the letter is dated on the 23rd, and the Pastoral on December 22, 1704. Probably the author means to give the date on which he received the letter at Madras. The Archbishop's letter and Pastoral are repeated in Part V., fols. 57-64.

Here is a copy of the Pastoral that the Most Illustrious the Lord Primate of Goa sent to the Reverend Father Friar Michel Ange, vicar of the Church in Madras, a similar one being sent to the fortress of Pondicherry, both to the following effect:[1]

The Doctor Dom Friar Augustinho da Annunciação, by favour of God and of the Holy Catholic Church Archbishop Metropolitan of Goa, Primate of India and other parts of the East, of the Council of His Majesty, *et cetera*.

To all faithful Christians salutation and peace in Jesus Christ, who is for every one the true Redeemer and Saviour.

We make known that on our shoulders, however unequal to it, the Catholic Church has imposed the burden of all Christian flocks, from the Cape of Good Hope even unto Tartary, as Primate for the whole of the Orient. Holy Mother Church relies on Our Vigilance for the defence of the vast Christian communities of all Asia, not permitting that any enter therein with any jurisdiction derogatory of the Primatial rights to Us entrusted nor under any other [228] title, until he shall first have promulgated his Bulls and powers, thereby proving the delegation entrusted to him by the Holy Catholic Church. This legal publication must be made in the form fixed by the said Church, adverting to the great inconveniences and abuses that might be introduced into the congregations and the houses of God, if the powers and delegations conferred by His Holiness were not examined, whoever may be the persons who have to exercise jurisdiction within any community of Christians.

As the Most Holy Father Boniface VIII. ordained in his *Clementina, 'Injunctae,'*[2] *'Sane de electione inter communes,'* no person asserting a delegation shall be believed or obeyed until he shall have previously made legal publication of his commis-

1. This Pastoral is referred to by Père Norbert ('Mémoires Historiques,' third edition, i. 153), but not quoted in full. It was abrogated by Pope Clement XI, by a Declaration, dated Rome, January 4, 1707 (see the same work, i. 159-171, where the Pope's covering letter of January 1, 1707, is also given, pp. 154-159). The Pope held that the Patriarch's powers had been sufficiently validated by communication to the Bishop.
2. See preceding note 46 to fol. 183. The passage begins: 'Sane quam periculosum existat.'

sion. He ordained that any interdicts fulminated by such a person should be null and of no effect. This law prevails throughout the Catholic Church, above all in Asia, which is at such a distance from the Apostolic See, where it would be difficult to redress any abuses introduced by a person who might thus act under his powers as delegate.

Therefore we declare that the Lord Dom Carlos Thomas, entitling himself Patriarch of Antioch and Legate à *latere*, has tried to introduce himself into the Christian communities of India, altering the laws and civil customs of the Christians without having experience of them, and perturbing these congregations. Those in Madras are, we find, deprived of the administration of the sacraments, the friars, their parish priests, being by him declared outside the law.

This mode of proceeding in a business involving the salvation of souls is violent, and in derogation of the privileges of His Most Serene Majesty of Portugal, which, if they are to be of any value, do not admit of such derogation. These acts were done entirely without the Legate's Bulls and the powers under his commission being made known in a legal manner to the prelates who were competent to grant such jurisdiction. In so acting he contravened the laws of the Church and the rights of the Royal Patronage [229] of the Crown of Portugal,[1] and usurped the powers of this Primacy.

We declare the interdicts so imposed to be null and void, admit the persons denounced in them to the administration of the sacraments, ordain to all friars and secular priests dwelling within this Primacy non-obedience to and disregard of his interdicts, until such time as he shall first prove his powers under the delegation, and establish its legality.

---

1. This right of patronage, including the right either to appoint or to sanction the appointment of all Bishops and Archbishops in the East, has been claimed by the Portuguese Crown within quite a recent period. Mr. Philipps has shown me the translation of a dispatch from the Portuguese Government to the Archbishop of Goa, dated August 8, 1863, claiming the right to exercise those privileges 'outside of the Portuguese territories.' On that occasion the British Government declined to acknowledge the force, within British territory, of the Concordats of February 21, 1857, and January 24, 1860, between the Pope and the King of Portugal, and repudiated the claim of the latter to be protector of the Roman Catholic Church in British India (F. C. Danvers, 'Portuguese in India,' ii. 464).

We hold the said Lord Dom Carlos Thomas as cited, inhibiting him, under pain of excommunication, from the exercise of any act of jurisdiction derogatory of the rights of this Primacy and of the Royal Patronage, until he shall first prove to Us legally the powers of his Commission.

Given at Goa under Our signature and seal on the 22nd of December of 1704,

> I, Henrique Bravo de Moraes, chief treasurer of the Primatial See of Goa, have caused this Act to be written and subscribe it.

(Signed) HENRIQUE BRAVO DE MORAES.
(Signed) ARCHBISHOP PRIMATE.

The Seal Ӂ Gratis
Moraes.

The said pastoral the Very Reverend Father Friar Michel Ange, Vicar of Madras, caused to be publicly authenticated in the chancery of the Lord Bishop of Mailapur, by procuring the order and attestation of the Vicar-General, so that all the people were satisfied. But the Dominician Father, Friar Diogo do Sacramento, declined to submit either to the Primate of Goa or to the Lord Bishop of Mailapur. For this purpose he fixed up a document, opposing submission, on the door of his church, but the people took no heed of his impertinence. This manifesto was as follows: [230]

Manifesto wherein is explained for the information of the ignorant the pastoral of the lord archbishop primate, thereby proving the Lord Dom Carlos Thomas to be a veritable prelate within this diocese and the indies, and therefore all he did and pronounced is valid and juridical.

The Lord Primate states in his Pastoral attached to the principal door of the church in Madraspatam that the Lord Dom Carlos Thomas entered this country without producing his powers to the prelates, to whom he should have showed them.

This is untrue, most untrue, and therein was the Lord Primate wrongly informed; since the Lord Dom Carlos Thomas showed and presented to the Lord Bishop Dom Caspar Alfonço a Brief wherein His Holiness declared him to be his Apostolic Visitor. This can be testified to and proved by the said Lord Bishop, for he had the Brief in his possession. The Lord Dom Gaspar Affonço was the authority to whom the Lord Patriarch was required to show his powers in this country. Hence all that the said Lord Patriarch did is valid, and must be respected and obeyed. The fathers of Madras named in the Pastoral are not absolved, for that pastoral is founded on wrong information sent to him by them. Were the Lord Primate rightly informed, he would never have given them absolution. It is to be clearly seen from the pastoral itself, in which the said Lord is cited to appear, and he is called on to show his powers, *sed sic est* [but so it is], that he did show them, and they are at this moment in the hands of the Lord Bishop Dom Gaspar Affonço. Thus it is certain that this act validates all the Patriarch did and shall hereafter do.

Sao Thome, on the 2nd of February of 1705.

(Signed) DOM GIULHELMO DE LA VALLE.
(Signed) FRIAR DIOGO DO SACRAMENTO.

The judicious reader can detect the passion of the above individuals, and how much truth there was in the allegation of their manifesto—viz., that the Lord Dom Carlos Thomas, Patriarch of Antioch, showed and presented his powers under his Commission to the Lord Bishop of Mailapur, Dom Gaspar Affonço. For the contrary is established by the letter that this same Most Illustrious Lord Bishop of Mailapur [231] wrote to the Capuchin Fathers in Madras, which is as follows:

VERY REVEREND FATHERS,

I reply briefly. I have received a copy of the Lord Primate's letter in which he lays it down that the Lord Patriarch ought to have presented his letters at the Primacy of Goa. On the whole it appears to me it was enough to present them to any bishop.[1] My mistake was to recognise him without asking him to produce the Letters for his Commission, and it was an error

1. In the end this was the view adopted by Pope Clement XI. (see previous note 127 to fol. 226).

to obey him [without his doing so]. You, Reverend Fathers, respected the obedience I gave to him, and supposing that I and you, Reverend Fathers, did obey him, I judge that what he did is not null and void. Thus it seems to me you, Reverend Fathers, ought to make use of the Pastoral sent you, and of the absolution granted to the Reverend Father Guardian. In regard to what concerns the letter of the Lord Primate you, Reverend Fathers, may act as you judge to be most just. I hold it to be good for you, Reverend Fathers, to publish the Pastoral sent to you, and if under cover of this, you make known the Lord Primate's letter, you may act as to you seems best. The certificate that was given to the Reverend Father Michel Ange is becoming justified, and if there is anything overlooked in my reply I will see to it a few days hence. May God have you in his keeping.

Sao Thome, 9th October, 1704.

The festival of the Rosary may be carried out by your Reverences as seems fit, but it would be preferable to move more slowly.

Of your Reverences the humble servant and friend.

(Signed) BISHOP OF MELLIAPUR (MALIAPUR).

To certify that this writing is genuine the notary public of this town of Madras draws up this certificate. The copy above given agrees with its original *de verbo ad verbum*, and for such I Joao Gago Pexouto attest it.

Madras, on the 13th January, 1705.

(Signed) JOAO GAGO PEXOUTO.

There can be no doubt that the missionaries who come from Europe bring with them much zeal.[1] They expect on their arrival in these Indian lands that their labours will be very fruitful. [232] But they know nothing, and have no experience of these people, nor the fitting way of dealing with them. I can give the following example. In the year 1680, being at the city of Aurangabad, I received a letter from a reverend father, a discalced Carmelite, whose name was Petro Paulo.[2]

1. This passage about the Carmelite missionary is repeated in Part V., MS. xlv., fols. 71-73, or in MS. 135, class vi., fol. 22b.
2. Petrus Paulus a S. Francisco (born 1643) was the heir to a principality in Naples, and through his mother was the nephew of Pope Innocent XII. (born 1615, elected 1692, died 1700). He joined the Car

Hearing me spoken of, he wrote informing me of his arrival at Surat from Persia. Then, without any beating about the bush, he went on to say I must speak to the king, Aurangazeb, and tell him to send an immediate order for the erection of a church at the port of Surat. He must also issue an order throughout his empire that missionaries should be admitted everywhere, and openly allowed to convert Mahomedans and Hindus. If he raised objections to these demands, he (the Carmelite) would force the King of Persia to declare war against India by land and sea. He would also take other measures by teaching a secret to the Mahrattahs. He knew about a matchlock that could be fired five to seven times after only once loading it, and whenever he chose to do so.

He really did know such a device, as I will explain presently. I replied to his letter by saying that when the Saviour of the

---

melite Order on May 20, 1673. and came to India in 1678. Returning to Rome in 1689, he was made Archbishop of Ancyra in Galatia Prima *in partibus* on September 20, 1696, and succeeded Bishop Custodius as Vicar Apostolic of Malabar. He obtained from the Dutch at Amsterdam a decree, dated April 1, 1698, permitting a Bishop and twelve Carmelites, Italians, Germans, or Belgians, to live in the territory, but not in the town of Cochin. As an equivalent, the Dutch obtained from the Emperor Leopold I, toleration for the Calvinist religion in Hungary. From Bishop Angelico Francis, in 1701, to Bishop Aloysius, in 1785, the Bull of appointment was submitted to the Dutch at Cochin, and permission obtained to reside at Verapoly. Father Petrus Paulus has been mentioned before in Part III., fol. 429, of Venice Codex XLIV. (Zanetti). Soon after reaching Surat, the Archbishop died (January 4, 1700), aged fifty-seven, and was interred in the church of the Capuchins (Müllbauer, 347, relying on Eusebius, 'Enchiridion.,' Rome, 1734, pp. 391, 399-403, and Raulinus [J. F. Raulin], 'Historia Ecclesiae Malabaricae,' Rome, 1745, p. 50, with additional details from G. T. Mackenzie, Madras Civl Service, 'Christianity in Travancore,' Trevandrum, 1901, pp. 29 and 30, and 'Madras Catholic Directory for 1878,' pp. 87 and 88). In F. Penny's 'Church in Madras,' p. 219, there is an extract about this missionary taken from the Madras Consultations, dated June 14, 1686. Mr. Philipps says 'discalced' is the word recognised in English, though I should have preferred 'bare-footed.' The Archbishop probably died in 1701 and not in 1700, for on November 15, 1700, there is a Declaration by him permitting the Jesuits to work at Surat and build a church; he styles himself Vicar Apostolic in the kingdoms of the Mogol, of Golconda, and of 'Idalcan' (Bijapur). See Archives Nationales, Paris, K 1374, document No. 43.

world came to this earth He showed humility in spite of His omnipotence, and by His tender words won over to Himself people in many parts of the world. I had not done what he asked, in order not to risk the loss of both our lives without any profit; and I advised him against communicating that secret to the Mahrattahs, for as soon as they had learnt it they would kill him.

In the year 82 [1682] I came across this reverend father in the city of Goa. He paid me a visit, and espying a matchlock in my room, he loaded it with five charges of powder, each with a ball rammed down on it. He then gave a salvo of five shots with great ease. But when he placed the powder-horn to the fire-pan, he did it so that no one could see. I was much amazed, and the Lord Viceroy Dom Francisco de Tavora having been told, he employed me as negotiator to get the Carmelite to teach them this secret. As a reward ten thousand *xerafins* (*ashrafis*) were offered, and other gifts. But the Carmelite informed me that the secret could be confided to no one but a leading member of his own house.

The [233] above-mentioned friar went to Rome and came back to Surat as archbishop [of Ansira (Ancyra)], bringing a number of missionaries. In a short time he died of a purgative administered to him by the Jesuit fathers, who, after his death, realized fourteen rupees for the dose.

On February 3, 1705, there arrived here in Madras a missionary priest of German race, called Andre Guilhermo Wil Thomacey, who had been one of the company brought out by the above archbishop. He had lived four years in the army of the Mogul; so I asked him what results he had obtained in all that time in that army. He answered me that he had worked a great deal with those people in the arts of medicine and mathematics. The only gain was to be changed from a very active man into one very weak and depressed. Owing to having been ill-treated for his complaint, he was unable to start in the monsoon for Europe.

I have already mentioned that King Aurangzeb was preparing to take the field for a fresh war, but his fast-month[1] was

1. The year 1704 is probably referred to, and in the corresponding Mahomedan year (1116 H.) the fast of Ramazān lasted from

the cause of his not moving. Yet, busy as he was with his prayers, he did not forget to make such efforts as were necessary. To this end he wrote different letters pledging his word, as he is used to do for the deception of the princes. There was one of them who ruled over several districts called Saguer (Sagar),[1] lying in the kingdom of Bijapur. He was induced by flatteries to attend the Presence, and was given many honours, and appointed a *Chahar Hazari*, or commander of 4,000 horse. This was accompanied by the gift of an elephant, horses, and a set of robes which he put on in the royal presence. Full of joy, he set out on his return to his tents, but on the way was attacked by violent fever. On the following day the flesh from his whole body began to peel off; on the third day he quitted his grandeurs along with his life.

King Aurangzeb made himself master [234] of the dead prince's lands, which adjoin those of a prince who is called Aguengivar (Wakinkerah).[2] They are also within the same kingdom of Bijapur. This powerful and valorous lord kept an army of eighty thousand matchlockmen, besides men armed with swords and spears. In past years Aurangzeb has made every effort to reduce this prince. The king sent against him the general Ranmastacan (Ranmast Khan),[3] but he and his

---

December 29, 1704, to January 27, 1705; or, if the next year be intended the dates were December 18, 1705, to January 16, 1706.

1. Nusratabad Sakkhar (Sagar), now in the Nizam's dominions, ninety-five miles south-east of Sholapur, lat. 16° 36', long. 76° 51'. Formerly the capital of a small State held by a Bidar or Dhedh, Naik or chief. On the 2nd Safar, 1099 H. (December 7, 1687), it was taken by the Moguls from peda, *Naik*, caste Dhedh. He was introduced at Court on the 2nd Rabi 'I. (February 5, 1688), and died five or six days afterwards ('Ma,asir-i-'Alamgiri,' 307).
2. This is the name of a place, and not of a person. Wakinkerah was a new capital, established by the Sakkhar family on a hill some distance to the west of their old stronghold. It was taken on the 14th Muharram, 1117 H. (May 7, 1705), and renamed Rahman bakhsh Khaira ('Ma,asir-i-'Alamgiri,' 490-494, 498-506).
3. 'Ali, entitled Ranmast Khan, Panni, the uncle of Da,ud Khan. He entered the service in the seventh year (1664-65); in the twenty-seventh year (1683-84) he joined the Emperor when he came to the Dakhin. He rose to be a *Panj Hazari* (5,000), and was killed in the thirty-fourth year (1690-91) during an attack on Wakinkerah ('Ma,asir-ul-Umara,' ii. 64).

soldiers were killed. A second time Aurangzeb, unwilling to desist, ordered the famous general Diler Khan to undertake the attack. But he succeeded badly, and leaving his dead behind him, had to flee at full gallop with his hands to his head. Not for a contretemps like this would Aurangzeb relinquish his purpose, but sent a third expedition under Rub Calacan (Ruhullah Khan);[1] but he was afraid to venture into the enemy's territory. By judicious letters he obtained his recall to court, and after a short time died.

At the present moment Aurangzeb, previous to attacking Maisur, purposes to clear out this place (Wakinkerah), in order that the cavalry of the Mahrattahs may not find a refuge there. Time will show what will happen; if this aged king is able to live on for some years, he will succeed in taking these principalities of the Karnatik. But he knows that his generals make no genuine efforts, and therefore he is obliged to go in person if he wishes to carry out his designs.

He continues to show himself devout and abstinent. During the fast he says his prayers for twenty-four hours on end, his head on the ground, eating nothing, and never moving his body. The queen, Udipuri, beholding all this make-believe, roused him, and told him he had been so many hours at his prayers that it was necessary for his majesty to eat something. Upon this he raised his head and sharply reproved the queen for having withdrawn him from the delights he was enjoying, by which he suggested that he had entered into heavenly glory, and now despised earthly enjoyments.

From time to time he plunges into similar fits of devotion [235], and among the ignorant common people the belief in his false saintship goes on increasing. Yet his army is a filthy, dirty place, more like a scourge sent by God, judging by the daily mortality of men and animals. The common people are

1. I can find no record of any expedition by Diler Khan: but on the 4th Zu,l Qa'dah of the thirty-fifth year, 1102 H. (June 10, 1691), Ruhullah Khan was sent against Wakinkerah ('Ma,asir-i-'Alamgiri,' 344). He died towards the end of 1103 H., between the 1st and the 18th Zu,l Qa'dah (July 15 to August 1, 1692) ('Ma,asir-ul-Umara,' ii. 313: 'Ma,asir-i-'Alamgiri,' 348). The subject of Wakinkerah is resumed in Part V., fol. 1.

dealt with as mere animals after they are dead. Their bodies are searched to see if they have any money, and after the feet have been tied together with a rope, they are dragged out of the camp and thrown into the first hole to be found. The same is done to the animals, and both serve as aliment for wolves, dogs, and crows.

A great stench is caused in this way, and no measures are taken to get rid of this filthiness. Many a time, under such circumstances, I have found myself unable to bear the evil smell, and been forced to urge my horse to the gallop to get away from it, holding my nose as I did so. Sometimes I was even compiled to vomit, human nature being unable to bear such a grievous thing. The flies are in such numbers that there is no means of eating your food in peace.

Travellers setting out from this army are not protected against the attacks of the Mahrattahs and other robbers; and when you are delivered from this peril, you fall into the hands of the *juncaneiros*[1] (customs officers), or publicans. These take what they please unjustly and by force, and if they know that anyone has money on him, they rob him, cut his throat, and bury him.

This is the condition into which the saintly rule of this king has fallen. The existing pretenders to this empire number seventeen princes of full age. First there are the sons of the king, already old men, as can be verified from their ages previously given.[2] Then his grandsons are men with grey beards, some of them already forty-five or forty-six years of age, some younger. There are great-grandsons, some of whom have reached twenty-four or twenty-seven years.[3] I say nothing of great-great-grandsons, or the women of the blood-royal belonging to his family. What an event to behold will be the tragedy following

1. For *junkaneers*, see note 183, Vol. II., Part II., fol. 130.
2. Although incidentally referred to, I cannot find any passages in the text giving these exact ages.
3. The male descendants of Aurangzeb to the third generation alive in 1705 were: Three sons—*viz.*: (1) Muhammad Mu'azzam, Shah 'Alam, aged sixty-two; (2) Muhammad A'zam Shah, A'zam Tara, aged fifty-two; (3) Muhammad Kam Bakhsh, aged thirty-eight—four sons and nine grandsons of No. 1, three sons and one grandson of No. 2, three sons of No. 3, or a total of twenty-three persons (see H. Bloch mann's 'Table of the House of Taimur' in the 'A,in-i-Akbari,' vol. i.; Calcutta, 1873). I have not included Prince Akbar, who, although alive in 1705, was an exile in Persia.

the death of this old man! One only of these princes can succeed, and thereby protect his family; the rest of them will be decapitated, or lose their lives in various other ways. It will be a much worse tragedy than that [236] which happened at the end of King Shahjahan's reign.

Hindu traders living in this empire are forced to pay every year in advance a personal tax, as I have once before stated (II. 182; III. 51; IV. 28). In return they are given a receipt to serve as a passport, but when they travel to another kingdom or province of this empire the said passport is of no value. On their outward and their return journey the same amount is collected. In this way the mercants suffer from great impositions, and thus many of them and of the bankers are ruined. Aurangzeb rejoices over these failures, in the belief that by such extortions these Hindus will be forced into embracing the Mahomedan faith.

END OF THE FOURTH PART OF NICOLAO MANUCI, THE VENETIAN.

[239][1] The inquiring reader will have already seen in various parts of my work that I have spoken of the chief minister and chancellor called Cazimir (Qazi Mir).[2] He left Shah 'Alam because that prince declined to listen to his good advice. He was the most learned man in the empire, always occupied in writings which were approved by the other learned men of that time. He composed a new work drawn from the Old Testament and the Evangelists. It was composed with his special acuteness of mind, forming a volume of considerable size. When it was finished, my friend Qazi Mir prayed for leave from Aurangzeb to travel to Mecca, since no one can be refused this, as it is a pilgrimage.

1. Here follow eight folios and two tabular statements, all of which seem to have been loose leaves subsequently bound into the volume.
2. This narrative appears again in Part V., fol. 128, and the passages in square brackets are added from that version. Qazi Mir is named again in Part V., fol. 109. That there was such a man, and that he had some special connection with Shah 'Alam, is shown by passages mentioning his nephew in Khafi Khan's 'History,' ii. 681, last line, year 1123 H. (171 M2), and 930, first line, year 1133 H. (1720-21).

On his arrival there he showed his book to the principal learned man of the Mahomedan faith, who is called the Xerif (Sharif). He collected all the most famous men of learning for the examination of Qazi Mir's opinions, and to decide whether it was right lo lay them before the public. After some months spent in examination, all of them with one accord said openly that what Qazi Mir had written was correct. The verdict was attested by the principal men—the Sharif and the other learned men of Mecca—with their seals and signatures.

He set out on his return to India, and on arriving at court he laid his book before his majesty. The principal doctors of the law within the empire, four hundred of them, were summoned, and received orders to read and consider the book, examining it most minutely. After the lapse of some months they returned the book, saying that on the whole it set forth the true faith, and its precepts might rightly be followed.

Aurangzeb, as a keen Mahomedan. was alarmed, and confiscated his (Qazi Mir's) property, and also caused the book to be burnt in his presence. He directed the chief *qazi* to pronounce a sentence of beheadal on the author [239*b*], Qazi Mir. The chief *qazi* replied that he found in him no fault requiring death, and if under royal compulsion he sent an order of execution, it would be a manifest injustice. After listening to these arguments, the king directed that Qazi Mir should be removed as a prisoner to the fortress of Aser (Asir), of which I have already spoken in connection with the conquests of the great emperor Akbar, as you will have already seen in my First Part (I 75).

When two years had elapsed Aurangzeb ordered Qazi Mir to be shut up in a palanquin and brought to court, and instructed the principal men at the court to use persuasion and induce him to disavow what he had written. But he was fixed and rooted in his opinions, and declined to vary them. Finding this the case, the king had recourse once more to the chief *qazi*, and with wheedling words besought him to find some way of putting the man to death. The *qazi* declined.

Next the king had the prisoner brought into his presence, and said: 'If you will disavow and show penitence for what you have done, your offences will be pardoned,' Qazi Mir replied ardently that he meant to give the truth to the public, by whom it was ignored. 'Your majesty must repent and ask God's pardon for having given the true faith to the flames, and for not following its commands. Nay, for acting contrary to it, seizing your father, slaying your brothers, usurping the dominions of others, and unjustly ruining many princes and vassals.' At this point Aurangzeb interrupted by saying that in the Quarn Muhammand enjoined the defeat and destruction of the infidel. Qazi Mir retorted: 'Muhammad acted as it pleased him; I follow what God ordains.' Upon hearing this, the king ordered him to be taken back to the same fortress, giving secret directions that as soon as he had arrived his life should be taken. This case happened in the year 1690.[1]

Years ago I might have written what I have now said, but I did not; I waited until I had assured myself thoroughly in the [240*a*] matter, it being of some importance. Finally, I became assured that it was true, from its being known as such all over the court and throughout the empire. To this day I have no want of friends at the court and in various parts of the empire, who send me information of all that happens. In addition there are the news-letters received by the governors and principal officials at least once a month. By these men I obtain reports of all that takes place, keeping up friendship with them effectually, as it ought to be maintained.

A similar case occurred in the city of Ahmadabad during the year 1699, when it was ruled over by Prince A'zam Tara.[2] There was a youth, the son of a learned man who dwelt dwelt in the town of Xalcot (Shyalkot),[3] situated in the province of Lahor. He forsook his father's house, and, abandoning his riches, took the garb of a poor ascetic; he wandered hither and thither, despising the great things of this world, and accepting nothing from anybody.

His business was to dispute with learned men and doctors of theology, and point out the road assigned to us by the Messiah. He made attacks on the Quran, as if already vexed with life and

1. The year 1690 corresponds with 1101 and 1102 H., but I can find no trace in the historians of any such event.
2. This story appears again in Part V., fols. 132 and 133. A'zam Shah was sent to Ahmadabad late in 1113 H. (in the spring of 1702) ('Ma,asir-i-'Alamgiri,' 442).
3. Part V., fol. 132, reads 'Xalcot,' which is evidently Shyalkot (Sialkot), a town in the Punjab, lat. 26° 30', long. 94° 59'.

longing to sacrifice himself. He soon obtained his desires. He visited the principal *qazi* when seated in public audience, and said: 'All men assert you to be the most learned man in this province; for this cause I have come to find if it is true.' Then began various disputations, the youth extolling the Gospel and decrying what Muhammad had enjoined.

At this point the *qazi* flew into a great passion, and along with all the other doctors present fell upon the young man, and endeavoured to force him into a disavowal. The beating they gave him produced no effect, so they dragged him away to prison. Every day he was sent for to be catechized; the questions were accompanied with many promises and honied words. Since there was no result, the beating was resumed. This martyrdom lasted for forty days. An appeal to A'zam Tara was equally ineffective, and finding all efforts fruitless, they cut off the young man's head, and threw his body on to a dungheap outside the city, to be devoured by dogs and wolves. As it appears to me, this man must have been some disciple of Qazi Mir.

[240*b*] A fine instance happened a few years ago in the city of Isfahan in connection with the great men of the Mahomedan religion.[1] In that city there was a Capuchin Father, of whom I fancy I have already spoken; his name was Friar Raphael, a man much esteemed by the king and all the court, who delighted in his conversation, he being both learned and sensible.

One day that he was in conversation with the greatest doctors of the court, they said to him, 'You are a sensible man; how can you say that the prophet Masih' (for so they style Him) 'is God?' The judicious Capuchin saw that an answer to this question required time if he were to deal with it satisfactorily, and expound the truth properly in a matter of such importance.

Next day the friar presented himself, when there was a still greater crowd of learned men than before. He was received courteously, and all were anxious to hear the promised answer. They interrogated him upon the subject. His reply was that in due time he would state his opinion. Meanwhile, it was more urgent to consider a business of some importance to him, and that completed, he would talk of the other.

---

1. This narrative appears again in Part V., fols. 134 and 135. For Father Raphael du Mans, see note 4 to Part I., fol. 12.

So saying, he produced a document which he handed to the leading man then present, making a claim for justice to be done. He demanded payment of a large sum of money, as detailed in that paper. As he spoke he indicated as the debtor one of the persons present. This man repudiated the debt by saying he had never had any dealings with him, and thus could owe nothing. Then all of the onlookers began to examine the acknowledgment, and saw that it was written by the self-same father, witnessed by him, and signed by him. Upon discovering these facts, they all said that in no court of justice [243*a*],[1] and by no system of law, could such a document be valid.

The father replied: 'If this acknowledgment is held not to be valid, from being signed and witnessed in my handwriting, credit being refused to it in the absence of persons who certify the debt, how can faith be accorded to the Quran of Muhammad? It was given to the world without any witnesses to certify that it was true and holy doctrine. In that case, why is not my document accepted? Posing for solution the above question as to how the Messiah is the Son of God and the only true God, I reply that the answer is to be obtained from the whole of the Prophets and from different parts of the Sacred Writings, both of the Old Testament, where the promises can be seen, and of the New, where is found the fulfilment of those promises by the coming of that same Messiah, certified and testified to by the mouth of many apostles—men who were illuminated by the Divine Wisdom.'

As the Mahomedan doctors listened they looked at one another in shame, for there was no answer to give. They turned the conversation and put the father off the track, and with a smile on their lips, depreciated him as mad and wanting in common sense; then declared that he did not know what he was talking about. The padre withdrew, and as he took his leave of them, he declared that what he had said was ascertained doctrine, accepted among all reasonable men and those learned in the true law of God.

[241a][2] . . . the tongue, others suffocated themselves, others

1. Here a leaf seems to have been misplaced in binding the manuscript, and the end of the story is found on fol. 243*a*.
2. The passage begins abruptly in the middle of a sentence, and some leaves must be wanting. The matter treated refers, without doubt,

threw themselves into the ponds. In the camp the greater number did the same, as I have stated. Rushing out of the tents and running about in the camp in desperation without finding any consolation, the women and wives of the Hindu princes who had died in the battle flung themselves with joy into the flames, in the way that will already have been seen described in my Second Part (II. 70, 71; III. 127, 133, 210).

The victorious princes were summoned to court. They entered the city [Agrah] in triumph, the streets being carpeted and adorned. Wherever they passed, rose-water was sprinkled and flowers scattered. The whole population shouted their huzzahs and uttered congratulations. They then entered the fortress. There they found the king seated on the throne; and on coming into sight of the royal person, they made a profound obeisance, and stood where they were, awaiting the royal orders. A sign was made to them with the king's hand, beckoning them to approach. When they reached him they bent their heads to his feet, while he touched their backs three times with his hands. Sultan Mu'izz-ud-din was on the right, and Sultan 'Azim-ud-din on the left hand. He said: 'You did your duty, and the profit shall be yours and your sons'.' Then he ordered them to rise.

Upon rising they made three obeisances, and then returned to their places and stood. Sultan Mu'izz-ud-din received a plume ornament, which was at once attached to the turban on his head. It was worth three hundred thousand rupees. Three strings of lovely pearls worth two hundred thousand rupees were also put on his neck, and round his waist a belt four fingers broad covered with precious stones worth five *lakhs* of rupees. The same presents were given to Sultan 'Azim-ud-din, but of less value. They were then given seats, Mu'izz-ud-din on the right and 'Azim-ud-din on the left hand.

On this day great rewards were distributed to those who had survived the battle. Their rank was increased, and new *jagirs* were conferred on them, while the relations of those killed in it were rewarded with good pay and *jagirs*. The sons of the Hindu princes belonging to the family of the ill-treated Jaswant Singh

to events following Shah 'Alam's defeat of his brother, A'zam Shah, at Jajau, near Agrah, on June 18, 1707, N.S., and possibly it was meant to follow fol. 324, Part V. The same subject is repeated in Part V. (Codex XLV.), fols. 342 *et seq.*, and begins there in the same manner.

received a grant of the revenues of Gujarat province for five years, and, in addition to this, the territories were restored to them which had been taken away by the new king's father [241*b*]. To Chhatar Sal Rae were granted the revenues of Ajmer; and others were also honourably rewarded as each one had deserved. On the third day the third son of Shah 'Alam, called Rafiulcader (Rafi'-ul-qadr), arrived in the royal presence, and received the same distinctions as his brothers.

On the same day it was ordained that a letter should be written to the general Ghyaz-ud-din Khan stating that until the arrival of the Prince Mu'izz-ud-din in those parts he should take charge of Barar, Burhanpur, Aurangabad, and Baglanah. Another letter was at the same time written to the new King of Bijapur, Kam Bakhsh, whereby he was enjoined to remain and take his ease at the city of Bijapur, and refrain from interference elsewhere (sad news indeed for that prince).

When five days had passed, he (Shah 'Alam) dispatched Sultan Mu'izz-ud-din to the Dakhin, appointing him lord over those regions, and conferring on him full powers. At the leavetaking Shah 'Alam with his own hands attached to his waist a valuable sword. Mu'izz-ud-din issued from the city of Agrah with one hundred thousand horse, having for his principal general Queamerdinchan (Qamar-ud-din Khan),[1] son of the fosterbrother of the old king, now dead. After the death of A'zam Shah all became quiet in these regions [? the Dakhin]; now we shall see, upon the arrival of this prince (Mu'izz-ud-din) in these parts of the Dakhin, what will happen. The only thing that troubles me is Kam Bakhsh, who will never come to the enjoyment of all that he imagined.

Here arises a point to be remembered. The judicious and inquiring reader will already have seen what happened to the King Paruoar.[2] All his courtiers were traitors to him except

1. There was a Qamar-ud-din Khan, son of Shams-ud-din, Mukhtar Khan, who became Mukhtar Khan himself in the twenty-eight year (1684-85). He was A'zam Shah's father-in-law, and in 1707 was Governor of the Agrah province. He surrendered to Bahadur Shah (Shah 'Alam), and may be the person intended. No mention is elsewhere made of an intended Dakhin campaign under Prince Mu'izz-ud-din, and the idea must have been soon abandoned. Shah 'Alam took command in person.
2. This name Paruoar is not recognisable; the Italian version

Jufacarkan[150], and Danisbankam (Danishmand Khan).[150] The traitors have died leaving no descendants, a castigation that fell on them from God. Readers have seen also the practice of the King Aurangzeb, and the payment he gave to the traitors who adopted his side in his revolt [242*a*]. He sent out orders secretly to deprive them of life; as he did to Jivan Khan who seized Dara, and to Khalil[ullah] Khan, who was the cause of his winning the battle, as already may be seen in my First (I. 266) and Second Parts (II. 85). As for Shaistah Khan, he did not kill him, because he was in need of his good advice.

Most of them had their lives taken in his (Aurangzeb's) life-time, while he rewarded the sons and grandsons of those traitors who were in the battle. All of the traitors came to their death with the exception of one—namely, Asad Khan. This man declined to join the party of Aurangzeb, and was sent to his court by an order of Shahjahan, after his becoming a prisoner, as will have been already seen (II. 14). Thus, of the ancient and noble persons in the empire, all were killed, except a few infants left with the baggage-train.

It is to be observed that in the ancient chronicles of the battles fought in Hindustan between powerful princes in those earlier days, as well as in the time of the Pathans and the Moguls, there is no description found of so fierce and sanguinary a battle as the one I have just described.[1] True, I was not there myself, but the agents of those lords who govern provinces, fortresses, and districts in this direction (the Dakhin), all of them wrote to their masters an account of these events. They are all under an obligation to make such reports, as I have already said (III 68). They all affirm to the same effect; and inquiring from men who were present, I always obtained the same result without any differences, and in all places nothing else is asserted.

The judicious reader will have seen already how King Aurangzeb, through his deceits, double-dealings, and treachery,

(Part V., fol. 344) has Xaaian (Shahjahan). It may be part of the honorific mode of address, *Gharib-parwar*, 'Cherisher of the poor.' In Part II., fol. 199, the two loyal servants are given as Mukarram (? Taqarrub) Khan and Danishmand Khan.

1. The reference is to the battle of June 18, 1707, at Jajau, between Agrah and Dholpur, fought by the armies of Shah 'Alarm and A'zam Shah. Shah 'Alam was the victor. There is a short description of it on fols. 323 and 324 of Part V.

made himself master of the empire. My prince, Shah 'Alam, has not adopted these methods, but overcame with humanity and courage.

[243*b*] There was a priest at Manila, a Castilian by birth, called Dom Joao Fratre de Gevara Capello.[1] As I have heard from many persons, he found himself compromised in a crime of murder, and a complaint was laid by the relations of the deceased before the tribunal of the Lord Archbishop of Manila, who was in some slight degree friendly to the accused priest. As sentence the court gave the priest his letters dimissory, and told him to quit Manila. Quitting that place, he landed at Tranquebar, a fortress of the Danes, and there for some three years he laboured as an active missionary, preaching and granting indulgences. During this period he captured the friendship and affection of the Danes by gifts and presents. By means of this intimacy he suggested to the Danes certain faults, real or imagined, of the vicar then in charge of the church at Tranquebar. In this way the Danes ceased to be on good terms with this vicar.

When this was put in train, the said Father Dom Joao Fratre left Tranquebar and came to San Thome to interview the Lord Bishop, nor did he fail to inform him of the complaints against the above vicar, and the desire of the Danes to turn him out of the church. After he had given the Lord Bishop this information, he requested the favour of being conceded leave to remain in San Thome, stating his desire to be enrolled in that diocese. He alleged that he was unable to travel owing to an attack of *beri-beri*,[2] which was not the case. On finding the bishop unwilling to give permission, he made friends with some favourites of his lordship, and in the end was enrolled in the diocese.

During this time there also arrived complaints to the bishop from the Danes against the vicar; they asked for the appointment of someone else, even if the bishop declined to reject the priest then in charge. This application had been planned by the said Father Dom Joao, the intrigue being firmly backed up by means of the bishop's favourites above referred to. He was collated to the said church of Tranquebar, and, taking possession, entered on

1. This story is repeated in Part V., fols. 335-338. There the name is given the Italian form of Giovanni di Guevara.
2. A kind of paralysis, prevalent chiefly in Ceylon (Yule, 87).

the execution of his office of vicar. When, as I say, he had become vicar, he made use of a Malabar native (the Lord pardon him!) for buying and selling.

At this time a Malabar [a Tamil] of this province of Karnatik, a Christian belonging to the mission of the fathers of the Society [of Jesus], had celebrated the betrothal of his daughter to a young man of his own race; and having concluded the ceremony, he started on a voyage to Manila. At the same time the man's wife and all his family moved to Tranquebar, and made it their abode, and remained some years during the absence of their husband and father. During these six years there grew up a most mystical friendship between the wife and the above-named native, who was in the service of the said Father Dom Joao. Such an intimacy was publicly accounted to be adulterous, both of them being young.

Having regard to this evil repute, there being no other way out of it, the woman arranged a marriage between her daughter and the said friend of hers, by this method neutralizing the current report. On receiving word of this, the other relations of the betrothed placed a protest in the hands of the said vicar. He declined to accept it, and performed the marriage ceremony during Holy Week, taking the girl to the church for the purpse at night time, although barely convalescent from small-pox. When they found this out the relations of the girl, as the only course they could pursue, had recourse to the father of the Society at the mission for advice touching this marriage—what might be the consequences, and what pleas they could submit to the Lord Bishop. But the Jesuit was not pleased to point out anything of the kind they desired; and thus the young girl remained the wife of the vicar's broker.

Some months after this event the bride's father came from Manila and learnt what had been done. He concealed his feelings for some days, then went to see his daughter and his son-in-law at their house. He took possession of the girl, and sent the bridegroom about his business, telling him there was no marriage between them, and that he meant to marry her there in Hindu fashion to some one to whom she had been betrothed. This occurrence was the cause that the man became a pervert with some forty other persons. When the bridegroom found this to be so, he, too, presented a petition to the Lord Bishop, either that the relations be compelled to hand over to him his wife, or that he be given permission to marry someone else. But the Bishop would give no decision whatever. So the bride was married to some one else, and the first husband was deprived of a wife.

[244*a*] In this same province of Karnatik, in the Christian community of Madura, under the fathers of the Society (the Jesuits), there was a married Malabar [Tamil] native. This man had four sons. He was in distress, and unable, where he lived, to find any means of supporting his family. Leaving them in charge of a neighbour, he made for Negapatam to see if he could find any employment. Having found something to do there, after a month he asked leave of absence from the person he was serving, and returned to his home at Madura to fetch his wife and children.

There he learnt the news that the very neighbour to whom he had confided his family had abducted them, telling the wife her husband had sent for her. Then he carried her off with her sons to Tranquebar, where he sold them all treacherously to the worthy vicar for thirty *pagodas*. The persons sold were not aware of it. In the end the husband heard of the sale of his wife and sons; he came to Tranquebar, and made efforts to recover them. The said vicar resisted, and by aid of the governor had the man seized, so that he could make no further attempts beyond [2446] effecting his own release.

When delivered from prison, he made complaint to the Lord Bishop, but a hearing was refused out of regard for the said vicar. Finally he prayed that he might at least have permission to re-marry, since the said father had already bought his wife and sons. The latter ware to be sent to Manila to be sold. Even this privilege was not accorded until he should pay sixty *pagodas*, when he might take back his wife and sons.

Since the Malabari was a poor man, the whole of his caste assembled and undertook to pay the said sixty *pagodas* in one month. Even this did not avail. But the Governor of Madras, being a heretic, decided that such slaves should not be embarked in the ship leaving for Manila. Thereupon the worthy vicar took them away, and sent them for sale elsewhere into the hands of the infidels. The husband in desperation, made off, it was never known where; and probably he returned to Hinduism, since he was unable to secure justice among Christians.

[245*a*][1]After Da,ud Khan had taken the fortress of Pilconda (Penukonda), as already stated (V. 168 and 185), he came to San Thome in the month of November (1706).[2] Before entering the town he rested for one day and one night in my house, situated at the foot of Monte Grande (the Great Mount), of which I have already spoken (IV. 106).[3] I was unable to go out myself to meet him by reason of the heavy rain then falling.

The following day he came on to San Thome, and went straight to see the Lord Bishop, prostrating himself at his feet, as is their custom in the case of religious mendicants. The Bishop received him in the church with music and instruments. On his leaving he presented three hundred and fifty rupees to the household of the said Most Illustrious, and then retired to his tents.

As I was anxious to pay him a visit, the governor of Madras, Thomas Pitt, asked me to go in company of the envoys he must that day send. [I acceded to the governor's wishes.] The envoys were the following: Mester Rabart (Raworth) and Mester Fedorik (Frederick), both of the Council; the third Mester Devenport (Davenport), secretary, the fourth Mester Canosbin (Coningsby), both well-born, well-instructed young men of good carriage. Joined with them was the doctor of the Honourable Company, called Doctor Botler (Bulkley).[4]

---

1. This section is repeated in Part V., fol. 196, and any additions found there are inserted in square brackets. For the position of Penukonda, see note 115, Vol. IV., Part V., fol. 166.
2. Part V., fol. 185, has August 11, 1706, as the date of the surrender of Penukonda, and this fixes the year.
3. As to this house of Manucci's near St. Thomas's Mount, see remarks in the Introduction. The India Office Records say that on November 1, 1706, the Nawab was at 'Pullamullie,' where the Company's 'Braminy and Mulla' were sent to 'compliment him.' On November 2 it is noted that the Nawab meant to stay at a 'garden house' south of Fort St. George, and desires to dine with the Governor. Messrs, Raworth, Frederick, and Davenport were sent to dissuade him, but a present was agreed to.
4. As to this visit on November 3, 1706, see also Wheeler, 'Madras,' ii. 45-48. He does not give the names of the deputation. I identify them as Robert Raworth, John Frederick, and Henry Davenport

The four above-mentioned gentlemen were mounted on handsome Arabian and Persian horses, while the doctor and I were in palanquins. During the march there went in front one hundred halberdiers, men of the country; behind them were carried two flags, and after these marched sixty-two European soldiers, commanded by a sergeant.[1] We went on and found Da,ud Khan in a large tent erected on the sea-shore and fitted with carpets. He was seated on a small bedstead and clothed in simple raiment. On our entering the tent he rose and embraced us all, then made us sit near him. He displayed much urbanity, and was most courteous. After exchanging compliments, we passed an hour and a half in conversation with him. He professed himself a warm friend of the governor, praising his good administration.

Upon giving us our leave he presented us each with an emerald ring worth two hundred rupees,[2] and placed in the hands of Mester Rabart (Raworth) a jewel to be presented to the governor; it was worth five hundred rupees [2456]. He remarked that he was sending it in sign of remembrance, and he would be glad to meet him and drink a glass or two to his health in his company.

The next day the governor sent him a messenger, a person of standing, with many compliments, to say that he would expect him during his march. Da,ud Khan started, but halfway reflected that the English would never permit his entry with a number of retainers, and that some dispute might arise between the soldiers on both sides.[3] Thus, stipulating with me to get his salute of guns from the city, he halted. He proposed going to a garden belonging to an English resident of that city, and sent word to

---

'canosbin' must be a Mr. Coningsby, whose name appears in the entry of November 3, 1706, in the India Office Records. For 'Botler' we have, in Part V., fol. 196, the variant 'Bocler' which, when pronounced with the last letter silent, gives us 'Boclé'—that is, Bulklcy. We hear of Edward Bulkley as far back as 1693 (Wheeler, i. 277), and he died in August, 1714, at Madras (see Penny, 'Church in Madras,' 144, and Mrs. Penny, 'Fort St. George,' 191).

1. The Portuguese has *twelve* instead of *sixty-two* Europeans.
2. Wheeler (ii. 46) has 30 to 40 *pagodas*—*i.e.*, Rs. 105 to 140— at Rs. 3 a. 8 per *pagoda*.
3. On November 4, 1706, Da,ud Khan had promised to come with twenty men, but wanted entry for 200. Pitt objected. Then Da,ud Khan suggested dining at the garden (Wheeler, ii. 46, 47).

the governor that from certain reasons he had changed his mind as to his visit. At once there started to greet him the same Englishmen as specified above, and with them a young man, a private merchant, named Mester Lester (Lister),[1] son-in-law of Daniel Chardin, also a famous merchant, and much esteemed by him (Da,ud Khan). I, too, was of the company.

The banquet which had been prepared was carried to the garden along with several cases of good wine. When the meal was finished they made him a present of eight pieces of broadcloth of various colours, different pieces of silver plate, such as candlesticks, *pan*-boxes, basins, inkstands, boxes, scent sprinklers, *et cetera*, two large mirrors in gilt frames, several chests of liqueurs, Persian wine and rose-water, a large quantity of dried fruit, almonds, walnuts, filberts, pistachios, apricots, *et cetera*, the whole amounting in cost to seven thousand rupees.[2] The Nawab, pleased and satisfied, resumed his journey, and passed six days in San Thome. I felt it my duty to pay him a visit every day in return for the obligations I was under, and also because he asked me.

As Da,ud Khan was suffering from sciatic pains, he sent a man to beg the governor of this place (Madras) to do him the favour of lending him the services of his medical man to treat him. In reply the governor sent his doctor with all the articles requisite.

[246*a*] At this time [when Da,ud Khan was laid up] the Lord Bishop went to pay him a visit, and gave him a present of some torches and candles of white wax. He explained that he was a poor 'darvesh,' and had no wealth with which to find presents. He was received most courteously. On the next day Da,ud Khan went to see him, and said good-bye. He was received in the way I have already described (IV. 245*a*), and

1. In March, 1704, Joseph Lister married D. Chardin's daughter Jane, and died on March 14, 1707. In June 1709, the widow took as second husband Charles Boone (Mrs. Penny, 'Fort St. George,' 118, note, 190, 196). D. Chardin died September 7, 1709 (*ibid.*, 191). Boone, a free merchant, acted as Manucci's attorney in 1712.
2. The English records contain no list of the articles. The total expenditure, according to the account presented to the Council on November 21, 1706, was *pagodas* 1,174.31.4 (or about Rs. 4,109). The articles given (valued at *pagodas* 956.23) are not detailed.

once more he gave the Bishop three hundred and fifty rupees. He drank a considerable quantity of wine, and the principal Portuguese inhabitants, to the number of four, were present.

One day before his departure I went to take my leave. We then had a long conversation, and he expressed his approval of the liqueurs and cordials that on several occasions I had forwarded. I now presented some more. He gave me a present of a costly set of robes, and of three hundred and fifty rupees. He added that it was only a small sum, and must be made over to the little children in my house; and he would not ask me to accompany him, so as to spare me the fatigue of the march, I being a man already getting on in years. He begged me to continue my friendship as before, and he would never forget me.

During the conversation a dispatch-rider arrived from the court with a number of letters. Among them was one from Zu,lfiqar Khan, of whom I have already spoken (III. 13, IV. 2, 15). By it he entrusted him with some business, and also in it directed him to make over to me seven hundred rupees as a present. Da,ud Khan executed this second commission on the spot. That noble (Zu,lfiqar Khan) had been condescending enough to write to me several times to ask for some lotions and medicines, by means of which his wife, who suffered from her eyes, had been cured.

Da,ud Khan started, and took with him the doctor. Before they left he gave him one hundred and fifty gold *pagodas*, which comes to 520 rupees in silver,[1] and a valuable set of robes. After he had reached his camp he detained the doctor for a month, allowing him thirteen rupees a day, and food sufficient for twenty persons. He had now recovered from his complaint sufficiently to be able to walk and mount his horse without any detriment.

At this time it happened that in the city of Madras an English lady [246*b*] of position and wealth fell mortally ill. To obtain help for this lady the governor wrote a letter to Da,ud Khan that the doctor was urgently required. Da,ud Khan sent him back [with a present of a thousand rupees and more robes], and thanked the governor. One day before the arrival of the

1. This makes the gold *pagoda* worth a fraction under 3½ rupees. In 1818 it was reckoned at 3½1 rupees exactly (Yule, 653).

doctor the said lady had died. Her name was Madam Pitt, the widow of John Pitt, the Consul of the New English Company, who died in the port of Machlipatam three years ago.[1]

[Endorsement] Account of the visit of Da,ud Khan in the year 1706.

1. The death of John Pitt occurred at Dharmpet, near Masulipatam, a little before May 14, 1703 (see 'Fort St. George Consultations,' xxxii. 84, 85; Hunter, 'History,' ii. 376). There is no entry forthcoming of the exact date of Mrs. Pitt's death; but between September 22, 1705, and June 7, 1706, the Madras Records have many entries about Mrs. Sarah Pitt, and her claim for money lent by her late husband to the New Company. She must be the Sarah Wavell who married J. Pitt before 1693 (see Mrs. Penny, 'Fort St. George,' p. 151). Her will is in the British Museum, Egerton MSS., 1,971; and MSS 22,850, No. 23, proves she was dead before February, 1707 (Yule's 'Diary of W. Hedges,' iii. 90, 91, 107).

PART FIVE
OF THE
STORIA DO MOGOR

By
NICOLO MANUCCI, VENETIAN

TRANSLATED FROM THE PORTUGUESE INTO ITALIAN BY
COMMENDATORE DIOGO CARDEIRA, PORTUGUESE[1]

1. From the Italian of Codex No. XLV. (Zanetti), in the Biblioteca Nazionale di San Marco at Venice. The Portuguese and French original from which Part V. was translated into Italian has come to my notice at the last moment; it does not appear in the Zanetti catalogue, but its present classification is No. 135, Class VI. I have compared a copy of it carefully with my translation from Codex XLV., and I find only slight verbal changes are required, which I have accordingly made.

[LETTER PREFIXED TO THE TRANSLATION]

'MY MOST ILLUSTRIOUS SIR, MOST RESPECTED SIGNOR,

'Your Excellency's most worthy sons, so promptly sent by you, have appeared here to receive the commission of the Most Excellent and Most Venerable Lords. To them has been entrusted the book referred to, entitled "The Fifth Part of the History of the Mogul," by Nicolo Manuzzi. It is bound, and runs from folio two to folio ninety, written partly in Portuguese and partly in French; with some detached leaves, to the number of eleven, in one or the other language. Upon your Excellency's exertions we rely for the labour of this translation, in order to submit this Fifth Part to their Excellencies. This will raise higher than before your merits and those of your sons, who with ardent emulation encounter willingly all difficulties and overcome them. Repeating my own exalted respect, I subscribe myself,

'Of your Excellency,
'The most devoted, most obliged servant,
'AGOSTINO GADALDINI.'[1]

'VENICE,
'*February 20*, 1712.'

1. I am indebted to Dr. Cóggiola for the information that A. Gadaldini was secretary to the Venetian Senate (Emanuele Cicogna, 'Iscrizioni Venesiane,' 1830, vol. iii., p. 258). The dates of his birth and death are not known. Like the rest of his family, originally from Modena, he was a physician.

[1] FIFTH VOLUME COMPOSED BY THE AUTHOR, SIGNOR MANUCCI, OF THE VENETIAN NATION,

IN THIS

FORTRESS OF ST. GEORGE OF MADRASTA-PATTAM

FIFTH PART OF THE NARRATION OF MOGUL HISTORY,

IN THIS PRESENT YEAR, 1705, IN THE MONTH OF JANUARY,

BY NICOLO MANUCCI, VENETIAN

Since God has preserved my life, I wish to finish the Fifth Part, already promised, of the reign of the existing king, Aurangzeb.

The kind reader will have seen at the end of my Fourth Part (IV. 234) that this king was preparing for a new campaign after his fasting month, which fell in the said year in January,[1] as above written. Cognizant that neither his craft nor his artifies would suffice to overcome the Prince Aguanguira (Wakinkerah),[2] he suddenly ordered his army to march, and attacked one of his fortresses which was situated near a great forest. Although at the first assault seven thousand soldiers were killed along with twelve valiant and famous commanders, while many other officers were wounded, Aurangzeb was not in the least discouraged. Continuing to invest the place more and more stringently, he forced it, after a siege of five months, to surrender. The loss of this fortress [2] induced the Prince of

1. The fast of Ramazan, 1116 H., lasted from December 29, 1704, to January 27, 1705, N.S.
2. As already noted, Wakinkerah is the name of a fort, not of a prince.

Wakinkerah to join himself to Shiva Ji,[1] and carry on the usual plundering. Up to this moment things are in this condition.

Until the time when the campaigns of Aurangzeb furnish me with matter for continuing the story, I will recount some events in the hope of amusing the inquiring reader.

The king has in his army a new commander called Chiniquiliscam (Chin Qilich Khan),[2] a Chacata (Chaghatae) Tartar by race, and lord over seven thousand horse. This man is much esteemed, and a favourite of Aurangzeb by reason of being of his own race. But not for that reason alone has he given him the command of so many troops and elevated him to so conspicuous a station. The object is the more easily to make use of him on an emergency; principally in the hope that after his death this noble may adopt the side of his son, Prince Kam Baksh, who is powerless. This most prudent king saw very plainly that his other sons, Shah 'Alam and A'zam Tara, with their sons, were powerful through their riches and governments, and he foresaw what grave disturbances would arise the moment he was dead. Therefore, not to leave this son, as much esteemed as loved, entirely forsaken, he raised this man, Chin Qilich Khan, to the dignity of a great commander. In addition he promised him in marriage [3] a daughter of the same prince, Kam Bakhsh, although this is opposed to the customs of the royal house, which from the time of King Akbar no longer allows such a practice. In this way Aurangzeb hoped to compel that commander to help Kam Bakhsh in case of necessity.

This grandee was treated by me for the stone during his infancy. He is the son of the great Quiliscam (Qilich Khan),[3]

1. Here begins a long note by Senhor Cardeira on Shiva Ji. There are many such notes on other subjects, but I shall omit them, unless by any chance they contain facts not otherwise known to us.
2. This is Nizam-ul-mulk, Asaf Jah, disguised under an early title. His original name was Qamar-ud-din; he was born on August 11, 1671, and this title of Chin Qilich Khan (previously held by his grandfather) was given him about 1690-91. His family belonged to Bukhara, but he was not a Chaghatae.
3. Asaf Jah was the son of Ghazi-ud-din Khan, Firuz Jang, and the *grandson* of the Qilich Khan who was shot outside Gulkandah on January 30, 1687.

who died before Gulkandah, struck by a cannon-ball. In the war above referred to Chin Qilich Khan was wounded in the left arm by a musket-shot, and his horse was killed.

I have already recounted in my Fourth Part (IV. 186) how the Dutch had blockaded the port of Surat. Since then some vessels of theirs have taken in the latitude of Malacca three barques, laden with valuable merchandise from China, which were the property of Surat traders. In spite of this loss the Mogul king gave no sign of a grievance, but rather concealed the insult. But the Dutch knew the king's intentions, which were to refuse them the satisfaction that they claimed. Therefore they decided that the general of their fleet should write [4] a letter to the governor of Surat, of which the terms were as follows:[1]

1. A somewhat similar letter of complaint was written on July 14, 1704, by Pieter de Vos, Director, to Afzal Khan, *Diwan* of Prince A'zam Tara at Ahmadabad, but I have no evidence as to any letter written in 1705. Pieter de Vos and all the Dutch Company's servants left with the fleet on April 6, 1705. The next entry about Surat in the resolutions of the Governor-General and Council at Batavia is dated July 14, 1705. They decided to send six chief merchants and six under merchants to renew negotiations. On July 24, 1705. further action was resolved on in regard to the quarrel with the Mahomedan Government, and on July 16, 1706, they ordered six ships to Surat as a check on the Mogul extortions, and to impede their trade. On July 23, 1706, they nominated Grotenhuis as Director there, and head of the expedition, with orders to settle the dispute. On March 27, 1707, they noted his success, and on July 25, 1707, they sanctioned his proposals. The Surat Mahomedans were to pay a compensation of 8,11,000 rupees, and the captured craft were then to be restored to them.

The capture of the Surat ship is reported in a secret letter of January 16, 1705, from Carel Bolner, Governor of Malacca. On the 9th the outlook from the hill saw a ship at anchor to the north, and at once the *Blaauwenbergh* set sail, and dropped anchor beside it. The sloop *Middleburgh* was sent out, and brought back the information that it was the *Faxz Rasan* from China, owned by 'Abdul-ghaffur, merchant, of Surat. On Sunday, the 11th, the *Blaauwenbergh* came into port with her prize. Following the Council's instruction to cruisers in the neighbourhood of the Sincapoura (Singapore) Straits, the captured ship was sent on to Batavia. Her cargo was not touched at Malacca. With her went two other ships recently captured—the *Faiz-ilahi* and the *Bassora Marchand*. The convoy consisted of the *Nederland*, the *Itershem*, and the *Blaauwenbergh*.

'LORD GOVERNOR,

'Several months ago we remained off this port incurring, great expenditure, solely to the end that we might get justice for the robberies and injuries done to us. Once more we give you notice that we mean to be paid that large sum of money which we have detailed in various statements. As, moreover, we demand the return to us of the bond binding us for the security of the [Mogul] ships; we shall take by force all vessels entering into and issuing from the said port, whether Mahomedan or Hindu. Furthermore, we demand, if you want to be left to live in peace, that you grant us permission to establish a factory near the sea, at the mouth of the river of Surat. We await an immediate reply, and if you are not prompt in rendering the desired satisfaction, we shall write to our prince and do as he orders us.'

This letter was sent on by the governor to the court, but up to this time they have seen no reply, the king being busy with the above campaign. Meanwhile the Dutch [5] are compelled, by the approach of the monsoon, to withdraw. When that season is over we shall see what will happen, nor shall I omit to give an account of it to the inquiring reader.[1]

The Portuguese also took a Mahomedan ship leaving a port in Bengal on a voyage to Mecca laden with the finest goods to the value of five *lakhs* of rupees. Their reason for the capture was the absence of a Portuguese passport, and therefore they only liberated some females who were going to Mecca on pilgrimage. When the news reached Aurangzeb he issued orders to the general Cotopcam (Qutb Khan) to make raids in the neighbourhood of Daman and Bassain. He carried out the orders of Aurangzeb so exactly that after invading the territories of Daman and Bassain, he was not content with sacking them, but put them entirely to fire and sword. In this way Aurangzeb took vengeance for the injuries that he asserted he had received from the Portuguese when they attacked the Arab ships in the port of Surat.

The Viceroy of Goa, when he saw all this destruction, wrote

1. The subject is resumed on fols. 167 and 204, where it is said that the blockade was raised in March, 1706, after a payment to the Dutch.

to the Father Rector of Agrah[1] that in the guise of an envoy he should repair to the court and make efforts to negotiate a peace. The father willingly undertook the task; but to this hour he has been unable to conclude the business, although actually present in the royal [6] camp, suffering much hardship, both from the marchings and the dearth of food.

Already the benevolent reader will have observed in my Third Part (IV. 77 to 81) what I had done to help the Christians of Tanjor during their persecutions. However, the Jesuits were not content with my action, nor would they acquiesce in my advice, but preferred that their own extreme opinions should be accepted. They enlisted the aid of the Lord Bishop of Mailapur, Dom Gaspar Affonço. This prelate, during the visit he paid to Da,ud Khan (IV. 246*a*), begged him to write a letter to the Prince of Tanjor in favour of the Jesuit Fathers. They wanted the Nawab to force the said prince to rebuild the churches and grant complete liberty in his territory to the said fathers for the exercise of their office; also that there should be no hindrance in passing along in palanquins, and other minute.

Da,ud Khan, a man of high courtesy, wrote the letter, well foreseeing that by this conduct he stood to lose nothing. The prince sent him a valuable present, and replied to his letter by saying that he was a tributary and vassal of the Mogul emperor. As his friend and protector he (Da,ud Khan) ought not to allow foreigners with new customs and rites to impose themselves on his people and throw down [7] his own religion. Should he be forced to allow the building of churches and the exercise of that new religion, then he, too, must be permitted to thoroughly restore

1. I learn from Father Van Meurs, S. J., through Father A. Brou, S. J., and Mr. Philipps, that in 1704-1705 the Rector of Agrah was Joao d'Abreu. He concluded his *triennium* in 1706, and was succeeded by Father Joseph de Payva, who was replaced in September, 1706, by Father Manoel Monteyro. In January, 1708, Father d'Abreu reappears as Rector. He was born at Odwellas in Portugal in 1669, entered the Society at Goa in 1684, and made his profession in 1702. He was two years Professor of Grammar, twice Rector of the Bassain seminary, curé of the north parish. Rector at Agrah (as above), *operarius* at the same place. curé at Salsette, and Rector at Chaul in 1719. On fol. 120, Part V., we are told of the failure of his negotiations, and his ejectment from the Mogul camp.

his ancient Hindu pagodas at Conjevaram and at other places in the Karnatik. In consequence, leave must be conceded to the Brahmans to live there and exercise their rites in accordance with ancient custom. Upon receipt of this reply, Da,ud Khan willingly received the present and wrote again to him at once that he must continue to pay his tribute to the Mogul; as for the rest, it seemed to him that his arguments were most judicious, and, as far as he was concerned, he would ever be found ready to favour the prince's interests.

The aforesaid fathers made the same proposition also to me, attempting to persuade me to put such pressure on Da,ud Khan as might induce him to declare war upon the prince in question, and to that intent they offered to give him at once 10,000 *patacas*;[1] but I declined to interfere on any terms in such a business, as will have been already seen (IV. 81).

The above expression of opinion by Da,ud Khan induced the Prince of Tanjor to impose on each Christian a heavy payment in money. Where they were unable to bear such heavy taxation, he forced them [8] under a severe penalty to frequent his pagodas, and through fear they obeyed. The same thing has already begun to be practised by the neighbouring princes, and this is the way in which the Christians of that territory are being treated. In this lamentable result has ended the indiscreet zeal of those who wished to force these powerful princes to bend to their will. Those zealots considered it beyond discussion and not open to doubt that they must obtain a fortunate issue for whatever they might dream of doing. At the present time there are no Jesuits in that mission, even the catechists have left, and thus the Christian congregation is already destroyed. Of this the following case will serve as an example.

There dwelt in Bengal a French merchant named Monsieur Bomom, who was married to a Portuguese lady called Senhora

1. Coins ordinarily worth the same as a *giustina*; they are of this shape ▭ (Cardeira's note). Manucci valued the *pataca* at two rupees. I learn from Dr. Cóggiola that the *giustina* was a coin struck in 1571, during the dogeship of Alvise Mocenigo, after a victory over the Turks near the Curzolari Isles. The day was the Festival of St. Justina, a renowned saint of Padua, and her portrait appeared on the coin. There were two *giustina* coins—one of two *lire*, and the other of one Venetian *lira* (see Schweitzer, 'Serie delle monete ...... di Venezia,' Trieste, 1852).

Apollonia. I knew her well; she was of the best behaviour, and of good family. This Monsieur Bomom built a sumptuous mansion close to the factory of the French Royal Company, and died a few years afterwards, leaving as sole heir to his wealth his consort above named.

The Jesuits were eager to usurp that mansion, it being in the best situation in the whole place. This purpose they sought to carry out by all the force such men can invent. [9] The artifices they attempted were all in vain, the lady objecting to be deprived of her dwelling. They did not desist, however, from trying other roads for arriving at their wishes, and out of the many they might have chosen they adopted the most perfidious.

Rabid with rage, the Jesuits resorted one day to her house, and spoke to her as follows: 'Senhora Apollonia, now that we see you do not mean to give us what we have asked, you will be no longer, as you believe you are, the heir of your husband; for, in addition to everything remaining in our hands, we mean to denounce you as an adulteress.'

The poor woman, on hearing such an unexpected assertion and manifest calumny, considered it better to lose her property than the inestimable prize of her good fame. Therefore she made them a donation of the house, and they retired highly pleased. After a short time she married a French friend of mine called Monsieur Boutuvil, and came to live in Pondicherry. All the (European) inhabitants of Bengal marvelled at this extraordinary story, and for a long time could talk of nothing else.

At this time there lived in Bengal a French surgeon called Monsieur Cattem. This man was in the service of the Royal Company, and, fearing that after his death the Jesuits might calumniate his wife, he put into his will this clause: that if by chance his wife were an adulteress, she should, nevertheless, remain his heir. But the Jesuits aforesaid do not mind in the least creating these scandals, and go on with such-like knaveries, of which I will give some examples.

There was also in Bengal a young Frenchman called Monsieur Pellé,[1] second in the Royal Company, and married to Senhora Catterina, of Portuguese race. She lived on good terms

1. Gabriel Pellé was one of those who represented the absent godparents at the baptism of A. B. Deslandes' eldest son at Hugli on May 24, 1689. Tliis may be the person intended. There was a Monsieur Pelé, second in Council at Chandarnagar, when Deslandes left it in 1701.

with her husband. Belonging to the Royal Company there was among the other Fathers one Father Quenin,[1] who interfered in every business, and therefore nowadays he is styled colloquially 'Monsieur Quenin.' This father, I know not why, took such a dislike to Senhora Catterina, that he sought every method of doing her an ill turn.

One day, on meeting her husband, the Jesuit was unable to restrain his anger, and said to him that he had better set to work to put his house in order. Monsieur Pellé, being a cautious man, paid no heed to this advice, never suspecting it to be directed against his wife. But the choler of Father Quenin was not appeased by this, but increased to such an extent that a few days after the first speech he said to the husband plainly that his

1. Writing from Pondicherry on September 30, 1703, Father G. Tachard names Pére Quenin as one of three Jesuits then in Bengal ('Lettres Edifiantes et Curieuses,' edition by M. L. Aimé Martin in 'Panthéon Littéraire,' 1840, vol. ii., p. 329). I suppose he was given the worldly style of 'Monsieur' instead of 'Pére' in derision, because he did not confine himself to spiritual matters. He is mentioned again on fols. 96 and 181. Thanks to Father Van Meurs, S.J., I am able to trace this missionary's career. The true name is Quencin, as in his autograph signature to his formula of profession. He was born at Angoulême on March 13, 1661; entered the novitiate in 1676, finished it in 1678, and joined the province of Aquitaine. He was at Pau, Agen, Bordaux, and again at Agen. We find him at Paris in 1693-96 'preparing to be a missionary.' He made his profession on March 25, 1695, at Blavet (Church of St. Pierre), a little town now in ruins, and replaced by Port Louis (Morbihan), close to Lorient. His voyage to India was made under the celebrated Guy Tachard, who took out also Gervais Papin, Pierre Mauduit, Maximilien Michel, Philippe d'Avril, Charles Beauvoiliers, and two brothers. In 1697-98 we find Fathers Beauvoiliers and d'Avril at Surat; the others had reached Pondicherry. In 1698-99 Fathers Quencin and Mauduit proceed with Father Tachard to Siam. In 1699-1700 Father Quencin is in Bengal with Father Papin; the former becomes Superior of Chandarnagar, and dies there on May 28, 1706. In 1705 there was a dispute about erecting Chandarnagar into a parish. The Augustinian Fathers of the Bandel parish, to which it belonged, protested that the Bishop of San Thome was by his Pastoral removing Portuguese subjects from Portuguese to French domination. The Bishop issued a second Pastoral, dated July 3, 1705, confining Father Quenin's cure to Chandarnagar, with the exclusion of Notre Dame, in building which the Jesuits had had no share, and limiting his spiritual charge to the officers of the French Company and their servants (Bibl. Nat., MS, Français, No. 6,231, fol. 36, 'Mémoire sur la Compagnie des Indes Orientales').

wife had committed adultery, and that he should therefore take steps against such misconduct. To these words Pellé replied [11] that his Reverence was ill-informed, he knew his wife to be an honourable woman, and all men saw with what modesty she behaved.

Some days having passed, the Jesuit met Pellé again in society, a number of people being present, and before them all the priest said: 'It seems to me I have sufficiently warned you, sir, of the adultery your wife commits, and yet you do not mind me; last night a man, (he gave the name, but it was not known to the bystanders) 'scaled the wall of your house, and you pretend to see nothing.'

To all these words the only answer of the patient Pellé was: 'Your Reverence is wrongly informed.' Thereupon the father added that no one better than himself could know, since he was her confessor, and that it was his business to send her to prison, assigning various arguments for this caprice of his. Although these words ought to have made no impression at all upon the mind of the husband, they had their effect—so much so that he allowed himself to be persuaded to shut up his wife in a room, leaving only one small window through which her food was passed, and that only sparingly.

Four days in the week Father Quenin visited the poor prisoner, the keys of the room being in his hands. The only consolation he afforded her was to abuse her, to threaten her with death, to say she ought to be buried [12] in that very room, and similar misplaced menaces. The lady, although in the flower of youth, and only eighteen years of age, supported all in patience, and, above all, the imprisonment, which lasted for nine months.

Nor would she have so easily obtained her liberation therefrom had not at that time occurred the death of her husband, The director, Monsieur Deslandres[1] interceded for and obtained her release. Although she gained her liberty, she was not allowed to inherit from her husband; she could not even recover her own dowry out of the hands of the Jesuits. The poor young woman, deprived of all means of livelihood, was forced to beg her food from door to door. Finally, forced by such distress,

1. André Boureau Deslandes, Director at Chandernagar from 1689 to 1701. He was son-in-law of François Martin (see note appended to the Introduction). There is some mistake, for Pelé was not dead when Deslandes left Hugli.

she married an Englishman, a Protestant, in order to live with more decorum. They took up their abode in Madras.

While I was living in Goa there happened a similar case. There was a pilot of Portuguese nationality called Salvador Bexiga. Finding himself already advanced in years, and in possession of a considerable amount, he gave up his calling and retired to the house of a married friend, Manoel Pereira, living at the Arch of the Conception. As the Jesuits knew that the man was rather well off, they went to visit him very frequently, and kept up [13] a friendship with him.

Then came the death of Manoel Pereira, his friend, when the poor old man was obliged to take shelter in another household, where he was not so well looked after as in his late friend's house. Hearing his complaints, the Jesuits gave him an invitation, and offered him every convenience in their college. Many times they repeated that he should have full liberty if he chose to live with them. The good old man knew not the astuteness of such fellows, allowed himself to be persuaded, and went to live with them, carrying there his heavy casket.

The Jesuits received him with the most courteous compliments and entrancing ceremony. They assigned to him a fine chamber, with a soft and lordly bed. They gave him to eat and to drink sumptuously. The old man was fully satisfied with his new shelter, retaining the liberty of going and coming at his pleasure.

After eight days had elapsed several Jesuits entered his room and persuaded him to take the habit and become a brother of the Society, by which he would earn many indulgences. The simple old man was caught by their persuasion, and when he had put on the habit, they made for him a sumptuous banquet, with instrumental music and singing.

The next day the old man wanted to go out, as was his custom. Brother Alexo, who was the janitor, barred his exit, telling him it was [14] necessary to have a permit from the Provincial. Hearing these words, the old man exclaimed at the affront, and lamented over this breach of their promises. The fathers, the further to annoy and irritate him, reproved him sharply, while he, being most violently angry, told them they had cheated him. His lamentations were, however, of no avail, since the fathers cried aloud, like men on whom has fallen some great misfortune. Then they began to say one to the other that the man had gone mad; therefore some said they must bleed him, others felt his pulse, and asserted he wanted a mixture to produce vomiting; others, again, suggested repeated purgings. Thus, simply on account of that fine rage he had fallen into, did they dispose of him maliciously as a madman, without his arguments having a chance of being heard. Finally, they laid hold of him violently and shut him up in a prison cell. They announced to the public that he was insane, and thus did he finish his days in misery.

When I was living in the island of Salsette, near to Bassain, a most curious affair came to pass. Near the settlement of Bandora, belonging to the Jesuits, there lay a village at a distance of two leagues from the town. It was commonly called Irlemparlem (? Warli Parela),[1] and the owner's name was George Gonzalves, a Portuguese by race [15].

In this village were several quarries of very fine stone, excellent for paving, road-making, and similar purposes. The Jesuits attempted in various ways to get possession of these, but Gonzalves would never consent to part with them. Finally, they made a novel and most curious attempt.

One night without any warning they brought several houses of straw, made ready beforehand for this purpose, and erected them among the palm-trees round the said village. They were at once occupied by men, women, and children with dogs, cats, cocks, hens, bringing their pots and pans, their goods and chattels. On the following morning George Gonzalves was thrown into wonder and amazement on beholding this novel and unexpected sight.

He began at once to question these people to find out by whose orders they had come to take up their quarters there. They answered that they were the tenants of the Jesuit fathers, and had lived in the place for many years. George Gonzalves perceived that this was a stratagem of the fathers in order to render themselves masters of his property. He collected his men,

1. This name may be intended for Warli and Parela (Parel), two villages at the north end of Bombay Island, but once in Portuguese territory. They lie approximately two and three miles south ot Bandora (see Constable's 'Hand Atlas,' Plate XXXIX., 'Bombay and its Environs'; and J. Gerson da Cunha, 'Antiquities of Bassein,' *Journal of the Royal Asiatic Society*, Bombay Branch, 1874, p. 337). The Jesuits used to have property at Parel, the income of which went to their college at Agrah.

and attempted to expel the intruders. But the Jesuits appeared with their servants, and after some struggling Gonzalves was forced to retreat.

However, he did not leave matters there. For, with the assistance of two companies of soldiers furnished by the general, Manoel Saldanha [16], he turned out the new inhabitants by main force and burnt the new settlement. The Jesuits were annoyed at this action of the general, and drew up against him a paper of complaints, styling him a tyrant for having burnt their new village and causing them damage to the extent of twenty thousand crowns (*cruzados*), that being the valuation thereof. They said he had burnt the church with the holy images and a large crucifix.

This plaint was sent to the court of Lisbon, and when the general arrived there he was cited on account of these misdeeds. He cleared himself, however, very easily, proving the justice of his cause by testimony worthy of implicit faith. This *fidalgo* came back to India as admiral of the Portuguese fleet, when he was denounced by the Jesuits to the Viceroy of Goa, Francesco de Tavora,[1] who was his personal enemy. Their calumnies, however, did not succeed, for the admiral pointed out that no one, with the exception of His Royal Majesty of Portugal himself, could proceed against general officers for any crime they had committed.

[Folios 17 and 18. I omit here a story about an elephant's reluctance to crush to death a Ceylon prince whose voice it recognised. This has already appeared in Part III., folios 150, 151. The only additional particular is that the king's name is given as Orilha, but no such ruler is known, Mr. Ferguson says.]

[18] It did not happen thus in the city of Goa when it was ruled over by Dom Phelipe Masquarenha.[2] There was an elephant which worked on the river bank, and its driven often made it pass through the city, taking it to the shops for fruit and other eatables. All the shopkeepers gave it something, as for example,

1. Francesco de Tavora was Viceroy from 1681 to 1686.
2. No. 49, Dom Filippe Mascarenhas, Viceroy, 1646-51 (Danvers, ii. 488).

Yams,[1] figs (bananas),[2] dried grapes, sugar-cane, mangoes, Jack-fruit,[3] rose-apples,[4] cashews,[5] guavas, *et cetera*.

Among the shopkeepers was one who gave the elephant a coco-nut, and, stretching out its trunk, he handed it to the driver who was astride on him. The man thought he would like to eat the coco-nut, and though he could have split it open with the driving-iron which he had in his hand, he broke it in two upon the elephant's head; one piece he kept for himself, the other he gave [19] to the animal.

It was not likely that the beast would eat it, when it considered itself (so to speak) insulted by its master's breaking the

---

1. *Batatas*, a fruit peculiar to India, and unnamed in these countries (Europe). It grows in the earth; when cooked and roasted, it has the flavour of a chestnut (Cardeira; compare Yule, 884, 'sweet potato').
2. The Indian fig (banana) is a soft plant, about the thickness of a man's thigh, 15 to 20 hand-breadths in height, with leaves more than 4 feet in length. They use the latter as platters and paper. The fruit is only gathered once; for as soon as there are sixty to seventy, or at times 100, bunches, they cut down the plant. The fruit is of two kinds: (1) Those of the length of a man's palm, of the thickness of a grape, and called *Assar* figs. They have a sweet flavour, and are very nourishing; they are eaten roasted, and sprinkled with cinnamon and sugar. The inside pulp is red and yellow; they are gathered green, and are left to grow yellow and ripe in the house. (2) The other kind is called *Figoso orta* (? garden figs); these are sweeter, and eaten uncooked. These last are 'cold,' the others 'hot' (Cardeira; compare Yule, 715, 'plantain').
3. *Jaqua* (Jack-fruit) is the largest fruit in the world, no man being able to carry more than one at a time. It grows at the foot of the trunk, as the branches could not bear the weight. The rind is yellow and green, with pointed spikes like those with which *pallone* (a game of ball) is played. The fruit is obtained from March to September (Cardeira; see Yule, 440). As Dr. Cóggiola points out, Cardeira's comparison refers to the wooden cylinder with which the fist is protected in playing *pallone*; it is studded outside with wooden spikes.
4. The *giamboja* (*jambon, jambu*) is a fruit as large, and of the same taste, as the grape, but smelling like rose-water. They are of several sorts, and ripen from January up to March (Cardeira; Yule, 448, 'jumboo').
5. *Caius*, a fruit shaped like an apple, red and yellow outside. It bears outside a nut, in shape like a crest; it ripens from February to May. Divided into four, the fruit is placed in cold water and macerated, the juice is extracted, and is found useful in chest complaints (Cardeira; Yule, 168, 'cashew').

coco-nut upon its head. He kept it in his mouth, and when they had arrived at the usual resting-place, as soon as his master had dismounted he seized him with his trunk, threw him at his feet, and, bringing down the half coco-nut on his skull, beat out his brains. He then threw the body as far as he could away from himself.

In old days, when the Portuguese had made themselves masters of many parts of Ceylon island, they compelled the inhabitants of the towns to come out to greet any soldier who might have started from the city on his way back to camp. They had to appear as soon as he gave a signal of his arrival in the village by discharging his musket. At once all the villagers came out headed by their chief men, and escorted the soldier with great politeness and respect into the village. They assigned to him the best house to be found in the place, and complied with all his demands in every particular. In addition, they were obliged when night came on to produce the best-looking woman of the [20] place. If she did not suit him, it was the custom to take several to him, so that he might chose the one he fancied most. It often happened that the daughters and wives of the village headmen were selected. But this was not felt any grievance, nor considered any sin, it being the custom of the locality—nay, rather did they hold it an extreme honour. Those inhabitants were obliged, in addition, to provide as many loadcarriers as were required to carry the baggage to the camp. These men were changed at each village.

But returning to the obligation they were under of giving their women, this applied not only to soldiers passing through their village, but also to the friars in the parishes. Nor were these selected at the will of the inhabitants from the most deformed or oldest, but from the handsomest and youngest to be discovered in the village. The duty of the poorer ones was to sweep out the convent and the church every day; that of the richer and better clothed to clean the corridors, the friars' cells, the refectory, and the garden.

I knew a soldier from Ceylon, a great friend of mine, called Joao Rodriguez da Silva.[1] From having served a long time in the island as a soldier, he had taken part in many fights, and told

1. Farther on (Part V., fol. 53) we are told he succeeded Bishop Gaspar Affonço as Portuguese ruler, or 'Capitan Mor,' in San Thome.

XLIII. URDU-BEGL, or woman Superintendent of Harem Camp

Vol. IV *To face page 144*

me of many incidents that had happened in them. This man once started from the city of Colombo on his return to camp. [21] He arrived at a village in the dark about seven o'clock at night, and found his way to a convent, where dwelt a friar named Fra Agustinho da Santa Cruz, a very great miser and little given to charity. The soldier on reaching the door asked the sacristan as a favour to open the church that he might say his prayers. The sacristan sought the permission of the said father, who very grudgingly consented to the opening of the church. The soldier fell on his knees at the foot of the altar and made a great show of piety. Friar Agustinho, irritated at all this delay, and in a hurry to go to rest, fell into a rage and went into the church. He complained that soldiers should be so overbold as to come at the wrong times to offer up their prayers.

Joao Rodriguez da Silva, on perceiving that the friar had reached the church, began to beat his breast and kiss the ground; then, rising, he made a deep bow to the altar. Beholding all these gestures of silent contrition, the friar was much amazed. Meanwhile the soldier advanced towards the priest with much humility, and, saluting him courteously, said: 'As it seems to me, this church must have few worshippers, for I see it is very poor. I shall not fail, however, to present for its adornment a chandelier, candelabra, candles, and some cloths from China.' Hearing such good news, the friar led him politely into his convent, and treated him exceedingly [22] well. Before the repast, in conversing with the friar the soldier gave him to understand that he was the nephew of a woman of some wealth, a wellknown widow living in the city, whose name was Senhora D. Maria de Guimar. Upon hearing such good tidings the monk went on treating him with more and more respect, and regaling him more magnificently. The soldier to encourage the friar indited a letter to the following effect:

'MY RESPECTED AUNT,

'You will do me a favour by making over to the Reverend Father Friar Agustinho da Santa Cruz, who is the bearer of the present, the chandelier that I received from China, with the two pair of candlesticks, four dozen of candles, and four pieces of cloth from China, two boxes of tobacco, and a quire of paper with a dozen pens. The key of my room is already with the serving-girl, Luiza, and therefore I pray her to make over the things I have mentioned. When I have completed the business with which your Honour has entrusted me in connection with the general, [23] I shall not delay my return. Further, I pray her to remember to send some one to demand the sword mountings that are at the goldsmith's, Diogo Fialho's, house, and God keep your Honour.

'Of your Honour
'The humble nephew and obedient son,
'JOAO RODRIGUEZ DA SILVA.'

'*March* 7, 1654.'[1]

When the letter was finished, he made it over to the friar, who, after reading it, was in a state of complete contentment and satisfaction. When supper was over, the friar found for the soldier a soft enough bed, and then politely said good-bye to him, as he proposed to start at four in the morning for the city. He gave orders to his serving-friar that next morning he must furnish the guest with everything that he wanted for breakfast, and comply with all his demands. Before day broke the good friar had started.

Upon getting up in the morning the soldier had a good meal, then sent for the head-man of the village, and gave him [24] orders to produce fifty load-carriers. Next he caused the room to be opened where the friar kept his provisions, and loaded these men with hams, large sausages (*paios*), black-puddings (*choricos*), olives, salted meat, wine, and the rest of the things out of the godown. Leaving behind many words of thanks to the reverend friar, to whom he was so much indebted, he started for camp, where he was received politely by his captain and all his company. When the friar reached the city, he discovered the deception, and ceasing to be merry, he came back in a rather melancholy mood. But he did not arrive in time to take any steps to redress the mistake.

What[2] is known of a certainty is that the money mentioned as collected by force was so taken by the royal orders. For

1. This letter is dated very early if its writer was Governor of San Thome in 1704. Fifty years is a long period for a man to remain in active service. Mr. Ferguson thinks the story may be true, though probably exaggerated.
2. The paragraph begins in this abrupt manner, as if there had been some omission.

Amanetcam (Amanat Khan),[1] governor of Surat, stopped the loading of goods on two French ships, and made a demand for money beyond all reason. The director, Monsu Depilavan (de Pilavoine),[2] persisted in his refusal to pay the money demanded, and in spite of its being the property of his countrymen, he decided to set fire to the whole of the merchandise. Meanwhile he complained to the governor of his trying in this way to break the friendship and peace agreed upon with his nation. The governor, to prove that his own feelings of friendship had not changed, showed him the letter with the orders received from his Majesty (Aurangzeb). [25] These complaints were, nevertheless, of some benefit to the French, for the governor, recognising that the French were resolved rather to die than to pay the money, and that much loss would ensue to the town, allowed their merchandise to be put on board.

This governor is the one who took by force from the hands of all the European nations bonds assuring all [native] ships sailing from that port. This was done by the king's order, as already stated (IV. 34). The very same order had been given to the prince, Sultan 'Azim-ud-din, son of Shah 'Alam, but he had declined to execute it.[3]

1. Muhammad Husain Khwafi, Amanat Khan No. 11., died at Surat between the 4th and the 25th Jamada 11., 1111 H., forty-third year of Aurangzeb (October 28 to November 18, 1699) ('Ma,asir-i-'Alamgiri,' p. 412). The 'Ma,asir-ul-Umara,' i. 287, says he was buried outside the city. near the wall. He was the paternal grand-uncle of Shah Nawaz Khan, author of the 'Ma,asir-ul-Umara.'
2. It could hardly have been Pilavoine, as in 1699 he was on leave in France. He was relieved at Surat by J. B. Martin, who arrived from France on January 4, 1696. Owing to the French Admiral's quitting Surat in a hurry in April, 1696, Pilavoine was left behind. He then made the journey by land to Goa, where he embarked in the *Pontchartrain* on November 26, 1696, and reached France on July 17, 1697. He returned to Surat in the St. *Louis* near the end of 1700. Meanwhile J. B. Martin had died at his post in June, 1698, and the Sicur Regnard took over temporary charge. The loading of French vessels had been stopped by the *faujdar*, and leave to resume work was obtained at the Court with some difficulty (Dr. Jules Sottas, 'Histoire,' 386, 393, 409, 413). In the Bibliothéque Nationale (MS. Français No. 8,971) there are some 'Notes Critiques sur l'Histoire des Indes Anciennes et Modernes de Mr. l'Abbé Guyon,' by Pilavoine, 'Ancien Conseiller k Pondicherry.' These must be subsequent to 1708.
3. The reference is to Bengal. 'Azim-ud-din was appointed to that province in Ramazan, 1108 H. (March, 1697). A Dutch translation

Amanat Khan sent the said bonds to the court, and the king was as pleased with him as he was discontented with 'Azim-ud-din, to whom he wrote a letter full of censures. He pointed out to him the services done to the crown by Amanat Khan, and the little capacity he ('Azim-ud-din) appeared to possess, although a prince and powerful, in not having done the same with the European nations in his government of Bengal.

The prince replied that it gave him quite sufficient occupation to deal with the disturbances raised by the Hindu princes in the province. If he had attempted to interfere with the Europeans also [26], as required by the royal orders, they would have taken part with the rebels, and the province of Bengal would have been lost. Upon receiving this answer, the king's mind was quieted, and he was satisfied.

After prince 'Azim-ud-din had answered his grandfather, he wrote a very bitter letter to Amanat Khan, accusing him of imprudence and stupidity in carrying out the royal orders as he had done. He had ignored the ruin that without a doubt must ensue. He told him he was certain he had only acted in that manner in order that for the rest of his life he might be remembered as the man who was praised for doing a service to the crown, which a prince of the blood-royal had not the spirit to undertake. He swore an oath that not many days would have gone by before he had secured satisfaction from him for such overweening vanity. The letter occasioned the governor so much grief and such profound melancholy that he died in a short time.

It must be over forty years ago that I knew this lord's father. His name was Mirec Maiudinn (Mirak Mu'in-ud-din Ahmad);[1] he was *diwan* first of the Kabul province and then of Lahor, [27] and, as it seems to me, I have spoken of him there (I. 103). This man, through his services to the crown, was raised to the dignity of Amanat Khan, and all his family entered the king's service on good pay. He was a great friend of mine, as, indeed, he was of all Christians, a most affable and kindly man, much devoted to alchemy, and always trying to make gold. Every year he wasted

---

of the bond (*Muchalkah*), forcibly taken from the Dutch at Surat by Amanat Khan, and dated February 4, 1699, can be seen in Valentyn, 'Oud en Nieuw Oostindien,' iv. 169. It is signed by Pr. Ketting and seven others.

1. 'Ma,asir-ul-Umara,' i. 258, Amanat Khan No. 1. Manucci has already mentioned him in Part I. 103 and II. 158.

thirty thousand rupees, and yet never in all those years attained the desired result, although always busily occupied with retorts and stills, as is the habit of alchemists.

Many a time he invited me to join him in these researches, in the belief that I was experienced in such matters. But I always undeceived him, and told him he was spending uselessly both money and time, and could never conquer impossibilities. Yet these words of mine did not move him from his opinions, he pressed on with the undertaking then in hand, and constantly renewed his experiments. It was his habit to say to me that by this means one day or another he would recover the method of making gold, and that, should he not have found it, his son Miroseni (Mir Husain) would certainly do so. This is the son above spoken of.

After his father's death this son obtained the title of Amanat Khan, and was appointed, as I have said, governor of Surat. It happened that after [28] some years I met in the city of Aurangabad with the said elder Amanat Khan. The old man was still at work on his projects without ever having succeeded. In spite of that, he did not lose hope of attaining his desires, and still went on with new experiments.[1]

While I was in his house one day he sent for a vicious black snake to show me. He placed it in a pot along with ten ounces of crude mercury, then luted the lid on skilfully with clay. Next the pot was placed on the fire, and a learned Arab was ordered to recite the Quran over it. Beholding this rash act with alarm, I departed. Observing this move, he sought the reason of my leaving the place. I replied that I did not think the spot was safe. At that moment the pot was overturned, the Quran fell from the Arab's hand, he was struck, and fell senseless on the floor.

In spite of this accident he did not intermit the pursuit of the fancies he had in his head; on the contrary, he left as an inheritance to his son, Mir Husain, these methods of attempting to make gold. When the latter died at Surat there was found among his effects a large provision of retorts prepared for these purposes.

1. Amanat Khan the elder was appointed governor of Aurangabad early in the twenty-seventh year (it began August 24, 1683), when Aurangzeb marched against Ahmadnagar. He was left behind because he objected to taking up arms against Mahomedans. He died there in 1095 H. (1683-84), and was buried near the shrine of Shah Nur, Hamami (Ma,asir-ul-Umara,' i. 264).

This was attested by the Reverend Father Lorenzo of Angoulesme,[1] who was present. It is a fact that this governor never discovered the way to manufacture gold; but, on the other hand, it is true that he found a mode, by his astuteness, [29] to force much money out of the hands of the merchants at that port (Surat). But by this action he was unable to profit, for when his life left him [so soon afterwards] the money was lost too.

[Here follows an account of the doings of the French fleet, beginning with July 11, 1704. It is omitted, it being substantially the same as the version in Part IV., fols. 223-226. There are a few additional statements which I have introduced into Part IV. within square brackets. I resume at folio 34, which seems an amplification of the narrative in Part IV., fol. 224, referring to the Dutch commissary.]

[34] The said commissary [Phoosen] was received in Pondicherry with great civility: after fifteen days they released him, and made him a present of all his plate, and some cases of merchandise which he claimed as his private properly. When he left he was escorted by fifty soldiers, the captain over whom was called Monsieur Deligondes.[2] They conducted the commissary as far as Cuddalore, and on reaching it he opened one of his boxes and took out from it a casket of valuable jewels, and wished to give the officer a valuable diamond ring, but the Frenchman declined to take it, though thanking him for his kind offer. Thus the commissary quitted Cuddalore [35] and went to Negapatam to take charge of his government, and remained ever afterwards on good terms with the French of Pondicherry.

On February 20, 1705, the four French vessels set sail for

1. This Lorenzo is evidently the same as the Friar Laurent of Angoulesme, Capuchin and Apostolic Missionary, who signs François Martin's burial certificate on December 31, 1706 (see P. Margry's article in 'Biographie Universelle,' new edition, vol. xxvii., pp. 121-124). Father Lorenzo (Laurent) was temporarily Chaplain at Madras in 1704, when the Patriarch of Antioch suspended Father Michel Ange (see *ante*, Part IV.).
2. Desligondes is mentioned once in the French records. M. Boissieux writes from Pondicherry on February 5, 1703, recommending 'the Chevalier Desligondes, "garde de la marine," who had been a very long time first lieutenant of the garrison,' for the company whose captain was returning to France (C^2 67, fol. 18, 1703).

France.[1] The *Phenix* went to Bengal under the command of Monsieur Bono (Bouynot), and the vessel called *Marchand des Indes*, being old, was sold to an Armenian merchant named Mallegujas.

NOTE ON BERNARD PHOOSEN AND THE CAPTURE OF THE *GOUDE VOGEL PHENIX* (FROM THE DUTCH ARCHIVES)

[In Phoosen's defence of his conduct submitted on January 15, 1706, to Joan van Hoorn, Governor-General, and Council at Batavia, in compliance with their resolution of December 21, 1705, there are some details worth preserving—(1) about the fight at sea; (2) about the negotiations for a local truce.

Phoosen sailed from Malacca on January 19, and reached Balasor roads upon March 18, 1704, on board the *Ellemeet*, having in company the *Goude Vogel Phenix* and six other vessels. After loading new goods on the *Goude Vogel Phenix*, and transferring to her the cargo of the *Ellemeet*, Phoosen and some other officials set sail in her for Negapatam on December 30, 1704, while the *Ellemeet and Molenwerf* started for Batavia. A French vessel, which was hovering about off the coast, got away in advance of them, and no doubt conveyed to the French the news of their approach. On the morning of January 12, 1705, the high land near Palicat was in sight, and about noon they passed Geldria, the Dutch fort there. Towards evening they were off Madras, and before sunset they sighted the hills behind Sadraspatanam. They then stood out to sea in the hope of passing the fortress of Pondicherry without being perceived.

As day broke next day, January 13, when they were about fourteen miles from the coast, they made out four sail to the north-west at a distance of four or five miles. Guessing them to be French, they made all sail, but the pursuers overhauled them hand over hand. About ten o'clock the nearest ship displayed a red ensign as a signal to one of the other ships. All four ships now flew white flags, the admiral coming up on the port and the second in command on the starboard. Owing to its position the Dutch could only attack the second ship with their swivel guns and musketry.

Meanwhile the *Goude Vogel Phenix* fought the enemy's principal ship with all available cannon. But owing to their being so heavily laden, only four of their lowest tier of guns on either side

1. The officially recorded date of sailing is February 21, 1705 (Dr. J. Sottas' letter to me of June 27, 1906). The subject of the *Phénix* is touched on again by Manucci in V., fol. 123, and Commissary Phoosen is again referred to on fol. 150. As for the sale of the *Marchand des Indes*, the fact appears from a Pondicherry letter to the French Company of October 8, 1705 (C^2 67, fol. 280, verso), but the name of the purchaser is not on record.

could be discharged. The French fired broadside upon broadside into them, a portion of their rigging and a good deal of their shrouds being shot into tatters so that they could carry no sail. The topsails were shot into bits and fell overboard; a large part of the tiller was destroyed. They drifted helplessly between the two largest Frenchmen, while the remaining two ships of their fleet were drawing close.

The skipper, Hendrik Mondiger, had fought on for nearly one and a half hours against an overpowering force. Many of the Dutch were killed, including Gerrit Katt, the third mate, whose leg was shot off early in the fight when standing near Commissary Phoosen, who all through the fight stuck to his place on the upper deck. The master now reported the impossibility of holding out longer. The casualties had induced a slackening of effort among the crew, and it was impossible to persuade them to fight their guns.

The commissary himself saw that out of twelve men only two stood to their work. Two or three times Cornelis de Graaf jumped down and tried to drive the men back to duty. Things being in this state on board the *Goude Vogel Phenix* as seen by the commissary and councillors themselves, the master, H. Mondiger, was pressed to say whether more could be done to save the ship from the enemy. His words were that to fight longer was mere stubbornness and obstinacy; the men would be butchered, and the end would be the same. The councillors expressed their agreement with the skipper.

It was resolved to strike the flag of the *Goude Vogel Phenix*. 'I (Phoosen) went to the poop to be ready, when from the French admiral came a broadside to salute us, one ball of which passed through the mizzen-mast and struck H. Mondiger and under-merchant Jaan Oosterling both in the breast, the first-named also having his left arm shattered. Both fell on the deck together dead. Undersigned was wounded by a splinter in the face, arm, and breast, but not dangerously.'

The flag having been struck, the French continued to call on the Dutch to launch their boat and come on board their ship. The tackle and ropes had been destroyed, and they could not comply; the French were forced to send boats to bring them off. Thus after resisting for two hours they had been forced to surrender, having thirteen men killed and about twenty severely wounded. They were received by the admiral, Baron de Pallieres. From the chief surgeon the commissary learnt that his captons were *L'Agréable, La Mutine, 'Aurore,* and the *St. Louis*, the details being the same as already noted from Dr. Jules Sottas' work. These ships had left Fort Louis in April, 1704, and in November, upon reaching the coast of Malabar, had taken one English and two Portuguese ships, of which the first was ransomed, and the larger of the other two was sent to Goa with both the Portuguese crews on board.

We come next to events at Pondicherry, and the course of negotiations there. The French ships with their prize anchored off that settlement on the afternoon of January 18, 1705. On the 20th Phoosen was landed, and taken to Governor Martin in the fort. A dwelling was assigned to him there, and sentries were posted. The chief Dutch officials and ship's officers were sent to other quarters. Some of the crew were locked up in a warehouse on the beach, and the rest of the common sailors were put aboard the two-masted French vessel from Bengal already referred to. On the 22nd two Dutch envoys arrived from Negapatam—Hendrik Grousens, chief administrator, and Hendrik Becker, then Fiscal and subsequently Extraordinary Councillor. They were authorized to treat for the release of the prisoners.

On the envoys being received by Governor Martin, Phoosen was sent for. De Pallieres and Du Dresnay took him apart, and a letter was given him from the Governor and Council of Negapatam, dated January 18, 1705. After he had read the letter, Du Dresnay whispered to him to keep up his spirits. This remark was communicated by letter to Governor Conans on January 23 as showing they had hope of success.

But almost from that moment the French began to tell Phoosen that he must agree to a cessation of hostilities in India. The affair was conducted by Du Dresnay through one of the Duchmen, Johan de Wolf, who knew French. They dwelt on the inconveniences to both nations from hostilities in India, and said that ratification and approval of the sovereigns on both sides could easily be obtained. Phoosen sent back word that we was in no way empowered to treat, but on reaching Negapatam he would consult with the Governor and Council there. Du Dresnay hinted that this refusal would not help on the release of the prisoners. De Wolf said the two things had not the remotest connection. Meanwhile the Dutch learnt from Negapatam that everybody said that Ariahpa, an interpreter, was very busy trying to thwart the efforts of the Dutch envoys. On their side they employed a native called Letje to find out what was going on. Through him they learnt that a leading merchant of Pondicherry, called Cammer Appa Chetty, was using influence against them with Governor Martin, and they were told at second or third hand that this man had offered Governor Martin 8,000 or 9,000 *pagodas* if the Dutch prisoners were sent to France, a proposal which Martin indignantly refused.

On the morning of January 24 (1705) the Council assembled at the Governors house, and the Dutch envoys when called in presented the Negapatam letter. After pursuing it the Council pointed out that on the taking of S. Thome [1674] and Pondicherry [1693] the Dutch sent their prisoners to Europe, De Flacourt, second in Council, having been one of those deported in spite of his protests. The French said they would gain reputation with their monarch by following the same course. As an alternative they urged Phoosen to agree to a truce both north and south of the equinoctial line, subject to the subsequent approbation of their respective sovereigns.

The Negapatam envoys tried to draw a distinction between those former events on land and the present capture at sea. They claimed that Phoosen should be treated as Martin was after the surrender of Pondichery [namely, he was released and allowed to proceed to Hugli]. Secondly, they pleaded want of authorization, and requested that Phoosen might be sent for. Phoosen repeated the claim to be treated as Martin had been, also relying on an agreement between the two States made in 1690 for the mutual release of prisoners, and as the French had themselves acted to the English after the capture of the *Canterbury*. But all this was 'like knocking at a deaf man's door.' The *cartel* referred to was confined, the French said, to the previous war, and had not been renewed. They asserted that a truce would be favourable to the Dutch. The Dutchmen denied the fact, for they were incomparably the stronger in those regions. The Frenchmen met this by dwelling on the better sailing of their ships, which redressed the balance at sea, while on land they had nothing to fear. Their state of defence the Dutch could see for themselves.

Heer Phoosen then brought forward the difference of their political position; the Dutch in India were subordinate to Batavia, the Dutch Company, and the States General, while the French were in direct dependence on their monarch in Europe. The French retorted by saying they were as little empowered to treat as were the Dutch; but they would stretch a point, seeing a common advantage to the two nations by a truce in India. Phoosen proposed to defer an answer until his arrival at Negapatam and the receipt of sanction from Batavia. To this it was answered that his open commission and the Negapatam letters were full credentials for negotiating. It was then pointed out by him that his open commission included no more than the Choromandal coast. The other side remarked that Rykloff van Goens had not in his day interpreted his powers so scrupulously. The truce ought to extend from Vingorla on the west coast right round the coast and up it to a place within twelve miles of the Ganges. Phoosen pleaded the limited extent of his powers, and refused to entertain this offer. The French then varied the conditions, and offered a truce from Point de Galle along the east coast to a point within twelve miles of the Ganges. This was equally declined. Upon this refusal the French declared frankly that they must send Phoosen and the chief prisoners to Europe.

Next the Dutch thought it wise to test the force of this threat by demanding as a condition precedent to any discussion that the prize *Goude Vogel Phenix*, with its crew and cargo intact, should be restored. 'This proposal acted on our opponents like a thunderbolt.' They were much astonished at such an incredible demand, and declined to listen to any further mention of it. They closed the interview by saying that all they could do was to submit the point for their sovereign's decision.

The Dutch officials now found themselves in difficulty and perplexity. They knew their superiors would never ratify any such agreement, yet if they did not enter into it they would be deported to Europe. They requested leave to withdraw, and take some time for reflection. The points now discussed by them among themselves were four: First, had their company any force in sight sufficient to attack the enemy and effect their release? This was decided in the negative; and as the monsoon was over, future arrivals could with difficulty be brought as far as the roadstead of Pondicherry. Secondly, a Dutch vessel, the *Pappensburg*, was daily expected from Japan, and would most assuredly be captured as the *Goude Vogel Phenix* had been. Thirdly, the presence of Commissary Phoosen on the Choromandal coast was absolutely necessary. Fourthly, the French possessed a fast ship, *Le Petit Marchand*, which could prevent all traffic by sea between the Dutch factories.

For all these reasons it was resolved to enter into the proposed agreement, which after all could only last a short time. It was choosing the lesser of two evils. If their Excellencies at Batavia refused to ratify it, it would fall to the ground of itself. There was a further stiff dispute over the exact terms, as the Dutch wished to strike out the condition making the truce extend to within twelve miles of the Ganges. Eight articles were drawn up, and were as follows:

1. A truce to be made between the two nations both by sea and land, commencing at Negapatam, and extending to Point Palmyras, and as far as 60 fathoms' depth out at sea.

2. Within those limits no injury should in any way be inflicted by the one nation upon the other.

3. The *pattamars*, or letter-carriers, and other expresses sent off by either party were to have free passage over either's territory so long as they remained no longer than required for the dispatch of business.

4. The Heer commissary, the ship's crew, and the servants taken in the *Goude Vogel Phenix* should be set at liberty.

5. Any French or Dutch ship taken thereafter within the agreed limits should be restored untouched with its crew, passengers, and cargo.

6. Fugitives from either side within the agreed limits should be extradited on demand, subject to the condition that no death penalty should be inflicted.

7. Governor Martin and Council undertook to furnish at the cost of the Compagnie Royale all the necessary vessels for the conveyance of the commissary and superior officers as far as Negapatam, the Negapatam envoys undertaking on their side to furnish safe conducts for the return voyage, protecting the ships from seizure by the English or Portuguese.

8. An engagement was made to procure ratification.

The French Council added a supplementary article, which they sent by the hand of Monsieur de la Prevostiére, their secretary. This fixed the limits as from Point de Galle to within twelve miles of the Ganges. Phoosen flatly declined to accept this alteration. There was a discussion next day, and the original words were restored. The agreement was then signed on January 27, 1705. Finally, Phoosen pleads the *force majeure* of circumstances, winding up his defence with the proverb, 'Nood breekt wet' ['Necessity has no law'].

On February 2, 1705, fifty of the men of the *Goude Vogel Phenix* were embarked for Negapatam under command of a petty officer. On the same day the head of Conimere Factory wrote to warn the commissary that the *faujdar of* Jinji had sent out horsemen to intercept the party while on their way to Tegenapatam (Cuddalore). In consequence, Governor Martin at dinnertime offered them an escort. The party of Dutchmen left Pondicherry on February 3, 1705, towards evening, accompanied by an escort of twenty-four French soldiers under a captain. They spent the night in a house about a mile from the fort. Next day early [the 4th] they passed within half a mile of Alechivabe, where the native attack was expected. There they were received by a captain and forty-eight men sent them by Mr. Gabriel Roberts, governor of the English fort of St. David at Cuddalore. They were conducted to the Company's factory at Tegenapatam, reaching it about mid-day. Continuing their journey, they camped on the 9th at China Pagoda, and finally, next day (February 10, 1705), marched into Negapatam.]

The above-named commissary (Phoosen), having started from Batavia, arrived at Hugli to inspect the factories of the Dutch situated in the province of Bengal. Before his departure from that port on his journey to this coast [Choromandal] he gave a sumptuous banquet, at which were present all the English factors, the principal officers then in charge at that [Dutch] factory, and the captains of the vessels in port at the time. The banquet lasted eight days in high joy and festivity. During those days the cannon were fired over three thousand times.

Among the many guests was Gart [Savt], an English captain, who the previous year, when on his return from China, had surrendered his ship to the French in the Straits of Malacca after a valorous defence.[1] The commissary directed [36] his conversa-

1. Probably this is a reference to the capture of the *Canterbury* by the French warships *Maurepas* and *Pondicherry*, commanded by the Chevalier de Pontenay, *capitaine* de *frégatte*. This took place on December 20, 1703, in the Straits of Malacca (see Archives de la Marine, now

tion to this gentleman, censuring him most severely, and calling him a coward and worthless fellow. He began to boast of how delighted he should be to come across some French ships in his voyage from Hugli to Negapatam. He would teach them how to fight. Only a few days had passed when the said captain (Gart) arrived at Madras, and while drinking cheerfully with some friends, the news came in of the commissary's capture. This increased the captain's joy, and he was consoled that Fate had avenged the insult he had received from the commissary, and he resumed his carouse by drinking to the honour of the event.

Being a friend of some of these [French] captains, I went to Pondicherry to pay them a visit and enjoy their company. After eight days they sailed.

Two days after the departure of these French captains the marriage took place of the Lord Governor Martin's granddaughter to Monsieur Ardancour (Hardancourt), commissary [37] and second councillor.[1] A grand banquet was given, followed by

---

at the Archives Nationales, 'Campagnes,' Register B^4 25, fol. 386, report dated August 15, 1704). The captain of the *Canterbury* was, however, Kingsford, and I do not know who this Gart or Savt could be.

1. I append a copy of the marriage certificate, extracted from the registers of the Elat Civil of Pondicherry, at the Ministére des Colonies in Paris, fol. 9: *'Mariage de Mc Dardancourt avec M[ue] Agnes Desprez*

'Aujourdhuy 22 Fevrier 1705, Monseigneur Leveque de Tylopolis et vicaire Apostolique a marié dans I'Eglise du fort de Pondichery Monsieur Claude Boyuin Dardancourt Conseiller Souverain de Pondichery, fils de Charles Boyuin d'Ardancourt gentil homme ordinaire de la grande fauconnire de France et De Demoiselle de Rabec ses pere et mere avec Demoiselle Agnez Desprez fille de Michel Desprez Bourgeois de Paris et de Dame Agnes Martin ses pere et mere ont été temoins les Soussignés (Signds), Marin Eveque de Tilopolis, Martin, et f. Deflacourt.'

Hardancourt (as he always signs himself) served both at Pondicherry and at Surat, and between 1700 and 1705 he signs all the letters from Pondicherry along with Martin Challonge, Delabac, and Desprez. For instance, on March 13, 1703 (C^2a II., 67, fol. 115 *et seq.*), there is a general report by him on the situation at Surat. He signs 'Claude Hardancourt,' councillor and merchant, to a letter from Pondicherry of April 3, 1705 (C^2 II., 67, fol. 244). He must be distinguished from the Hardancourt (a brother) who went to India in 1710 to report on the affairs of the Company (see Archives Coloniales, Compagnie des Indes Orientales, Administration en France, Registre 13, C^2, fols. 192 and 193). A son was born in 1706, and baptized in the Fort Church at Pondicherry on

music and dancing, at which were also present the son of Governor Ruberto (Gabriel Roberts) of the fortress of Tevenapatam, and a councillor called Mester Barlu (Mr. Berleu).[1] When the

April 18, Madame Marie Cuperly, wife of F. Martin, Governor, being godmother. On May 20, 1708, a daughter, Marie Agnez, was baptized, the same lady, now a widow, being again godmother. Claude d'Hardancourt must have died before June 5, 1719, as on that date Agnes Desprez signs herself as his widow when witnessing Jeanne Albert's first marriage (Bib. Nat., Nouvelles Acquisitions Françaises, MS No. 9,346, fols. 1-16, extracts from Etat Civil made by the late P. Margry).

As for the brother, Louis Boyvin d'Hardancourt, we find that he received letters patent of nobility in April, 1726, being then one of the Directors of the French East India Company (Bib. Nat., Nouveau d'Hozier 64, Dossier Boyvin, fols. 6 and 7). His previous employments, beginning with 1699, are recited, and his descent is then described. His great-grandfather, Tristan Boyvin, Sieur d'Hardancourt, was a commissary of artillery in 1621, and was killed at the Siege of Montauban. Charles, his grandfather, took the style of *écuyer* in all legal documents; he served in the army, and then retired to Normandy, where he married Demoiselle Le Roi. His father Charles, second of the name, entered the office of Colbert, and on September 6, 1674, received a charge of *greffier* in the Grand Chancery. In 1685 he was made a *gentilhomme* of the Grand Falconry. The arms granted are then stated.

Desprez is mentioned as *procureur de Vamirauté* in the 'Voyage du Baron de Pallieres' (Archives de la Marine, Campagnes, Registre B^4 26, fol. 493); he has been already mentioned by Manucci as sent to San Thome in 1702 to negotiate with Da,ud Khan. The officiating Bishop, Labbé-Marin, was born near Caen, and in 1678 was appointed to the mission of Cochin China. Having been recalled in 1697, in 1702 he was consecrated at Paris as Bishop of Tilopolis by the Cardinal de Noailles, and was sent out as Coadjutor Bishop in Cochin China to assist Francesco Perez, Bishop of Bugie. He died in Cochin China on March 14, 1723 (see Chaudon and Delandine, 'Dictionnaire Universel,' Paris, 1810, ix. 408; L. E. Louvet, 'La Cochin Chine Religieuse,' Paris, 1885, i. 311, 341). Manucci calls him Bishop of Tiripolis in Part V., fol. 255. For the witness F. de Flacourt, see note 78, Vol. IV., Part V., fol. 100.

1. Tevenapatam, the original name of Fort St. David, two miles from Cuddalore. The land was bought by the English in 1690 ('Madras Manual of Administration,' vol. iii., p. 297). Gabriel Roberts took his seat as Deputy-Governor of Fort St. David on June 11, 1702 (Fort St. George Public Consultations, xxxi. 123, 124). John Berlu (or Berleu) is mentioned in 1698 in the account of Sulaiman Khan's attack on Cuddalore (February, 1698). In December, 1699, he became one of the Council there ('Public Dispatches,' xi. 187-190). There are other mentions of him.

festivities were ended, they returned to Tevanapatam, and I in their company, wishing to pay a visit to Governor Ruberto (Roberts), my old friend. This gentleman received me with great politeness, and after several healths were drunk we had music and dancing.

In the midst of this joyous intercourse there reached me almost at midnight a mounted orderly bearing a letter, which recalled me with all urgency to Pondicherry. I was wanted at once to treat the Lord Governor Martin, who was seriously ill. Upon hearing this sad news I and the rest of the company were much pained, not merely at having to break up our feast, but equally at learning of the grave indisposition of an old and affectionate friend. At once I was given my leave to depart, on condition of paying another visit to Tevanapatam, which I promised to do.

I began my journey at once, and at break of day arrived in Pondicherry. I found the good old man, then seventy-three years of age, in a high fever, with pains in the head, absence of sleep and other symptoms. [38] I started on the treatment forthwith, and held a consultation with the doctors of the Royal Company, one of whom was named Monsieur Maqari, and the other Monsieur Albert:[1] By our efforts and the drugs we administered he was placed out of danger, and by dieting and care was restored to perfect health.

Not to break my word, and in compliance with the messages sent me, I went back to Tevanapatam, to the contentment of all my friends, thence back to Pondicherry, and finally to my own house at Madras. Here I received news that a Monsieur Dela-

1. Jacques Albert (father of Madame Dupleix) was at Pondicherry in 1710 (see P. Cultru, 'Dupleix,' Paris, 1901, 179). His son, Jacques Théodore, by his first wife, Marie Madelaine Molle (of St. Eustache parish), was married at Pondicherry on June 15, 1700, to Marie, daughter of Florent Mainferme and Isabelle Madére. The first marriage of his daughter Jeanne (by a second wife, Elisabeth dé Castro, born at Pondicherry) to Jacques Vincent (son of Jacques Vincent and Jeanne Ramosse, of Montpellier) was celebrated in Nótre Dame de Anges at Pondicherry on June 5, 1719. The witnesses were Esprit de Tours (curé), De la Prevostière, Agnez Desprez (widow of d'Hardancourt), Cuperly, Albert, Hébert, and Dulivier (see Bibliothèque Nationale, Nouvelles Acquisitions Françises, MS. No. 9,346, extracts from Etat Civil of Pondicherry, fols. 2 and 13).

vale, a married man and resident of Juncalam (Ujung Salang),[1] a land belonging to the King of Siam, had turned pirate. It is three years ago that he came to Madras in the guise of a merchant. I gave him money to trade with, as did many other persons of this settlement. Having acquired enough money and a supply of goods in this country, he left it. To disabuse his creditors of any hope they entertained of being repaid—at any rate, the capital amount he captured an English boat loaded with cloth from Bengal, and took its captain a prisoner.

The governor of the place [*i.e.*, Ujung Salang], on the facts being reported, sent orders to seize Delavale; but he fled, followed by all his companions, taking with him the prisoner, but abandoning his house and wife. The governor of the [39] country took possession of his wife and of all the merchandise. Monsieur Delavale sought refuge in another province of the same kingdom, ruled over by a man who was an enemy to the other governor. The followers of this pirate Delavale are two in number, one called Monsieur Masson, the other Monsieur de Roubal. These events have caused such consternation among the merchants that not one of them will venture on a voyage to that port.

Although the King Aurangzeb had occupation enough in fighting the Mahrattahs, in conquering different rajahs, and many other enterprises, he never overlooked the question of getting his son Sultan Akbar into his power. This son, then in Persia, was invited back by many letters, none of which had any effect. At last, in the year 1689, he wrote him one in the most loving terms. It was also the last one sent; its terms were as follows:[2]

1. Apparently the same as the Junk Ceylon of English navigators (Yule, 473). It is an island off the west coast of the Malay Peninsula, and belongs to Siam.
2. Letters to this effect are to be found in Persian in 'Khatut-i- Shiva Ji,' Royal Asiatic Society's MS., No. 71. fols. 25 and 30; British Museum Additional MS., No. 18,881, fols. 77*a*-79*b*; India Office Library, Persian MS., No. 1,344, fol. 25*a*. They were written about 1680-81, when Akbar was in rebellion, and there is no evidence of their having been written when he was in Persia. I have compared Manucci's version with the British Museum Additional MS., No. 18,881, and the Royal Asiatic Society's MS., No. 71. In the first named the substance is the same, but the second half of Akbar's letter as given by Manucci is wanting: it is, however, included in substance in the other transcript. These two letters are repeated (in Italian) in Codex XLV. (Zanetti). fols. 328-334.

'My beloved son, light of my eyes, part of my heart, Akbar! I write to you, swearing upon the word of the Ruler over kings, and be God my witness [40], that I esteem and love you more than my other sons. You were ever my solace and consolation, and lightened my afflictions when you were present. Now that you are so far away, I feel their whole weight, and must endure them. You became disobedient, and were led away by the Rajputs, those demons in human form; thus you lost the favour of Heaven, and were abandoned by it. What can I do? and what remedy can I offer you for the troubles under which you are now suffering? When I think on these things, I continue in travail and great sorrow, so that I have lost the desire for longer life. I endure the greatest grief at seeing you so far from this realm, deprived of your princely title, removed from power, stripped of your dignities in the State. Because I love you deeply, I weep bitterly over your wretched condition. Yet did you disregard your youth and loyalty to your family, and are forced to live thus far separated from wives, sons, and daughters. From your self-will you fell a prisoner into the hands of those demoniac Rajputs. They treated you like a ball, struck first by one side and hurled back by the other [41]. Thus were you compelled to take refuge first in one place, then in another. In spite of all these things, although you have been guilty of such heavy crimes, yet, impelled by the love I bear you, I have no desire to inflict farther punishment.'

After these words followed two verses, which continued the letter; their sense was as follows:

'In spite of a son being only a little ashes,
Yet is he a salve to the suffering eyes of parents.[1]

'Now, Fortune seeks to favour you. If you have repented of your errors you can come to my Presence, and advance to meet me sure that your sins will be remitted; that I shall not forget to favour you and aggrandize you even in a manner that will exceed your wildest dreams of greatness. Thus will you be recompensed for the sufferings and the labours you have undergone.

1. Couplet:

'Garchah pisar tudah-i-khak ast,
Surmah-i-chashmah-i-pidar o madar ast'

('Ruqa'at-i-'Alamgiri.' British Museum Additional MS., No. 18,881, fol. 78*a*).

This invitation is not given solely from a desire to see you present here, but to obviate your being, as you are now, ruined, solitary, lost, and dishonoured.'

'I do not speak of the Rajah Jaswant Singh, who was the [42] chief of all the Rajputs and the follower of Dara. O son! Trust not in such nor heed their words, for they will sell you falsified goods yielding you no profit, and in the end causing nothing but regret. Understand, and accept it as infallible, that what I tell you will be for your good, and points out the only right road. Retain it, therefore, in memory, for never again shall I write to you.'

COPY OF THE REPLY WHICH WAS SENT TO THIS LAST LETTER BY PRINCE AKBAR TO HIS FATHER AURANGZEB

'I state, being the meanest among your Majesty's sons, I, Akbar, in reverent obeisance and humility and respect, that I have received your Majesty's letter. A thousand times do I give thanks for the honours, kindnesses, and favours that your Majesty metes out to me. Thereby have I received great joy and much consolation. The letter arrived at an auspicious moment, and I took it with all the humbleness and obedient duty that is owing to your Majesty's high dignity. Its mere receipt has brought me comfort. I am now informed as to your orders, and continue to be very joyful at seeing and reading again and again all [43] that your pen has condescended to write to me, and the instruction thereby imparted. I reply on all the heads, which I record with brevity, as is fitting for one who adheres to truth and justice.

'Your Majesty writes to me that you love me, although I became disobedient, and was deprived of rank and dignity because I had placed myself in prison [among the Rajputs]. My lord, just as the son ought to be the obedient servant of his father who has conceived him, and ought to follow rightful orders as his father dictates, so must a father give reasonable commands in order that the son may find himself under a necessity to obey. Thanks be to God! I have not been wanting in due respect and reverence, nor in any way have I failed in my obedience as a son. I acknowledge the great grace and favour of your Majesty; so grateful am I that I cannot display it sufficiently. In fact, of all that you promise me, were there only to be granted a small fraction, or even of that small fraction only the minutest particle, I should rest content.

'As it seems to me, since I was the youngest you ought to have shown me love and done me favour greater than that accorded to your other sons. However, I do not live devoid of hope, knowing you to be a tender-hearted father. Your Majesty has acted against the world's rule. You favoured your other sons; me you outraged. To your eldest son you conceded the title of king,[1] and in [44] addition have declared him heir to the throne. In what system of justice or from what tribunal was there ever such a decision heard of? All the sons ought to share in the paternal estate. Your Majesty, to the very contrary of this, has raised one to greatness, has enriched another and overweighted him with titles, while the others are forsaken and in poverty. But where is the code and system in which such things can be discovered? O veritable king of truth, in thy equity all are equal! His mode of conduct is clear, and notified to all the world, and His works are registered in His scriptures. God will assign greatness to him who the most pleases Him.

'Your Majesty was my teacher, who showed me the road I ought to tread, and your example was imitated and followed by all others. And who is he who can decry my acts, when I followed the road that my father had taught me to go? Our first father, Adam, forfeited the favour of Heaven for two grains of corn, while I have been sent to perdition for one grain alone. But I[2] should be a fool if I did not know how to sell it profitably.

'Bygone kings, such as the great Taimur-i-lang and [45] King Shajahan, went through and endured great labours, and to the end continued to be powerful and happy. He who refuses to undergo hardships can never become great or obtain the favour of Heaven or live in prosperity. Flowers do not exist without thorns, nor mountains without serpents.'

---

1. That is, he conferred on Prince Mu'azzam the title of Shah "Alam, or 'King of the World.'
2. This is a verse:
   '*Pidaram rauzah-i-Rizwan ba du gandum ba-farokht,*
   Na-khalaf basham agar man ba jane ba-farosham?'
   (My father sold Paradise for two grains of wheat,
   Am I an unworthy son for selling it for one barleycorn?)
   ('Ruqa'at-i-'Alamgiri,' British Museum Additional MS., No. 18,881, fol. 79*a*).

[Here follow two verses to this effect:]

'If Fortune means to favour me,
A sharp sword will not wound me.'[1]

'As is usual, fatigue is followed by repose; therefore I hope by the grace of God to be thus favoured, and freed from the hardships and troubles that at present I am suffering. In regard to your remark about Jaswant, who was the greatest of the Rajputs and a friend of Dara, as all the world knows, you advise me not to trust such people. To this I reply that your Majesty says well; but your Highness should be careful to speak no further thereof. For it is quite certain that Dara was not loved by that tribe; he was their enemy. Had he retained their friendship he would not have been defeated. King Shahjahan was fond of that tribe, being (as he was) related to them, and by their weapons [46] made himself King of Hindustan.

'By the help of these people the great Mahabat Khan made a prisoner of King Jahangir, and chastised his enemies. Let your Majesty remember what Rajputs, men of this tribe, have done in your very presence at the Court of Dihli. They fought with such bravery that their deeds have been entered in the world's chronicles. In ancient story no record of equal valour can be anywhere discovered. Jaswant was the man who in the

---

1. The Persian original reads thus:

' 'Arus-i-mulk na sazad magar ba damadi,
Kih bosah bar lab-i-shamsher-i-abdar zanad'

(A royal bride takes no man to her breast
Who kisses not the edge of the sharpened sword)

('Ruqa'at-i-'Alamgiri,' British Museum Additional MS., No. 18,881, fol. 79*b*).

Cardeira's Italian lines are as follows:

'Di quest 'occhi vezzosi se la sorte
Getta sopra di me cortese un sguardo:
La spada aguzza non mi fà codardo
Ne temo che al mio cuor dia mai la morte.'

Professor Jadunath Sarkar points out to me that Akbar makes here a covert allusion to Aurangzeb's words at the Battle of Khajwah, fought against Shuja' (1659). He then quoted:

' 'Arus-i-mulk kase dar baghl girad tang
Kih bosah bar lab-i-shamsher-i-abdar dahad'

(He only clasps firmly a kingdom as his bride
Who kisses the lip of the sharp sword's edge)

('Ahkam-i-'Alamgiri,' Irvine MSS., No. 252, fol. 4*b*).

battle against Shah Shuja' was guilty of such a defect that he merited to be rigorously punished instead of being pardoned. Yet your Majesty passed this over because you not only knew the man, but feared him. It is he who, being corrupted and deceived by your Majesty's pretences and magic arts, omitted to espouse the cause of Dara. If he had taken that side your Majesty would not at this day be reigning; for it was he (Jaswant) who won you the victory.

'Who can doubt that these Rajputs deserve to be praised for their fidelity? This right they earned when, although deprived of their chieftain, they took the little children of the deceased rajah under their charge, and fighting desperately, offered up their lives. Three hundred of their [47] horsemen held out for twelve hours continuously against all the forces at your court, killing many famed and veteran warriors, finally retreating in safety. They are, then, worthy of praise, this tribe, as much for their fidelity as for their valour.

'When the kings of Hindustan, its princes and potentates, or the chief generals, desired to enrol soldiers, for each one whom they required a hundred offered themselves. At the present time it takes you three years to recruit a few men. From what does this difficulty proceed, and what fact could tell you more? Yet from the first day in your Majesty's reign all are lords, governors, and generals, but none have any loyalty; the soldiers are impoverished and unprovided with arms, famous writers produce nothing and have no employment, the traders are assassinated or deprived of their goods, and the people destroyed. The lands of the Dakhin, which are so vast, and once seemed like a terrestrial Paradise, are nowadays uncultivated, unproductive, and uninhabited.

'What can I say about the kingdom of Bijapur, once the jewel of India, and now entirely undone? The city of Aurangabad, founded by your Majesty, and the chief place in that province, [48] was devastated by the enemy because it bore your name, and is now like a little quicksilver that disappears suddenly, being at this day no more than a mound of earth.

'The cause of this ruin was the tax imposed on the Hindus, which was converted into a profit to the enemy, who have done so much harm to the population, and subjected them to such hardships and tyrannies, worrying them on all sides, until the whole land has been reduced to desolation.

'Upon what subject can I say anything good of your Majesty? The ancient and noble families are all extinct. The government, the rules, the counsels and advice needed for the welfare of the State, are all in the hands of low, ill-bred persons, such as weavers, washermen, barbers, carpenters, blacksmiths, tailors, and suchlike. Your Majesty puts your trust in hypocrites wearing huge turbans, and accepted as theologians because they carry a Quran under the arm and hold a chaplet in their hand. Yet are these men nothing but snares of Hell, with their hypocritical exterior of piety. They give false counsel, and by their appearance mislead the world. From this class of riffraff your Majesty has selected your privy councillors and courtiers. These are your guardian angels, your Gabriel, Michael the Angel, Raphael, and Michael the Archangel, men who are dealers in adulterated wares. In public audience [49] they produce a feather or a straw, which to your Majesty they can make appear as a mighty mountain.'

To this discourse are added some verses, of which the sense is as follows:

'In Aurangzeb's reign the vile and low are favoured;
They pass by in mighty state and arrogance,
These are his companions and counsellors; they govern all:
The noble and learned are undone, he uses not such, they
have no place at his court.
The whole world wonders at seeing such misrule;
Behold to what condition we are reduced!
Asses plant kicks on noble horses, great men ride in fear.
Not a soul pays any attention to the King's orders;
The officials trade, buying and selling offices at court:
To-day, when done eating, they break their salt-cellar and
pay him with ingratitude.' [1]

---

1. The original Persian of these lines, as given in 'Khatut-i-Shiva Ji,' Royal Asiatic Society MS., No. 71, fol. 37, is as follows:

'Ba daur-i-Shah 'Alamgir Ghazi
Shudah sabun-faroshan sadr wa qazi.
Bud julahah wa bafindah rae naz.
Dar in buzm-i-malik gardidah ham-raz;
Arazal ra shudah an dastsgahc
Kih fazil bar dar-ash joyad panahe;
Ba dast-i-jahilan an ast pavah
Kih hargiz 'aliman ra nist mayah.
Ma'zallah! az in daur-i-pur-ashob
Kih tazi az kharan bashad lakad-kob.

'Seeing the destruction of this kingdom, and your inability even then to rule it, I felt forced to withdraw in deep dejection at the sight of such disorders, in order to restore my equanimity and live in peace, with the decorum befitting the refinement of my habits. May your Majesty live long! Quit the government, and I will rule the kingdom as it ought to be done. Journey [50] to Mecca, and when you have done so all men will tell of your greatness. During all these years you have ruled in grandeur and done what you pleased. Now that the shadows fall it is time to retire and begin to care for your soul. Your Majesty urges me to return to the Presence. Willingly would I do so if my youth did not inspire me with some fear. However, if your Majesty were only at the head of a small company, I, as the least among your sons, would come and throw myself at your feet and obey you in every particular.

'I refrain from writing here anymore, as I might, not wishing to weary you; and may the sun ever shine on your Majesty along with your sons.'

The inquiring reader will have already seen in the Fourth Part (IV. 187) what happened last year to the Portuguese of San Thome and their new chief captain, who had come from Goa to govern their quarter of the town. After his wound had healed he wrote to the Viceroy of Goa that he resigned the office of captain, and requested him to order someone else to take charge [51] of the government. The Viceroy, who was then Caetano de Mello,[1] issued an order to the Lord Bishop, Gaspar Affonço, to take over charge from the captain, and if he declined the task he could chose anyone he considered best fitted for the office.

Upon receipt of this order the Bishop assumed command, and governs up to this day. In the very first days of his rule he assembled the officials of the Portuguese quarter, and enjoined

---

Professor Jadunath Sarkar renders the first and second lines thus:

'In the age of Shah 'Alamgir Ghazi
Soap vendors have been made Sadr and Qazi.'

The rest is in the same strain; there is a general, but not verbal, agree¬ment with Manucci's version.

1. No. 69, Caetano de Mello de Castro, Viceroy, 1703-1707 (F. C. Danvers, ii. 489). The chief captain's name was N. S. Frade.

on them the imposition of a tax to meet the cost of a new standard; for it was already obvious that the old one, having been long in use, could not serve much longer. The officials remonstrated, pointing out to him the impossibility of the matter owing to the poverty of the inhabitants, who had hardly enough to eat. After meeting with different objections the Lord Bishop grew angry, and said to them, if they would not provide the money for the flag he would have the flagstaff removed. At this answer they were a little upset, and finally conceded what he desired.

But this did not end the discussion. The greatest impediment in this affair, they considered, was not knowing how, having no money, they could pay every month nearly one *pataca* (two rupees) to the person who would have to raise, fix, and lower the flag. This new difficulty caused the officials to ask for time before deciding.

[52] Finding there was great delay in giving the desired answer, the Bishop, after waiting eight days, sent again for the same officials and held forth to them at great length. He said to them that in olden days the city of San Thome was much renowned, and held in respect by both Mahomedans and Hindus. Let them not forget that at this city the Apostle St. Thomas had converted many men to Christianity. Thus it was fitting to raise aloft the standard of his Portuguese Majesty, and secure for him respect in these regions.

Some of the officials explained that the year before, while the flag was flying, the Mahomedans had come into the Portuguese ward and murdered some of the inhabitants, whereby up to the present the matter had remained in suspense. But to wind up with, the real difficulty in preparing the new Royal Standard was that the person who looked after the old flag demanded his pay for the year and a half then due to him. To start with, it was necessary to pay him, seeing there was no one else throughout the city fit for this duty.

The Lord Bishop was worn out by this affair and other government business, and being already advanced in years, he foresaw that he would have no peace. He therefore made over the direction of affairs to Nicolao Rodriguez, of whom I have already spoken (V. 20). The first [53] judgment pronounced by this new ruler was as follows:

A man in the Lord Bishop's employment sold a slave girl to a ship's captain living in Madras, a Catholic, named Francesco Noult (or Hoult). The price was twenty-six *pagodas*.[1] The girl absconded and took shelter in the Bishop's house. Upon receiving information the captain went to the Bishop's house to ask for his slave girl. The answer he got was that she was in no way a slave, but a free person, and this in spite of his producing the certificate of slavery and the contract of sale attested by the judge. Finding that he had lost the negress, the captain demanded the return of his money. They got rid of him by saying that the cleric had spent the money and had nothing wherewith to pay.

Some days after the said Rodriguez had assumed charge the servants of the clerics in the Lord Bishop's house assembled to the number of eleven, and at midnight went and set fire to the gate of Joa de Moraes Mixias, his Majesty's auditor.[2] Seeing the fire burning, this gentleman went to the window and shouted for help. The only answer he got from the students was a discharge of muskets. The bullets struck the window, and some fell inside the house. The auditor in turn seized his arms, and the fight went on for the rest of the night. This happened twice. The auditor was compelled in the end [54] to make a complaint to the Bishop, who replied, like the Paulist (*i.e.*, Jesuit)[3] he was, that if complainant would hold his tongue he would see the thing was stopped. Finding himself thus interfered with, and that there was no justice to be got, the auditor was forced to remove to Madras, and now he is on his way to Pegu.

In the year 1705, on the 2nd of October, I went to visit the Mahomedan ruler of San Thome, whose name is Molla Morat (Mulla Murad). While I was in conversation with him there came before him a poor *faqir*, all bruised and bleeding, with his head broken and his body covered with marks of blows. He

1. *Pagodas* are gold coins of the Hindu rajahs or kings. They are so called because they bear the figure of a *pagoda* (temple). They are equal in value to the Venetian *zecchino* (Cardeira).
2. In Portuguese *ovidor*, a kind of magistrate.
3. Paulist means a Jesuit. They have acquired this name from the Church of St. Paul in Goa, which they founded. It is outside the city, and at present there are only two Fathers, the air being bad (Cardeira).

cried out for justice to be done for the injuries inflicted on him. The governor [*i.e., faujdar*] inquired how it happened that he had been so badly treated. He arrived at the conclusion from the description that the culprit was a student serving-man of the Bishop of Mailapur. The *faqir* had asked him for alms at the house-door, instead of which he was given a sound bastonading.

The governor (or *faujdar*) was very much angered at such an act, and therefore ordered the hot-headed student to be brought before him; his name was Francesco Borges. The order could not, however, be executed, as the man hid in the house of the Most Illustrious Bishop, where he believed he would be safe. When the business is to deal out punishment, the Mahomedans have respect to no one, and make no distinctions. They attempted [55] to get hold of the delinquent. The governor sent several times for four days to ask the Lord Bishop to give the man up; but it was all in vain.

In the interval, by the interposition of friends, the criminal court was propitiated by a present made to it of fifty *patacas*. This money was realized by a tax imposed upon the people, as it is the custom to do in such cases. The affair just recounted caused two evils: one was that the money having been employed to satisfy the criminal court, it could not be used to make the flag; the other, that they omitted the usual procession of the Rosary in order not to have to deal with any tumult such as that occasion might give rise to.

On December 15 of the year 1705 began the Novaine of the Virgin Mary. This festival it is usual to hold every year at Monte Grande (Great Mount). On that day the musicians of the Lord Bishop appeared to take a part in the solemnities. Those gentlemen went for a stroll in the garden of the Honourable English Company [56], which is situated at the foot of the mount, and has in it a fine house for recreation. During this walk, without having any consideration for the Governor of Madras, these clerics and students took the liberty not only of removing fruit from the trees, but also of giving the gardeners a shoe-beating when they forbade them to pick the fruit. This piece of temerity came to the ears of the governor, and he sent twenty-five soldiers, Mahomedans and Hindus, who took the insolent clerics, and, dragging and pushing them, marched them off to the fortress of Madras, where they were locked up. Subsequently they were brought into the governor's presence. He released the culprits after they had begged their liberty and expressed repentance for their misdeeds.

In the month of March of the said year [1705] the Arabs returned with sixteen vessels to the territory of Daman. They landed four hundred soldiers and sacked several *aldces*, or villages. Without delay this invasion was reported to the governor of the town. But being very intent on his game of cards, he gave no sort of answer. A second message was brought; still he answered nothing, but went on with his game. Finally, on the third summons he answered that he would set things right at his own time, and went on playing.

The inhabitants of the [57] place, seeing their villages plundered and burnt, and the enemy advancing on the town, laid hold of the governor, and, collecting a few horsemen and some infantry, went out to meet the enemy. They behaved so bravely that they forced him to retreat. They killed fifty of his soldiers, and recovered a little of what had been plundered from the villages.

The governor of the place was sent to Goa in irons. It is quite likely that the man will be appointed to some greater position, since I have seen many a time such a thing happen to that sort of official; while those who are faithful and exert themselves for the Crown of Portugal are very soon either ruined or murdered.

[Omitted, fols. 57-64, a letter from the Archbishop of Goa of December 23, 1704, and his pastoral, dated December 22, 1704. These are a mere repetition of what was already appeared in Codex XLIV., Part IV., fol. 226. I resume on fol. 64.]

[64] At present there are living in Madras many Armenian merchants and a number of other persons of this race who frequent this port. Not many years ago they received a report from Persia that their race had suffered much by the gross injuries committed and the calumnies invented by those of their own nation. The Armenians are themselves the originators of these evils from the want among them of unanimity and concord. It is already known that the principal Patriarch of this race lives

usually not far from the city of Arivam (Erivan). His abode is about three days' journey from that city; the town is of considerable antiquity, and is called Uchiquilicia (Uch Qilissah),[1] which in our tongue means 'The Three Churches.' Great veneration is paid to the place because of the numerous and ancient holy relics there.

In the town called Zulfah, close to Isfahan, are three bishops; the first is called Alexandre, the second Mobies, and the third Ovanes. The last mentioned turned renegade, so nowadays his place has been taken by someone else. These bishops decline to obey the aforesaid Patriarch of the [65] Three Churches (whose name is Naapiet),[2] although anciently this was the custom; and this refusal has caused great enmity. On this account a great dispute arose among the population of Zulfah about the Patriarch, some being ready to obey him, and some declining to do so.

When the three bishops saw it was impossible for them to become absolute masters of the situation, they planned to take the Patriarch's life. To this intent they concocted a letter in the Patriarch's name, in which a great deal of ill and many abusive words were written about the King of Persia and the false prophet, Muhammad. Then they so manoeuvred that the letter should fall into the king's own hands through Armenians, who were friends of theirs and enemies of the Patriarch—men who professed to be zealous supporters of the Persian Crown.

The letter was in the Armenian tongue, and thus the king, like a wise man, was reluctant to believe the traitors. Therefore he called to the presence an aged Armenian from among the principal men, and ordered him to read out the letter. The old man, who was called Kalantar,[3] fearing some treachery, feigned to be ill, stood all in a tremble, and being nearly blind, was in that way able to excuse himself from reading it. Anxious to find out the truth, the king called in an old man from the

1. *Uch*, Turkish for 'three.' The place is about seventy miles south-west of Erivan, and lies on the Murad River. It is called Echmiadzin by the Armenians.
2. Mobies (possibly to be read Mobses) is properly Movses (Moses); Ovanes is meant for Yovhannes (John), pronounced Hohannes or Hohann; Naapiet (the Nahapiet of fol. 64) is properly Nahapet. (A. G. E.)
3. *Kalantar*, Persian, chief person or headman.

residents of Zulfah, called Gregorio Jamal, and giving [66] him the letter, ordered him to read it aloud.

When this man reached the passage which touched the honour of his Majesty, he began to tremble from head to foot to such an extent that he was unable to utter a word. Seeing this, the king told him to have no fear, but to read every word that was written, assuring him that he would not take any offence with him personally. After these reassuring words he managed to read, and when it was finished the king, being a young man, felt it deeply, and ordered a household slave to cut off the Patriarch's head.

The executioner reached the Three Churches when the Patriarch was saying Mass on Good Friday in the principal church. It was full of people, and various Armenian bishops and priests were present. The executor of the harsh order entered the church. It is impossible to describe sufficiently the amazement and confusion that at once spread among the bystanders. The man sprang up the altar steps, seized the Patriarch, and dragged him by main force out of the church preparatory to decapitating him. Among all those present there was not one who dared to hinder such a lamentable act.

Only [67] the principal men who, as good luck would have it, were present succeeded in persuading the executioner to allow the Patriarch to be divested of the ecclesiastical vestments before the carrying out of the royal orders. This short delay saved the Patriarch's life, for in the meantime a horseman arrived with a revised order from his Majesty: the Patriarch was no longer to be beheaded, but to be taken to prison instead.

The origin of this new order was traced to a faint suspicion that reached, I know not how, the ears of his Majesty that there had been the treachery we have already described. Anyhow, it is certain that when the king gave the first order the bishops already mentioned, with all the rest of their faction, betrayed great satisfaction. The renegade bishop also boasted among his friends of having been the causer of the royal order. Our Lord, who is a just ruler over all things, and the defender of the innocent, so worked that his Majesty penetrated the deception, although some doubts remained.

Therefore, to find out the rest of the facts, as told above, he caused the renegade bishop to be arrested, and ordered him to be questioned to find out if he was to blame. Although he did not confess the crime, his answers to the demands and cross-questioning of the judges had not been consistent. Therefore he was put to the torture vigorously. The man, unable to stand the torture, confessed that the letter had been drawn up by him at the instigation of the three Armenian bishops, and that for he same they had [68] given him a reward in money. At once, upon receipt of this confession, men were sent to arrest the three bishops, and after being well examined they confessed they were the culprits.

After their conviction they were subjected to a punishment as degrading as it was painful. It took place in the public square in front of the royal palace. The three bishops and the renegade were bound with their feet raised, so that half of their bodies touched the earth. Such a beating was then administered on the soles of their feet that their toe-nails and some of their toes dropped off. They were then released. A new tribute was imposed on the church of Zulfah, whereby they were called on to pay twenty thousand *patacas* in addition to the usual annual demand. However, the Patriarch was released from prison, subject to the penalty of paying yearly ten thousand patacas. These insults caused to the Armenians loss and to the Mahomedans profit; and the latter are guilty of a thousand outrages on the Christians. It is the custom of the Armenians, in whatever part of the world they have churches, to pray God on behalf of their patriarch, Nahapet, venerating him as their Pope, equally in their public as in their private prayers. It is only in the three churches of the above-named bishops that he is not prayer for. The above events happened in the year 1703.

It must be nearly five years since a similar thing happened in the town of Zulfah. Among their principal men was one called Abiett,[1] who became a renegade. He hated the bishops of his own people, and by a plot similar to that recounted above he obtained the torturing and condemnation to death of the chief bishop, whose name was Estefanus.[2] I do not dilate on it farther, or give any minute account, knowing that there is no deficiency of inquiring persons in Persia who write to Europe on these same events more clearly than I can do.

1. Avet (Promise), a Christian name.
2. Stefannos was the name of the interim patriarch at Uchkilissah for ten months in 1697: he was then imprisoned and died.

NOTE ON ARMENIAN TROUBLES IN PERSIA, 1703

I am much indebted to Mr. A. G. Ellis for the following notes from Armenian writers. They place the events referred to by Manucci in the text in their true historical setting.

'History of New Julpha in Isphahan,' by Yarouthiun Th.
Ter-Yovhaneants, Chancellor of the Convent
of the Universal Saviour in new Julpha
(new julpha, 1880)

I.

Vol I., pp. 210-221.

Martyrdom of Gregory . . . . . who is commonly called 'Loys Grigor' [Light Gregory], which took place in the reign of Shah Sultan Husain in the year 1703.

This Gregory was a native of the neighbourhood of Erivan, the son of poor parents. When eighteen years old he entered the service of a certain English merchant in the city of Isphahan. One day his father happened to be in the bazaar, when the skirt of his coat chanced to transgress against the water-pot of a certain shopkeeper, whereupon the latter beat him violently and wounded him for polluting the vessel. In his wounded condition the father went to the house of the English merchant, and related to his son what had happened. Moved with his father's injury, Gregory took with him two Moslem servants of the Englishman, and proceeded to the bazaar. They sought out the offending shopkeeper, beat him and wounded him, and dragged him to the house of the Englishman.

The other shopkeepers, indignant at such an act on the part of the servants of the English merchant, sought to retaliate violently upon Gregory, who had been the cause of this disturbance. For this purpose they concocted a false charge against him, and taking false witnesses, went to the Shaikh al-Islam, and declared that this Gregory had reviled their sacred Law, and demanded judgment according to law. The Shaikh al-Islam gave answer: 'If your words are true, this man must either die, or save his life by embracing our faith.' The complainants corroborated their words by means of their false witnesses, and obtained a judgment of death or apostasy. This judgment they carried to the Kazi of the city, and got it legalized by his seal, and then went to the governor of the city, who was a Georgian by race and a grandson of Shah Nawaz Khan, and laid it before him. The governor, seeing the crowd of shopkeepers and their zeal for the faith, was pleased thereat and impressed in their favour. Thereupon he sent some of his servants to the house of the English merchant to bring

Gregory and his fellow-servants, who had committed the assault. On their arrival there they made known the order, and demanded the surrender of the men.

At this time the English merchant, who had fallen ill, died, leaving behind him two English colleagues who were ignorant of the language and laws of the Persians. Being intimidated, they gave up to the governor's servants Gregory's two Moslem fellow-servants, who had joined him in assaulting the shopkeeper. These two were taken to the governor and put in prison, but Gregory was kept back.

The crowd were not satisfied, but went with the governor to the viceroy, to whom they complained clamorously, shouting: 'Have pity upon your people, Lord, and help us, for an infidel has violently beaten and wounded our fellow-believer, and dragged him with great insult and reviling to the house of his English master, and, not satisfied with this alone, has even reviled our law and faith.' In proof of this they produced the Fatwa of the Shaikh al-Islam and showed it to him, and again raising their voices, they shouted: 'Avenge our insulted Law, which is despised and contemned and brought low level with the dust. For an infidel has openly and freely reviled our Creed and our Prophet.' They kept repeating their shouting in these same words publicly, so that everyone could hear, and the viceroy was compelled to listen to their complaint, and promised to try the case the next day.

On the following day the crowd collected again at the viceroy's door, and importuned with the same words. The Englishmen, seeing that the vindictive passion of the shopkeepers increased daily, and becoming alarmed for the consequences of the affair, sent Gregory away and ordered him to hide in one of the villages until, as they said, the excitement of the mob should subside. Gregory went to his father's house, and remained there three days without seeking a hiding-place elsewhere.

During this time the complainants were perpetually at the viceroy's door, incessantly importuning him. He therefore called the English merchants' dragoman, and with intimidation and threats demanded Gregory of him. To this the dragoman answered: 'Since our servants raised this disturbance, we have dismissed them from our house, and sent them away, Gregory amongst them.' The viceroy would not listen to him, but urgently demanded Gregory, for he said he wished to examine him concerning this affair, and gave the dragoman to hope that, if he were found not guilty, he would release him without harm.

Gregory's father, who had been wounded, had remained in the Englishmen's house, and the dragoman mentioned him to the viceroy in order to free himself from his importunity, and said:

'He knows the place where his son is, and we do not.' The viceroy sent men to bring Gregory's father, who when they came, seeing the Englishmen careless with regard to him, seized him and bound him, and carried him to the viceroy, who ordered him to be put in prison, where they threatened him with death if he would not divulge where his son was. The viceroy's servants, seeing the supineness of the Englishmen in the matter, informed the complaining shopkeepers of it, and exhorted them not to abandon the cause until they had converted Gregory to their creed. Gregory's father they sometimes terrified with threats, sometimes led him by persuasive and deceitful words to think that there need be no fear on account of his son, for they said: 'He is not guilty, and the man he has wounded is walking about quite safe and sound. So do not be afraid, but tell us where your son is, and we will not allow a single hair of his head to be harmed, but the viceroy will release him after briefly examining him about this affair.' By these words of theirs, confirmed by an oath, Gregory's father was deluded, and called a certain Armenian, whom he made to write to his wife (for he himself did not know how to write) to have no apprehension with regard to Gregory, but to let him come. This letter was taken by the viceroy's servants, who went and gave it to Gregory's mother. She read it, and, deceived by her simplicity, gave her son into their hands, and they took him and returned with much exultation to the city.

When Gregory's accusers heard that he had been taken, with great joy they crowded round him and tried to intimidate him by threatening him with death if he would not embrace their faith. Gregory, however, refused to be frightened. When they saw that he made light of their words, they took him and brought him before the officer, to whom the viceroy had committed the investigation of the case. He endeavoured to shake Gregory's resolution by promising him money, possessions, and a handsome wife if he would apostatize, but the young man steadfastly refused. When the officer saw Gregory's firmness in his faith, and the boldness of his answers, he decided to report to the viceroy. When the shopkeepers learned this they crowded to him, and said: 'To you is committed the carrying out of this affair, and you ought to bring this man by force to our creed. If he refuses to be converted he ought to be put to death.' By various arguments they persuaded the officer to become their accomplice, and said to him: 'Do you inform the Viceroy that we wish Gregory brought to the public square of the city, so that we may finish the affair there by making reconciliation between the shopkeepers and the English merchants. Nevertheless, our real purpose is to kill him as soon as he arrives at the place.' Covering their intention by such deceit, they went in a crowd to the viceroy's court, and, repeating their accusations and protests, said: 'This young man has treated our laws with contempt, and has publicly beaten and wounded our co-religionist and dragged him with violence. And now, if it be your Lordship's pleasure that we should endure such an insult from this young infidel, your Highness shall be obeyed; but if not, do justice between us and him, and exact vengeance for our outraged laws.' With clamour of this kind they exaggerated the case, and demanded of the viceroy an order to bring Gregory publicly into the city. When those who were in attendance upon the viceroy heard their words, they all with one accord, as vindicators of the laws, said: 'He ought not to live.'

Then the viceroy ordered his servants to bind Gregory and bring him to the public square, and to make an effort to convert him, but, if he should refuse, to inform him, so that he might notify to the king concerning the young man. The viceroy gave this order because he was unaware of the real intention of the mob.

Upon receiving this command the executioners stripped Gregory, leaving him only his shirt and drawers, and drove him towards the market-place, the mob surging round him and continually endeavouring to terrify him with horrible threats, telling him to embrace Islam, or if not they would kill him with stone and steel. They tied his arms behind his back with such severity that the blood flowed from the cords. They lashed and beat him, and were incessantly striking him on the head and subjecting him to every kind of ill-usage. Crowding round him, the mob kept dragging him about in the market-place, and everyone kept exhorting him to be converted, some with threats and some with persuasive arguments. But Gregory, steadfastly enduring all his sufferings, boldly answered, refusing to apostatize. When the Christians who were present heard his answer and saw him bound in such wretched plight, they were touched with compassion and wept aloud.

Hereupon the executioners laid hold upon Gregory and brought him to the city square, where at sight of him the multitude of the aliens crowded together on all sides. Here they brought him through the crowd to the King's Inn, which is opposite the Mint, and haled him up to the top of it.

An aged shopkeeper approached him, and, whilst others of the mob stood round him, addressed him persuasively, endeavouring to bring him over to Islam, and promising him various rewards. They brought also at the same time a handsome mantle, and a number of the shopkeepers said to him: 'This is a sign of our promise to you, and now do you put it on. and do not continue obdurate, but go and kiss the hand of the chief of the merchants.' Gregory, however, absolutely refused to comply.

When the mob of aliens despaired of converting Gregory, one of them struck him on the back with a stout stick. When the crowd saw this they rushed upon the young man and threw him down to the ground. One of them drew his sword and struck at his chest with it, but others, snatching Gregory away, threw him into a chamber in one of the shops and locked the door, preventing his execution, in the hope that it might yet be possible to win him over. They called to him from without, saying: 'Now be persuaded by our words, for then you will certainly live.' But he from within courageously confessed Christ God.

When the mob heard this, with a great shout they attacked the chamber, broke open the door and rushed in. One of them slashed Gregory on the face with a sword; others stabbed him in the heart; others, again, stoned him. The yelling of the stoners chilled with horror those who were near.

The body of Gregory was carried to Erivan, and buried there before the altar in the Martyr Chapel of the Church [? of St. Sergius]. His martyrdom took place in the eighth year of Shah Sultan Husain, in the year 1153 of the Armenian Era [*i.e.*, A.D. 1703], on July 20, the Feast of St. Nerses the Patriarch and St. Haggai the Bishop.

NOTE BY THE AUTHOR.—The original of this narrative is a small pamphlet, the author of which, although not known by name, was contemporary, and was perhaps identical with one of the Armenian eyewitnesses who were present at the time of Gregory's martyrdom. It is an obscure and confused piece of composition.

II.

Ibid., Vol. II., pp. 30-33.

Ter stephannos, Bishop of Julpha, pupil and disciple of Ter Dauith (David), after the death of his teacher, by the desire and unanimous election of the people of Julpha was ordained prelate in the year 1684.

In the first year of his prelacy he imposed the diocesan tax, or contribution, upon the clerical priests of India, issuing a Bull concerning this, in which, after severely reprimanding the insubordination of those priests who had gone to India without a Bull or order from the prelate, he adds, saying: 'This tax we have laid upon the priesthood in India in the same manner as it is levied upon the priests here, and it is our will that each priest give yearly two *tomans* to his impoverished and tribute-burdened Church.' He exerted himself diligently to pay off the tribute of the Church of Julpha, which had been imposed by Shah Sulaiman, and in respect of this having paid 400 *tomans*, he obtained a farman of freedom, although the tribute itself was not completely paid off until the time of the prelate Moses.

In the time of Stephannos a great disturbance arose between the Gregorians and the Armenian Papists of Julpha. The Shahrimaneans aided and protected the Papists, and desired to propagate their tenets amongst the Gregorian Armenians of Julpha by means of a prelacy of the Jesuit Fathers. Stephannos, with the other magistrates of Julpha, vigorously opposed them, and, appealing to the king Shah Sulaiman, obtained a *farman* for the expulsion of the Fathers and the demolition of their church. Of these matters I shall give a full account in their own place.

Stephannos printed in the Convent of the Universal Saviour a book against the Papists called 'Hakacharouthun' ('Counterblast'), concerning which the Papists falsely alleged to the alien Government that the words of the book were against the doctrine of the Koran. On account of this they obtained 200 tomans damages, whilst on the other side other 200 *tomans* had to be paid as a bribe to the alien Government. Of these sums 200 *tomans* were obtained from the magistrates and notables of Julpha, whilst the rest was assessed on the poorer people.

In the year 1697 Stephannos received a letter, bearing the signatures of all the bishops of Holy Echmiadzin, urgently entreating him to accept the see of the catholicate, the Catholicos Nahapet having been expelled. Having obtained, therefore, a mandate from the people of Julpha and a decree from the king Shah Sulaiman, he proceeded to Echmiadzin. Here, however he did not prosper. He was denounced and slandered to the alien governor of Erivan by the partisans of Nahapet, who induced the latter by bribes to transmit their accusations to Shah Sulaiman. The king condemned Stephannos to pay a fine of 1,000 *tomans* (which was discharged by the Convent of the Universal Saviour), and caused him to be thrown into prison, where he died under torture on January 4, 1698.

After Stephannos had resigned the prelacy of Julpha, and had succeeded to the See of Echmiadzin, the Convent of the Universal Saviour was still liable for debts counting to 1,000 tomans, which had been contracted in the time of his prelacy on account of various works of public and private utility, as well as for 1,000 *tomans* in respect of fines over and above the before-mentioned burden.

Ibid., Vol. II., pp. 34, 37.

Ter Alexander, Bishop of Julpha, by the desire of the people of his diocese succeeded to the see in the year 1669. He governed his spiritual flock with excellent policy until 1706, in which year, having been elected Catholicos of Echmiadzin by the hierarchy of the Armenian nation, in accordance with a royal decree he left Julpha, and proceeded to Echmiadzin to take possession of the throne of the patriarchate He died on November 22, 1714.

Ibid., Vol. II., pp. 49, 50.

Ter Movses, after the resignation of Bishop Alexander in 1706, by unanimous election succeeded to the See of Julpha.... He died on March 1, 1725.

III.

Ibid., Vol. II., 264-267.

The Roman Armenians came from Armenia to Isphahan with the great migration of 1605. From the beginning they were always hostile to the Gregorian Armenians.

In 1064 A.H., 2 Rabi' I. (January 21, A.D. 1654) the Gregorians obtained a decree from Shah 'Abbas (1642-1667) prohibiting churches of the Frank from being built in Julpha. Nevertheless, the Latin Armenians succeeded in obtaining permission to found seven churches, either through the intervention of the French Consul or by their own interest. These churches were: (1) St. Avetikh, founded by the influential Roman Armenian family of the Shahrimaneans; (2) St. Elias, commonly called the Carmelite Church; (3) St. Joseph, called the Jesuit Church, because it was founded by that Order; (4) the Dominican Convent; (5) the Augustinian Convent, in Husainiyah; (6) the Carmelite Convent in Godmir; and (7) the Capuchin Convent, in Ghalatabaruk (Kal'ah Tabarik). The last-named three churches were within the city of Isphahan, each in a specially assigned quarter, whilst the first four were founded in Julpha. Of four of these churches not a trace now (1871) remains. Of two others the ruins are still visible—namely, those of the Jesuit Church and of St. Avetikh of the Shahrimaneans. The Dominican Convent alone is still intact, in the Khocher quarter.

The Papist missionaries endeavoured in various ways to convert the Gregorian Armenians to Romanism, such as by monetary aid to the needy, specious persuasion, or by receiving sympathetically and kindly those who had incurred the rebuke of their spiritual superiors. The prelates of Julpha, on the other hand, strove to prevent their progress by vigorous opposition, either by invoking the aid of Government authority, or by the exercise of their own episcopal power.

This hostile activity has remained unextinguished until this day. The Papists labour incessantly to sow dissension in the Armenian Church, whilst the guardians of the Gregorian community endeavour by every means in their power to protect their flock from the wiles of these strangers. The smouldering hostility between the Gregorians and the Papists was first blown into flame in the reign of Shah Sulaiman (1667-1694) in the year 1688. Jesuit fathers had come to Isphahan, and had founded the church which is called the Jesuit Church. They opened schools in Julpha for the education of children, and began to preach after their fashion, and endeavoured to win over the people. At this time the Prelate of the Convent of the Universal Saviour was Bishop Stephannos, who was possessed with an implacable hatred against the Papists. In championing the cause of his people he brought great tribulation upon the Jesuit preachers. He complained to the King, Shah Sulaiman, that strangers had come to

Persia from European parts, and were disturbing the peace of the Armenian people; that they had opened schools, and were endeavouring to lead astray the children of the simple-minded, and were inciting the people to quarrel with one another; that such was their apparent object, but that their secret purpose was to spy out the incoming and outgoing of Persia, and to report upon all the passes of the country to the European Governments. By such ingenious and plausible accusations the Jesuit fathers were rendered odious in the eyes of the Persian Government. The Shahrimaneans, however, came to the aid of the Jesuits, and by expending large sums in bribing both the religious heads of Isphahan and the officers of the Government, they obtained a farman that the schools of the Jesuits should not be closed, and that there should be no hindrance to their preaching. The magistrates of Julpha on their part also acted in the same way against the Shahrimaneans, and did not spare the expenditure of large sums of money. The party of the Gregorians was in the end successful, for in the year 1689 they obtained a *farman* from Shah Sulaiman. One of the churches of the Romans, that of the Carmelites, was demolished, and some of the Jesuit preachers were expelled, amongst them the priest Jacobus, and the Papist party was much humbled.

At this time a book was printed in the Convent of the Universal Saviour, directed against the Dyophysites.[1] Hereupon the opportunity was seized by the Papists to declare falsely to the Government that the Armenians had printed a book against the doctrine of the Koran, and in order to clear himself from this slander the Prelate Stephannos was compelled to expend a sum of 500 *tomans*. In consequence of this determined hostility, Stephannos, together with his clergy, went in procession, wearing chasubles and bearing blackened candles, to the *Maidan* of Julpha, and solemnly excommunicated the house of the Shahrimaneans, because that, through the help which they had afforded to the Jesuits, such great trouble and mischief had resulted. When the Gentiles, on seeing this ceremony, asked what the Prelate and his clergy were doing, they replied: 'Just as you curse your Sunni heretics, so we curse our heretics.'

The rest of this miserable story would neither be worth relating nor pleasant to read, *et cetera*.

IV.

'Biographical Dictionary of Eminent Men,' By Mattheos Maghakh-Theophileants. (Venice, 1839.) Vol. II., p. 4

NAHAPET, Catholicos of Armenia, was a native of Edessa and a

1. Dyophysites—*i.e.*, the adherents of the doctrine of two natures in Christ, otherwise the Romans.

disciple of the Catholics Eliazar, his predecessor. He was a good and gentle-spirited man. On the death of Eliazar in 1691 he was elected Catholicos. He rebuilt the church of Shoghakath and its belfry. Having heard that certain Armenians in Rome had accused their people of heresy, he wrote to Pope Innocent XII., praying him not to give ear to vagabond persons from Armenia. After this letter was sent, a certain lover of strife stirred up the people to hatred against the Catholicos because he had written a letter to Rome, with the result that in 1695 they expelled him from his see, and put in his place Stephannos [of Julpha]. The latter, however, on account of his turbulent conduct, was himself expelled after ten months by the monks, and was put in prison, where he shortly after died. Hereupon Nahapet returned to his see.

At this time there reached the Catholicos an epistle of congratulation from Pope Innocent, which was at the same time a reply to his own letter, sent by the hand of the priest, Khachatour of Karin, and accompanied by presents suitable to the honour of his see. In his letter the Pope advised Nahapet to offer a declaration of faith to the banished malcontents in the West, and the Catholicos wrote him an answer of acceptance, gratitude, and submission. The succeeding Pope, Clement XI., also wrote to Nahapet a letter of love and friendship, commending to his care the Western priests Joseph and Peter, who were sent to preach in Persia, and exhorting him to remain firm in union and friendship, and to continue in intimate correspondence with the Holy See of Rome.

Nahapet lived a few years longer, and died on June 13, 1705. His see remained vacant a whole year on account of the difficulty of choosing his successor, but at length Alexander of Julpha was elected.

V.

Ibid., Vol. I., p. 25.

Alexander of Julpha, Catholicos of Armenia, sat in the seat of St. Gregory in 1707. He wrote a letter of submission to Pope Clement XI. in his own name and in that of the whole Armenian nation, and received in return a letter of blessing from his Holiness, and died in 1714, lamented by the whole nation on account of his piety.

In the same season there arrived from Persia two Armenian friars of the Order of St. Dominic,[1] one called Friar Minas de Siave and the other Friar Thomas Abarenes. These friars had come with the sole object of collecting the money due to Father Friar Domingos, deceased, of the same order, of which I have sufficiently spoken, as will have been seen (IV. 165). As soon

1. This has been already touched on in Part IV., fol. 165.

as they arrived they endeavoured to recover the money which was in the hands of Armenian agents living in Bengal, to whom the deceased had consigned it. Immediately upon the arrival of the friars these Armenians handed over the money in their possession, as they were in duty bound to do if they wished to carry out the will.

There were, however, four thousand *patacas* in possession of another Armenian trader, a renegade called Coja Ovan (Khwajah Ovan),[1] who lived [70] in Madras. The Reverend Father Michel Ange, Vicar of Madras, went and demanded that money from the above Armenian on behalf of the Abate di San Giorgio,[2] whose command was that the money be deposited with him in the space of twenty-four hours. To this demand the renegade replied that he could not do the contrary of what was laid down in the will. He fled from Madras and took up his abode in San Thome, as he owed money to various merchants.

The Abate di San Giorgio was then living in San Thome in the house of a French merchant called Monsieur Gueti,[3] This gentleman did his utmost to make the said Abate understand things, so that he might not throw the Christian community into confusion. All was, however, fruitless. Never would he be content to desist; he was too eager for the money of the deceased friar. This I assert by the tokens thereof he gave in San Thome.

It is necessary to explain that in the territory of San Thome lived an Augustinian friar called Frey Manoel das Neves. He gained a living by buying and selling cheese, shoes, handkerchiefs, *et cetera,* between Paliacate[4] and Madras. It is a ten-hour

1. This must be the Coja Awan of the Madras Records. On March 27, 1704, he is reported to have used influence with the *faujdar* of San Thome to procure the imprisonment of his creditor, Coja Timore. On April 6 Governor Pitt ordered Awan's house to be broken open, and his goods seized for the benefit of his creditors. The *faujdar* then sought an interview with the Governor. Finally, in July, Coja Timore was released, and a settlement (in regard to the estate of Coja Usuph) was arrived at on July 24, 1704 ('Press List of Ancient Records in Fort St. George,' No. 7, entries Nos. 1457, 1469-1471, 1524, 1533, 1542, 1557).
2. As to the Abate di San Giorgio, see note 4, Vol. IV., Part IV., fol. 165.
3. For Monsieur Guety (or Guelly), see also IV. 70, 188: V. 241. 242, 244, 261, 284.
4. Pulicat, the Dutch factory, twenty-four miles north of Madras ('Madras Manual of Administration,' iii. 670).

journey from the one place to the other. The Abate wanted the Frate to give him a little something out of the gains squeezed from this miserable trade. While the two were arguing and the poverty-striken friar was defending [71] himself, I, too, turned up, and just in time; for I was forced to separate them, if I did not wish to see them give each other a hearty shoe-beating.

But returning to the above-named friars the two Dominicans from Persia): for all the efforts they made to recover the money from the renegade (Khwajah Ovan), they could never obtain it, for their debtor was in Mahomedan territory. The Reverend Father Fra Michel Ange made over to them a few things that he had in his custody.

[Omitted, fols. 71-73, the account of Father Peter Paul, the barefooted Carmelite. It has already appeared in Codex XLIV., Part IV., fols. 231-233. I resume on fol. 73.]

[73] In the month of February in the year 1705 the wife of A'zam Shah died; her name was Jani Begam,[1] and she was the daughter of the prince Dara Shukoh. The death of this princess caused great sorrow in the army, but greatest of all among the principal men and the older nobles, as it revived in them the memory of Dara's good qualities, the prudence, the good administration, with which he ruled over the things put under him. This princess never showed any pain or anger at the act of her husband, A'zam Shah, in bringing into his palace a public woman as his consort. From this time henceforth there is no survivor of the blood of Dara. His son Sultan Sipihr Shukoh was married to a daughter of Aurangzeb, and [74] was kept a prisoner in the fortress of Salimgarh, as I have already stated in my First Part (I. 256, 278). In these days nothing is said of him, and it is not known whether he is alive or dead.

The above-mentioned Jani Begam left a good name behind her for generosity and liberality, and for never having given protection to injustice. Thus many times she stopped her own

1. Jahan Zeb Bano Begam, known as Begam Jani, daughter of Prince Dara Shukoh, wife of Prince A'zam Shah, and mother of Prince Muhammad Bedar Bakht, died in Shawwal, 1116 H. (January 28 to February 25, 1705, N.S.), at Ahmadabad Gujarat (Tarikh-i-Muhammadi,' 1116 H.). For this lady, see also note 195, Vol. II., Part II., fol. 144.

husband when he wanted to plot rebellions and revolutions against King Aurangzeb. But such a good name was not left behind her by the queen Tagimal (Taj Mahal), wife of the King of Gulkandah, and mother of two princesses, who by a piece of cruelty which she committed lost both her good fame and her reason, as I will now recount.

King Abu, I Hasan of Gulkandah[1] one day, when out hunting, passed through a village where he saw a young and good-looking shepherd woman. Falling in love with her, he demanded her from her parents, assigning to them several villages for their maintenance. He carried the lovely shepherd girl away with him to his palace. Although she was of lowly birth, and of a somewhat black complexion, she was otherwise perfect both in body and mind. Therefore the king showed her great affection, but without any intention of annoying others.

The queen Taj Mahal betrayed jealousy at this act of her husband's, and looked on this poor young woman with an eye of severity. She showed the disdain and hate she bore to her rival. Finally, unable any longer to repress her rage, she chose a day when the king had gone [75] to the chase, and ordered the shepherdess to be tied to a tree in the garden, and her clothes, after being stepped in oil, were to be set alight. These orders were executed. She, too, wished to be a spectator of this barbarity, and visited the fatal spot at the time when the miserable girl was enduring all the agonies of that torture, and, although almost ready to give up the ghost, her body was still writhing and struggling. Her movements were so horrifying to the sight that Cruelty itself could not have beheld them without some sentiment of compassion or, at any rate, of horror.

So it happened to the cruel queen, for in spite of her looking on in great contempt at the mortal anguish of the unhappy shepherd girl, she was unable to control herself at such a dreadful sight, and fell into such a serious plight herself that she became mad. During the whole of the rest of her life she never ceased to tremble and go through all the contortions of the burning shepherdess. Thus the women who had the charge of her were frequently frightened. Nothing could cure her. Neither this affliction of the queen nor her death caused any grief either to

1. Abu,l Hasan, Qutb Shah, reigned 1672-87.

her subjects or the king. The latter never went even to see her, and everybody spoke against her cruelty.

In order that the reader by the variety of matter may pass his time more agreeably, I will relate an incident that happened in the year 1665 at the Court of Dihli.

There arrived at the court of Dihli a merchant of precious stones; [76] he had made frequent voyages between India and Europe. As the man knew he would be unable to sell his goods as easily as in the time of King Shahjahan, he had recourse to a doctor of his nation"[1] who was in the service of Aurangzeb, and fairly well esteemed at the court. He took up his quarters at the physician's house with a view to obtaining his help in selling the jewels he had brought. The astute trader dealt with the doctor politely and showed him respect. He was aware that he and his wife did not live on very good terms. She was the daughter of Francisco de Souza, a Portuguese, of whom I fancy I spoke in my Third Part (III. 253). The trader told the husband that he had made a mistake by marrying in India, and if he were in France he assured him His Most Christian Majesty would have greatly honoured him, on account of his ability to afford so much information about the Mogul court. The trader only said these things in order to make him happy and be able to negotiate his own affairs.

While this conversation was proceeding there tumbled out of the doctor's bag the portrait of his wife. The trader said if only he had not been married, he could have returned to France, where he would have found a wife both richer and more beautiful than this one. The frivolous surgeon was put into great good-humour by this talk, and conceiving great affection for the friendly merchant, Monsieur Tavirnier (J. B. Tavernier), made all possible [77] efforts to sell his jewels for him. In fact, his efforts were successful, and the merchant, highly satisfied, started for Europe.[2]

1. The diamond merchant intended is J. B Tavernier (see a little further on). In his 'Voyages,' edition of 1692, iii. 94, he speaks of knowing in 1666 a physician at the Court named François de la Palisse, *alias* Saint Jacques. This man had a Portuguese wife.
2. Tavernier and Manucci do not seem ever to have met. In 1665-66 Manucci was not at Dihli, but in the Dakhin or at Lahor. By 1698-99, when he began to write, I surmise that Manucci was in possession of Tavernier's book, which appeared first in 1677.

The surgeon, too, was anxious to take his departure for Europe, and bought some diamonds. At that time the king ordered him to undertake the treatment of an officer called Fazulacam (Faizullah Khan),[1] one of Begam Sahib's guard, who lived in a province six days' journey from court. Before he started he got hold of an ancient matron to direct his household, and she consented that while he was absent she would give his wife a poison that he had prepared for the purpose. He rewarded her with a little money, and held out hopes that on his return he would again reward her.

The good old woman, knowing the estimable conduct of this most upright wife, took compassion on her, and revealed what was going on by showing her the money and the paper holding the poison. The wife reflected on the bad conduct of her husband. For, instance, he allowed her to go only once a year to church, and disliked her meeting her brothers and relations. She therefore wrote to one of her aunts, who lived in the city of Lahor, whose name was Maria de Ataides,'[2] the renegade wife of 'Ali Mardan Khan, of whom I have spoken several times (I. 124, III. 228). In her letter she stated all that had happened.

On hearing from her niece, Maria de Ataides started from Lahor, and soon reached the court. She presented herself before the king, and told him the whole story adding that her niece was desirous of becoming a Mahomedan [78]. At once the king gave an order to send soldiers to the surgeon's house and bring back his wife and sons to the palace, using force if necessary. This order was executed with all speed. The lady, appropriating all that was most valuable, took her little son of eight, named Ignatio, and removed to her aunt's dwelling. The elder son of the lady, at the time she left her home, had gone on a visit to some of his relations. When they heard rumours of what was going on in her house they concealed him, and thus, at the age of thirteen, he was sent away to live at Daman.[3]

1. Faizullah Khan may be intended for the man of that name (son of Zahid Khan, Kokah), who was brought up by Begam Sahib. He was long *faujdar* of Muradabad, and died there. He had a craze for keeping a menagerie ('Ma,asir-ul-Amara,' iii. 28).
2. Spelt 'Taides' in Part III., fol. 228.
3. The outline of this story about St. Jacques, the surgeon, and his family will be found in the Annual Letter from the Jesuit Mission of the 'Mogor' for 1670-78, written by Father Joan Paulo Oliva (British Museum

The surgeon's wife pressed the king for an order to have her elder son returned to her; his name was Joao. The surgeon was at once summoned to the court, and he was ordered straight to prison, without knowing what was going on at his house. The miserable man received first a thorough beating, to see if he would state where his son was; but he was never able to say anything, the truth being that he did not know. Finally, he was liberated, and his pay reduced by two rupees a day, one being applied to his wife's and one to his son's support. Afterwards the king ordered Maria de Ataides to return to her home at Labor. She started, taking with her the little Ignatio and all the wealth found in the surgeon's house. These events [79] happened in 1666. Some years afterwards—that is, in 1669[1]—I left Goa, and transferred myself to the city of Lahor, where I practised as a medical man, as already stated in my Second Part, and made the acquaintance of Maria de Ataides.

The afflicted surgeon made great effort to recover his little son, but never succeeded. The child's detainers were too strongly protected. Maria de Ataides taught him in the Mahomedan way, and he learnt to read the Quran. The Maria de Ataides in question had an ancient eunuch in her service who directed her household. He was a very avaricious man, and advised his mistress to kill her niece and take possession of her property. The lady, without further consideration, accepted the proposal and gave her niece poison.

While the niece was in the throes of death, an old woman-servant of hers came secretly to call me in. I started in all haste, but did not arrive in time to be of any use to her, the whole of her body having already become black. Therefore, when I had enjoined her to ask God's forgiveness, she called upon the name of Jesus as well as she could, and shortly afterwards expired.

Additional MS., No. 9,855, fol. 896). By his Portuguese wife, born in Bengal, St. Jacques had two sons, Joao and Ignatio. Taking the elder boy with him, he followed the Court to Agrah. His wife's aunt, a renegade widow, then came to Dihli, and carried away the wife, the younger son, and all the man's property. St. Jacques, by the advice of the Agrah Jesuits, sent off his son Joao at once to the Jesuit College at Hugli. The qazi seized St. Jacques, and he was promised liberty if he would renounce Christianity, but he remained firm in the faith.

1. Perhaps this date should be read '1667,' for 1669 seems too late for Manucci's departure from Goa, according to his statements elsewhere.

When the surgeon heard of his wife's death he was quite happy, and over and over again asked the king for leave to return to his own country, but all in vain. Once more he wrote a letter to Maria de Ataides, in which he said she ought to send back his son at once. If she did not, he had decided to make the boy over to Begam Sahib, who [80] would send men to seize him.

Maria de Ataides was annoyed at this threat, and was, in addition, afraid of some censure against her being issued by the court. Thus, she had the boy circumcised at once, and continued his training in Mahomedan tenets. Whenever I had the opportunity I never omitted to console the boy, to teach him, and hold out hopes that his father would still be of some benefit to him. Seeing that the youth received consolation from, and believed in, my words, and being also anxious to deliver him from Mahome-danism, I took the liberty of saying to him that if he wanted to leave that house and go to his father, I would help him and provide the necessary expenses. I knew that his father was waiting for him, and meant to marry him to the daughter of the officer in command of the fortress of Daman, who was providing her with a dowry of twenty thousand rupees.

To these overtures the youth replied that he would carry out all my orders. At once and in secret I found four guardians who could represent the youth before the courts, if upon obtaining his liberty he should endeavour to recover part of what belonged to his mother. The youth left the house secretly and joined these guardians, who were in waiting. They took him without delay to the *qazi's* court, a man who was my friend, and to whom I had [81], in addition, recommended this client's interests in the shape of some presents I had given him.

The guardians' action was such that the boy Ignatio was restored to liberty, and recovered something, though nothing of consequence, out of what had belonged to his mother. This small effort cost me two thousand rupees, which equal one thousand *patacas*. I reported to his father, then at the court in Dihli, what had been managed, at the same time advising him that as soon as his son arrived he should send him into Portuguese territory, so as to be protected from Mahomedan outrage.

When Ignatio reached the paternal dwelling he was very pleased, but, finding that his father was not sending him away from Mahomedan territory, as I had suggested, he said to him:

'My father, why do you keep me in the house, and do not at once send me into Portuguese territory? Do you not see that one of the days the Mahomedans will come to steal me?' The ignorant father answered that he kept him in his house to revenge himself on Maria de Ataides, and to be able to recover the plunder that his wife had robbed him of. What an impossibility!

Thus my counsels were of no use to him, nor did in aught avail the words and repeated insistence of his son. We shall see what things came to pass. After twelve days the men of Maria de Ataides went to Dihli, and asserting that the youth was in his father's house, they went before the king and recounted to him the above circumstances. Forthwith the king ordered [82] soldiers to be sent to seize the youth and bring him to the Presence. As soon as the king saw him he appointed him one of his pages, with charge of carrying his sword during audience, being a well-formed and graceful youth. Then after some years he was appointed captain of artillery, and at the present time he is married and has sons and daughters.

Let us now turn to the case of his brother, Joao, who, already having reached a young man's estate, went to live in Portuguese territory. There he married a Portuguese lady, giving himself out as a Portuguese of good birth, and adopting the name of Don Joao Jaques de Menezes. In this he was aided by the Jesuits, who were his father's friends; but his father supplied him with the necessary expenses. This wife of his was of noble blood, and her name was Donna Roza de Castro. I know not how, but her parents found out that he was in no way of Portuguese blood, as he had declared. They therefore set on foot a conspiracy to murder him.

This plot did not remain concealed from Joao; he therefore decided on flight to Masulipatam. There he married again the Portuguese widow of a very rich English captain who had a little son. They transferred themselves to Bengal and led an extravagant life, and in a few years all the money was at an end [83]. He led his wife and his stepson a very unhappy life, and the latter in desperation went to his stepfather when he was asleep and shot him through the head by several balls from an arquebus.

The old surgeon stayed on at the court without obtaining leave to depart. Then he decided on flight from Aurangabad for Daman. This he managed to do, but the end was not favourable. At the time I arrived at Surat orders had been received to catch the surgeon who had fled from the court. He was very easy to recognise, for he bore a knife-scar across his face from one ear to the other, due to a wound inflicted by one of his compatriots. I was then in Dihli newly from Persia.[1] The governor, in his attempts to find the surgeon, learnt that a surgeon (that being I) had arrived from court.

At once he sent off a messenger to my house, who informed me, on behalf of the governor, that I must at once appear in his presence. At the time I had fever, and the insolent fellow (they are all like that) would not take my excuses, or accept the complimentary message that I sent to the governor, whose name was Cartalapan (Kar-talab Khan).[2] The man spoke with great rudeness, and made as if he meant to take me away by force. At this movement I lost patience, and, getting to my feet, I laid hold of him, gave him several shoe strokes, and threw him downstairs. Thus beaten as he was, he returned to the presence of the governor with outcries, making out [84] a little more than he had suffered. As the governor was a cautious man he sent a person of standing, making over to him the letter from the court, in which was entered the mark on the face as a means of recognising the surgeon.

On his reaching my house, as soon as I saw him I recognised that we were old friends. He reported the facts to the governor, and he sent word to me that as soon as I was well again he would come to see me. Three days having elapsed, the fever left me, and I repaired to the governor's. I was well received by him, as he required medicines from me. Whilst we were in conversation they brought in the surgeon. He was taken away for that night to another house, and next morning was sent back to court. These events took place in 1680,[3] in the month of

1. Surely he must mean 'in Surat newly from Aurangabad'!
2. There was a Kar Talab Khan, Muhammad Beg, removed from charge of Surat in the twenty-eighth year, 1095-96 H. (August, 1684, to August, 1685). but I do not know when he was appointed (see 'Ma-asir-i-'Alamgiri,' 247).
3. There was a Kar Talab Khan, Muhammad Beg, removed from charge of Surat in the twenty-eighth year, 1095-96 H. (August, 1684, to August, 1685). but I do not know when he was appointed (see 'Ma-asir-i-'Alamgiri,' 247).

September. In 1686 the king consented to his leaving, looking on him as a man already old and no longer of any use.

This same doctor in 1672 had another mishap. Being then, as I have said, desirous of leaving for Europe, he expended seven thousand rupees on diamonds. He showed his purchase to a young man, who in his wanderings had arrived at his house. Being a fellow-countryman, he placed great faith in him, and never dreamt of his plotting [85] treachery against him.

One day when the doctor had gone to make his appearance at court, the ungrateful youth opened the casket with a key that he had got made, and took the diamonds and as much money as seemed to him necessary for expenses. He then fled. He might have carried off a great deal more than he actually took, but this he refrained from doing, not wishing to carry such a weight as would hinder the celerity of his movements. When the surgeon returned from the audience hall to his house, he perceived the loss he had suffered. By much exertion he sent off different persons in many directions to search for the thief. He also wrote to the [European] factors living at the seaports. But all his efforts produced no results, for never more was that young man heard of. It may well be that he was robbed by other thieves and his life taken, as on many occasions I have seen happen.

I pray the prudent reader not to grow angry at such advice, but if I write it so often, I do it solely to warn any inquiring traveller who may wish to wander through the world, and teach him at others' cost how to look after himself. In voyaging prudence is required, and, above all, patience, for in most instances it is only through the rashness of youth that such difficulties arise; and men are generally the originators of their own ruin, and may risk even the loss of life. The following story will serve as an example:

When I was a youth [86], at the beginning of Aurangzeb's reign, it was my custom to go out on Thursdays. On that day there is a great concourse of men and ladies of the city [Dihli], who come out to visit sepulchres and obtain recreation in the gardens of Khwajah Qutb-ud-din, outside the city of Dihli—as I have said before—some to pray and some to enjoy themselves. I, too, went to take the air in those gardens. I was also curious to see certain festivals that it is usual to hold several times in the year in the fields, in gardens, and on the banks of streams, reservoirs, *et cetera*.

While returning one day from the garden of Khwajah Qutb-ud-din on the way to my house, I saw a carriage coming a long way oft. It withdrew out of the direct road, and went down into the open fields. Seeing this manoeuvre, I assumed that it had moved out of the highway for fear I might do it some harm. I knew that in the carriage was a public dancing girl; it was surrounded by fifteen pages, and followed by a horseman. Without taking time to reflect, I turned my steps with all possible speed towards the carriage, shouting to it to stop. It paid no attention, however, to my voice, but went on its way peacefully.

Seeing that I was not obeyed, I decided to make a display of courage, so I seized a stick, and, going up to the carriage, gave the pages several blows. Seeing that the game was not a joke, these men followed the example of the horseman, abandoned the carriage, and took to their heels. At that point I raised the cloth that [87] covered the carriage, and saw the dancer. I gave her some abusive language, not forgetting, however, to keep my eyes open to see if any succour was on its way.

This precaution of mine was not uncalled for, since at this moment I saw afar off a troop of cavalry coming in my direction. I left the carriage at once, and directed my steps slowly towards the horsemen in question, while I adjusted my turban firmly on my head, and handled my sword to see that it would come easily out of the scabbard, just as if I was making ready for a fight, should I be opposed. During this interval I had drawn near the horsemen, making these preparations meanwhile. They now drew rein; one of them, however, who was in advance, came on towards me. In spite of having his face half concealed, I could see he was a man of some age. When he was near me he spoke to me politely and modestly. However, I gave no answer to his words, and went on my way with my eye fixed steadily on the other horsemen, who were standing still. I believed they meant to bar my way. I was greatly mistaken, however, for on my passing quite close not a man of them said a thing to me.

The following day I made the same excursion, taking my lance with me this time. While I was in a plain of some size and fairly level, I saw [88] the carriage of the previous day a little off the road guarded by some horsemen. I knew at once that these were the same men as before. Nevertheless, not to show I had any fear of them, I would not retrace my steps, but continued my journey, flourishing my lance about a bit until I was quite close to them. Then the elderly horseman, with the greatest politeness and a smiling face, asked the favour of speaking a word with me. Directly I heard the voice I stood still, and turning towards him the point of my lance, I asked what it was he wanted.

He answered modesty that he was the brother of Allahwirdi Khan, that he had fallen in love with this dancer, on which account the king had reduced his high pay. Out of love for her he endured all this hardship, and gave up everything. Therefore he asked me the favour of permitting him to go and come freely. Without changing my position I answered that I granted what he asked, on condition, however, of his throwing over the carriage a scarlet covering, so that I might identify it. He answered that he would do so, and went away after saying goodbye.

The man's name was Mirza Arjani,[1] brother of that Allahwirdi Khan who betrayed Prince Shah Shuja4 when he delivered battle [89] against Aurangzeb, as will have been already seen in my First Part (I. 230). This Mirza Arjana (*sic*), being resolute in not giving up the said dancer, was content that the king should take away two hundred horse from his command and leave him only ten, with twelve thousand rupees of yearly pay. He endeavoured to become friendly with me, but I declined to waste my time on him or put any trust in him.

One day, while I was out on one of the above excursions, I amused myself in those gardens for longer than usual, and night came on before I had half completed my journey. By the light of the moon, which was not very bright, I observed coming towards me some strings of camels and oxen laden with goods, guarded by some mounted soldiers. To afford myself a bit of a game, I drew my sword and charged them, with

1. I have failed to identify this Mirza Arjanj (? Arzani). It may be a pen-name or a nickname. Nine sons of Allahwirdi Khan are on record; but the only brother spoken of, Mukhlis Khan, died before Aurangzeb's succession. There was a Mirza Jani, Kabuli, the *Diwanah* (madman) who died in 1106 H. (1694-95), but no connection with Allah-wirdi Khan is noted.

shouts of 'Mora, mora!' [*Matro, maro*! (Strike, strike!)]. On hearing my cries all the men fled and abandoned the animals. When I had arrived quite close, and found there was no one there, I rode my horse in all directions, crying out that I was only joking; moreover, I was no thief, therefore let them return and look after their animals. My voice was given to the winds, since no one appeared. I resumed my journey, and made for my house. Afterwards I learnt that it was the baggage of a viceroy, who was proceeding to his government of [90] the province of Ajmer; but no one ever found out that it was I who had caused the stampede.

It is the custom in the Mogul country for the royal elephants, whether those meant for war or those which fight before the king, to be kept outside the city near the gardens. They stand in a field below some trees, they are bound with heavy chains, and their keepers live with them, I went once at night to tease these animals with fireworks. They broke their chains and rushed wildly over the fields, doing a great deal of damage. Next I received word that some cavalry soldiers had been posted on guard to seize the insolent intruder; thus I forbore to molest the elephants any more. Just let the judicious reader imagine what would have been my punishment had I been taken, and into what disgrace I should have fallen. To-day, although now in old age, when I remember this and other similar escapades I committed, I never fail to sigh over them and grieve at my misdeeds.

I have noticed that these people of India, generally those of low extraction, are not fitted for the drinking of wine, and when they drink they become like animals, both in body and in intellect. If they have drunk only a little, you can tell it by their hesitating speech. The following instance will serve as an example:

[91] In Masulipatam there was a Mahomedan, a seafaring man, of the caste of Chulia (Chūliā),[1] men who follow no other occupation than that of sailor. This man gained a lot of money at that work, and in time became rich. He went to live in the kingdom of Pegu, where he grew still richer, and he married a woman of the country, who was both noble and

1. *Chulia* is the name of a class of South Indian Mahomedans (Yule, 207).

handsome. Upon finding himself so well off, he began to drink the spirits of Pegu, made from the rice called *polo*, which are of rather good quality. Some lime after his marriage his wife fell seriously ill, and died of that illness, to the great grief of her husband, he being very fond of her. All the same, he did not give up drinking.

Three days after her death all the slaves in his household assembled dressed in morning, and went to present themselves before him in the gardens, where he had been shut up the greater part of the night drinking.

They made great demonstrations of affliction. When he saw this novel performance he asked what all this sorrow meant. They replied that they had lost a well-conducted mistress, a woman of great kindness, and they would never be able to find another like her.

The tipsy Chulia then remarked to them: 'Do not be cast down. By the power of God the Messiah died and was brought to life, and I, too, will resuscitate your mistress by ordering her to arise.' He shouted at once for lights to be brought, and [92] he started for the cemetery, stumbling about first here and then there. When they reached the spot he caused the tomb to be opened, and the coffin containing the dead body was exhumed. The coffin was opened, and the grave-clothes loosened. He approached with the light; he beheld his late wife with her tongue projecting from her mouth and quite black, her face horrible, and the whole emitting a strong, fetid odour. He fell into a swoon, from which he was unable to recover himself, and they were forced to carry him home in that condition. Then they returned to re-inter the deceased. Two days afterwards the Chulia opened his eyes; he was in a state of terror, trembling all over, and unable to eat. After five days he died. This case was told to me by some Armenian merchants who were on the spot, and had several times dealt with the said Chulia.

In this kingdom of Pegu is a province called Siriam,[1] which is reached in boats through canals debouching into the river. It takes three days' travelling to reach the town where the merchandise has to be sold. The inhabitants of this country are accustomed to hold several festivals in the course of the

1. Evidently this is the Syriam in the Hanthawadi district of Lower Burma (see Pate XXXIII. of Constable's 'Hand Atlas,' and Yule, 886).

year in honour of their idols. But the principal festivity is celebrated outside the city at the foot of great mountains. The idols are on the summit. This feast falls in the month of 193] February; it is called the Digum (? Dagon)[1] festival, which means, 'Of the fire.'

On that day the governor and the chief men of the place attend and the greater number of the inhabitants. They solemnize the festival by consuming a considerable quantity of spirits; there are also performances and dances and fireworks, which are discharged at night-time. In the preparation of these fireworks they labour for many days.

The machine in which they enclose the powder is in shape and size like a large barrel, hooped with iron, and having a long tail. This barrel, in order that it may fly into the air, is attached to a high tree, of which there are plenty in the place, the forest being a vast one. Before the thing is set alight they resume their drinking, then the chief men draw near and bow to it as a mark of veneration.

Once when they were performing these solemn acts one of the officials of the law courts, being more tipsy than the rest, boasted that he could rise into the air along with the firework and come down to earth again unharmed. Over this assertion several wagers for large sums were entered into, because some believed and others disbelieved him. To sum up, to avoid any [94] fraud that the man might attempt, they bound him by his hands to the end of the firework. The end, shaped like a tail, is made out of a large tree called *bambu*, a great number of which grow in that forest, and they are eight cubits in length.

When ten o'clock at night arrived, following their custom they set alight to the firework, and all the people began to run and shout as is their fashion. The next day they found the firework a league away from the place where fire had been applied to it, and the drunkard who had been tied to it was found to have been burnt.

The Jesuits at Pondicherry do not give over the performance of their extravagant comedies, one of which they produced the other day. In it they represented a knight of good family

1. The reference is apparently to the great Shwe Dagon temple just north of Rangoon. It is ten miles or more west of Syriam.

who had married a rich and noble lady. By gambling and other dissipation he came in a few years to the end of his wealth, and fell into extreme poverty. Oppressed by his needs, and finding no one would lend him any money, he had recourse to the Devil. Satan lent him the money on condition that, should he not find the wherewithal to satisfy the debt, he must make over his wife in payment.

The term fixed having passed, the Devil appeared to demand his money; but [95] the knight, having nothing from which to pay the debt, contended for a long time with his creditor. Finally he agreed to produce his wife at a place appointed by the Devil. In order not to break his word the husband enticed his wife away from the house on a pretext of taking a walk in some gardens. On the way they passed close to a church, when the wife craved leave from her husband to enter and offer a prayer to Our Lady the Virgin Mary, for whom she felt great veneration.

Whilst the woman was at the foot of the altar engaged in prayer, it came to pass that the Virgin descended from the altar and said to her; 'Stop where you are, for your husband is taking you away deceitfully. I will take your place.' The Virgin issued from the church, joined the knight, and they continued the journey. Upon arriving at the place fixed upon, the knight said to the Devil: 'Here is my wife in place of the cash.' The Devil approached to seize the woman, but received a great shock of terror, and with a backward leap cried: 'This is not thy wife as thou promised me; it is the Virgin Mary, whom I am impotent to lay hands on.' The knight assured him it was his wife; but meanwhile the Virgin had disappeared.

The character was played by a black man dressed in woman's clothes [96]. The Devil's and the knight's parts were taken by two white men, who now commenced to shoe-beat each other, and thus the play came to an end. This play was acted by the Jesuits in the month of July, 1705, in the presence of all the officials of the settlement, as also of the Malabari population, to a noisy accompaniment of drums and trumpets and the discharge of fireworks.

From and to this port of Madras there go and come every year many ships trading with Bengal; hence one of my friends promises to send me by these occasions a statement drawn up by a person worthy of credit, dealing with these subjects [*i.e.*, the conduct of the Jesuits]. Should this reach me, I will without fail communicate it to the enquiring reader.[1]

In Manila in the year 1703 there was another ridiculous instance. Early in the month of August there set sail from this port of Madras a Portuguese vessel called *Nossa Senhora do Rosario*. Many merchants of different nations took passages in her. When these people reached Manila they took up their quarters in a town half a league from the city; its name is Santa Cruz.[2] The greater number of the merchants live there as finding it [97] more agreeable.

In the place is a church called Santa Cruz, belonging to the Jesuit fathers. They performed in it a representation of our Lord Jesus Christ's passion with living figures, being black men residents of the country. It took place in the middle of Lent, and they represented Christ carrying the cross on His shoulder. Upon that day, moved by piety, many of the merchants from this city of Madras, as well as many from Macao, attended at the church. They found the Jesuit father Mansilha in the pulpit. He preached in three languages—that is, Chinese, of which nation there are many in that country; Tagalla, the vernacular of the place; and Spanish.[3]

When he was at the end of his sermon, they set up a sound of drums and trumpets. In a short while there appeared close to the high altar a masked black man wearing white gloves and carrying a heavy cross upon his shoulder. Round his neck

1. This must be a reference to Father Quenin, S.J. (see *ante*, IV., fol. 195; also V., fols. 9 and 181).
2. That there was such a place close to Manila is shown by the references to it as the seat of the Jesuits' college at the end of the seventeenth century (see 'Morale Pratique des Jésuistes' (1691), vol. v., pp. 265, 268, 269.
3. F. Jagor, Travels in the Philippines,' English edition, 1875, spells the word 'Tagalo.' He says (p. 55) it is one of the five most important dialects, Spanish having acquired scarcely any footing. One-fourth of the population of the islands, or over 1,250,000 persons, speak it, chiefly in Luzon. In the province of Manila in that island it is the language of 323, 683 persons, but Spanish and Chinese are also spoken there. Mr. A. G. Ellis tells me the correct name of the language is *Tagálog*, and he has a 'Grammaire *Tagálog*' by Aristide Marre, 8vo., Leiden, 1902, pp. 47.

XLV. A noble interviewing a Hindu Ascetic

Vol. IV *To face page 200*

was a thick rope, and he came forward step by step very slowly, followed by twelve masked black men holding spears and swords. As the man carrying the cross was about to mount the altar-steps he was so held back that he could not advance another footstep. It was the others following him who had put their feet upon the rope, which was dragging on the ground [98]. This stoppage gave rise among those low fellows to some disputing. Then those who took the parts of the Hebrews laughed at the Christ. He fell into a lage, and turned towards them, and gave them a lot of abuse. This abuse they returned; from words they came to blows, and interchanged shoe-beatings.

On seeing this outbreak, the father scrambled down from the pulpit as quick as he could, and with a rattan administered several blows to the Christ and the Hebrews, rushing after them in all directions. Thus ended the Passion. The principal persons present, chiefly foreigners, were unable to maintain' their gravity, and gave a loud laugh. On the other hand, the Jesuit was all indignation and scolded them severely, ordering them to leave the church at once and never enter it again. In fact, the merchants of the country were from this time forced to go into the city to say their prayers, which occasioned them great inconvenience. However, after some months they obtained leave to go back and enter the church, but only upon Christmas Day, and even that was the effect of several donations that from time to time they gave the Jesuit.

At that church it is the custom of those fathers to enter the pulpit holding a rattan cane. If while [99] they are preaching they see any man and woman of the country talking together (as is the habit all over India, as I have noticed), and not behaving devoutly, the preacher leaves the pulpit and, without reserve, applies the cane several times. This admonishment finished, he mounts to his desk again and resumes his sermon.

At nine o'clock at night upon September 5, 1705, the Jesuits of Pondicherry entered a Hindu temple by forcing in the doors.[1] At the time a festival was being celebrated, which had been sanctioned in the hope of increasing the number of new Hindu settlers. Several of the Brahmans were beaten with shoes, and

1. This affair is referred to in Father Thomas's 'Littre Apologétique,' dated Madras, September 7, 1733 (see Norbert. 'Mémoires Historiques,' Besançon, 1747, ii. 280-283).

their hair was pulled, which is the greatest dishonour that can be inflicted. The other men present were treated in the same way. The idols they defiled by making water upon them, and then broke them into pieces.

Owing to this insult the whole Hindu population rose in revolt, quitted their houses, and assembled preparatory to departing. In number they were close upon forty thousand persons. The governor, Monsieur Martin, when the facts were reported to him, doubled the sentries at the gates, thus preventing these Hindus from getting away, but this only gave rise to greater confusion. The shops were shut, the fishermen took to flight, the officials disappeared; so also did the masons and carpenters working upon the erection of the new fortifications. These men, to the number of two thousand, were forced to leave, owing to the cessation of all supplies. This exodus was a great loss [100] to the population. The rising lasted for twelve days, when by the governor's wise conduct the people were appeased, though still far from well content. For this was the second time that the Jesuits had behaved badly to them.

Many traders who had means of living comfortably left the territory owing to the insults of the Jesuits, who would not let the people live in peace. When they met Hindus in the street they spat in their faces, making use of various abusive words about them and their idols. When the whole of the Hindus had assembled, as I said, in a street of some width and length preparatory to quitting the town, Father Taxar [Tachard],[1] the Jesuit general, who was the principal leader in this disturbance, resorted to the fortress in a passion, and urged the governor to fire cannon at the people. The father suggested that it was a good opening for killing them.

The father behaved rudely to Monsieur Flacour (Flacourt),[2]

1. Guy Tachard, born at Angouleme on April 7, 1651, went to Siam in 1685; then moved to Pondicherry, circa 1689. After a visit to Europe he returned there, and preached François Martin's funeral sermon at Pondicherry, 1706; he died in Bengal on October 21, 1712 (see Sommervogel's 'Bibliographic,' vol. vii., s.v. Tachard).

2. This is evidently the F. de Flacourt who signs as one of the witnesses to the 'Acte de Mariage' of F. Martin's grand daughter on February 22, 1705 (see *ante*, V., fol. 36), and is also mentioned as 'Premier Marchand,' under date of February 18, 1705, in 'Voyage du Baron de Pallteres' (Archives de la Marine, Campagnes, Registre B^4 26, fol. 493).

who is the second of the Royal Company, and abused him. Nay, he behaved in the same way to all who were not of his faction, uttering the further menace that he would write to France and would secure their dismissal from the service. All the persons present were thrown into a state of amazement, and were wearied out by this sort of talk. They cooled him down with gentle words, and then sent him away. The governor convened all the militia officers, [101] and made them sign a long letter wherein they laid before the French Court how the Jesuits had unjustly raised disturbances among the people. This paper it was intended to send to France for the information of His Most Christian Majesty. When this news reached the ears of the Jesuits, they used every effort to sow discord and enmity among those officers, in the hope of securing some loophole for exculpating themselves.

A few particulars about François de Flacourt have been gleaned from the Bibliothèque Nationale and the registers of 'Correspondance Générale' at the Ministère des Colonies. On February 5, 1703 (C^2 II., 67, fol. 9), we learn that De Flacourt had lately gone to Masulipatam to provide some goods. In addition, there had been some trouble about his wish to marry the widow of a Dutch fiscal; he had promised not to carry out this intention until permission was given. On January 2, 1703, they received his letter, dated December 16, 1702, reporting his marriage on November 26. One plea was that the Governor of Negapatam had ordered the widow and her children to be sent there from Masulipatam. In 1705 we find him on the Council at Pondicherry, and he signs, as second in Council, a letter of April 3 (C^2 II., 67, fol. 244). According to Pilavoine (Bib. Nat., MS. Français, No. 8,971), De Flacourt, on the death of F. Martin in December, 1706, succeeded as *ad interim* Governor from October, 1707, to January, 1708, when he was relieved by P. Dulivier from Bengal. In 1708 he went to Hugli to fill the place of chief vacated by Dulivier. He thus speaks of himself in a letter of December 26, 1708 (C^2 II, 68, fols. 208-210): 'The Sieur de Flacourt and his family arrived here on September 7 last on a Danish ship. The Chevalier Hubert, Governor of Pondicherry, gives us some interesting details in his letter of February 12, 1709 (C^2 II., 68, fol. 264): 'When I reached India [July, 1708], I found that De Flacourt, a good enough fellow in himself, had refused to come to the Fort since M. Dulivier had superseded him. He said he had been longer in India, was abler, and was more zealous in the interests of the Company. He married a Dutchwoman of the Reformed religion, the daughter of a preacher of Utrecht. In this he behaved badly, and, had M. Martin known the King's requirements in the matter of adherents to that religion, he would have prevented the marriage.' As he had no one else at hand, Hebert was forced to send De Flacourt to take charge in Bengal.

Nearly five years have gone by since Da,ud Khan came to govern the Karnatik. The Dutch, always energetic in business, sent an envoy to him at once with a valuable present. They asked as a favour that he would cede to them a small town called Coniumeri (Conimere or Kunimedu),[1] close to the sea and five leagues from Pondicherry on the north. The place was granted to them, and as the Dutch wanted settlers for it they invited people from Pondicherry and elsewhere to come there, offering them the fullest liberty and an absence of all interference. At the present time this town is growing with considerable hurt and damage to those who do not know how to make their subjects contented.

I must not forget to tell what happened to me on the day of the Virgin's Feast—that is, on December 18, 1705. It was at this Monte Grande (Big Mount) at three o'clock in the afternoon.[2] I was in the middle of entertaining several guests, who on that day never fail to appear, for a great crowd assembles there for this solemnity.

While I was in the middle of conversation with my friends, men of different nations, [102] I noticed that a serious dispute was going on at my gate. My servants were hindering the entrance of certain audacious persons who wanted to come in by force. I, too, proceeded to the spot. Although I saw they did not mean to listen to argument, all the same I attempted to prevent any violence, but quite m vain. The insolent fellows persisted in their attack, but were finally put to flight.

There remained in our hands the captain of the men; he

1. It is in the South Arcot district, eleven miles north-north-cast of Pondicherry. A factory was established by the English in 1682, and the place bought in 1688, but the factory was withdrawn in 1698 upon the erection of Fort St. David. The factory stood on a sandhill, 500 to 600 yards from the sea ('Madras Manual of Administration,' iii. 209). References to the Dutch interference appear in 'Fort St. George Public Consultations,' vol. xxx., pp. 68-72 (April 24, 1701), and 'Letters' from Fort St. George,' vol. x, pp, 41, 42; see also Wheeler, 'Madras,' i. 368.
2. Apparently he was writing this paragraph at Big Mount. This house must be a different one from that he owned in Madras, between Fort St. George and Black Town. The festival here referred to must have been that of the Conception of the Virgin, December 8, N.S., which by Old Style would have fallen, in the eighteenth century, on December 19.

was a Brahman officer, who ruled over some villages not far from Big Mount. He was drunk. I ordered the man to be tied to a tree over against my gate, and he received a good thrashing. He was then taken before the Mahomedan governor [*faujdar*], Mulla Murad, in San Thome. He is the present governor of the territory, and is a nominee of the great *diwan* and minister of the Karnatik.

When the captive reached the *faujdar's*, the principal officers and some of his relations presented themselves. They tried hard to throw the whole blame of the misdeed upon me, and they accused me as the culprit. Some of the Mahomedan officials supported their contentions. The judicious governor was not taken in by these fabrications, but on dismissing my servants he sent me a letter full of ceremonious expressions. He paid no heed to the contrary suggestions of the Brahmans, my enemies.

Perhaps he had doubts that if he acted otherwise [103] he would be either reproved from court or dismissed from his office He knew very well that the chief ministers were my friends. The man who has no friends in these lands is nowadays despised, and it is of no use for him to be in the right.

As it seems to me, I have not explained in detail the way in which I was treated when in the service of the prince, Shah 'Alam. Now, to demonstrate once more their policy, their style of government, and the mode in which their business is done, also how much the ladies at this court can accomplish, I will resume the subject. By this means the reader will learn what is the value of friends upon an occasion.

There was at the court of the prince Shah 'Alam a European blood-letter who, when he entered the service, was granted two rupees a day, and after some years was raised in salary up to seven rupees a day. This was done by the influence of the chief physician, Muhammad Muqim of whom I failed not to speak on other occasions (III. 43, V. 185). The blood-letter, finding the prince had a good opinion of him, and having by this time acquired a little money, made a most unreasonable demand from the prince to the detriment of the said physician. He said to the prince that Muhammad Muqim had an annual salary [104] of over one hundred thousand rupees, besides the other great profits that he received. But Muqim was not any wiser than he, the European, was, and therefore he, too, was worth quite as much pay. The prince upon hearing this preposterous claim was much put out, but concealed the fact, and gave not a word of reply. The physician, Muhammad Muqim, heard of the affair by means of his friends. He was much annoyed, but made no sign, and did not betray his feelings in the least.

I have already been known in the empire for many years when I reached the court after the heavy loss of money in Portuguese territory of which I have already spoken (II. 178). I was then much in need of money for my support. As soon as my arrival was heard of, I was at once invited by the prince and several of his princesses to accept service with him. The message was conveyed to me through a eunuch of some standing named Meccaian (? Miskin). To this proposal I replied that I would be really glad to accept the honour done to me by his Highness, but I must decline to accept his service unless the physician, Muhammad Muqim, conducted the negotiations with me. Thereupon it was at once ordered that he should present me to the prince, as is the custom.

At this time Shah 'Alam was making his preparations for starting to take charge of the Dakhin. The physician, Muhammad Muqim, remembering what the European blood-letter had [105] done to him, feared the same conduct from me also. He farther reflected that I had cured several persons of quality whom he had given up as beyond hope, whence he was afraid he might lose his reputation and be ejected from the service. Thus, in spite of his promises, he took no steps to push my interests.

The leading princess, as a sign of her affection for me, sent me food daily, and made me presents of different kinds of fruit. Seeing that the date of departure was close at hand, she asked my permission to deal herself with the prince on my behalf, since the physician had done nothing. Before this I had requested her not to speak on the subject. My reply to her now was that I begged as a favour she would not speak to the prince on the subject, as I had left it to the discretion of the physician. This I said in spite of my being in great straits from the want of money, and my sufferings from the persecutions of my adversaries, the aforesaid [European] blood-letter [of the prince! and the [European] surgeon of the king, of whom I have spoken above (V. 75-85). I stood strong and firm in my decision, in order to prove to the physician, Muhammad Muqim, and those others the vast difference there is between one person and another, and that he might see my upright modes of action.

I held my tongue for several days, looking out for some movement on the physician's part. Finally, seeing that he was not forwarding [106J my interests, in spite of his making a great show of wishing me well, I left the court, gave up my house, and took refuge in the house of a friend named Luis Gonzalves, intending subsequently to remove to the city of Lahor, where I had lived for a number of years. On the day that I disappeared the princess as usual sent me some gifts of food. When it was reported to her that I had gone, and it was not known where (the news reached her rather late), she was much grieved. She shut herself up in her room, and would not go to the garden to join the prince, as was her custom. He passed his time there listening to music and in other pastimes.

The prince noticed the absence of the princess. Not aware of the cause, he sent to invite her, letting her know that he was waiting in the garden most impatiently, for without her there could be no joy. The princess, aware of the great love the prince bore to her, sent back to say that she had been kept awake and troubled by a slight ailment; would he, therefore, excuse her for that day? Hardly had the news reached the prince's ear than he quitted the entertainment, and with all possible haste [107] made for her apartments. He saw she had nothing the matter beyond being in low spirits, so he pressed her to tell him the cause of her melancholy.

But the princess in a graceful way made excuses, just exactly as ladies know how to do when they are intent on having their own way. Finally, being forced into consenting to explain her ill-humour, she said it all sprang from the thought that his Highness did not love her to the extent he asserted; because, if his love were really such, he would not have neglected to entertain at court, and take into his service, the physician Manuchi, a man who knew her constitution, and had nursed her as a little child in his arms.

Taking her by the hand, to these words the prince replied that when morning came he would send in search of me, and pledged his word of honour that he would do so. Women can do much, and demand a good deal as soon as they perceive that they are held in estimation. On this occasion that was how the princess acted; therefore she replied to the prince that that very moment he must write an order to the principal eunuch, Nazir Daulat,[1] directing him to send off a troop of soldiers, who at the time were on guard, to trace me [108] out. Prince Shah 'Alam gave way to the wishes of the princess, and the soldiers, rushing about all the night, made a fruitless search for me.

However, they came in the end to know that if I were in any place in the suburbs of the city, I should not be found anywhere else than at the King's artillery park, in the house of my great friend, Luis Gonzalves. In fact, when it) was already full daylight, being seated in the garden, I observed one of the prince's guard thrusting his head in at the door, but as soon as he saw me he withdrew it at once. Having seen this man, I was a little reassured, guessing what it might be for, when in a minute or two there entered twelve troopers in the highest glee. They treated me most ceremoniously, and in a few words conveyed to me that the prince was waiting for me, and I must start quickly.

At these words I pretended to turn a little uneasy, as if they had need of me for some case of illness. They assured me that everybody was in good health, and I was sent for solely with a view to do me honour. The men urged me to start, and, to tell the truth, I was extremely eager myself, yet concealed [109] it, and gave signs of the exact contrary to what I desired. I told them to let me go to sleep, during which time they, too, could sit down and rest. To sum up, we began our journey about nine o'clock in the morning.

Meanwhile, let us look at what was going on about me at the court. By this time the princess had given up hoping for my return, and carried her lamentations to the prince. Shah 'Alam went forth to hold audience, and asked his chief minister and counsellor, Casmir (Qazi Mir)[2], where Manucci had gone to

1. Most probably this is the same man as the eunuch Daulat mentioned in the 'Ma,asir-i-'Alamgiri,' p. 343, under the year 1102 H. (1690-91), as being sent to Dihli to bring Shah 'Alam's family to the Dakhin.
2. This man and his heterodoxy have already been mentioned in Part IV., fol. 239; but, beyond indications that there really was such a person, I have failed to find out anything about him. One 'Abd-ul-qadir (or 'Abd-ul-qadir) Khan, his nephew, is twice named by Khafi Khan,

The Qazi, knowing nothing about my disappearance, replied that I was in the city. Shah 'Alam then ordered him to include me among the servants of his Highness. Upon receipt of this order Qazi Mir suggested that Manucci had heavy expenses; it was therefore necessary to give him an honourable rate of pay. The prince thought over this for a little, and then instructed him that he should give me seven rupees a day, the sum that his blood-letter had received. My friend Qazi Mir put on a dejected air, and made this suggestion: 'Your Highness ought to know that the father of your blood-letter was barber to the father of Manucci; thus he will never accept that rate of pay.'

At these words another friend of mine who was present, named Mirecautaula,[1] came forward three paces, and making obeisance [110], said: 'If your Highness permits me to speak, I will inform him of what I know about Manucci.' The prince turned his eyes in his direction, and with a smiling face said he might speak. Mirecautaula then stated: 'Does your Highness know that Nawab Mahabat Khan offered him through me three hundred rupees a month, with a palanquin, robes, and food, yet Manucci would not enter his service V Having said this much, he bowed, and returned to his place. The prince asked him whether, if he were to offer me three hundred rupees a month, and create me a *mansabdar* (noble) of the court, would I accept. Mirecautaula replied: 'Maybe he will agree, this being a royal establishment.' The prince ordered Qazi Mir to settle with me, and obtain my consent. This is the way they are accustomed to act in this court when they want to give a helping hand to anyone.

While this was in progress, I arrived at the house of my friend, Qazi Mir, not far from the court. He was not long in making his appearance. As he was coming in at the door I went to meet him, and paid him the usual compliments, but with a very long face, in spite of my now knowing all that had taken place.

---

ii. 681, last line, and 930, first line. In the second instance, Qazi Mir is qualified as the 'Bahadur Shahi'—*i.e.*, a person who had served Shah 'Alam, Bahadur Shah. There is some suggestion of the family having come from Tattha in Sind.

1. Codex CXXXV. adds the epithet 'viador da fazenda' (literally, 'Comptroller of Establishments'), probably intended for *Mirsaman*, or Lord Steward. The name, as spelt, is obscure; it may represent Mir 'Ifiqad-ud-daulah, Mir 'Itiqadullah, Mir 'Izzatullah, or Mubarikullah. I have failed to trace him under any of these forms.

The moment he saw me he put his hands to his sides, halted, and showed all the signs of being quite worn out, telling me: 'To-day I laboured in a cause which very seldom is carried to success in the Mogul court: you are already made a servant of the prince Shah 'Alam, and have [111] as pay three hundred rupees a month, and in addition you are a noble of the court.'

With a humble countenance, making an obeisance, I rendered him sincere asseverations of my gratitude. But Qazi Mir, observing that I had not changed my expression one little bit, nor shown any sign of gladness, came to the conclusion that I was dissatisfied. Therefore, coming closer to me, he suggested that for the time being I ought to accept the pay that had been fixed. He could assure me it would very soon be increased, and this he repeated at least twice. Discovering by these remarks that he had not perceived that I was more than content, in order to let him see the truth, I drew back one pace, and lifting my head and my voice, I said: 'I accept with all goodwill the honour that, through your mediation, his Highness has done me, and I live in the hope of receiving through your protection still greater'. Thus, did I reassure Qazi Mir, and inform him that I was satisfied. Embracing me, he took me by the hand and led me into the house. We had dinner together, then he presented me with a horse (which I was much in want of) and a valuable set of robes; thereupon I returned to my own house.

As soon as I reached my house the princess sent me her usual gift of food, together with a thousand rupees, giving me to understand that this money should serve as a help for the expenses I might have to incur in connection with the ensuing march, which was to begin a few days afterwards.

The eunuch Nazir Daulat sent a man to [112] call me, whereupon I paid him a visit and sat down in his presence. On seeing me, he shook his head and said: 'You are the man who had the royal gates opened at night at unsanctioned hours—a thing never allowed in the royal palace.' I replied that to have the royal gateway opened at that hour was due to the generosity of his Highness, who desired to favour a foreigner.

This man (Daulat) was a great friend of mine, as I experienced on many necessary occasions, as will have been seen. In opposition to the habits of his class, he was of a good disposition, and very liberal. He had sixty horses in his stalls and sixty camels loaded with pieces of cloth and other valuables. His tent was like a general's, and in his suite were noble horsemen. He was much esteemed at the court because he behaved prudently; his income was very large, owing to the offices he held; and his words were listened to by the prince.

I likewise give an account of the manner in which it is usual to bleed the princes, at what seasons it is done, and what happened to me on such occasions.

Ordinarily the princes and princesses have themselves bled twice in the month of March, and the interval between the two bleedings does not exceed twenty-four hours. The operation is begun half an hour before the setting of the sun. Three days afterwards they take a purge; but if necessity demands a shorter interval [113] they do not wait the three days, but are governed by the requirements of the case. In the month of September the same procedure is repeated.

The first time that Shah 'Alam had blood let by me I was summoned to the *Maal* (*mahal*), which means palace, and went into the *saral* (*sarae*)—that is, seraglio. He showed me his arm, inquiring if his veins were visible, and asked if I should give him any pain when I drew the blood. When I heard this question, I took hold of his arm, and looking at it, said without a pause that the vein could be opened without the least difficulty, and he would be quite satisfied. I quickly tied his arm with a bandage of fine broad cloth without stretching the skin very much. As I took up my lancet to make the incision, he stopped me, and said I ought to stretch and rub the arm well, as other blood-letters did. I answered that his Highness need not be alarmed, that I knew what I was doing.

I took hold of the arm again, and at once made the incision, opening the vein without going so deep as other practitioners do, by which practice some days must be passed without being able to move the arm. What I noticed on this, occasion was that the prince betrayed signs of fear, turning away his face until the blood had been taken. It is customary to keep ready for these [114] occasions a set of silver scales and weights; the basin for receiving the blood is also of silver.

On the ground is spread a large sheet, in order not to dirty the carpets and floor-cloths; over the body of the prince is cast another sheet, somewhat smaller. All the princes are present at the operation, as also the principal eunuch and some undereunuchs who act as attendants. It is the business of one of these to throw a little charcoal into the blood that is collected from the vein, also a little bit of iron, some small coin, and a few grains of raisins[1] for the preservation of the blood. After all these ceremonies they buried the blood in the garden, also performing other customary superstitious observances. When the incision is made all those who are present make profound bows, adding the words: 'May the blood-letting be to your benefit.' The same ceremonial is followed in the case of a princess.

As soon as the surgeon has left the room alms are distributed. When I had finished the blood-letting the prince ordered them to give me four hundred rupees. At the time of my reaching the gate a eunuch handed me the said money on a salver, telling me it was proper for me to make a bow with my face turned towards the palace. I did so, according to the custom of this court.

When I gave an order to my servant to take charge of the said rupees [114], the insolent eunuch said to me: 'It seems to me you could never) have had as much money in all your life.' At once I took the salver and emptied out on the ground all the money in it in the presence of the gate-keepers, telling them I made them a present of it. Then I turned to the eunuch: 'Do you not know that I am the son of the chief physician of the King of Spain, who is lord over half the world and owns the mines of silver? My father, being tired and in a hurry, on one occasion missed the vein; but, seeing that the king required to be bled, he made another stroke, and hit the right place. In spite of this my father was so sorrowful for the error he had committed that the consolation offered by the king had no effect upon him. Therefore, out of the love he bore him, and in the hope of restoring him to happiness, the king gave him a town as large as the town of Sihrind, together with a galleon laden with silver, which had just reached the port of Cadiz. Out of these revenues and moneys my father sends me twenty-four thousand rupees for my expenses, since the pay I receive from this court barely suffices for the expenditure in my kitchen.'

---

1. The Portuguese text has *mantimento*, 'aliment.' Cardeira translates this into *cibo* (Italian). How *food* or *victuals* could preserve the blood I do not see. Looking at the Italian versicn only, Dr. Cóggiola took *cibo* as a copyist's mistake for *cibibo=zibibo*, 'raisin.' It is in 'grains,' and in the Middle Ages medical virtues were attributed to it as a purifier of the blood (see Redi, 'Etimologie Italiane' [in 'Opere,' vol. iii.], Napoli, 1778, p. 293, and Mangelius, 'Bibliotheca Pharmaceutica-Medica,' Coloniæ, 1703, vol. ii. [sub 'Vitis vitifera']).

All this I did and said solely to the end that it should not be thought I was needy, and also to let them know my lofty way of looking at things. My prince [116], when he knew what had happened, said that he felt I must have been brought up in the midst of riches. He sent me the money over again, recovering it from the porters, and added to it a valuable set of robes and a fine horse. He said he must maintain the customs of his court, but without my being subordinate to anyone, and that I should have entire liberty.

Another mysterious thing happened to me when I first drew blood from the wife of the prince, called Nurnixam (Nur-un-nissa) Begam. The lady thrust her arm out from the curtain, as is the custom, and holding my lancet, I moved forward to open the basilic vein.[1] was still at a distance of six inches from the arm, when suddenly the princess turned round and threw up her arm violently towards the lancet—I know not whether through fear, or simply in changing the position of her body. The instrument went into the basilic vein, and blood flowed.

The prince, who was present, patted me with his hands on the shoulders (a sign of pleasure), and applauded my ability in having opened so skilfully so difficult a vein as the basilic. At this unrehearsed success I cannot tell you how I felt. Pallor spread over my countenance at the thought that all that portion of the lancet which projected beyond my finger-ends had entered [117] the basilic vein, and might have cut the artery. Having this in my mind, I stood watching the blood flow with no little apprehension. However, when four ounces had been lost, I noticed that I had not in any way touched the artery; on the contrary, I had struck exactly on the basilic, and thus I was reassured without having betrayed my concern.

The princes who were in attendance, although they had observed the difference of method in this extraction of blood, nevertheless did not attribute it to accident, but to the dexterity of my hand; and as such they spread it abroad, talking me up

1. The median sephalic vein is always chosen now to bleed from instead of the basilic, which runs over the artery. Shah 'Alam married Nur-un-nissa Begam before 1081 H. (1670-71). She was the daughter of Sanjar Khan, Najm Sani, and the mother of Rafi'-ul-qadr. She exercised great influence over her husband ('Ma,asir-i-'Alamgiri,' 106, 107; Khafi Khan, ii. 330). In Part IV., fol. 3, Manucci has told us that she died at Kabul in February, 1701.

as a great master of surgery, although it was really an accident. In this way I left the court after obtaining great honour and valuable gifts, in addition to being praised by everybody.

What I have observed and learned about the Jesuits is that, when unable to find out by public channels all that is done in private houses and in the city council, they endeavour to learn it by private means and through the medium of the confessional. They make the penitent understand that to observe silence or not to reply to their interrogations will trouble his conscience—a maxim, as it seems to me, the principal end of which is to secure knowledge of everything that is discussed in public and private gatherings.

Above all [118], however, they make use of women, knowing thoroughly well that they are unable to keep anything a secret. By these means they govern the world and courts, as we see them do in Europe. But these arts are of no use to them among Mahomedans; with them they are somewhat more politic. The Jesuits know what Mahomedans are, and therefore behave with moderation; nevertheless, when they find a little opening, they endeavour to draw to themselves as much as ever they can. Experience shows this to be true, and I will relate a case in confirmation of this dictum.

In Bengal there was a Portuguese married man, who placed full reliance on Jesuit hypocrisies. The man drew up his will, the terms of it being that he bequeathed all his goods to the said fathers for the benefit of the Madura mission. The estate consisted of three thousand rupees in ready-money, besides all the other property he owned. The moment he was dead the Jesuits took possession of everything, leaving the wife and three marriageable daughters without a penny. Thus, at this time they are houseless wanderers, through not having) the means to get married.

I might recount many such cases, but I [119] pass them over, believing that to the cautious reader this one instance can serve as his guide, if he will only reflect on it.

In the month of March, 1706, the Shiva Jis [*i.e.*, the Mahrattahs] came again to plunder the suburbs of Surat and all the surrounding country. Among other places they sacked a large town called Gandoui (Gandevi),[1] lying half-way between Surat

1. For Gandevi, see Constable's 'Hand Atlas,' Plate XXXI. It is in the Broach district, and now a station on the Bombay and Baroda

and Daman; it was a place of considerable wealth, owing to many traders living there.

At that time the *qazi* of Surat found himself there; he had gone not only to amuse himself, but to make rent collections from, and audit the accounts of, his villages. The unhappy man was unable to flee before the arrival of the Mahrattah troops, and he was taken prisoner. They pierced his hands, passed a cord through the holes, and dragged him about everywhere in the country, demanding money from him and a statement of where his hoards were buried. From these tortures he died. This was a merited punishment, for the man was not only an oppressor, but an unjust judge.

The Mahrattah princess, widow of Ram Raj and mother of the new prince, Shiva Ji,[1] caused the head of the general, Danojado,[2] to be struck off. His crime was that he had not, as he ought to and could have done, made a prisoner of Da,ud Khan; another crime was that he had not conquered the kingdom of the Karnatik [120]. On the contrary, he had retreated from that conquered country after the payment to him of some sums of money by the aforesaid Da,ud Khan. At this punishment all the captains and soldiers rejoiced.

The merchants whose ships had been taken by the Portuguese while on their way to Mecca, as I have already stated (IV. 153; V. 3, 24), never ceased to make complaint to King Aurangzeb and demand justice. Wearied by their supplications, his Majesty sent several dispatches to the Portuguese demanding restitution of the vessels, but they would never consent to give them back. Enraged at this conduct, the king suddenly expelled from his camp the Father Rector of Agrah,[3] after having subjected him to some disagreeable treatment.

Next he ordered the Governor of Surat to punish the Portu-

Railway, about thirty miles south of Surat, lat. 20° 46′, long. 73° 2[1] (Thornton, 'Gazetteer,' 359). It belongs to the Gaekwar of Baroda.

1. Shiva Ji, son of Ram Raj by Tara Bae. He was born about 1690, and died in January, 1712 (Grant Duff, 'History of Mahrattas,' 175, 188, Bombay reprint).
2. The spelling Danojado points to Dhana Jadon, Senapati, as the person intended. But the facts of that man's history do not bear out Manucci, nor did he die until 1709 (Grant Duff, p. 188).
3. For Father J. d'Abreu, S.J. see note 8, Vol. IV., Part V., fol. 5.

guese at Daman. A march was commenced at once at the head of six thousand men, cavalry and infantry. As soon as the governor approached the Portuguese villages, the frightened peasants took to flight. Upon noticing this the governor sent for the village headmen, and treating them courteously, reassured them, and told them that they ought to remain in their villages and go on cultivating their fields as usual. For, so he assured them, no one would interfere [121] with them. He sent them away contented, giving presents to each according to his merits.

After this he marched onwards and attacked a small Portuguese fort, situated two leagues from Daman. It was provided with five pieces of artillery, and defended by forty soldiers. They surrendered to superior force after a contest of one half-hour, during which one man was killed and several wounded. The rest of the garrison were made prisoners. Just then the news was brought to the governor that seven Dutch ships had come into the port of Surat.[1]

This news made the governor desist from his invasion of Portuguese territory; he acted prudently enough, for he was afraid that the Dutch might take possession of the Surat fortress. For this reason he gave hasty orders for the march of his army back to that town. The demands of the Dutch were as I have already recounted (IV. 153).

It may now be closed on twenty years ago that a most curious incident arose at the port of Surat. A European living there had been married to a lady who was a native of India. During a voyage that he undertook [122] he lost through robbery both the wealth he possessed and his life. His wife was known as an honourable woman, virtuous and charitable, ready to help the sick poor and gather into her house orphan girls, bringing them up to good habits. Thus, she was held in esteem by everybody.

In the neighbourhood of this lady dwelt a very wealthy Mahomedan trader, married to a lady of good family. This man, on leaving Surat in the pursuit of his business, made over his house to the charge of his consort. The woman committed adultery, and became pregnant. Seeing her fault thus exposed, and expecting on her husband's return to be put to death, she resorted

1. The date of their arrival was September, 1703 (see Part IV., fol. 153).

to the above lady, her neighbour, and sought her advice, telling her what had happened.

The virtuous lady, in order to protect the honour of the Mahomedan woman, and at the same time to gain for the Faith her offspring, made pretence that she was with child, at the sacrifice of her own reputation and of the esteem in which everyone held her. Everyone spoke evil of her and she became universally abhorred; nor was there anyone who would help her with alms as they had hitherto done. In the end the Mahomedan was delivered in secret [123], and the Christian lady carried the infant to her house, had it baptized, and brought it us as her son. In this way the Mahomedan continued to be held chaste, since there was no one else who knew the secret.

The charitable Christian lady, when she had brought up the child to the age of seven years, in the fear that he might be perverted sent him to France. When he had grown up he returned to India, and travelled from one part to another, earning his livelihood and living as a Christian, and he believed himself to be the son of the Christian lady who had brought him up.

After some time the Mahomedan woman became a widow, and when at the point of death, remembering the charitable act done by the Christian, was secretly baptized by a Capuchin father, thus in this last extremity embracing the Catholic religion. Not many years after her death the Christian lady fell mortally ill. When she was dying she confessed publicly what I have above stated.

It will have been already seen (V. 34) how Monsieur Bono [Bouynot] set out for Bengal on being appointed captain of the [Dutch] commissary's [captured] ship, the *Phénix*. He arrived safely at that port, and loaded his ship [124] with a valuable cargo. In the month of November, 1705, he set sail, passing in front of the English and Dutch factories, flying at his masthead and poop a captain's flag of scarlet colour. He passed through twenty-five ships of various nations which were anchored there [in the Hugli]. Upon coming out of the river, not far from the entry to the port, he encountered two Dutch ships, the one of 54 cannon and 550 Europeans, the other of 24 cannon with 250 soldiers, also Euro peans.

As he was coming out they stopped him and attacked. He tried to set fire to one of the ships, but his attempt did not sueceed, for the ship escaped and he only damaged himself. The two ships, finding they had cut off his retreat, fought him most vigorously. On his side Monsieur Bono [Bouynot] made a stout resistance, and used his utmost efforts to get away into the open sea and continue his voyage. But he was not able to proceed farther as his ship was not well found, and was defended by only two hundred fighting men of different nations. Thus he was obliged to beat a retreat, and, using judgment and courage, he went back into the port of Bengal [? Hugh], disembarked his cargo at the French factory, and there laid up his ships till the times permitted of his departure.[1]

1. That the new commander of the *Phénix* was named Bouynot, and not Bono, is shown by his report in the Archives, C^2 68, fols. 4 and 5, which begins: 'My Lord, I have the honour to send particulars of several adventures which I have undergone between my leaving France and my appointment to command the *Phénix d'Or*, a prize taken from the Dutch by the Baron de Pallieres.' Under Governor Martin's orders, he sailed on March 6, 1705, for Bengal. On March 25 he anchored before the factory on the Hugli. On October 26, 1705, re reached a place he calls 'Cajoury,' near the mouth of the river, where he was attacked by three Dutch ships of fifty-six, of thirty, and of twelve guns. He forced them to retreat, and put 180 of their men *hors de combat*. The Dutch sought a position where he could not follow them. He repeats the story in another letter from Hugli of January 5, 1706 (fols. 6 and 7). On fol. 9 Fournier, a pilot, certifies that the Prenix was saved by the skill of Bouynot. On fols. 10-14 we have three more reports of the fight. Some of his subsequent doings are unfavourably noticed in 1707. In May he came back to Pondicherry, bringing 25,000 crowns, two families, and six filibusters. Complaints came from Madras that France should give countenance to such doers of evil. Bouynot had promised the inhabitants to bring them slaves to break up the soil (Bib. Nat., MS. Français, No. 6,231, fol. 39, verso).

Bouynot not more or less of a pirate in his methods, thereby adding to the troubles of the Company. In his tenth letter of February 12, 1709, the Chevalier Hebert (F. Martin's successor) mentions Bouynot's having taken a Mahomedan vessel, much to the Company's incovenience. The purser of his ship accused him of having embezzled Rs. 5,000 worth of supplies and war stores. The Council also charged him with cruelty to natives, and with plundering a Mahomedan vessel. He was condemned to pay 6,000 livres, ordered home to be admonished and was declared incapable of obtaining a command. He was also condemned to pay 200 and 300 *pagodas* to those whose hands he had cut off, and to deliver 120 *pagodas* to each religious house (C^2 II., 68, fols. 305, verso, and 307).

This sentence was not strictly carried out, for in 1714 we find

[125] I will insert what is commonly said by all the Hindus, though for myself I do not believe it will happen as they assert. In all their prophecies and documents, it is said that after the death of King Aurangzeb the line of Tamur-i-lang's descendants will cease to rule, and that once more the Hindus will reign over Hindustan as they did of old time. They tell, however, a fable, which is very widespread in the empire, and is as follows:

They say that long ago, while Taimur-i-lang was still a lad, as he was going through his village on his way to graze his camels, her met a poor *faqir* walking along that road and crying out: 'He who will give me to eat and to drink once only, I shall make him a great king.' Taimur-i-lang, who even then cherished ambitious thoughts, believed in the *faqir's* words, and told him to wait where he was and he would satisfy his wants.

He ran in all haste to his own house. When his mother saw him she cried out at him for coming back to the house so soon, and not keeping with the camels as he was used to do. Taimur-i-lang told her what had happened, and gave his mother no peace until she had made over to him some food. [126] He carried it to the *faqir*, who, after eating, informed Taimur-i-lang that if he wanted to be a king he would make him one, but in the case he must patiently suffer the pain he should inflict. Taimur-i-lang replied that he would suffer glady all that might be done to him.

Then the *faqir* ordered him to throw himself on the ground, covered him with his cloak, and struck him with the hand, using all his strength, eleven times on the posterior. He would have gone on administering blows had not Tamur-i-lang, unable any longer to endure the pain, risen up and flung the cloak far from him. He then sat down some paces from the *faqir*. The man said to him that if he had been able to endure, as many more descendants of his as there were additional blows would have reigned as

---

him commanding two vessels, the *Saint Louis* and the François (Dulivier's letter of July 18, 1714, C[2] II., 69, fol. 85). In spite of all, he continued his plundering, but this time the accusation referred to the Chinese (same letter, fol. 85, verso). In another letter of the same date (C[2] II., 69, fols. 97 and 100), Dulivier again details the accusations against Bouynot. But he could not be removed, as was right and as the King had ordered, because there was no one else to whom the command of the ships could be given. The spelling of his name cannot be doubted, as it occurs so often, and his own signature is very plain and distinct.

kings. Thus, the fault was his if there were to be no more than eleven generations of rulers. This tale is very well known, but I have not seen it in the royal chronicles of Taimur-i-lang.

In connection with the narrative I have already inserted, I will recount what happened in the year 1702. Reflecting on the great sins he had committed [127], and desirous of knowing which of his sons would become emperor and destroy the rest, Aurangzeb caused a famous magician to be sent for several times. The man repeatedly excused himself from attending. But as kings are powerful and can do what they please, he was obliged in the end to go to him.

The king had him brought into his room, and then set forth the desire he had to know which of his sons was fated to be emperor. The magician became rather terrified at this proposal, and attempted to protect himself by finding out what were the king's wishes. But finally he was persuaded by he king's soft words, and encouraged by a promise that no one should be allowed to hurt him.

In about twenty minutes he caused four severed heads to appear at the four corners of the royal bed; they were the heads of Aurangzeb's four sons. Whilst the king stared in horror at such a sight, the magician told him none of the princes would be allowed to reign. Without uttering a word, Aurangzeb waved his hand for him to go, ordering the eunuchs to let him pass out and conduct him home in safety.

When the magician had left the four heads disappeared, and for that night the king did not sleep [128]. After having ordered the bedstead to be burnt, he knelt on the bare earth in prayer.

Time will show what is to happen, and if God gives me life I shall not fail to draw up a report thereof, and satisfy the reader's curiosity.

[I omit the following, which have been already given—*viz.*, the story of Qazi Mir, his unorthodox treatise with Christian tendencies, and his death in prison (Part IV., fols. 239, 240); that of the young man from Syalkot, who met his death in Ahmadabad (Part IV., fol. 240); and that of the Capuchin friar at Isfahan (Part IV., fol. 2406). I resume on fol. 136.]

[136] It will be about five years ago that I went to visit Nawab Da,ud Khan to carry out some negotiations, as I have

stated in my Fourth Part (IV. 88).[1] One night while I was in conversation with him there arrived a letter from the court containing a strict order that immediately on perusal he was to place in prison the captain, Bader Kam (Bahadur Khan). In execution of this order, the Nawab sent for the officer under the pretext that good news had come from court which he required to communicate at once.

The officer believed this was the truth [137], and came at once to his superior's presence without even a single follower. There he was seized suddenly and bound, without being able to have recourse to his arms. He was removed to a house in the fortress of Arkat, where he lay with irons on his feet, watched by vigilant sentinels. This Bahadur Khan was a subordinate of Da,ud Khan, had the command over three hundred cavalry, and possessed many elephants.

He was sent to prison on the pretext that he was a traitor to the crown, in secret correspondence with Shiva Ji the Mahrattahs) and the other allied princes who had revolted. In fact, we are obliged to believe that this was truly the case, owing to the numerous methods in which they (the Mahrattahs; tried to get him released, and to obtain his services on their side. In these attempts they succeeded.

These princes, in their efforts to get him out of prison, made use of a shepherd. This man carried daily to the captive a vessel of milk for him to drink, and inside it they placed some files, by means of which in time he got rid of his fetters. The day fixed for his flight was the day following the conclusion of their fast in the year 1706,[2] a day on which Mahomedans have great festivities and dances. When this day had arrived he (Bahadur Khan) feigned severe illness [138], threw himself on his bed, and groaned just as if he had really been attacked by a mortal malady. The

1. As the reference is to the visit to Da,ud Khan at Arkat in 1701, this passage proves that Part V. was being written in 1706 or 1707.
2. The day after the end of the Ramazan fast would be the 1st Shawwal, and in 1706 A.D. this day fell on January 16, N.S. (1117 H.). But, judging by the opening sentence, the occurrence belongs to 1701 A.D., when it would correspond to the 1st Shawwal, 1112 H. (March 11, 1701), or 1113 H. (March 1, 1702). Manucci was back in Madras on February 3, 1701.

sentries, believing that Bahadur Khan was really suffering from illness, went off to watch the dancing and the fireworks.

The prisoner lost not an instant, but, embracing the hoped-for opportunity, left the fortress, and joined his Mahrattah friends, who were waiting for him with horses. He took the road to the mountains, and was soon in safety. He continued his flight, however, in all haste, and went to join the Mahrattahs, who were encamped in the lands of Aduni. The extravagant delight with which the Mahrattahs received him can be easily imagined; this can also be collected from the sign of it they gave in assembling an army for him, with which to take satisfaction for the affront done him by Da,ud Khan.

Bahadur Khan, while engaged in scouring the country in that neighbourhood, came cross a despatch-rider carrying letters to Da,ud Khan. Speaking politely to the man, but without revealing his identity, he made over to him a letter [139] directed to Da,ud Khan, to the following effect: 'I left my scull-cap on the bed where I slept. Keep it safe, for shortly, when my horsemen and elephants are ready, I am coming to inquire for it from you.' When this letter reached Da,ud Khan he was far from content, for he knew the nature of his own tribe when they entertain a hatred to anyone.[1]

[Here follows (fols. 139-148) a story of a herdsman and Shah 'Abbas the Great, of Persia. As it has no reference to India I omit it, as also another about the same Persian king (fols. 148-149).]

[149] At the present time the kings of Persia are a good deal different from the former kings. They are now much addicted to wine and women, besides such diversions as music and dancing. They pay no heed to what concerns the crown. The government is left in the hands of eunuchs and persons learned in religion. The new kings do not make a display of their ability in governing like the former kings did.

In the reign of Shah Sultan Husain,[2] the son of Shah Sulaiman and grandson of [150] Shah 'Abbas the lesser, there was a famous general called [blank in text]. This man noticed the

1. This Bahadur Khan is spoken of again as commandant of Penukonda (see V., fol. 168).
2. Sultan Hussain, Safawi, reigned from 1694 to 1722 (S. L. Poole, 'Mohammadan Dynasties,' 259).

great difference between this king and his predecessors. In place of making much of and showing esteem for officers who had grown grey in battle-fields, he insulted them by refusing them the offices that they had merited. In this fashion the affairs of the state went from bad to worse. Therefore that general said boldly in the king's presence at a public audience: 'Your Majesty is incapable of governing, since you do not rule like your predecessors; they raised to high place those who merited it, and could be serviceable to them. Your Majesty, quite to the contrary, appoints low men to places of authority, men of little judgment, and therefore you will be the cause of your own destruction.' On hearing these reproofs the king directed him to withdraw, and never appear at court again. The command was executed, and to this day he lives in retirement in his own house. To say the truth, this was a great piece of courage, not to say temerity, by which this general was deprived of his king's favour, although he had been highly thought of previously.

You will have already seen (IV. 224, V. 34) the agreement made by the Dutch commissary Bernard Phoosen [151] with the French of Pondicherry when he was made a prisoner. The Dutch gentlemen who live in Batavia, and have control over Indian affairs, when they heard of the agreement that he (Phoosen) had made, deprived him of his office, as they did also to the other officials who accompanied him, and dismissed even the officials at the town of Negapatam who had signed the agreement.[1]

We come now to speak of King Aurangzeb. During the time of the rains the king cantoned his army near the river Quessina (Kishna), which flows past the territory of the prince Aganguiri (Wakinkerah).[2] Not to , be idle, he dispatched General Zu,lfiqar Khan to make war against a prince who was a vassal of the kingdom of Bijapur; he also ordered the general

1. For notes on Bernard Phoosen and his truce with the French, see Part IV., fol. 224, and Part V., fol. 34. The Dutch records show that he was called upon by the Batavia Council to explain his conduct. His defence is dated January 15, 1706. On June 12, 1705, the Madras Council heard that the Batavia Council had disapproved ('Fort St. George Public Consultations,' vol. xxxiv., pp. 149-151).
2. See Vol. IV., Part IV., fol. 234, note 135, on Wakinkerah.

Chinichiliscam (Chin Qalich Khan) to march with his army and invest the principal fortress of another prince, equally a vassal of the Bijapur kingdom.

The first of these princes offered thirty thousand, the other twenty thousand rupees in order that the king might allow them to live in peace. This offer was referred to his Majesty, who directed that these sums of money should be taken, and the cash should be kept as a present by the said generals [152]. Yet he instructed them to continue their best efforts to destroy these rebels. This is a habit of this king, although his orders are not carried out as he gives them.

Meanwhile he sent men to reconnoitre the route along which, as he pretended, his army would make its advance on its way to attack the prince of Massur (Maisur). The same was done in regard to Taniaur (Tanjor) and Triginapali (Trichino-poly); it was meant only as a means of intimidation and the extraction of money from them. With the same object he gave a fresh order for Da,ud Khan to return to the Karnatik. The Khan, assuming pleasant ways, feigned himself the friend of those princes, and advised them to offer handsome tribute to the Mogul if they wished to be liberated from imperial interference.

These princes are so ignorant that they paid what was demanded of them, without foreseeing the destruction which would overtake them therefrom. The said Da,ud Khan amassed all the money that he could from them and from the Europeans, since he had bound himself to pay to the court a revenue fifty per cent, in excess of that usually paid. From this cause the people had a good deal to suffer.

The Shiva Jis (the Mahrattahs) quitted the neighbourhood of the royal camp, started for their own territory, and in less than three months recovered the fortresses of which the conquest had occupied Aurangzeb so many years.

[153] Da,ud Khan left the court and came back to the Karnatik, and when he reached it all the European nations sent him their presents, which he accepted.[1] From the French alone

1. The English letter of congratulation was passed in Council, and the dispatch of a present approved upon, on June 1, 1705 (Fort St. George Public Consultations,' vol. xxxiv., pp. 133, 134). A horse was received from the Nawab in return on September 22, 1705.

did he refuse to take any, in spite of his declaring himself to be their very great friend. Instead of receiving their tribute, he rejected it with displeasure. He said to their agent that he was not a man fit to carry on their affairs, he must therefore write to Monsieur Martin, Governor of Pondicherry, to send him some person of judgment to arrange certain interests of the greatest importance.

At once Governor Martin sent a Hindu inhabitant of Pondicherry, named Anomond, bearing a substantial and notable present. When this man reached the camp of Da,ud Khan, he was not well received; on the contrary, he was spoken to in a somewhat arrogant and menacing manner. He was given to understand that the French ought to restore to the Dutch the ship *Phénix*, taken from their commissary, with all the valuable cargo in it;[1] otherwise he (Da,ud Khan) should proceed to destroy the fortress of Pondicherry.

This discussion took various turns, and in the end Da,ud Khan announced that if they gave him one hundred thousand rupees he would leave them alone. This settlement was not accepted by the French of Pondicherry; they were resolute to pay nothing, and began to prepare for defence [154]. At the same time. Governor Martin did not relax his efforts to adjust the claim; and, with the aid of some friends, he succeeded in settling matters. Up to the present time Da,ud Khan has done him no injury, although he has uttered many threats. But that is what they always do.

The prince of Maisur was aware that, as soon as the rainy season was over, King Aurangzeb would make war upon him. He therefore made ready to resist him with a force of fifteen thousand horsemen of different tribes—Pathans, Rajputs, and Moguls, *et cetera*. The whole of these men came out of the Mogul empire; not finding employment at that court, they went and took service with this prince. I do not believe that these men will be faithful to him; on the contrary, I know that Aurangzeb, following his custom, will be sure to invite them to desert to his standard by an offer of higher pay, if he has not done this already, as he has practised in the kingdoms of Bijapur and Gulkandah, and in other principalities.

1. For the case of the *Phénix*, see Vol. IV., Part IV., fol. 223, note 119 and Vol. IV., Part V., fol. 34, note 30.

The said prince suspected, however, that this tampering had taken place, and called a council of his principal officers. He asked them, in case such a desertion happened, what would be the remedy for the evil. They replied to him that he should place no reliance on those horsemen; in time [155] of need his Highness had forty thousand captains, not to speak of the soldiers who fought under their standards, making a total of three hundred thousand men, all of them ready to defend his Highness.

Within their own country this tribe consider themselves valiant soldiers, and are very tender on the point of honour. If by chance, in going out from or coming into any place, their clothes are touched unintentionally, or when passing each other they cough or spit, they hold that there has been an affront, and they forthwith challenge each other to a duel. This sort of duel happens customarily two or more times in a day. They are fought in the presence of the prince, who allows them because he cannot prevent them.[1] These officers and soldiers are highly paid, and live very well; they are rather skilled in the use of weapons, and are accustomed to wear on their arms small armlets of gold or silver. In a few months from this time, if Aurangzeb lives, we shall see what sort of valour these soldiers have, and I shall not fail to give a clear report.

Although this prince might easily lead this great army against the Mogul, he is an enemy of war, and it pleases him better to live in peace and amity. He offered to his Majesty fifteen millions of rupees and five elephants, promising, in addition, to double his annual tribute, on condition that he was not interfered with. Aurangzeb accepted [156] the proposal, and at once sent off a thousand horsemen to convey the money to his camp. The Shiva Jis (the Mahrattahs) had information, and pursued the convoy with twenty thousand horse, hoping to relieve them of the cash, but the pursuers were not in time. The

1. The Resident, Mysore, has kindly consulted for me the archaeological officer of that State, who suggests that *jetties,* or professional wrestlers, must be intended; they are very jealous of their honour, and challenge each other to duels on the slightest provocation. The Dasahrah contests are well known, and still take place in presence of the Maharaja. See also Wilks, 'South of India.' i. 32. note. Spitting as a mode of affront is not peculiar to Maisur.

escort had retired with the utmost promptitude into a fortress, end up to this moment the money is locked up there.

In the month of September of the said year [1705] King Aurangzeb fell ill, and for twelve days he did not appear at the public audiences. [1] The news caused a great commotion in the royal camp, since the greater number believed he was dead; the fact being that he unexpectedly fell into a swoon, and for three hours on end he was unable to speak a word. When Prince Kam Bakhsh heard of it, he, too, jumped to the conclusion that his father was dead. With the idea of getting command over the whole army, he sent a letter to the grand *wazir*, Asad Khan. In this letter he told him to remain without apprehension; he undertook that no one should interfere with him. The *wazir*, in answer, made use of similar phrases, saying, 'May God preserve his Majesty's life! If it happen otherwise, and he die, I am constrained to make over the treasure, the property, and the whole of this army to that one of the emperor's four sons who succeeds in ascending the throne and crowning himself, and to him I shall render [157] an account of everything.'

Aurangzeb was informed of what had passed between Prince Kam Bakhsh and the *wazir*, and he was satisfied at finding the latter so loyal; as an inducement to be still more faithful he promoted him in rank. However, suspecting there might be some treachery or rising if he were not seen at audience time, Aurangzeb, when his illness had subsided a little, went, weak though he was, to the public audience, and remained for half an hour. By this means the populace were quieted, and the pretensions of every man were rendered vain.

During the time when the king was thought to be at the point of death, some grandees loaded twelve camels with gold coin, intending to place the money in some neighbouring fortress, as on such occasions is customary. But the financial officials who were in charge and the tax-collectors prevented this removal. When the king gave audience again, the matter was reported to him; he sent men to seize the money, its guards

1. In the rainy season (June to October) of 1117 H. (April 24, 1705, to April 13, 1706) Aurangzeb fixed his camp at the town of Dewapur, there *kos* from Wakinkerah. Here he fell ill, but concealed the fact as long as he could; then fainting fits supervened, and it was ten or twelve days before he could appear again in public ('Ma,asir-i-'Alamgiri,' pp. 507-509).

having already abandoned it for fear of its being known who the owners were. The cash was used to pay the army, which had not been paid for years, and this distribution caused great joy. The owners of the money were not discovered.

The physician who treated his Majesty was the son of Mossancam (Muhsin Khan),[1] of whom I have already spoken (III. 43). This man has received the title of his deceased father. As a reward for the cure, an order was given to weigh him against silver rupees, which came to six thousand five hundred, then five hundred were added, making in all seven thousand rupees.

[158] When the king could move about, having recovered from his indisposition, the rainy season had ended. He sent men to measure the quantity of water in the rivers, preparatory to an attack on the prince of Maisur, to whom he forwarded violent threats. At this time news was received by his Majesty that the villagers in the province of Agrah had risen and plundered the suburbs of the city, and closed the roads in those parts.[2] Very shortly afterwards other reports were received that some Pathan chiefs, who ruled between the province of Kabul and the Indus river, had risen in rebellion, and killed several soldiers of Prince Shah 'Alam, his son.

From the coming of these reports the design of fighting the prince of Maisur was frustrated; and the king withdrew his army to the neighbourhood of Aurangabad [*read* Ahmadnagar], having continually at his heels the Mahrattahs, who follow him everywhere. Here the report was received that Prince A'zam Tara, the son who was in charge of Gujarat province, had taken the field with a great army, and was advancing on the road to Agrah, in the belief that his Majesty was dead.

Against this prince came out a Rajput leader called Doruc-dax (Durga Das),[3] belonging to the territory of Jaswant Singh,

1. In the 'Majasir-i-'Alamgiri.' 510, the physician named is Haziq Khan.
2. Sansansi, near Mathura, the stronghold of Raja Ram, Jat, was stormed a second time on the 2nd Rajab of the forty-ninth year, 1117 H (October 20, 1705) ('Ma,asir-i-'Alamgiri,' 498).
3. Durga Das became the hero of Marwar after the death of Jaswant Singh in 1678. The 'Ma,asir-i-'Alamgiri' does not mention this fighting specifically, but there is a possible allusion to it in Tod, ii. 73, under Sambat, 1762 (A.D. 1705); also in the entry, on p. 498, line 4, of the 'Ma,asir-i-'Alamgiri,'

XLVI. A SATI. or widow-burning

Vol. IV *To face page 228*

at the head of twelve thousand cavalry. This is the Rajput who took Prince Akbar's side when he rose in rebellion. A'zam Tara was under the impression that Durga Das was coming to effect a junction with him. Therefore he wrote him a letter [159] of thanks; but he found by experience that things were very different from what he had expected. When the prince's force arrived in front of that of Durga Das, the latter barred its passage onwards, resulting in a loss of four hundred Rajputs and twelve hundred of the prince's men. This opposition forced A'zam Tara to retreat.

The cause which led Durga Das to resist A'zam Tara was his contention that the throne belonged to Prince Akbar, in the maintenance of whose rights he had taken the field. When the king heard of this movement, he called upon Prince A'zam Tara to return to the Presence, under promises of many high dignities and appointment as lord over still greater provinces. After the retreat of the prince, Durga Das also withdrew to his own territory, which is that formerly belonging to Jaswant Singh.

His Majesty's retreat towards Aurangabad was against his will,[1] his desire being to make war against the prince of Maisur; but he had to postpone that campaign in order to attend to the above rising. The king was greatly exercised in mind by these uprisings, the more so when he recollected that his undertakings had not been very successful, and the common people had begun to speak desparingly of his continual and fruitless marches. He issued a proclamation [160] that, if anyone spoke abusively about the royal marchings, his tongue would be pulled out the next morning early.

After such a proclamation the royal army marched without giving any sign of life and without sound of instruments, wishing to convey thereby that they would have to return a second time. Marches in this style continued for fifteen days. It happened on the second day of this journey that the

---

saying that Durga Das, Rathor, had left the Prince's camp, and then returned to it on the 10th Sha'ban, 1117 H. (November 27, 1705).

1. The Emperor left Dcwapur, near Wakinkerah. on the 16th Rajab, 1117 H. (November 3, 1705), reached Bahadurgarh on the 1st Ramazan (December 17, 1705), and Ahmadnagar on the 16th Shawwal (January 31. 1706) ('Ma,asir-i-'Alamgiri,' pp. 510, 511, 519). For 'Aurangabad' in the text, read 'Ahmadnagar.'

Mahrattahs reached the rear of the advance tent, in which the king took a rest, and killed one thousand Mughals, burnt the tent, and carried off the officer, whom they blinded, to prison in a fortress. For his ransom they demanded five *lakhs* of rupees. The Mahrattahs had many openings for attacking the king himself, but declined to avail themselves of them, owing to the profit they find in his continuing to live. Being king of the Mogul country, there come to him various subsidies in treasure and merchandise, by capturing which the Mahrattahs benefit.

Aurangzeb was also informed that the Mahrattahs had crowned as their prince Shiva Ji, son of Ram Raj.[1] He was also told that the new rajah was to take the field, although a minor. At the present time these Mahrattah peoples keep on foot a huge army of cavalry, to the number of two hundred thousand. They never cease from skirmishing and plundering in all directions with the greatest boldness.

[161] Among all the princes, sons of Aurangzeb, one of whom must succeed to the throne, the most esteemed and loved at court is A'zam Tara, and he is spoken of there much more than all the others. The reason for believing that he will become king is that the princes at court take his side and object to Shah 'Alam as king. This animus of the princes against Shah 'Alam can be understood by the attitude adopted to him by the grand *wazir* (Asad Khan) and other officials.

For it is known that when Aurangzeb ordered him, (Shah 'Alam) to be seized, the chief *wazir* removed the prince's sword from his side, the powerful general Gueazudi Karn (Ghazi-ud-din Khan, or sometimes Ghiyaz-ud-din Khan) placed the fetters on his feet, other officials seized his sons, others plundered his palace and behaved disrespectfully to his women. For these reasons all the persons I have named and the rest of their faction are on the side of A'zam Tara.

In addition to this he (A'zam Tara) is also the most esteemed for being the son of Xenevescam's (Shah Nawaz Khan's) daughter, and is therefore of Persian [royal] blood. These reasons will, however, prevail nothing, but all will be as God pleases. Prince Shah 'Alam has already reached the age

1. Shiva Ji, son of Ram Raj by Tara Bae, was born about 1690, and died in January, 1712 (Grant-Duff, 'History,' 175, 188).

of sixty-six years.[1] He does not look after his soldiers, who suffer much from want, nor noes he attend to other important affairs. His time is occupied in wine-drinking and lascivious practices quite in excess of all reason.

[162] The large sum of money sent by the prince of Maisur as a present to his Majesty had been taken to a fortress called Sirpi,[2] situated in the vicinity of that prince's territory. This money was recovered by the prince of Maisur, and the fortress taken, in the following manner. When this prince saw that the king had retreated, and that his affairs were in a bad state, he made use of the opportunity and bribed the soldiers who garrisoned the place. This was done very easily, since they were dying of hunger and had received no pay. They delivered up the fortress on April 18 [? 1706].

In spite of all these losses, the mind of Aurangzeb remains intent on these operations, and in spite of his recognising that his strength produces no result, he still relies on his astuteness. He brought out of prison the son of Sambha Ji, of whom I have spoken (II. 246), and made him over to the general Zujfiqar Khan. Then he wrote letters to several Mahrattah officers, inviting them to appear and take service under their legitimate prince, to whom liberty had been granted. He promised to give them for their maintenance the tenth part of the revenues from the Dakhin province and its territories.

These men replied to the king's letters that they had already a prince, Shiva Ji, son of Ram Raj, whom they had acknowledged [163] as their legitimate lord and ruler. They had pledged themselves to obey him, and were dependent upon his orders. On no terms would they recognise the released prisoner. As for the promised tenth, they would excuse his Majesty from troubling, since they meant to collect it by their own armed force.[3]

1. Shahnawaz Khan was a scion of the Safawi house of Persia; he was killed at Ajmer in 1659 (Part I., fol. 244). Shah 'Alam was born at Burhanpur on the 30th Rajab, 1053 H. (October 14, 1643): thus, assuming this passage to have been written in 1706. He was then sixty- three (solar) years of age.
2. This may be intended for Supa in North Canara (sec Constable's 'Hand Atlas,' Plate XXXIV.). The treasure is that referred to *ante,* fol. 156.
3. 'Sahu, son of Sambha the Accursed, whose quarters were within the imperial enclosure, was on the 21st Shawwal, 1117 H. (February

After the officers had sent this sort of answer to his Majesty, Shiva Ji and his army crossed the river Narbada and invaded Hindustan, and also reached as far as the province of Hrixa (Orissah), situated in Bengal. There can be no doubt that they would have gone still farther and plundered the cities of Dhakah, Rajmahal, *et cetera,* if the Prince Almiragi,[1] a Hindu, had not used his army to close the passes through the forests and mountains, which it was impossible for them to avoid on their way. They were therefore obliged to turn and march back to avoid being all killed in the forests. In spite of their having been unable to sack Dhakah, they came back with much booty, and found no one to contest with them on their line of retreat. This is the third time that the Mahrattahs have been in that direction.

In the month of February (? 1705), a body of forty thousand horsemen, detached by the said Shiva Ji, plundered anew the province of Surat, penetrating as far as the city of Barrochi (Broach) [164], situated in the province of Gujarat. From this city there came forth to repulse this great army no more than six thousand horsemen under the command of two officers, one called Nazar 'Ali Khan and the other Coja Amit (Khwajah Hamid). They were cut to pieces, being unable to stand against such a multitude of enemies. These two officers lost their sons, who were made prisoners along with themselves, and they were carried off. For their ransom Shiva Ji demanded eight *lakhs* of rupees.[2]

6, 1706), with regard to certain political considerations, placed in charge of Khan Nusrat Jang [*i.e.,* Zu,lfiqar Khan]. His tent was erected close to the camp of that lord, and a *khila't* was conferred upon him' ('Ma,asir-i-'Alamgiri,' p. 511). The offer of 10 per cent, on the revenue (*sardeshmukhi*), and the letters to the Mahrattah officers, are mentioned by Grant-Duff, pp. 179, 180, his authority being Khafi Khan.

1. Mr. H. Beveridge suggests that this should be read 'Almas Rajah' (Diamond King), an epithet applied in the seventeenth century to the Rajah of Palamau in Chutia Nagpur. See articles by V. Ball, *Journal of the Asiatic Society of Bengal,* vol. 1., 1881, part ii., pp. 31-44, and Colonel Dalton, *ibid.,* vol. xliii., 1874, part i., pp. 240-244; also Ball's 'Tavernier's Travels in India,' ii. 458 and map. For Palamau, lat. 23° 50′, long. 84° T, see Constable's 'Hand Atlas,' Plate XXVIII.
2. This campaign is again mentioned on fol. 168. It must be the same as that put by Khafi Khan, ii. 518, in the forty-seventh year, 1114 H. (1703-1704), and by Grant-Duff, p. 177, in 1705. Khwajah,

In 1705, in the month of February, there was a terrifying occurrence in the province of Gujarat. In the district of Goga (or Gogo[1]) there was such a trembling of the earth that the ground opened for a length of five leagues; in some places the fissure was from ten to twenty cubits wide, and even as much as thirty cubits. The governor of the country sent men to take measurements of the depth, and they brought back the report that at a depth of fifty cubits they did not reach the bottom of the cavity. After a few days of these terrible quakings of the earth there came on a rain of blood in drops of considerable size, the earth becoming red and the reservoirs full of it.

At the same time there appeared a comet, which was visible for fifteen days. The Brahmans and astrologers found herein an occasion for talk, and they declared that these signs were [165] demonstrations of Aurangzeb's (approaching) death and of devastation in many places in the empire, together with the loss of the port of Surat.

Since we are upon the subject of the earthquake in Gujarat, I will record the one which happened three years ago in the city of Batavia. The earth was so terribly shaken in the city that a great number of the houses fell, and many people died in the ruins, both natives of the country and foreign traders. The earthquake lasted continuously for a month, forcing the governor and all the inhabitants to leave the town, and go out into the open country to live in tents. At the time there were many Hindu traders from this place (Madras) in Batavia, and many suffered the misfortune of being crushed under the sad ruins of the city. These events caused much weeping in their families here (Madras).

It is impossible sufficiently to express the sufferings endured by the poor inhabitants who were obliged to live in the open

---

'Abd-ul-hamid Khan, the *Diwan,* was Deputy-Governor of Gujarat until the arrival of Prince A'zam Shah. Nazar 'Ali Khan, adopted son of Shuja'at Khan, the recently deceased governor, was one of the commanders of the force sent out. The defeat was due to a surprise after the Mahomedans had unsaddled and had begun cooking. Khafi Khan says the force was 13,000 or 14,000 strong. For Shuja'at Khan, Muhammad Beg, Turkman, who died 20th Muharram, 1113 H. (June 26, 1701), and Nazar 'Ali Khan, see 'Ma,asir-ul-Umara,' ii. 706.

1. Gogo, a town and port on the eastern shore of the Kathiawar Peninsula, now superseded by Bhaunagar (Yule, 382; Thornton, 'Gazetter,' 340; Constable, 'Hand Atlas.' Plate XXXI.).

fields. Means to satisfy thirst were wanting, the rivers having lost all their sweet water, and the little water that remained tasting of nothing but sulphur. All the fish died. Nor could the inhabitants make use of the ponds, since they, too, had the same [166] unpleasant flavour. However, with great labour and expenditure, they did their best to restore the damage, until at last the earthquakes ceased.[1]

Three years ago Aurangzeb sent a subordinate officer named Riza, a Palhan by race, to take over charge of the government at Ramguir (Ramgir)[2] from Mamudu Kam (? Muhamdi Khan). The latter objected to his supersession by Riza Khan, and disobeyed the king's order. Thereupon the other man recruited some soldiers and seized Muhamdi Khan, and took possession of his property. Then, when once in possession of the government, he (Riza Khan) rebelled against Aurangzeb, and at the present moment, at the head of fifteen thousand horse and thirty thousand foot, he makes expeditions to sack and ravage the Mogul territories. He exacts from one district after another the tributes that they pay to the King. Thus, last year he collected a large sum of money from the province of Gulkandah, and devastated it right up to the port of Machhlipatanam. In this way he goes on pillaging and making himself powerful, after the example of Shiva Ji.

In the month of March in the above-named year of 1705

1. For an account of this earthquake, Mr. D. Ferguson has kindly referred me to Valentyn, 'Oud en Nieuw Oost-Indien,' Deel iv., Beschryvinge van Batavia, p. 231, the exact date being January 4, 1699. Before this earthquake the river used to distribute its waters throughout the town by canals, but since it occurred those canals lie quite dry at low water, especially in the dry season.
2. From the combination of names, I suppose this must refer to the appointment in Rabi', 1117. H. (July, 1705), of Muhammad Riza to succeed his deceased father, 'Ali Mardan Khan, Haidarabadi, as commandant of Ramgadh. 'Ali Mardan Khan was the man twice captured by the Mahrattahs—once in 1691-92 (Part IV., fols. 16, 118, 156), and again in 1696 (see 'Ma,asir-i-'Alamgiri,' 516: 'Ma, asir-ul-Umara,' ii. 824; Grant-Duff, 168). But Muhammad Riza was a Sayyid, and not a Pathan (Afghan). Which Ramgadh is meant I know not; possibly it was a fort in Barar. If Ramgir is the right name, it might be either the town in the Yelgandal district of the Nizam's territories, or Ramgiri on the western edge of the Vizagapatam district.

another army of Shiva Ji took the great fortress of Pelconda (Penukonda),[1] the key of both the Kamatiks, and formerly the capital of the Narsingh emperors [167]. Da,ud Khan was at the time with his army near the sea-coast, collecting money from the European nations. But, hearing the above news, he abandoned his claims, and withdrew his army to the territories of his government. He feared that Shiva Ji might obtain possession of one or other of his strong places.[2]

The Dutch ships which had gone to Surat[3] stopped there up to the month of March in the year 1706, and no ship was allowed by them to leave or enter the port. Finally, in the above month, they set sail, taking with them a ship coming from Mecca and carrying a very valuable cargo.

The Mahrattahs took measures several times to disturb the Portuguese living in the direction of Goa. The last time they troubled them was in February of the said year [1706], when they sacked and plundered Salsette;[4] nor would they have stopped there had not the Viceroy, Gaetano de Mello, taken the field in person and chased them away, with some casualties on both sides.

Prince A'zam Tara met his father, Aurangzeb. at the city of Aurangabad.[5] His Majesty made a display to him of great

1. Penukonda (= great hill), a town, fort, and mountain in the Anantapur district, one hundred and ninety-five miles west-north-west of Madras. The rulers of the Vijayanagar Hindu dynasty, founded by Nar Singh, made it their capital after their defeat at Talikot in 1564. The town is strongly fortified, and commands the passes up to the Maisur plateau ('Madras Manual of Administration,' iii. 675). Its capture (1704 or 1705) by Hindu Rao and Peda, Bedarah, is mentioned by Bhim Sen (British Museum, Oriental MS., No. 23, fol. 156*a*).
2. The subject of Penukonda is resumed on fol. 168. and that of Da,ud Khan on fol. 184.
3. See *ante*, Part V., fol. 4, and forward, fol. 205. I cannot tell whether by the 'ship from Mecca' is meant the captures on September 17, 1704, by the *Zuyddorp*, or some other and later seizures (see letters of Pieter de Vos, to XVII., November 13 and 28. 1704).
4. From the reference to Goa, and the appearance of the Viceroy in the field, it is clear that Salsette Island near Goa is intended, although Cardeira, the translator into Italian, gives in a note a description of the other Salsette near Bombay.
5. For 'Aurangabad,' read 'Ahmadnagar.' Aurangzeb got no farther, but died there. A'zam Shah was sent for to Court of the 24th

affection, and gave him many signs of a special love. He said to him that, since his age forbad his continuing longer the war against [168] the infidels, it had become his son's business to take vengeance and destroy them now that he had become lord of the whole Dakhin, of the kingdoms of Bijapur, Gulkandah, and all their dependent territories. He (Aurangzeb) intended to go away and seek repose, and then he buried in the mausoleum of the emperor Humayun. The prince replied to the proposal by requiring from his Majesty a month's time to come to a decision whether he ought to accept this charge.[1]

The army of Shiva Ji, which had, as I have said (*ante*, 164), crossed the Narbada river to the number of forty thousand horse and seven thousand infantry, penetrated into the province of Gujarat and sacked the city of Ahmadabad, from which they acquired considerable treasures.

The man Bahadur Khan, who, as I said (*vide* fol. 138), escaped from prison, has now been made Governor of Pelconda (Penukonda).[2] For its defence he keeps on foot fifteen thousand soldiers and all the baggage train and victualling supplies necessary for maintaining himself in the possession of such an important fortress.

Let me state here the way in which this fortress fell into the hands of the Shiva Jis (the Mahrattahs) without its costing them a single drop of blood. The commander of the fortress was a Rajput officer called Ram Das, a friend [169] of Bahadur Khan. He knew very well that this Ram Das had not been paid by the king, and he wrote to him that if he would leave him an opening for entrance into the fort, and allow him to make himself master of it, he would present him with ten thousand rupees, also retaining him and his soldiers at good rates of pay. The commandant accepted the offer, and one morning very early allowed Bahadur Khan to pass in.

He found the governor asleep, seized him where he lay, and confiscated his goods; he now demands three *lakhs* of rupees

---

Jamada I., 1117 H. (September 13, 1705), forty-ninth year (see 'Ma,asir-i-'Alamgiri,' p. 496, line 16). He arrived at Ahmadnagar on the 21st Shawwal, 1117 H. (February 5, 1706), fiftieth year (*ibid*., p. 512, line 10).

1. The subject is resumed on fol. 170.
2. For this place, see note 115. to fol. 166. Penukonda crops up again on fols. 177 and 185.

before he will set the captive free. When this enterprise was carried out, and the fortress was quite safe, Shiva Ji's army started again, and laid siege to the city of Sara, where he still is.[1] Da,ud Khan, having heard of this progress of his enemy, lives in great dread, and continues his preparations as best he can. At this time orders reached him from the court to watch carefully over and relieve those territories. He is therefore preparing to march, and his pay was raised, the King making him a six *hazari* without any regard to the rules of the great emperor Akbar.

It is now forty-six years since King Aurangzeb began his campaign against the Mahrattahs, the Kings of Bijapur and Gulkandah, and other princes and potentates. In the early days of the war he left the command [170] in the hands of his generals while he looked after the administration of the empire. But finding that these officers did not act as he wished, and were not energetic enough, in the year 1680, as I have already stated, he took the command of the army in person. It is therefore twenty-six years that this king has been in the field, and during that space of time has effected all the conquests of which I have spoken.

In the month of March, in the year 1706, he withdrew to the city of Aurangabad,[2] leaving behind him the fields of these provinces devoid of trees and bare of crops, their place being taken by the bones of men and beasts. Instead of verdure all is blank and barren. The country is so entirely desolated and depopulated that neither fire nor light can be found in the course of a three or four days' journey, and you are in continuous dread of coming across the enemy.

When the period fixed by Prince A'zam Tara for giving his answer to his Majesty had elapsed (see *ante*, fol. 168), the reply that he gave was as follows: 'During six-and-twenty years your Majesty with your whole strength and treasure has not been able to subject your enemies as you desired. How, then, can

1. Sara, in the Nanddrug district of Maisur (Constable's 'Hand Atlas,' Plate XXXIV.). From 1687 the Moguls made it the headquarters for their *fanjdar* of the Bijapur Karnatik (L. B. Bowring, 'Haidar Ali' ['Rulers of India'], p. 17).
2. Read here, as before. 'Ahmadnagar' instead of 'Aurangabad.' The date of arrival there was January 31, 1706 (see note 105, to fol. 159).

I do it, being a prince of small strength and wealth? I am not eager to involve myself in an affair of such great importance. My only desire [171] is to remain in your presence and serve like any other captain. You ought rather to employ on this enterprise Prince Shah 'Alam, who is much richer than me, and is supported by four sons." After hearing his son's arguments, his Majesty made no further suggestion; things continue up to this time in the same state as before, and the enemy prosecute their undertakings with great success.

In these days it happened that the foster-brother of Prince Kam Bakhsh killed one of the royal eunuchs for no other reason than that the man had been insolent. The culprit heard that the king was sending to arrest him, and he took refuge with the prince, who raised no objection to receiving him, and decided to protect him. The king was highly incensed, and, unable to conceal his rage, let the prince know that the man would be brought out of his palace by force.

In obedience to command, the prince appeared in his father's presence, but look with him the criminal, they walking arm in arm. In this manner he appeared before the king and cried out aloud that if anyone interfered with the man he would die in his company. When the king beheld this resolute proceeding on his son's part, although his anger was not calmed, he feigned that it was appeased. In soft words he told his son that his favourite's life was granted, and promised that the man should not be molested.

[172] Inconsiderately the prince believed the paternal promises, and released the man from his arms. Hardly had he done so when the prince was seized and disarmed, and his friend also, the prince being locked up in the royal palace and the criminal in another prison. After the lapse of some days the prince was released at the entreaty of his mother, Queen Udepuri. But he received a severe reproof, and was ordered not to appear at court unless sent for by his Majesty. In this mode Aurangzeb showed how great was his anger at this want of obedience to his orders.

In March, 1706, Captain Ignatio[1] arrived at Madras; he

1. Captain Ignazio Manocl, of the frigate *Santa Cruz*. He was an Armenian citizen of Tranquebar (Cardinal C. T. de Tournon's diary

is the man in whose ship the Lord Patriarch had sailed for Manila, as I have stated (IV. 175). He reported that the Patriarch was received there with great honour, as was due to his office. After three days the governor of the place sent an official to ask him the reason of his coming to Manila. The Patriarch answered that he was on his way to China, where the authority he possessed would be exercised. Before the monsoon came on he set out for China in the ship in which he had arrived, and the city gave him thirty thousand *patacas* to meet his expenses, while Captain lgnatio was relieved from all harbour dues.

Before Captain Ignatio left Madras, I entrusted to him a ceremonious letter for delivery to the Lord Patriarch, with a valuable cordial and an antidote effective [173] against every sort of poison and all bites of snakes or other venomous animals. After the voyage had lasted some days, the captain delivered my letter and present to the Lord Patriarch. As soon as he learnt that they were from me he flew into a rage, and, without opening them or giving them a thought, threw the whole into the sea.

The Abate di Sidotti,[1] a man of exceptional virtues, remained behind at Manila, intending subsequently to proceed to Japan. He obtained great support in alms, with which he erected a new college, and gave help to the needy, affording an example of singular piety to the faithful. In the same way the Abate di San Giorgio[2] was helped by arms, in order that he might afford aid to his parents, who were, as he said, very poor This he did without the harshness with which he had behaved at Madras.

When the Patriarch reached China, he was met by courtiers sent by the emperor's orders. They escorted him with all courtesy to the city, and up to this time we do not know what has happened there.

This Captain lgnatio, of whom I have just spoken, brought

---

in Father Norbert's M6moires Historiques,' Besanqon, 1747, i. 175). In 'Memorie Storiche' (8 vols., Venice, 1761), viii. i, the captain is called Ignazio Marcos; he took the Cardinal on to China in the year after he had left him at Manila.

1. Already named in Part IV., fol. 178, as being at Pondicherry, and see note 32, at that place.
2. For the Abate di San Giorgio, see *ante*, Part IV., fol 165.

from Manila three dogs, two of which were ferocious, killing men and cattle, and were held in by strong chains; the other was tame, and always followed the captain, of whom it was very fond. It was large and handsome, white in colour. Da,ud Khan was told about these dogs, and becoming desirous of possessing them [174J, he wrote to the governor of this place (Madras), sending a present of a set of robes, and requesting him to procure the dogs which had come from Manila.[1] The governor asked for them from the captain, who gave the two fierce ones, and retained the third for himself. They were sent at once to Da,ud Khan, who was highly delighted at seeing them. He set to work at once to test their fierceness, and loosing a bull, they forthwith tore it to pieces. The following day he made the experiment whether they would do the same with men. They were let loose at two criminals, who were tom to pieces in a moment.

Da,ud Khan believed that they were sending him the tame dog also, but having waited many days in vain, he came to the conclusion, which was correct, that his owner, out of the affection he bore to him, refused to part with him. Accordingly, he sent a principal official of his court, escorted by some cavalry, carrying a letter, accompanied by a set of robes, and a horse, his orders being to bring back with him the third dog at any cost. When the letter was received, Captain Ignatio delivered the dog to the official, and wrote a letter in reply, giving the Nawab to understand that he only sent the dog as a favour.

During the journey this dog was placed in a palanquin, attended by various servants, some of whom were entrusted with the duty of feeding him, others [175] of bathing him daily owing to the great heat; others, again, brushed the flies away. He was produced before Da,ud Khan, who was highly pleased. At once he began to caress him, kissing him, and styling him, 'Brother' and 'Faithful Friend.' Forthwith an order was given for the preparation of a handsome silver chain, by which the

1. From March to November, 1706, presents were several times sent to Da,ud Khan, but in none of the entries is there any mention of dogs. The ship St. Joan de *Canterbury*, belonging to Armenians, arrived in the Madras Roads on February 9, 1706, and the 'ship St. *Johanna de Canterbury*, Senhor Ignatius Marcus commandar, belonging to Armenians, sailed for Manila, July 1, 1706' ('Consultations at Fort St. George, Madras Public Proceedings,' Range 239, vol. lxxxiii.).

dog was tied to the leg of the Nawab's bed, and his food was given from the Nawab's own table.

This Da,ud Khan is very much interested in the chase, and has great delight in different kinds of animals. In his train he always keeps tigers, leopards, hawks, falcons, etc. Of ducks alive he has one thousand, besides many other birds. For the maintenance of all these animals he expends every year two hundred and fifty thousand rupees. Whenever he hears of any parrots, cokatoos, or similar rare animals, he sends at once to purchase them without any regard to price.

There lived in Madras a Dutch Jew called Abendana,[1] who owned a rare kind of ape. Da,ud Khan heard of this animal, and by the intervention of the governor obtained possession of it. The new owner made it over to one of the men in his household, but a few days after he had received charge it was found one morning lying dead. Unable to control his feeling at what was to him such heart-rending news, Da,ud Khan was so overcome by anger that he caused the servant who was in charge to be bound and put to death [176] by driving a stake into his anus until it came out at his neck. Not being yet appeased, he ordered the ears to be cut off of the man who had to attend to the lights in the room occupied by the ape. The first man was punished for not reporting the illness of the ape, and not finding any medicine to treat it with, or taking any other steps to save its life. The second man's punishment of having his ears removed was for not hearing the groans made by the animal, caused by the pain of its complaint, or, if he did hear them, for not making a report to his master. In addition, he ordered the house where the ape died to be destroyed by fire; it stood in front of his audience-hall.

On learning that Captain Ignatio was to leave shortly for Manila, Da,ud Khan wrote him a letter full of ceremonious language, by way of testifying to the obligation that he professed to be under, and the gratitude he felt for the gift of a dog which he esteemed as much as a son—indeed, must more than a son, for you will have seen (IV. 149) that he declined to preserve the

1. Abendana is mentioned frequently in the Madras Records of 1706. He and Sarah Pitt, widow of John Pitt, had a claim for money lent to the new Company (see Press List, No. 8, entries Nos. 190, 259, 279, 281, 283, 293, between September 22, 1705, and June 7, 1706).

life of his own sons. Therefore he prayed the captain to allow five men to proceed with him for the purchase of different rare animals with the money sent to him. To open a correspondence and obtain [177] his object, Da,ud Khan wrote a letter to the Governor of Manila, paying him many compliments, and enclosed thirty-one lengths of gold and as many of silver cloth.

At this time four mace-bearers (*gurz-bardars*) arrived at the audience-hall of Da,ud Khan with orders from the king. He was commanded to march at once with an army to the fortress of Pelconda (Penukonda),[1] and make an attempt to recover it from the hands of the Mahrattahs. Upon July 1, 1706, in execution of the royal commands, he commenced his march. We shall see what happens to this enterprise, and I will without fail report the result.

Meanwhile, until something new comes to pass, let us divert ourselves. In the year 1706 there arrived at Madras two ambassadors from the King of Pegu, on their way to the court of the Mogul.[2] They were, to tell the truth, two men of strange appearance, both youths, of complexion not entirely black; their eyes were rather small, as also their nostrils. Their dress was a piece of cloth folded several times round the waist, and hanging down to the middle of the leg. They went barefooted, and had a fine shirt which covered [178] the breast and came half-way down the arm.

The chief of the two men wore on his head a cap of scarlet cotton-cloth. The other man covered his head with a cap resembling a long funnel.[3] On their waists they bore a mark

1. See *ante*, fols. 166 and 168 for the loss of, and forward, fol. 185, for the recovery of, this fort by the Mahomedans.
2. On April 11, 1706, a letter from the Prime Minister of Pegu was considered by the Madras Council; he desired assistance for the safe conduct of their embassy to the Mogul's Court ('Public Consultations,' vol. xxxvi., pp. 56, 57). Mr. Taw Sein Ko, Government archaeologist, informs me that there is no Peguan record extant, nor any mention of the embassy in Mason's 'Burma,' 1860, or Phayre's 'History of Burma,' 1883.
3. Probably the cap referred to is identical with that worn by Siamese mandarins, as shown in the plate opposite p. 90, vol. i., of La Loubere's 'Royaume de Siam' (Paris, 1691). Mr. J. E. Bridges, late of the Indian Civil Service, who knows Burma well, confirms the above

in the flesh, which lasted for the whole of their life, and it was a sign of their nobility,[1] in the fashion of us Christians who have been to Jerusalem and bear on the arm the mark of that place.[2] These people passed most of their time in smoking tobacco through a long cane.

When their servants, whom they had brought with them from their country, served them with tobacco, or water, or food, they entered their masters' presence with the whole body inclined, the hands held close to the ground; and, retaining this position, they withdrew backwards without ever turning round. I mention all this because I have seen this ceremonial more than once, and, out of curiosity, I went several times to visit them. They were lodged in a small house, for the hire of which they paid one pataca (= two rupees) a month. They were seated on a large mat, and the house was very dirty and full of smoke, their cooking being carried on where they received visitors. I was not much delighted by my visit to them, and did not stay very long, since the smell of putrefying meat disturbed me.

When Da,ud Khan heard of their arrival [179] he sent for them, and they started for the court in the month of June (1706). It is quite certain that, upon their arrival at court, they will be considered by everyone a strange novelty, and everyone will talk about them. When I went to visit them they asserted that they had no intention, even at court, of abandoning their constume, in spite of advice to the contrary.

---

surmise, adding that the Pegu official costumes were copied from those of Siam, and that this pyramid-like hat belonged to the war dress.

1. Mr. Taw Sein Ko, the Government archaeologist for Burma, writes to me that these tattoo marks were a sign, not of rank or nobility, but of belonging to some royal regiment, such as the Natshinywe. As hereditary slaves such men enjoyed the royal favour, and often rose to high office. The still living Kinwun Mingyi, C.S.I., a former Prime Minister, bears such marks, and is the son of a private in the Nat-shinywe infantry regiment. Beginning as a Buddbist monk, he passed late in life into the service of King Mindin, and gradually rose to be chief Minister.
2. This reference to pilgrim marks at Jerusalem long proved a great puzzle, about which no one could tell me anything. At last, quite by accident, I found an explanation in E. Terry's 'Voyage to East India,' reprint of 1777, p. 61. Terry saw them on Tom Coryate's wrists when they were living together at Ajmer or Mandu: 'At Jerusalem this our traveller had made upon the wrist of his left arm the arms

The chief of these ambassadors is called Giadum (Kya Dun), and the other Neconaoc (Nakkan Nga Ok), both good names. Along with them there was an official called Chiampiu (Kyan Bu),[1] who bore the present, consisting of two big rubies, two thick sapphires, and a large lump of amber. They also carried a letter, the contents of which I do not know, in a round bottle about the length of a finger, closed with Spanish wax, and placed in a bag of azure-blue colour. Their interpreter is a Mahomedan, born in the kingdom of Pegu, called Quedarguli (? Khidr Quli). The Nawab (Da,ud Khan) provided them with necessary supplies, as they are without money.

When the King of Pegu sent off these ambassadors he ordered six soldiers of his tribe to accompany them, giving to each a sword, and promising that the voyage should not cost them anything, going or coming. To my thinking, this order was out of place. Now that I have spoken of these ambassadors, I will recount what happened to the ambassador of the Persian king, Shah 'Abbas [180] the Little, at the court of the Grand Turk.[2]

Shah 'Abbas was a man of fine appearance, prudent, and of

---

of Jerusalem, a cross crossed, or crosslets; and on the wrist of his right a single cross made like that our blessed Saviour suffered on; and on the side of the stem or tree of that cross these words written, *Via, Veritas, Vita*; some of the letters being put on the one side of that stem or tree, and some of them on the other; and at the foot of that cross three nails, to signify those which fasten'd our Saviour unto it. All these impressions were made by sharp needles bound together, that pierced only the skin, and then a black powder put into the places so pierced, which became presently indelible characters, to continue with him so long as his flesh should be covered with skin; and they were done upon his arms so artificially as if they had been drawn by some accurate pencil upon parchment. This poor man would pride himself very much in the beholding of these characters; and seeing them, would often speak these words of St. Paul, written to the Galatians (Gal. vi. 17)—though far besides the Apostle's meaning—"I bear in my body the marks of the Lord Jesus." '

1. I am indebted for these corrected spellings to Mr. J. E. Bridges, late of the Indian Civil Service; 'Nakkan' means an 'accredited agent.' Mr. Taw Sein Ko, Government archaeologist, suggests 'Gyadun,' 'Nekonauk,' and 'Shampri,' and adds that they are in the Talaing language.
2. Shah 'Abbas II. reigned 1642-67. The story of the Pegu' Ambassadors is resumed on fol. 185.

the most excellent judgment, as is ordinarily the case with Persians. He sent an ambassador to the Grand Turk to secure some benefits. After this ambassador had been for some time at the court, the grand *wazir*, during a visit, wishing to mock at him, said: 'Which is the better, to wear on your head a white turban, the sign of modesty and gravity, or, instead, one of cloth of gold, as is usual among the ladies of this court?' The ambassador, aware they were trying to laugh at him, said on the instant that things were not as the *wazir* said. He had seen many ladies of the court who, when they visited him, covered their lower parts with exquisitely fine white cloth, just as with their turbans the nobles of the court covered their heads. At such a ready and unexpected answer the wazir knew not what more to say.

The same ambassador left the court of Constantinople in the company of the Grand Signor, and once uttered an excellent repartee. While they were journeying, followed by a large number of cavalry, the Turk [181] said to the ambassador: 'Keep a little distance from those horses, so that the dust may not irritate your face.' The ambassador hardly replied, still like a prudent knight, however, by a verse which is a Persian proverb, of which the sense is: 'The dust raised by the hoofs of sheep rejoices the face of wolves.'

I have in a previous passage (V. 96) promised to give a clear account of the manners, the life, and the death of the Reverend Jesuit Father Guini,[1] or, as others called him, Piune. As I said then, I was expecting the arrival of information from one of my friends, who has in the end sent it to me. When I read it I trembled, and became so grieved, and at the same time so disgusted, that without a second thought I burnt it, to deliver myself from any need to publish it. Therefore let the reader forgive me if in part I break my word to him.

I wish to report nothing beyond the manner in which he died, anticipating that in this form everyone will be able to under-

1. Father Quenin has been already mentioned in IV., fol. 195; V., fols. 9 and 96. The Chevalier Hubert, Governor of Pondicherry, in his letter of February 12, 1709, incidentally remarks: 'Le Père Quenin qui fut tué malheureusement du tonnerre' (O II., 68, fols. 252 and 253). According to the Jesuit records, the date was May 28, 1706.

stand what was his mode of life. For from the manner of death it usually can be inferred what a man's life has been. I finish, then, my talk about this reverend person by saying that, one day in the month of May, while he was in his room writing, a thunderbolt fell and consumed him. I pray to God [182] the Creator that this instance may serve as example to persons like him, and turn them from intruding into matters which appertain not to ecclesiastics, nor even to laymen. But let them endeavour to find out and do what God commands. Many, both where it happened and elsewhere, will receive consolation from this event, which has delivered them from such a person.

In the same way I will state what happened to the two reverend Armenian fathers, Fra Thomas Abaranaguer and Fra Minas de Siave. One of them proceeded to Bengal to realize the money of the deceased Fra Domingo, which had been placed in the hands of Armenian merchants. This is the money that the Abate di San Giorgio wished to recover from the Reverend Father Fra Michel [Ange][1] (IV. 165, 166). He (Minas) went to Bengal, but he died there, and the affair came to a standstill.

His companion Fra stopped in Madras, where he fell ill; he was treated by a Hindu belonging to the country, who in a few days succeeded in transferring him to the other world. The Capuchin father, Fra Michel Ange, gave notice of the death at once to Father Friar Diogo do Sacramento, Vicar of San Thome, deceased being of his order. That father received the letter, but gave no answer. Friar Michel Ange, Vicar of Madrasta, looked for his coming to remove the corpe and carry it to San Thome. But finding [183] that the day was passing, and he did not appear at four o'clock, all the friars of the convent, with other priests, came, some from San Thome and others from Madras, to the number of nineteen in all, besides a large assemblage of laymen, removed the body from the house, and placed it on a bier ready to carry to the church for interment.

Just as the bier was being lifted Father Fra Diogo issued hastily from a neighbouring shop, having on his head a cap such as is worn by soldiers in this country. He flung himself on the bier, and objected to the removal of the corpse, or its being placed

1. That is, Michel Ange or Miguel Angelo, Capuchin, chaplain of Madras; Father Michael of the English records. For the Armenian Dominicans, see *ante*, V. 69, where 'Abaranaguer' is spelt 'Abarenes.'

in the church of Madras instead of San Thome. Everyone was amazed at such a disorderly act. The priests, both regular and secular, pleaded that the defunct should be taken to the church for the celebration of the offices, and should afterwards be carried to San Thome. But obstinate Fra Diogo declined to hear any argument; on the contrary, with loud cries, causing a large crowd to gather, he continued his opposition. In spite of all this, seeing that the friar was interfering needlessly, they carried the body to the church, sang over it the burial service, as was fitting, and during the night transferred it to San Thome, to the church of Fra Diogo, where it was placed in the earth.

For this good deed of a Christian and a priest the father Friar Michel [Ange], in place of reward, received a reproof from the Lord Bishop, Dom Gaspar Affongo, upon advice given [184] by Brother Nicolo Rodriguez, first councillor, and other enemies of the Capuchins. Such disputes should be avoided; otherwise the Mahomedans and Hindus recently converted to our Faith will begin to murmur on seeing such disorders, and little by little will forsake their new faith. Little store do they set by certain grand orators who preach the truth, but never act up to it. These converts begin to suspect that all must be a deception, and that in the Christian religion there is no truth; and this I have heard murmured in many places. I do not fail in attempting what I can to remedy this, by referring to various noble examples. For the rest, let those it concerns take thought about it.

Let us go back once more to Da,ud Khan.[1] During his march he occupied his time with his dogs. He set them to attack now animals, now poor men and beggars. Then one day, in his delight at such bestial sports, he set these dogs at some of his captains. Expecting they might be torn to pieces by these beasts, the officers collected their soldiers, killed the three dogs, and wounded Da,ud Khan, who attempted to defend them. From this event there was a great outbreak in the army, and declaring Da,ud Khan to be mad, the principal officers tried to put him in chains.

When Da,ud Khan heard what his officers intended to do, he apprehended [185] that he would be ruined, and therefore went to visit the officers whom he had insulted. He threw himself

1. The subject is continued from where it left off on fol. 177.

at their feet, and asked pardon for what he had done. In this way the army was pacified, and pursuing the march, they arrived within view of the fortress of Pelconda (Penukonda). Da,ud Khan was convinced that the place could not be taken by force of arms, and he offered to the fort commander, named Indu Rao (Hindu Rao),[1] who held it on behalf of Shiva Ji, the sum of seven lakhs of rupees for surrendering the place. The commander accepted the offer, and on August 11, 1706, made over the fortress after a simulated defence. This is the ordinary course of action adopted by these officers, after which they receive from the king greater honours and greater pay, while they retain the friendship of the enemy. The Mahrattahs collect money in all directions for the upkeep of their armies.

NOTE ON DA,UD KHAN, PANNI.

As we here part company with that genial ruffian, Da,ud Khan, some account of his origin and family, with the date of his death, may be fitly inserted.

The Panni tribe of Afghans, to which he belonged, migrated to India some centuries ago, their chief settlements being in Bianah, south-west of Agrah, in Sind, and in the Dakhin. They were the chief adherents of the Mahdawi sect, founded about 1553 by Sayyid Muhammad of Jaunpur, styling himself the Mahdi. Khizr Khan, father of Da,ud Khan, began life as a trader, but soon entered the service of the Bijapur kings, his patron being one Bahlol Khan ('Abd-ul-karim, Miyanah), a high-placed Afghan officer of that state. Khizr Khan was stabbed to death in 1674. Da,ud Khan was apparently born in the Dakhin about 1671 (or, if Mirza Muhammad, in the *Tarikh-i-Muhammadi*, is right in saying he was nearly sixty at his death, his birth took place as early as 1656), and he was taken into the Mogul service while still a youth. When the Bijapur and Haidarabad kingdoms fell in 1686 and 1687, Zu,lfiqr Khan, son of Aurangzeb's *wazir*,

1. There was a Mahratta officer named Hindu Rao, who was captured during a pursuit of Sambha Ji in 1689, but escaped almost immediately. In 1116 H. (1704) Hindu Rao, probably the same man, shared with Dhana, Jadon, the command of a Mahratta force sent to relieve Wakinkerah (see 'Majasir-i-'Alamgiri,' pp. 327, 328, 500). This is probably the officer referred to in the text. Bhim Sen ('Nuskhah-i- dil-kusha,' British Museum, Oriental MS., No. 23, fol. 158*a*) speaks in 1704 of a Hindu Rao, Ghorparah (probably Sidu Ji Rao, Senapati, of that family), whom the Rani tried to imprison; he fled to Korkal, 14 *kos* from Aduni, and finally retired to his home at Sundur, about twenty-five miles from Ballari.

became governor of the conquered provinces, and in time Da,ud Khan was appointed his deputy, remaining the most prominent Mogul official in the Dakhin until Zu,lfiqr Khan's fall and death in 1713. Upon Nizam-ul-mulk's appointment as that noble's successor, Da,ud Khan was removed to Ahmadabad Gujarat.

In a short time Sayyid Hussain 'Ali Khan, Barhah, brother of Farrukhsiyar's *wazir*, superseded Nizam-ul-mulk. The emperor and his party, in the hope of destroying the Sayyid, to whom they were secretly opposed, transferred Da,ud Khan to Khandesh, one of the six Dakhin provinces (May 3, 1715). His secret instructions were to oppose and, if possible, kill Husain Ali Khan; his reward, if successful, to be the government of the six provinces with the title of Sher Shah.

On reaching the Narbada bank, Husain 'Ali Khan heard that Da,ud Khan was at Burhanpur, the capital of Khandesh, preparing for resistance. Crossing hurriedly by a ford, the Sayyid's men managed, although the river was rising, to reach the other side in safety, but the artillery and baggage had to be ferried over in boats. Da,ud Khan advanced to Bahadurpur, about six miles from Burhanpur; but, evading his adversary, the Sayyid, on August 15, 1715, effected his entrance into the town.

At length, on September 6, 1715, Husain 'Ali Khan advanced and surrounded Da,ud Khan's position. Da,ud Khan himself sat quite collectedly on a bedstead, to which were attached his two favourite Persian greyhounds. From early morning on one day until noon on the next he never stirred; and as he was a believer in the god Lachhman's powers, he prayed: 'O Lachhman! send down rain, and put out the cannon fire.' Clouds appeared, rain began to fall, and the touch-holes and powder-pans were so wetted as to check the firing.

The Afghan onset was now successful, and the Sayyid's ordnance artificers and gunners took to flight. Da,ud Khan rode in search of Husain 'Ali Khan, killed one pretender to that name, put to flight the Sayyid's brother, and by a blow on the back from his elephant-driver's goad cleared another general out of his road. Thus Da,ud Khan fought on until his followers were reduced to three hundred men; at length a bullet pierced his forehead, his turban fell off, and in a minute or two he was dead. His body was exposed for two days in Burhanpur town to convince disbelievers that he was really dead.

He left only a small amount in money, a hundred elephants, seven hundred horses, some Persian greyhounds, tigers, leopards, and a number of birds. Neither tents nor equipage had he; he lived like a trooper or a mendicant. Perhaps the best summary of his character is one extracted from the Madras Records of 1709: 'Very precarious in his temper when sober; free and generous when supplied with the liquors he asks, which we always take care to supply him with; a great favourite with the late and present king as a soldier fit for rough work.' The last remark is borne out by a saying current in those days: *Bane* to *bane, nahin to, Da,ud Khan, Punne* ('Do it if you can; if not, try Da,ud Khan').

In Farrukhsiyar's reign (1713-19) a brother, Bahadur Khan, became *faujdar* of Qamarnagar Karnul, now the chief town of a Madras district. From that time the family became established as titular Nawabs of Karnul, and remained prominent in the Dakhin until nearly the middle of the nineteenth century. In 1838 the then nawab rebelled, and was deported; soon afterwards he was stabbed by a servant at Trichinopoly. A pension was granted to his son, which lapsed on his death in 1848.

AUTHORITIES.

Kam Raj, ' 'Ibratnamah' (India Office Library, MS. No. 1,534, Ether 'Catalogue,' p. 146), fol. 51b; Kamwar Khan, 'Tazkirat-us-salatin-i- Chaghatae,' my copy; 'Ma,asir-ul-Umara,' i. 124, ii. 63-65; H. G. Raverty, 'Notes on Afghanistan,' 1883; 'Madras Manual of Administration,' 1885, ii. 86, 87; Mark Wilks, 'Historical Sketches of the South of India,' 1810, i. 225, note.

As I know the court well, I venture to say that the above-mentioned ambassadors from Pegu [*ante*, fols. 177-180] will be received by the Mogul king as if they were apes or monkeys; it will be the same with the courtiers, and, generally speaking, with the whole population. There will not fail to be plays produced about them, as I have seen in similar cases; pictures of them will also be made and hawked in the streets, as something most marvellous and extraordinary [see forward, fol. 195].

[186] I have already spoken of the Persian physicians, and of their inability to believe or admit that European doctors are acquainted with medicine; but I will insert, nevertheless, an instance that occurred in 1679.

While I was at the court of Shah 'Alam in Aurangabad, there arrived a Venetian physician named Angelo Lengrenzi.[1] He came from Aleppo, having quitted the service of the Most Serene Republic, and at the age of thirty-five had set out in search of fresh fortunes. He had thought out various ideas, and collected in his head many thoughts.

He came to see me, and delivered to me a letter of recommendation from the Reverend Father Fra Ivo, Capuchin, of

1. As to this man and his book 'Il Pellegrino in Asia,' see the introduction, pp. Lxxiii-Lxxvi.

Surat.[1] I received him with every civility, making an offer to him of a share in my house, including a companion of his called Signor Protazio, a German gentleman. I was highly delighted by his arrival, in the hope of ridding myself of several patients, who all day long came in search of me personally. Forthwith I gave him out to be my relation, in order to obtain him more respect. I took him to the presence of the chief physician, Mamed Muquin (Muhammad Muqim), of whom I have already' spoken, with the object of getting him, too, entry to the court, with handsome pay from the prince, and thereby prevent any hindrance to his practising. The chief physician promised me the new-comer should have a place, but patience was required.

The worthy patrician, seeing how well I was treated, was full of joy, but would not comply with my advice. He showed he was in too great a hurry to enter [187] the prince's service and draw his pay. As a proof of his ability, and that he was not a surgeon, but a physician, he prepared a pamphlet in which he discoursed on the four principal fevers, of their causes, and the remedies for driving them away. Seeing that he had little confidence in my word, and none at all in that of other friends, I took him with me to the said chief physician. Legrenzi presented the pamphlet, and its contents were explained.

Muhammad Muqim, while listening to his talk, seemed pleased and contented, and by his face indicated that he approved of such good arguments. On his side Legrenzi was equally satisfied, in the belief that he had done rather well by presenting his work, which would cause him to be valued at the court. Knowing the contrary, I said to him how much I should rejoice if he met with success. At the time of saying good-bye the chief physician said to him that he could repeat his visit to the court.

I continued to aid him with a horse and servants, who every day attended him, for the chief physician lived over half a league from my house. This going and coming lasted for a year without the chief physician making over to him any patient, or speaking any more to him. Our patrician did not perceive what it meant. Finally, one day, to undeceive him, Muhammad Muqim ordered one of his servants, an Armenian, called Joseph, who acted as interpreter, to sit down near him.

Our patrician was offended at this act, and on his return

1. Father Ives, Capuchin of Surat, is named by Tavernier.

[188] home he reported it to me. I did not know what else to say to him than that he must have patience. The following day he went back to the court, and wasted his time seated there for over three hours. Finally the chief physician accosted him by asking whether he knew what thing God was. At such a demand Legrenzi was stupefied, and made no sort of answer. By this request he understood that he had received his dismissal, and his joy was turned into sadness. Thus he went back the way he came with lamentations over his strange fate. He was well received, and appointed again to the place that he had quitted. Mr. Protazio remained with me, having no money to pay for his journey. After a year, however, he started, and I helped him so far as I could, and I heard no more of him.

In April, 1706, Shah 'Alam sent a letter to his father Aurangzeb, enclosing other letters from several spies who were with Prince Akbar. By these the news was conveyed that Prince Akbar had died in that month near the fortress of Qandahar, belonging to the King of Persia.[1] Aurangzeb, when he received this joyful news so long awaited, pretended to feel the greatest sorrow, stating how much he grieved at the prince's dying in a strange land; that it was at his own desire he had left India; that it was God's punishment for not obeying his father's counsels, for having decided to act contrary to Mahomedan law.

[189] Equal to the king's joy was that of the princes A'zam Tara and Shah 'Alam, although from reasons of high policy they professed to be greatly disconcerted by it. For they knew they had been delivered from one great obstacle to securing power after their father's death. For he (Akbar) had many friends at the court, and the King of Persia would have helped him.

When the said prince fell ill and knew he had no hope of life he made his will, and named the King of Persia, Xasulten assen (Shah Sultan Husain), heir to all his property. This king directed Akbar's body to be conveyed to the city of Maxat (Mashhad), where the Kings of Persia are buried. He caused a grand sepulcher to be built for the prince close to that of his

1. Akbar died at Mashhad, in Khurasan, on the (March 31, 1706) ('Tarikh-i-Muhammadi').

own father, Sultan Sulaiman,[1] who had been a great friend of Akbar. He also directed that all the precious stones which had belonged to the prince should be inserted upon the tomb; he would not accept for himself a single thing from the inheritance.

In connection with his interment he also distributed bountiful alms, and assigned to the tomb an endowment, by which three hundred poor were fed daily. These acts caused the praise of his generosity to become universal. This king lives at this day in peace, and shows himself extremely devout, never missing on any day his appointed prayers, beseeching God to maintain peace. He does not slaughter [190] numbers of people, as had been the cruel practice of his ancestors.

In ten years of this king's reign not more than one man has been killed by his order. It is the habit of these Persian kings when they go to the chase, or travel from one city to another, to take with them their ladies guarded by cavalry and eunuchs. These attendants go in advance of the king, and look about in the fields to see if they can find anyone. Anyone found near the route is made to hide and withdraw until the king has passed. One day while he was marching to the city of Qazwin he came across a peasant under a tree, his face to the ground and his hands clasped over his head, resting there out of mere stupidity. He was noticed by the king, who, recognising that it was ignorance and not evil intent, threw his cloak over him with his own hands, and went on his way.

The chief eunuch, who preceded the queens and the women, found the man, took away the cloak, and killed him. When the king reached his tents he asked the chief eunuch if he had found anyone within prohibited limits. The reply was that one man had been found and killed. By the king's order the eunuch himself was killed for want of respect to the royal cloak with which the peasant was covered, it being a plain sign of the royal protection.

When this king was at the city of Isfahan, they told him there were many inhabitants who drank wine, and he issued a prohibition at once in accordance with the orders of the Quran. A few days after the issue of this order a Dutch ambassador

1. Sultan Husain reigned from 1694 to 1722; he was expelled by Mahmud, Ghilzai, of Qandahar. The King's father, Sulaiman, reigned from 1667 to 1694.

arrived at the court to negotiate certain business [191], and he brought a handsome present for his Majesty. Among a number of the other things were some birds, such as parrots, cockatoos, et cetera, which sang, talked, and whistled most cheerfully. It would be hard to express the amount of pleasure that his Majesty received from this gift.

One day, as was his habit, he went to sit in his garden, and caused those birds to be brought, hoping to increase his enjoyment by listening to their songs and talk. He was a good deal disappointed, since they uttered not a single sound of joy, although there was no want of the fruits or other products which are their food. His Majesty waited five days to see if they would speak; but finding they were more and more depressed, he sent for the ambassador, and asked the cause of the birds' silence. The ambassador replied that when he brought them to his Majesty he had given them a drop of wine; this caused them to sing and talk cheerfully. The king tried at once an experiment in compliance with the hint given by the ambassador, and on seeing the effect, he declared that he did not know that the privation of wine caused sadness in those accustomed to drink it. This experience caused the king to sanction once more the use of wine by those who had need of it. But a certain punishment was fixed for those who got drunk.

[192] I have already mentioned that the officials governing the Karnatik requested leave from the Mogul to build a new fortress at the port of San Thome. His Majesty refused his permission upon the excuse that the Europeans would take possession of it, since it was so close to the sea. Nay, he would be highly pleased if they could be deprived of those towns where they already resided.

At the port of Puliacat in the Grand Mogul's territory, lying at a distance of eight leagues from Madras towards the north, the Dutch have a fort within the town.[1] Five years ago the

1. Although the details do not correspond, the text must refer to one Agha Raza, a Persian merchant. He assaulted a goldsmith about the ear ornaments of Pieter Josephsz' widow and daughter, and disobeyed the summons of the deputy-fiscal, Dirck Haekaart. The Governor of Choromandal (at Negapatam) deplores the want of means to maintain respect for the Company. Although Zia-ud-din Khan, the *diwan*, forbade

daughter of a Dutchman fled from it. The Dutch, who are not a careless people, made an inquiry into the facts, and found out that a Mahomedan had carried her off out of the place with her own consent.

After five years had elapsed the Mahomedan returned to his home in Puliacat in the belief that no one would know anything about what he had done. The Dutch were told of everything, and therefore sent for three ships from Negapatam. They disembarked a sufficient number of soldiers, entered the Mahomedan's house without any warning, and removed the woman with her three sons. The whole force of the Mahomedan who governed there was useless. This event happened on September 12, 1706.

[193] The reader may have observed that the nobles of India take notice of any generous actions which happen to be done in their sight. The following case may serve as an example:

There was a good-looking young Frenchman named Monsieur de Lae,[1] who had been guilty of a homicide in France, and for that reason had taken refuge in India. In Hindustan he entered the service of certain nobles and learnt the language of the country to perfection. In the year 1703 this young man appeared in the city of Gujarat, then under the rule of Prince A'zam Tara. Returning one day from the chase with his magnificent retinue and numerous followers, the prince saw the young man. He recognised by the man's complexion and his clothes that he was a European. The young man took off his hat and made a very deep bow.

---

the Persian to enter Puliacat, he also demanded the surrender of the two Dutchwomen, asserting that they had become Mahomedans, and had lived two years in Agha Raza's house. Then the former *diwan*, Muhammad Sa'id, was reinstated, and the surrender was not pressed by him; but the Persian obtained help from Sundar Das, Havildar (sergeant), and 'Gidersie,' the *faujdar*. Fearing the enmity of Da,ud Khan in such critical times, the Dutch said nothing (see letters of Choromandal Governor to the Governor-General and Council at Batavia of October 13, 1706, and March 31, 1707).

1. As may be seen a little farther on, the correct spelling is, apparently, De la Haye. The occupation of San Thome by the French took place in 1672, and its recapture by the Gulkandah king in 1674. De la Haye had made a fine defence.

The prince halted and made him a sign to come forward and asked him of what nation he was and his name. He replied that he was a Frenchman, and he was called Monsieur de Lae. Upon hearing this the prince gave a sign of joy, and asked him if he were related to the Monsieur de Lae (= De la Haye) who took the city of San Thome. The young man replied that he bore the same name, but was in no way related.

Thereupon the prince resumed his road with all the signs of dejection. Had the young man said he was a relation of Monsieur de Lae (de la Haye), he would have been given high pay, and would have been much esteemed [194] by the prince and all the other persons at the court.

In the territory of the King of Persia there was a rebellion of the Baloch tribe, of whom I spoke in my First Part (I. 246, III. 75) when treating of the tribes in Hindustan who dwell on the borders between the Mogul country and Persia. These people attacked and ravaged several provinces of Persia. The king sent a division of soldiers to allay the tumult and subdue their pride. But the army was defeated and routed.

Then his Majesty ordered a general called Gurgi Kam (Gurgin Khan), a Georgian by race, to proceed with an army and reduce the country to order.[1] The general carried out his Majesty's orders, and had the good fortune to overcome the rebels. Not content, however, with that success, he entered their country at the head of his army, putting the whole country to fire and sword. He burnt down houses with entire families and killed the prisoners in the most brutal way. The principal men he roasted on spits. The little unweaned infants he dragged from

1. The trouble really arose round about Qandahar, and was caused by the Ghilzais, who are Afghans, not Baloch. Perhaps the best European account of Gurgin Khan (Shah Nawaz Khan was his Mahomedan title) is found in La Mamye-Clairac's 'Histoire de Perse' (3 vols., Paris, 1750), vol. i., book i., Sections IX., X., XV., XXII., XXIV. He was a renegade Georgian of the sovereign house of the Bagrathioni, and was appointed to Qandahar in 1702, where he behaved with great cruelty (work quoted, p. 22), and was assassinated by Mir Wais, Ghilzai, in 1709 (ibid., p. 68). Interesting details are also given on fols. 1-8 of 'Majma'-ut-tawarikh,' by Muhammad Khalil, son of Sultan Da,ud Mirza, son of Shah Sulaiman-us-sani, Safawi. This MS. belongs to Dr. R Denison Ross, of Calcutta.

XLVII. Caparisoned War Elephant

 To face page 256

their mothers' breasts and hacked to pieces, while other mothers were cut open. By these means he intimidated the tribe and brought it under subjection, and made it obedient to the king. When this general found himself thus victorious, he asked his Majesty's to invade the Mogul Kingdom in order to [195] eradicate entirely the above tribe; but his Majesty would not consent to his application.

Let us return to the ambassadors of the King of Pegu and see what happened to them.[1] They started from Madras with the intention of attending the court of the Great Mogul, as their king had directed. When they reached the camp of Da,ud Khan, they were prevented from going farther until they had agreed to put on better clothing than what they were wearing, and they were told that if they wanted to go to court they must ask permission; otherwise they might return at once whence they came. This order had been received by Da,ud Khan from Aurangzeb, who also directed the purchase of one hundred elephants. These were to be sent in company with the ambassadors, on the condition, however, that the latter had changed their style of dress.

When the ambassadors found that their progress to the court was barred, they decided to dress themselves in another way. They ordered some fine clothes and put shoes on their feet, covering their heads with a hat of straw having extended and rather wide wings, of which the lacquered crown was in shape something like a reversed flower-pot.[2] Pictures of them thus attired were sent to his Majesty. Thus accoutred, and with the above-named retinue of one hundred elephants, which Da,ud Khan had bought, they were sent on to court.

The friendly reader should reflect here on the designs of this

1. This is a continuation of the story which broke off upon fol. 185.
2. Mr. J. E. Bridges, Indian Civil Service (Retired), who served long in Burma, writes: "The king's ministers wore head-dresses similar to those described. The one like a glazed pot is probably the hat of the Council dress.' Mr. Taw Sein Ko, Government archaeologist in Burma, adds: 'It refers to an official head-dress, consisting of a plain crown, with ornamented flaps behind the ears. It may still be seen on some images of Buddha, but with the difference that the crown is of pyramidal shape.'

aged king, who gave this order to Da,ud Khan solely that the ambassadors and agents of different princes, as also the spies of various rajahs who are found in numbers at the court, should be able to write [196] to their princes that to his (Aurangzeb's) court had come ambassadors from a strange king bringing a magnificent present. Aurangzeb thought that by so doing he could make a display of his greatness, and that he would be looked on as a mighty potentate, a reputation which he desires to have.

There can be no doubt that some princes among the Rajputs do entertain this belief, as Aurangzeb wishes them to do, since, as I have said, they are in the habit of accepting what is commonly asserted. The Shiva Ji, however (*i.e.*, the Mahrattahs), are not highly impressed by these artifices; on the contrary they press on him straitly more and more. When the doings of the Mahrattahs are reported to him, he has no other answer than that there are robbers everywhere. This is to save his dignity, but in his heart he is acutely pained without being able to devise a remedy.

[Here I omit an account of Da,ud Khan's proceedings at San Thome and Madras, which I have already given from the Portuguese version in Part IV., fols. 245, 246. I have inserted there one or two emendations from the Italian and Portuguese versions in Part V. I pass on to fol. 202.]

[202] King Aurangzeb repents of having entangled himself in this war with the Mahrattahs, for it has not succeeded as he had hoped; thus he has been compelled to remain in these Dakhin lands as the only condition of keeping what he has conquered. At this moment he is encamped at a place near Aurangabad, called Ahmadnagar[1] of which I have spoken (I. 75). There is not one of the princes his sons who will undertake to carry on the campaign. Meanwhile the Mahrattahs move about with their armies and pillage the empire of Hindustan in all directions. Such is their power and audacity that they penetrated as far as the capital at Dihli and plundered wherever they pass. While one army was on this expedition another army,

1. Aurangzeb reached Ahmadnagar on the 16th Shawwal, 1117 H. (January 31, 1706) ('Ma,asir-i-'Alamgiri,' p. 519). The place is over seventy miles south-west of Aurangabad.

also belonging to the Mahrattahs, was active in plundering the city of Gulkandah. Every day they display their power to a greater extent in every part of the Mogul empire.

[203] The old king never ceases issuing his orders for the suppression of all these disorders, but they little profit him. He lives in constant dread that his sons A'zam Tara and Kam Bakhsh may rise against him; hence, as an impediment to any such revolt, he sends out the larger part of his troops to fight under the standards of generals, ordering them away on expeditions first in one direction, then in another.

In the month of November, 1706,[1] the old king fell ill once more, and for five days did not appear in audience. This illness was the cause of an outbreak in the army, men thinking the king was dead. Already many officers had gone over to the side of Prince A'zam Tara, others had adopted that of Kam Bakhsh, while the rest made ready to lay hands upon all they could find.

The astute old man was told of these things, and, ailing and weak though he was, had himself carried to audience on a small throne propped up by a number of cushions, and having men behind to hold him so that he should not fall. As soon as he made his appearance the instruments of music began to sound, and by the beating of the drums the army was informed that the king was alive and was engaged in giving audience. Thus the mutiny was stayed, which until that time had gone on increasing.

The sagacious old man, thus seated on the throne, gave first some orders to the chief *wazir*. He then had recourse to an artifice such as had been customary with him in early years. Taking his handkerchief, he pressed it upon his eyes and pretended to cry. This act raised acute compassion among the bystanders; and whether it were genuine or merely a stroke of clever policy, they demanded the cause of his grief. Aurangzeb [204] then removed the handkerchief from his eyes, and, tears running down his face, said: 'I weep bitter tears, and grief overwhelms me at finding myself so feeble, also because I foresee much destruction

1. Aurangzeb fell ill at the end of Shawwal, fifty-first year, 1118 H. (February 3, 1707, N.S.), but recovered ('Ma,asir-i-'Alamgiri,' p. 520). On fol. 339, Part V., the same ground is gone over, but with other details.

and many innocent deaths. The chief anxiety which torments me is that my prayers are unanswered wherein I ask God daily to take me from this world.'

Having said this much, he straightway fell to weeping again, and with many sighs went on with his story. 'Last night Muhammad appeared to me and told me I was unreasonable in calling for death, since God had decided that I should live another thirty years. The Creator had thus decreed, and my insistence could not prevail.' The astute king had invented this fable, so that if he fell ill again and was unable to appear in public, there should be no disturbance in the army, they being persuaded that he had so many years yet to live. He never doubted that all his words would be swallowed by everyone, since he knew that the majority of people held him to be a saint and a truthful man. As for myself, I have not a doubt that this fable of Aurangzeb's was rejected as untrue by all the princes.

At this audience the traders of Surat appeared again to supplicate his Majesty to get them back [205] the trade which had been stopped by the Dutch, as I have already stated (V., fols. 4, 167). His Majesty ordered twelve lakhs of rupees to be paid to the Dutch, with which they must be content. The Dutch agreed to accept the amount and cease to blockade the trade of the port. They had suffered no loss, having at various times taken possession of several valuable prizes. In this way they had triumphed.[1]

I now state what happened to me. On December 15 in the year 1706 it was the pleasure of the Divine Power to remove from this world my wife, with whom I had lived more than twenty years. The grief I underwent at that melancholy moment I neither know how to, nor ought I to, recount. All I will say is that it was the more profound for never having been experienced before. But,

---

1. For previous mentions of these Surat disputes, see Part V., fols. 4 and 167. On the 14th Muharram of the forty-ninth year (May 5, 1705), Mulla 'Abd-ul-Ghaffur wrote to Joan van Hoorn, Governor-General at Batavia, complaining of the capture at Malacca of his ship the *Faiz-Rasan*, and its dispatch thence to Batavia along with two other Indian prizes. He values the cargo at between $1\frac{1}{2}$ to 2 lakhs of rupees (£ 15,000 to £ 20,000). As stated in note 6 to fol. 4, Part V., Vol. iv., the amount finally paid to the Dutch by the Moguls in 1707 was 8 lakhs and 11,000 rupees.

just as it appears to be the way of the world that sad events always come in company, and are never solitary, on the 29th of the same month Monsieur Martin died; he was the Governor of Pondicherry, nowadays called Fort St. Louis. By this second death I was plunged into nearly the same grief. He had been very much my friend, my true and ancient friend, and I had received from him great—very great—kindness, civility, and honour.

[206] Still, in spite of all these misfortunes, I was able to console myself by placing reliance on the Divine will. Very few days had passed before there came upon me an occasion of still greater depression and sorrow. I know it to be a manifest injustice, not to be supported by those who cherish the slightest zeal for innocence. I see the true servants of God persecuted, men who have undergone the greatest labour for His service. These priests have never caused the least scandal, or given anyone the smallest occasion of murmuring against their doings; nor is it right that their work of charity should be censured.

To this state are the Capuchins of Madras reduced, flagellated by enemies of the soul's welfare and of the propagation of the Christian faith; solely, as I believe, because they are, as befits an Apostolic missionary and a parish priest, zealous for the good of souls and the honour of the Christian religion. Yet their merits are known to all, and as blameless priests they are praised by everyone. The inhabitants of Madras are ready to bear witness to how much they have done there, and what they endure for the profit of the Christians.

Who is there who does not know that Madras is a city of considerable size, with very scattered and rather populous suburbs? Yet the Capuchins, by night as well as by day, move about and attend there upon everyone. They are present assiduously at confession, both of [207] the healthy and the sick, administering holy unction and all the other sacraments. They help the widow and the fatherless, supporting them with alms. In addition to all this they also keep open two schools, one for the Portuguese and Latin tongues, the other for the Malabar (Tamil) language.

Nor do they overlook the needs of the poor mendicants, of whom there is in this city a plentiful supply. They help the travellers of many nations, and on every holy day and Sunday console Christian souls by their virtuous preaching. This is the manner in which they have acted, and for this they are persecuted instead of being praised and rewarded. The truth of these things can be discovered by a brief relation that I shall give of what has lately happened, and let it serve as a stimulus to those whose business it is to see these grave disorders remedied, for the consolation of the newly-converted Christians, and of those others who might wish to embrace our holy faith. For I am a good witness to the fact that, owing to these persecutions, a very large number of those once eager to become Christians have changed their minds.

[NOTE BY SENHOR CARDEIRA.—'Here follows the relation of the persecution in the French language.' Folio 208 is blank.]

[209] Account of the Persecutions Endured by the Reverend Capuchin Fathers [Translated from the French by Count Andrea Cardeira, Portuguese (Public Professor)].[1]

Sirs, although for the space of nearly eight years we have been persecuted in deadly war by the reverend Jesuit Fathers, who have unjustly deprived us of the cure of the Malabar natives, have made us endure many disagreeables, and as you, too, are aware, have had for us no compassion: we, on the contrary, have continued to submit to everything with unspeakable patience, and have never attempted to discredit them. Now, however, they are no longer content to aim at us as persons, but wish also to injure our reputation. Thus, the Lord Bishop of San Thome and the reverend Jesuit fathers are working hard before your Tribunal to besmirch and blacken the reverend Father Esprit, and in his person all the other Capuchins, as mad, disobedient, and scandalous persons. We have therefore judged it well, for the maintenance of our reputation and that of the whole Capuchin Order, to justify our conduct, that we may not pass for such in your opinion.

You know, gentlemen, that until about eight or nine years

1. This text is in Italian, but I have since compared my translation with the French original, which is in Codex No. CXXXV., Class VI. These manifestoes are the work of one of the French Capuchins at Madras, and not of Manucci; apparently, they were addressed to the Governor and Council of Pondicherry early in 1707, after the Bishop's letter to that Council of November 10, 1706, against which these two manifestoes protest so energetically.

ago the Capuchin fathers were pastors of the Malabar people in Pondicherry. Without the Malabaris making any complaint of us. or our doing the very slightest thing possible to which an objection could be made, we were deprived of that mission on the false allegation of an order from the king [of France]. The falsehood is made clear by the letters we have received from His Most Christian Majesty.[1] Although there was every reason for us to complain about such an injustice as the above, have we ever declined to obey the Lord Bishop of San Thome, when his Eminence made over the charge of that cure to the reverend Jesuit fathers? No! In what, then, have we been disobedient, that we are treated thus basely?

Finding, then, that we could not obtain justice from the Lord Bishop of San Thome in things appertaining to this mission, we appealed from him to the Holy See and the Sacred Congregation. The latter, moved to compassion at the injustice done to us, has declared in formal terms that its intention, and that of his Holiness, was that the Capuchin fathers should be admitted to the possession of their former cure. With the object of preventing the reverend Jesuit fathers from alleging ignorance [210], it has sent out decrees, in which it declares that such was its final decision. We presented these [decrees] to the Lord Bishop, who after perusal approved them, as may be seen on the margin of one particular decree sent to him by the Sacred Congregation. Not only has he approved them, but also directed that they should be communicated to the reverend Father Tachard. This we have done, gentlemen;[2] but what was the reverend father's answer

1. The transfer of the native parish to the Jesuits in 1699 was made under pressure from Governor Martin. He seems to have vacillated in his attitude to that powerful Society. If G. de Challes is to be believed ('Journal d'un Voyage,' Rouen, 1721, vol. iii., pp. 114-165), Martin, in 1691, was strongly adverse to them, although his official letters of the same period express a contrary feeling. After the dispute began, he writes on March 15, 1700: 'We have a perfect understanding with the Capuchin Fathers. In spite of the complaint they have brought against us, we do not fail to give them their due; they are the parish priests of the French, Portuguese, etc. As for the cure of the Malabaris, it is a point for the Jesuits and Capuchins to settle between themselves. Nor on that head do we believe we have acted against the orders you (the Company) gave us' (C 65, fol. 83).
2. The affidavit of March 12, 1706, by De Flacourt and d'Hardancourt, of the French Company's Council at Pondicherry, given

when we showed him the above-named decrees? 'My fathers, you are wasting your time and wearing yourselves out fruitlessly.' Do you not think that a fine answer from a man of judgment, as he is? By it he makes out these decrees to be no more than a jest,[1] and the penalties recited therein mere trifles of no importance. Neither he nor the other reverend fathers have ceased to carry on their functions in the ordinary way, just as if nothing had been said. Now we pray you, gentlemen, to tell us which of the two parties is the more disobedient, the Capuchins or the reverend Jesuit fathers?

Since we knew that all things done by the reverend Jesuit fathers since the announcement to them of the decrees of the Sacred Congregation are null and void—for they are *ipso facto* under suspension, and deprived of all the privileges conferred upon missionaries, as stands recorded in the decrees themselves—we came to the resolve of publishing the decrees in our church at Pondicherry. With the object of not being afterwards blamed in any way, we presented a petition to the Lord Bishop of San Thome on the eve of St. Michael, September 28, 1706, wherein we prayed His Most Illustrious Lordship to put into execution the orders of his Holiness and of the Sacred Congregation; or, if he objected to do so, would he attach at the foot of the petition a formal refusal, for the sole purpose of proving to his Holiness and to the Sacred'Congregation that we had taken or urged all the possible steps for causing their orders to be executed.

Finding himself driven into a corner, and knowing, in addition, that he would be censured at Rome if he opposed the execution of the decrees, the Lord Bishop of San Thome replied that he could not grant, the petition for certain reasons known to him. But we could publish the decrees in our church, seeing that no one could hinder us. Upon hearing these words from the mouth of a prince of the Church, whose words ought to be oracles, Father Michel Ange, pleased in the highest degree, put a question to him in these words: 'Most Illustrious [211] Lord, we may, then, publish the decrees in our church?' His lordship responded:

in Norbert, 'Mémoires Utiles et Nécessaires,' 1742, p. 189, shows that this formal notification look place on February 10, 1706, whereupon the Lord Patriarch's decree in favour of the Jesuits of June 14, 1704 (ibid., p. 200), was produced by Father Tachard.

1. A bibus, a term of contempt, of unknown origin, for a thing of no value or importance (Littré).

'You can publish; who is to prevent it?'[1] After hearing these words the Reverend Father Michel Ange took leave of Monsignor, and wrote to the reverend Father Esprit that he could make the publication. Gentlemen, as you are just and reasonable men, mark a little, I pray you, the scandal raised by the Capuchin fathers, for which they are dealt with and disgraced, as is now the case!

Upon the reverend Jesuit fathers finding they could not openly oppose the decrees, do you know what they have done?! We should never utter it were not our reputation, and, above all, that of our order, involved, and did they not calumniate us unjustly, as they are doing. They have persuaded the Lord Bishop of San Thome to say that we have published the decrees without any permission from him—a most extraordinary statement to be made by an honourable man, but still more so when made by a priest and a prince of the Church. Gentlemen, we have not a permission in writing given to us by His Most Illustrious Lordship for the publication of the decrees. We had not thought it well to demand that from a bishop, whose words ought to be more than sufficient for acting upon in security, Wherefore are we thus made dupes of, that Monsignor should declare in his Pastoral that we have published the decrees without his licences? I leave it to the thoughts of all honourable men to decide what sort of act this is; we beseech God, however, not to exact vengeance for it, but to inspire my Lord Bishop with a desire to testify the truth.

Gentlemen, I pray you to join me here in making a reflection. The infamous old men who accused the chaste Susannah of having committed adultery were triumphant until she was led to the place of execution (Dan. xiii.).[2] But their joy was of no long duration, because God, who cannot endure detraction and calumny, as the Scripture saith, 'Detractores, Deo odibiles' (Vulgate, Rom. i. 30), raised up the Prophet Daniel, who laid bare the deceit, and caused the culprits to be condemned. The same thing, gentlemen, happened, as it were, in our case, but in a still clearer shape; since God, who is the protector of oppressed innocence, took our cause visibly in hand. He has willed that those

1. The original French narrative gives the question and answer in Portuguese, which was the Bishop's mother-tongue.
2. In the Authorized Version this chapter is set apart from the Book of Daniel, and placed in the Apocrypha.

who made us out to be disobedient should be our justifiers, and that their manifest contradictions should be demonstrated. This is how it happened.

[212] After the Pastoral of Monsignor the Bishop of San Thome had issued, in which he accused us of having published the decrees without his permission, the reverend Father Michel Ange wrote him a quite civil and courteous letter, wishing to hear from his lordship's own mouth the assertion that he had given no permission for publishing the above-named decrees. His lordship, in reply to the letter of the reverend Father Michel Ange, wrote upon its margin the following words:

I have given no permission to your Reverence, not even in thought, much less in words' (notice, gentlemen, the accusation). 'I said to you that you could publish the decrees of your own authority, just as you could publish any other order whatever that you liked within your church, without my permission and without anyone hindering you' (See here, gentlemen, our justification, and the most authentic permission that could be desired). 'For I did not issue the Pastoral to stop the decrees of the Sacred Congregation' (notice here, gentlemen, the contradiction, since by a Pastoral his Lordship took away jurisdiction from the Capuchin fathers and gave it to the reverend Jesuit fathers, against whom the decrees were issued), 'but only to repress the audacity with which the reverend Father Spirito announced in his church that the reverend fathers of the Society [of Jesus] were not the parish priests of the Malabaris, but that all those people belonged to his (Esprit's) parish' (Gentlemen, it was not the reverend Father Esprit who made this declaration, but the decrees which said so, as you will hear a little farther on), 'interfering in our jurisdiction in a matter which had been disposed of by the authority vested in me as bishop, under the sacred canons and the decrees of the Sacred Council of Trent, concerning the erection and the division of parishes according as I may believe the welfare of my flock requires.'[1]

Gentlemen, I have certainly read the decrees of the Sacred Council of Trent, but I have never seen there that a bishop could withdraw a cure from the hands of a friar of one order and place it in those of religious of another. But to convince you, here

1. The French original in Codex CXXXV. here gives the Bishop's exact words in Portuguese.

are the very words of the Sacred Council of Trent, Chapter X., 'De Reformatione,' Sessio 14: 'Regularia beneficia in titulum regularibus professis provided consueta, cum per obitum, aut resignationem, vel alias ilia in titulum obtinentes vacare contigerit, religiosis tantum illius ordinis, vel iis qui habitum omnino suscipere, et professionem committere teneantur, et non aliis, ne vestem lino lanaque contextam induant, conferantur.'[1] [Bene fices of Regulars, which it has been the custom for professed Regulars to hold, when they happen to become vacant by the death of the titulary incumbent, or by his resignation, or otherwise, shall be conferred on religious of that order only, or on persons who shall be absolutely bound to take the habit and make that profession, and upon none others, that they *may not wear a garment that is woven of woollen and linen together* (Deut. xxii. 11).

It is quite true that in the same Council of Trent, Cap. 4, Sess. 21 [213], it may be read that when a congregation becomes so numerous that a single *cure* is not enough, then the bishop may order him to engage as many priests as he knows to be necessary to administer the sacraments and celebrate the Divine office. But not even here is it provided that the bishop may remove the legitimate pastor, particularly when he is leading an irreproachable life, and appoint another. 'Episcopi,[2] etiarn tamquam sedis apostolicæ delegati, in omnibus Ecclesiis Parcrhialibus vel *Baptismalibus* in quibus populus its numerosus sit, ut unus Rector non possit sufficere Ecclesiastics Sacramentis ministrandis et cultu divino peragendo, cogant Rectores, vel alios ad quos pertinet, sibi tot Sacerdotes ad hoc munus abiungere, quot sufficiant ad Sacramenta exhibenda, et culium divinum celebrandum.' [In all parish churches, or those wherein baptism is administered, in which [churches] the people are so numerous that

1. 'Canones et Decreta Sacrosancti Œcumenici Concilli Tridentini . . . ,' Romae (Typis S. Congregation is de Propaganda Fide), 1845, 8vo., p. 427; Waterworth, 'Canons and Decrees of Council of Trent,' p. 119.
2. 'Canones et Decreta,' edition 1845, p. 115; Waterworth, p. 147. The words in italics are omitted in the printed text. See also 'Dictionnaire Encyelopedique de la Théologie Catholique' (translation of Wetzer and Welte's 'Kirchenlexicon'), v. 510, for the Council of Trent's definition of a parish; new parishes can be created or old ones modified by the Bishop only (Sessio XXIV., cap. xiii., 'De Ref.').

one rector is not enough for the administration of the sacraments of the Church, and for the performance of Divine worship, the bishops, even as delegates of the Apostolic See, shall compel the rectors, or others whom it may concern, to associate to themselves for this office as many priests as shall be sufficient to administer the sacraments, and to celebrate Divine worship.]

It is equally true that there is to be found in the same chapter a direction that in places where the dwellers in the parish live sufficiently far from the church to make it a great inconvenience to get there, the bishop may, 'etiam' (*even*) against the will of the *cures*, erect new parishes. But we do not find that when Christians all live in a city which is not particularly large any action of that kind can be taken. 'In[1] iis vero, in quibus ob locorum distantiam, sive difficultatem, Parochiani, sine magno incommodo ad percipienda Sacramenta et Divina Officia audienda accedere non possunt, novas Parochias, etiam invitis Rectoribus, iuxta formam constitutionis Alexandri Tertii quae incipit "Ad Audientiam," constituere possint.' [But as regards those churches, to which, on account of the distance, or the difficulties of the locality, the parishioners cannot, without great inconvenience, repair to receive the sacraments and to hear the divine offices; the bishops may, even against the will of the rectors, establish new parishes pursuant to the form of the constitution of Alex-ander III., which begins *Ad Audientiam*.][2]

You gentlemen who live in Pondicherry, tell me, I conjure you, whether the Christians are so numerous that four Capuchin friars, all in priest's orders, are not sufficient. Tell me also, if you please, whether the distances between the places are so considerable that the Christians cannot get to church without great inconvenience. The first of these is not true, for, including the French gentlemen, the *Topasses* (persons of mixed blood), and the Malabaris (Tamils), there may be three thousand Christians,

1. 'Canones et Decretal edition 1845, p. 115 (Sessio XXI., cap. iv.), and Waterworth, p. 147.
2. Alexander III. was Pope from 1159 to 1181. His 'Ad Audientiam' is in the 'Decretales' of Gregory IX. (1227-41), book iii., title 48, cap. iii.: 'Propter nimiam distantiam ecclesiæ potest nova ecclesia in ipsius parochia ædificari et certa portio de antiqua sibi deputari' ('Corpus Juris Canonici,' ed. J. H. Boehmer and Æ L. Richter, 4to., Leipzig, 1839, part ii., column 628).

and at the outside that is the total number [214]. But, in addition to this fact, the second condition is even less true, and there is also another circumstance worth remembering. If the Lord Bishop of San Thome has taken the cure out of the hands of the Capuchin fathers and placed it in those of the reverend Jesuit fathers by reason of the distance between the places, which is the only ground of action that can be rightly adduced, the Christians are not relieved in any way by transfer to the reverend Jesuit fathers, which church stands at the gateway of that of the Capuchins.

If the Lord Bishop of San Thome had this object in view as his motive in removing the Capuchin fathers from their cure of the Malabaris and making it over to the reverend Jesuit fathers, it seems to me that he ought to have erected new churches in addition to appointing new pastors, so as to deliver the parishioners from the inconveniences previously suffered by them, instead of forcing them to attend a church quite close to that of the Capuchin fathers, from whom his Lordship has taken the cure of the mission to the Malabaris and transferred it to the reverend Jesuit fathers. By this detail you can see, gentlemen, that they bring forward quite out of place the Sacred Council of Trent, since this proves to be opposed to the Bishop's intention.

But since the Lord Bishop of San Thome and the reverend Jesuit fathers allege the Sacred Council of Trent as the justification for their conduct, and as proof of the good grounds they had for taking away from the Capuchin fathers the said mission to the Malabaris, I would beg them to tell me how it is necessary to understand those words, which you will find, gentlemen, in Caput 9, Sessio 25, 'De Reformatione,' where can be read in clear and plain words that cures and benefices, *et cetera,* which have been acquired 'per subreptionem' (clandestinely), and by illegitimate means, ought [215] to be replaced in the hands of those who previously possessed them. 'Quae vero [accessiones] a quadraginta citra annis factæ, effectum, et plenam incorporationem sunt consectuæ; hae nihilominus ab Ordinariis, tamquam a Sede Apostolica delegatis, revideantur, et examinentur; ac quae per subreptionem, vel obreptionem' (Reflect well, gentlemen, on these terms, I beg of you) 'obtentae, fuerint, simul cum unionibus irritae declarentur; ac beneficia ipsa separentur et aliis conferantur.' [But as regards those augmentations which, having been made within the last forty years, have come into effect and complete incorporation, such shall nevertheless be reviewed and examined by the Ordinaries as the delegates of the Apostolic See, and those which shall be found to have been obtained by deceit or stealth shall, together with the unions, be declared invalid, and the benefices themselves shall be separated and be conferred upon other persons.][1] Therefore, if there ever has been a cure that has been taken away surreptitiously and by illicit means, it is the very one which has been taken from the Capuchin fathers and given to the reverend Jesuit fathers; hence, as a true inference, there never was a case which more legitimately calls for restoration of the cure to the Capuchin fathers than does that of Pondicherry.

As it seems to me, gentlemen, it is impossible to inform you more clearly of the injustice which has been perpetrated, and which they continue to perpetrate in what concerns us, than by quoting to you the Sacred Council of Trent, adding thereto the chapters and sessions, whereby you can discover whether I quote incorrectly.

Although all this that I take the liberty of writing is clear and simple, I must pray you, in order to convince you completely of that truth, to tell me whether you can persuade yourselves that the Sacred Congregation, which is the Council of his Holiness, on whom the Supreme Pontiff has conferred absolute power over all missions, both in general and in particular, a body which these same pontiffs have designated by the [216] exalted title of Sacred Congregation 'de Propagande Fide,' does not know as well as the Lord Bishop of San Thome the meaning of the Sacred Council of Trent, and, further, what the sacred canons allow them to do. Whence it arises that, if the said Sacred Congregation, after having been informed that the cure of the Malabaris at Pondicherry had been taken from the Capuchin fathers and given to the reverend Jesuit fathers, ordered the Lord Bishop of San Thome to make over once more the said cure of the Malabaris into the hands of the Capuchin fathers; and in order to carry the same into effect dispatched such clear and precise decrees; no one who is not a Jesuit could have any doubt in the matter.

We know very well, gentlemen, though in no way thereby surprised, that the Lord Bishop of San Thome has written to your Council that the decrees of the Sacred Congregation spoke

1. 'Canones et Decreta,' edition 1845, p. 211; Waterworth, p. 266.

not a word about the parish priests of Pondicherry. But to obviate exaggeration, I will place before your eyes the precise words used by His Most Illustrious Lordship, that you may see, gentlemen, whether those words correspond to the original which you have in your possession.

'The[1] reverend Father Fra Spirito (Esprit) came forth with an unlooked-for and scandalous resolution' (Does it seem to you, gentlemen, a great scandal that we should have published, with his permission, the said decrees of the Sacred Congregation and of his Holiness, issued in our favour, in order to obtain once more our old cure?) [217] 'without more foundation than that of his many letters, when he ought to have awaited the decision of France, to which this affair had been remitted' (Here is a fine piece of respect, gentlemen, to the Court of Rome, the preferring to it of an inferior tribunal; and here is a fine method of gaining the good graces of a monarch whose title of Most Christian King was acquired in no other way than by continual submission to the Holy See!), 'and assumed the right to decide about those decrees of the Sacred Congregation' (Here is a heavy burden that his Lordship casts on us; when, then, ought we to come to a decision and be satisfied, if not when we hold the orders of his Holiness and of the Sacred Congregation?) 'which he (Spirito) says have reference to the division of the parishes which we have carried out, making over the cure of the Malabaris to the reverend fathers of the Society.' (Here we have, gentlemen, a fine piece of reasoning. Why and wherefore did the Sacred Congregation send out decrees in favour of the Capuchin Fathers? Did it, perhaps, issue them in jest—*ficar chouma*,[2] as the Portlguese say?) 'If you, gentlemen, send for and inspect the decrees, you will see if any one of them says a single word about the Pondicherry parishes.' Gentlemen, although the Lord Bishop of San Thome could not know how to respect or esteem you too highly, to me it seems, according to my feeble under-

1. Here begin excerpts from the Bishop's letter of November 10, 1706, which is given continuously in full on fol. 282. In Codex No. CXXXV. these are left in the Bishop's original Portuguese.
2. Mr. D. Ferguson writes: '*Chouma* is an Indo-Portuguese word from the Tamil. See Monsignor S. R. Dalgado's "Dialecto Indo-Portuguěs de Ceylao" (Vocabulario); "*Chumá*, sem motivo, sem proposito, Dial. Mang. [Mangalor]— Tam. SiLDIDLT (*Chummé*)." The word is common among Ceylon planters.

standing, that his Lordship has no right to make you judges in an affair which three great bishops, when deputed by His Most Christian Majesty, declined to examine because they learnt that the Sacred Congregation had passed a decision upon it.

Gentlemen, if the Lord Bishop of San Thome and the reverend Jesuit fathers had obtained decrees against us, as we have against them, they would be able to see very distinctly that those decrees dealt with the cure of the Malabaris in Pondicherry. But as we hold decrees against them instead of their having them against us, those decrees are couched in a language which our opponents decline to understand. In truth, gentlemen, must not men be very prejudiced, not to say ...,[1] who talk like that? We made an appeal to his Holiness and to the Sacred Congregation about the cure of the Malabaris in Pondicherry, which had been so unjustly [218] taken from the Capuchin fathers, and the Reverend Father François Marie of Tours, Capuchin and apostolic missionary, started from Pondicherry on his way to Rome with the object of informing his Holiness and the Sacred Congregation about all that had happened, and there (at Rome) he prepared his statement, which we reproduce in its own words:[2]

1. Blank in original.
2. This petition is printed in Norbert, 'Mémoires Utiles et Nécessaires,' Luques (Lucca), 1742, p. 180, where it is dated March 26, 1703. Mr. Philipps has also found it in the 'Madras Catholic Directory/ 1867, pp. 212, 213. Passages omitted in these versions I have put in italics, and additions made in them I insert in footnotes. Mere differences of spelling and punctuation I have corrected according to the above printed texts. Action seems also to have been taken at the Court of Louis XIV. through Father Paul of Vendome, Capuchin, as Procurator for the whole Capuchin Order of all ranks. There is a copy of his 'Mémoire' in Bib. Nat., Nouvelles Acquisitions Françaises, MS. No. 9,352, fol. 274, a copy made by P. Margry; but he does not state the provenance of the original. The attached documents, of which a list is given, would have been of value if forthcoming. They were (1) extracts from the registers of baptisms and burials; (2) a deed of gift for the Capuchin church outside the fortress of Pondicherry; (3) letters to prove that the Capuchins returned (? in 1699) at the request of Governor Martin; (4) letters from the Bishop of San Thome, who is, they say, entirely under Jesuit influence; (5) various letters addressed to Father Michel Ange, of Bourges, Superior at Madras; (6) a letter from the Bishop to Father Esprit, of Tours; (7) a letter from Governor Martin to the said Superior, dated July 7, 1699, asserting that he (Martin) would not have written to the Bishop asking for a transference of the parish had not Father Beauvollier written from San Thome that the Capuchins made him (Martin) pass for a *fourbe*. The petitioner remarks that he had already earlier in the

"Frater Franciscus Maria Turonensis Ordinis Capucinorum Missionarius Aposttolicus, humillimè exponit Eminentiis Vestris quod contra Mandatum,[1] sub die 28 Aprilis 1698, Illustrissimus Dominus Episcopus Meliapurensis absque causa, nec consultâ hac Sacra Congregatione, abstulit k Patribus Capucinis Provincial Turonensis Missionariis Apostolicis Pudicherii in orâ Choromandel existentibus, curam animarum gentis Malabaricae, quam a plusquam triginta annis fundaverant, et non sine fructû et edificatione populorum gerebant illam; quam dedit Patribus suæ Socie-tatis Jesu: quod dicti Patres Capucini videntes mandatis[2] Illustrissimi Domini Episcopi obtemperaverunt, ne scandala[3] *excitarentur oppositione quamvis iusta,* maxime quod sperarent[4] ut Eminentiæ Vestræ justo illorum juri faverent statim atque de illis informarentur. Quapropter Devotus Orator humillimtb supplicate quatenus[5] Eminentiæ Vestræ dignentuh super hoc mandatum particulare dare predicto Illustrissimo Domino Episcopo Meliapurensi ut dictos *Patres* Capucinos pristino juri restituat, pro qua gratia Deus, *et cetera.*' [F. Francois Marie of Tours, apostolic missionary of the Capuchin order, most humbly sets forth to your Eminences that, in opposition to the Decree [of the Sacred Congregation], the Most Illustrious Lord Bishop of Meliapur without cause, and not having consulted the Sacred Congregation, has taken from the Capuchil fathers of the Touraine Province and Apostolic Missionaries at Pondicherry upon the coast of Choromandal, the cure of souls of the Malabar folk, [a mission] which they had founded more than thirty years ago, and were carrying on not without good results, and to the edification of the people. This [the bishop] transferred to the fathers of his own Society of Jesus. Seeing which, the aforesaid Capuchin fathers obeyed the commands of the Most Illustrious Lord Bishop, in

year (1703) presented letters from the Pondicherry Capuchins to Mr. de Pontchartrain. There are also ten letters of 1702 and 1703 connected with these Pondicherry disputes in the Archives Nationals, Paris, No. K 1,374, Nos. 39-43 and 51-5.

1. Insert [ab hac Sacrâ Congregatione emanatum].
2. Insert [dicti].
3. Insert [ex ipsorum quavis de causâ, justa oppositione orirentur],
4. Insert [fore].
5. Insert [ut].

order that no scandals might arise from their opposition, however just, and this [they did] more especially in the hope that your Eminences would see them righted as soon as you were informed of the matter. Wherefore your devoted Petitioner most humbly prayeth that your Eminence will deign to issue a special order in this matter to the aforesaid Most Illustrious Lord Bishop of Meliapur that he restore the aforesaid fathers to their former rights. For which favour may God, etc.]

Here, then, gentlemen, is the petition of the Pondicherry Capuchins, not of those at Madras or Surat, in Persia or in Turkey. What, then, is the reply of the Sacred Congregation?, You have it, gentlemen, written at the foot of the very petition of the Pondicherry Capuchins. Let it be specially noticed that if it were not written at the foot of the petition itself, but on a separate sheet of paper, may be something could possibly be found to say against it. But when the answer of the Sacred Congregation is engrossed at the end of the petition from the Pondicherry Capuchins, who can deny that the said decrees are issued with reference to the cure of the Malabaris in Pondicherry? No one[219], gentlemen, except the Lord Bishop of San Thome and the reverend Jesuit fathers!

'Dentur decreta Episcopo emanata die 28 Aprilis [1698] super dubiis propositis a Pa tribus Capuccinis Provinciæ Turonensis in Urbe Suratensi missionariis; videlicet.[1]

[6] 'An in missionibus qui sunt magis antiqui missionarii Parochi in tali missione censeantur, maximè si Capellam seu Sacellum, aut Ecclesiam et sepulturam habeant publicam.

[7] Ubi sic Missionarii Parochi censentur, novis missionariis advententibus, Vicarius Apostolicus vel Episcopus[2] ad libitum possit Parochiam ab eis amovere[3] ut novis Missionariis concedat.' [Let the Bishop be given the decrees which were issued on the 28th day of April, 1698, regarding (certain) doubtful

1. This decree of the Sacred Congregation, dated, like the petition, on March 26, 1703, appears in Norbert, *loc. cit.*, p. 182, and in the 'Madras Catholic Directory,' 1867, p. 213. The corrections are made as described in the previous note. The decree of 1698 relating to Surat was adopted as applicable to the Pondicherry Capuchins' petition of 1703; there are seven 'doubts' dealt with, of which our text quotes the sixth and seventh, and the findings thereon.
2. Variant, insert [loci possit].
3. Variant, insert [ut].

points propounded by the Capuchin fathers of the Province of Tours, missionaries in the town of Surat—to wit:

(6) Whether in missions the older missionaries, acting as parish priests, are to be reckoned as in the mission, especially if they hold a chapel or oratory or church with a public churchyard.

(7) Where the missionaries are thus to be considered parish priests, can the Vicar Apostolic or Bishop at will, on the arrival of new missionaries, remove the parish from their charge and make it over to the new-comers?]

You have now seen, gentlemen, the doubts propounded by the Capuchin fathers; hear now, if you please, the answer of the aforesaid Sacred Congregation:[1]

'Ad sextum, "non esse vere Parochos"; ad septimum[2] "posse nisi ex gravi causâ, et consulta prius Sacra Congregatione." '

[As to No. 6 (the answer is): 'They are not really parish priests';[3] as to No. 7, 'they cannot be (removed) except for weighty reason, and after consulting the Sacred Congregation.']

It seems to me, gentlemen, that the above is quite clear and plain, and as a necessary consequence, the Lord Bishop of San Thome having had no urgent reasons, nor having consulted the Sacred Congregation, his Lordship could not legitimately take away the said mission; and though he did take it from the Capuchin fathers, and give it to the reverend Jesuit fathers, the latter, nevertheless, have never been, and are not now, the legal pastors of the Malabar Christians of Pondicherry.

My Lord Bishop of San Thome says in his letter written to your Council: 'I have sent forth a Pastoral by which I declare afresh, as I have already declared provisionally, that the reverend Fathers of the Company are the parish priests of the Malabaris, an office which in no shape belongs to the Capuchin Fathers, neither by order of his Holiness nor by mine, as they falsely allege.' If. say I, the Lord Bishop did write these words to your Council, what is there we can do when our adversaries are our judges?

Although His Most Illustrious Lordship says it, this statement is very hard of digestion: 'neither by order of his Holiness

1. Norbert, work cited, p. 184.
2. Variant, insert [non].
3. 'In other words, they remain members of the mission, and have their status as such' (J. K.).

nor by mine, as they falsely allege.' Here is his authentic permission, which I write one more, to clear us [220] of his Lordship's calumny: I did not give your Reverence permission, not even in thought, much less in words. I only said . . .' Weigh well these words, gentlemen, I beseech of you, and think how a bishop, who ought never to act unless by God's Spirit, could address to you these words, 'as they falsely allege,' after having expressed himself in the following terms: I only said to him that he could publish the decrees on his own authority, just as he could publish any other order (as he thought fit) in his church, without my permission and without anyone hindering him.'

Gentlemen, if it had not been a bishop, to whom I owe all imaginable respect, but any other person who had written these words, 'as they falsely allege,' after having given so valid a permission, I might make use of the expression in Holy Scripture, 'De ore tuo te judico' [Vulgate, Luke xix. 22]. But remembering, as I do, the respect I owe to his Lordship, all I will say is that he accuses us very much out of place of having falsely alleged an order of his Holiness. For the Sacred Congregation, which does no act without his orders and without his consent, has sent us the decrees, dated January 11 of the year 1656, of which we insert here the tenor.[1]

'Sacra Congregatio censuit nullo modo [in] posterum licere, pro bono Religionis Catholicae ad tollendas inter Missionaries dissentiones, et litigia, in locis in quibus existunt mission- arii Apostolici unius ordinis, novam missionem aliorum Religiosorum, et etiam Societatis Jesu, fundare, vel illam sub quovis praetextu, aut authoritate exercere absque express'd licentia ejusdem Sacræ Congregationis, sub poenâ privationis officii, privilege, et facultatis, ipso facto incurrenda, non obstantibus quibuscumque.'[2] [The Sacred Congregation has decided that for the welfare of the, Catholic religion, and to prevent litigation and disputes among missionaries hereafter, it shall in no way be permitted, under any pretext or authority whatsoever, that missionaries of a different order, not even those of the Society of Jesus, shall establish a new mission in places where there is

1. This decree of 1656 is printed in Norbert, work cited, p. 204, and in the 'Madras Catholic Directory,' 1867. In the latter version the date is January 22, but Norbert has January 11, as in the text.
2. Insert [in contrarium facientibus].

already an established mission without having an express permission from the Sacred Congregation, any transgressor being subject to privation of office, privilege, and faculty, to be incurred by the very act itself, in spite of all objections that may be made for the invalidation of the present order.]

After such an authentic decree, drawn up in terms so strong, how can the Lord Bishop of San Thome attribute to us error and falsehood because we allege an order of his Holiness? And how is he able to assert that the mission to the Malabaris in Pondicherry does not belong in any manner to the Capuchin fathers: [221] 'and that in no way do they appertain to the reverend Capuchin fathers either by order of his Holiness or mine, as falsely alleged.'

After that, gentlemen, his Lordship dares farther to write to you that, by a consideration of the decrees, it will be seen that not one of them says a single word about the parishes of Pondicherry. 'Let your lordships call for the decrees, and you will see whether any one of them speaks a single word about the parishes of Pondicherry.' But if the decrees do not speak of them, to what end, then, gentlemen, upon their presentation to Monsignor with a request to have them put into execution according to their tenor, did he write the following words? 'The Reverend Father Guy Tachard has already seen this petition and the decrees of the Sacred Congregation. Dated San Thome, February 12, 1706. (Signed) The Bishop of Meliapur.'

Whence proceeds it, then, that when the decrees were notified to the Reverend Father Tachard by the order of the Lord Bishop of San Thome, his Reverence produced a sentence of my Lord Patriarch in order to hinder their execution? If his Lordship had purposed to write to you that the said decrees did not speak in any shape of the mission or cure of the Malabaris of Pondicherry, to me it seems that he ought not first to have approved and then subsequently disapproved of them. If the reverend Jesuit fathers had meant not to obey the Sacred Congregation, to me it seems that neither ought they to have met us with the above sentence[1] in order to hinder the execution of its decree as not meeting with their approval. Thus the Lord Bishop of

1. Apparently by this is intended the order of 1704, given by Cardinal de Tournon, Patriarch of Antioch and Papal Legate to India and China (see Norbert, 'Mémoires,' 1742, p. 200). It is dated June 14, 1704.

San Thome would have been to some extent in a reasonable position, and the reverend Jesuit fathers also, by the non-production of that sentence. In addition, they would have spared the Lord Patriarch a well-earned reproof, which might well fall upon him from Rome for having interfered in an affair which had been submitted to the adjudication of the Holy See. By this course we should have been spared the spectacle of the bad faith with which they have acted in producing a sentence passed two years before, of which we should still be ignorant had we not notified to them these decrees [of the Sacred Congregation]; so true is it that, whatever expedient may be resorted to, the Divine oracles are bound to be fulfilled.

[222] For God, who is a just God, gentlemen, and cannot suffer iniquity, but must punish it, has chosen to make public all that these reverend Jesuit fathers had plotted to do in secret. 'Nihil enim est opertum, quod non revelabitur, et occultum, quod non scietur.' ['For there is nothing hid that shall not be revealed, nor secret that shall not be known' (Vulgate, Matt. x. 26).] However much they may seek a means of quieting their consciences, when they continue to perform their duties as usual after the receipt of these decrees, I find it difficult to believe that they will find any. Since whatever they choose to say, whatever sort of authority they may allege, whatever sort of argument they may adduce, it is necessary for them to give me an answer to two things: either the decrees have been given to the reverend Capuchin fathers for their re-entry upon the mission that had been taken away, or the decrees have not been given for that purpose; and if they say that verily his Holiness and the Sacred Congregation have sent them for our restoration to our ancient mission to the Malabaris, why, then, do they oppose these decrees?

If they say that his Holiness and the Sacred Congregation have not sent them [the decrees] to re-establish us in our ancient mission, and that this subject is not in the least touched upon in the said decrees, will they tell me how they would in that case interpret the following words: 'In locis in quibus existunt missionarii unius ordinis?' etc. Perhaps, because they are Jesuits, they are exempt from that rule. Then what does this mean: 'Aliorum Religiosorum et etiam Societatis Jesu'? Their acts proceed, perhaps, from their having arguments and pretexts which support what they are doing. In that case, what is the meaning of this: 'sub quovis pratextu'? Perhaps it is because they hold in their hands the authority of his Lordship the Bishop of San Thome. Then what does this mean: 'aut authoritate exercere'? Once more, it may be they have permission to act at their own pleasure without the consent of the Sacred Congregation. What [223], then, mean these words: 'absque expressa licentia ejusdem Sacræ Congregationis'? Can it be that if they disobey the said Sacred Congregation their acts will not be open to condemnation? What is this, then: 'Sub pœna privationis officii, privilegii, et facultatis, ipso facto incurrenda, non-obstantibus quibuscumque'? Perhaps, lastly, the Lord Bishop of San. Thome and the reverend Jesuit fathers are not subject to the Sacred Congregation. Perhaps the Sacred Congregation has no authority over them. If so, let them put before me the whole of that in writing; I will then hold my tongue and be at peace.

Gentlemen, I am absolutely certain that they will do no such thing, which is sufficient proof to any person of discernment, and an obvious revelation that the reverend Jesuit fathers, in acting as they have done, are not devoid of ill-will. If you are in doubt, ask them this yourselves, and you will find them tell you so orally, but will never reduce it to writing. Now, if the Sacred Congregation has the power to issue commands to them whenever judged appropriate, and to inflict on them penalties in case of disobedience, how can they appease their conscience after defying the orders of the said Sacred Congregation, which orders them to obey 'sub pœna privationis officii, privilegii, et facultatis, ipso facto incurrenda, non-obstantibus quibuscumque'?

Before the receipt of the decrees of his Holiness and of the Sacred Congregation, the Lord Bishop of San Thome and the reverend Jesuit fathers were possibly acting in an excusable manner, for it might be assumed that they did not know, in spite of its being a thing of which they should not have been ignorant. But after seeing the decrees, after having approved them, after having notified them to the reverend Jesuit fathers, after having proclaimed them in our church, after being convinced that his Holiness and the Sacred Congregation meant that the Capuchin fathers should re-enter upon their ancient mission, how could Monsignor entrust that mission to the reverend Jesuit fathers by a Pastoral [224] expressly issued? The reverend Jesuit fathers know quite well that the thing is no longer in Monsignor's power, for, as the decrees state, 'sub quovis pratextu aut authoritato exercere absque expressa licentia ejusdem Sacræ Congregationis,' how, then, can they continue to exercise their functions in the usual way? It is no longer a sin of ignorance; it is—pardon me, gentlemen, I hardly dare to say what, and leave you to place upon it the interpretation that you please, and to judge calmly whether the Lord Bishop of San Thome and the reverend Jesuit fathers are right and clear in conscience, or, rather, have all of them incurred the censures set forth in the Sacred Canon?

However great the injustice committed against us, which cries aloud for vengeance before God and in the sight of men, that is not, however, what most weighs down our hearts. It is a certain letter delivered to the Reverend Father Espirit of Tours on November 3, 1706, concerning which the Lord Bishop of San Thome, without reflecting upon whether what he imputed to us is true or false, has written a letter to you in such hard, cruel, sharp words that the public will hardly believe their eyes. However, I constrain myself to quote a few expressions, solely that you may satisfy yourselves, gentlemen, whether they correspond with the original in your possession: 'It concerns you, gentlemen; it is your business to preserve the peace, and uphold my jurisdiction as set forth by me, by compelling the reverend Capuchin fathers, through measures of the requisite rigour, to desist.'[1] You gentlemen who are at Pondicherry know how the Capuchin fathers have behaved. Tell me what is the scandal they have caused, that they should be dealt with in so harsh a way and spoken of in terms so hard? If the Capuchin Fathers had refused to obey, or, rather, had they been wicked men, persons given up to every vice, could worse have been done to them than jeonsigning them to the secular arm, with the direction [225] that they should be treated with the utmost rigour of the law? Before giving you orders like this, the Lord Bishop of San Thome, as it would seem, could never have read the contents of the Patents conceded to the Capuchin fathers by Henry III. of happy memory.[2] Because, had his Lordship read them, he would have

1. Quotations from the Bishop of San Thome's letter of November 10, 1706. In Codex No. CXXXV. they are all given in Portuguese.
2. Henry III. reigned 1575 to 1589. The letter is quoted by Lucas Waddingius, 'Annales Minorum . . . continuata P. F. Stanislao Melchiorri de Cerreto . . .' (Anconæ, 1844), vol. xxi., p. 2, on the authority of 'Boverius'—*i.e.*, 'Annalium . . . ordinis Minorum S. Fran cisci Capucini nuncupantur' (Lugduni, 1632), vol. ii., No. 10, p. 792, under year 1576. In the Italian

seen about half-way through the said Patent the following words: 'In order that we and our aforesaid subjects may benefit by the prayers and orisons of the said religious fraternity. We have taken and placed and hereby take and place the aforesaid religious fraternity called the Capuchins of the Order of St. Francis, as well as their monasteries, congregations, dependents, and all thereto appertaining, under our protection and special safeguard and that of the kings our successors, of our special grace, plenary power and legal authority . . .,' etc.

Most probably the Lord Bishop of San Thome has never read the words contained in the Patents of Louis XIV. now reigning. For his Lordship, who professes such great respect for our Invincible Monarch, since he places in his hands the decision about the cure of the Malabaris, would not in that case have made over to the secular arm friars whom His Most Christian Majesty takes under his singular protection and special safeguard. Here are a few phrases from the Patent we have obtained:

'Equally we desire and it is Our Pleasure that they enjoy the same in perpetuity, permitting them by Our grace and authority, as above stated, to establish themselves again and build convents and houses in all such places as may be offered or given to them hereafter, and that they may carry out therein their religious functions in pursuance of their laudable and saintly custom; the said places, as also every other thing that is and can be of service to them, we have freed and do by these presents free, permitting them further to remove the said convents and habitations to other more convenient spots, and to this effect, therefore, so far as necessary, we have taken and placed and hereby take and place under our singular protection and safeguard their persons, convents, and all the things [226] that they have or may hereafter have,' etc.

A little farther on we read: 'We forbid every sort of person, of whatever station or condition, whoever he may be, to disturb them or offer them any impediment under any pretext whatsoever, and in whatever manner it may be. These things we enjoin on our faithful and well-beloved lieutenants in our courts, parliaments,

---

translation, 'Annali dell' ordine de' Frati Minori Cappuccini, composti dal Molto R. P. Zaccaria Boverio . . . e tradotti da Fra Benedetto Sanbenedetti' (Venezia, Giunti, 1643), vol. i., part ii., pp. 446-448, where the date is July, 1575.

chamber of accounts, the court of aids, the procurators-general and their substitutes, bailiffs, seneschals, provosts and their deputies, and every other official whom it may regard,' etc.

Probably the Lord Bishop of San Thome, when he wrote those words to your Council [see *ante*], did not know that His Most Christian Majesty would not concede any respect to episcopal authority in cases where we were badly treated without cause. For there are many judgments by the councils of the parliaments of Paris, Toulouse, Grenoble, Rennes and elsewhere, of July 17, 1662, May 12, 1663, and of the council of Sens in 1667, and others fulminated against the Lord Bishop of alets, [the Archbishop of] Sens, and other prelates.[1] Yet these had not oppressed us in the severe way adopted by the Lord Bishop of San Thome. All these things you may see, gentlemen, in an

1. In an *Arrêt* of September 23, 1668, in favour of the Capuchins, previous orders of July 7, 1662, May 12, 1663, and April, 1667, are cited (see Pére Hilaire de Barenton, 'Les Capucins de la France,' 1903, 8vo., pp. 4-9). Throughout the *Ancien* Régime the French bishops fought for the maintenance of the rule that confession must be made to the parochial clergy and not to the regulars. In 1653 the *Assemblée*? *Générale* of the clergy denounced the Capuchins of Sens to all the bishops for this practice. H. de P. de Gondrin, Archbishop of Sens from 1646 to 1674, was suspected of Jansenism, and this led the Jesuits to support the Capuchins in their conflict with him. The struggle assumed many phases, and continued until the Archbishop's death (see André Mater, 'L'Eglise Catholique: sa Constitution, son Administration' [Paris, Armand Colin, 1906, 18mo.], pp. 364, 365, and G. Dubois, 'Henri de Pardaillan de Gondrin, Archeveque de Sens, 1646-74' [Alençon, 1902, 8vo.], pp. 413-447).

The dispute in the Diocese of Alet began in 1663, during the episcopate of Nicolas Pavilion (born November 15, 1597; died December 8, 1677). It was embittered by a league of the gentry against him, provoked by his denunciation of their excesses, the dean and one of the canons being allied with them, producing a situation somewhat resembling that in 'L'Abbé Tigrane' of Ferdinand Fabre. Proceedings of much complexity resulted, sometimes before the Parliaments of Toulouse and Grenoble, sometimes before the King and his Council. The Capuchins had added to their offences by intruding into this diocese without permission in their alms-collecting expeditions (see A. de la Chassagne and Lefêvre de Saint-Marc, 'Vie de M. Nicolas Pavilion, Evêque d'Aleth' [Saint Mihel, 1738, 3 vols., 12mo.], appendix at end of part ii., separate paging, and vol. i., chap, x., p. 7).

Alet is in the South of France, in the Department of the Aude; it does not seem to be now the seat of a bishopric. Sens is in the: Department of the Yonne, 115 kilometres from Paris, and still the seat of an archbishop (P. Joanne, 'Diclionnaire Géographique de la France,' vii. 4603).

extract from the Registers of Parliament entered at the head of our Rule,[1] from which we take a few phrases. 'Meanwhile, that the petitioners may be maintained in the possession of the rights and privileges of their Order, we forbid the Lord Archbishop of Sens and all others to disturb or interfere with their persons, or to hinder their ordinary functions, as also we direct all priests, rectors, rural deans and all others that they issue neither proclamation nor order in regard to any decrees, interdicts, or excommunications,' etc.

You can see this again, gentlemen, in an extract from the Register [227] of the Council of State, inscribed in the Rule of the Capuchin fathers, already referred to; and if you read you will find the following words: "His Majesty[2] ordained that their first place of establishment should be the city of Paris, in a spot adjoining his royal palace, the Louvre, in order that France, from the position of that site and the situation of that first foundation of the said Capuchin fathers in the realm, might hold in greater veneration the memory of the prince to whom the public were thus indebted. This desire was felicitously carried into effect by the said King Charles IX. selecting a site in the Rue St. Honore, close to his palace of the Tuileries, adjoining his gardens.' The Pope Gregory XIII.,[3] having received a

1. Three printed editions of the Capuchin constitutions are mentioned by Migne, 'Dictionnaire de Bibliographic Catholique' (Paris, 1867), vol. iii., columns 991 and 994 (vol. xli. of his 'Encyclopedic Théologique,' Series III.). But there is no prefatory historical statement like that in the text—at any rate, not in the French edition of 1644, which I have consulted. Words to the same general effect are found, however, in the Letters Patent of Henry III., granted at Paris in July, 1576, and registered in the Parliament on September 6 (see Iourdain, Isambert, Decrusy, and Taillandier, 'Recueil Général des Anciennes Lois Francises' [Paris, 1822-77, 29 vols., 8vo.], vol. xiv., pp. 302-304, and the recitals in the *Arret* of September 23, 1668 [Hilaire de Barenton, op. cit.]).
2. Apparently Charles IX. is meant; he reigned from 1560 to 1574.
3. *Note by Cardeira.*—'Gregory XIII. was a native of Bologna; he succeeded in 1572. and died on May 13 [1585], having governed twelve years. He was the successor of Pius V.' See also 'Degli Annali di Gregorio XIII.,' by J. R. Maffei, edited by C. Cocquelines, Rome, 1742, 2 vols., i. 300, year 1577, Section XXV., Introdusse in que' giorni nella detta Città [Parigi] con molto edificazione de' buoni i Padri Cappuccini . . . .'

report of the above fact, sent some Capuchins as a mark of his joy to found this establishment in France, praising and holding up to admiration in a Brief the zeal and piety of the abovenamed king, who for furthering the glory of God possessed a zeal which passed on to Henry III., and equally to the Queen Catharine dei Medici, his mother,[1] and to the princes of his house, as is apparent and results from the Letters Patent of the King Henry III., granted in the month of July, 1576. These prove with precision that the introduction of the Capuchin fathers and their convents into France was secured by the common desire of the royal family. Following them all the kings, predecessors of his Majesty now happily reigning, have approved of and imitated the said zeal, and above all, his Majesty just referred to, who has conceded a general permission to the Capuchin fathers.

But without having recourse to our Letters Patent or privileges, which debar the Lord Bishop of San Thome from thus making us over to the secular arm, you will see by turning to the Sacred Council of Trent, Cap. 14, Sess. 25, 'De Regularibus et Monialibus,' that his Lordship should have sent the case to our superior and head, and not to other persons, as he has done: 'Regularis non subditus Episcopo, qui intra claustra monasterii degit, et extra ea ita [228] notorie deliquerit, ut populo scandolo sit, Episcopo instante, a suo superiore intra tempus ab Episcopo prsefigendum, severe puniatur.' [A regular who, not being subject to the bishop, and residing within the enclosure of a monastery, has out of that enclosure transgressed so notoriously as to be a scandal to the people, shall at the instance of the bishop be severely punished by his own superior, within such time as the bishop shall appoint.][2]

1. 188. Henry III. reigned from 1575 to 1589; his mother, Catherine de' Medici, lived from 1519 to 1589. Under Paul III. (1534-49) the Capuchins were not allowed to establish themselves in France. In 1573 the King, Charles IX. (1560-74), asked Gregory XIII. (1572-85) to send some of them to him. They established themselves first at Picpus, then at Meudon (both near Paris), and lastly in the Rue St. Honoré, where they built a spacious convent, having 150 friars. They also had other convents (Helyot, 'Histoire des Ordres Monastiques,' 1718 vol vii p. 376).
2. 'Canones et Decreta,' edition 1845, p. 195; Waterworth, p. 246.

And as if it were not enough to make these entirely innocent Capuchin fathers over to the secular arm, in the teeth of the decrees of the Council of Trent, his Lordship goes on to direct that they should be punished with all possible severity. 'With all possible severity!, These words are formally opposed to the same Council, Cap. 1, Sess. 13, 'De Euchar,'[1] of which the exact words are: 'Quos tamen si quid per humanam fragilitatem peccare contigerit, ilia Apostoli est ab eis servanda praceptio, ut illos arguant, obsecrent, increpent in omni bonitate, et patientia; cum saepe plus erga corrigendos agat benevolentia, quam austeritas; plus exhortatio, quam comminatio; plus charitas, quam potestas.' [Towards whom, however, should they happen to sin in any manner through human frailty, that injunction of the apostle is to be observed by them [the bishops], that they *reprove, entreat, rebuke them in all kindness and patience* (2 Tim. iv. 2), seeing that benevolence towards those to be corrected often effects more than austerity, exhortation more than menace, charity more than power.]

Gentlemen, although I have set before you much more than was necessary, I have done it to show you that it is nothing but simple passion, and not the Holy Spirit, which drives his Lordship to such acts against the Capuchin fathers. Yet I cannot refrain from calling your attention to the manner in which a bishop ought to bear himself in committing a priest or friar to the secular arm, to be degraded and receive chastisement according to his offences. Those provisions are to be found in the Roman Pontificals of Clement VIII. and Urban VIII.:[2] 'Turn Pontifex degradator elficaciter, et ex corde, et omni instantia, pro miserrimo illo derelicto intercedit apud judicem Saecularem, ut citra mortis periculum, vel mutilationis, contra degradatum sententiam moderetur, dicens: Domine Iudex, rogamus vos cum omni affectu quo possumus, ut amore Dei, pietatis et misericordiae intuitu, et nostrorum interventu precaminum miserrimo huic nullum mortis, vel mutilationis periculum inferatis.' [Then doth the bishop, who

1. *Note by Senhor Cardeira.*—These words are in chap, i., Session XIII., 'De Reformatione, ('Canones et Decreta,' edition 1845, p. 62; Waterworth, p. 85).
2. Clement VIII., 1592-1605; Urban VII., 1623-44 (see 'Pontificale Romanum dementis VIII. ac Urbani VIII.,J Rome, 1868, p. 284, under the heading 'Degradatio a Prima Tonsura'). This ritual was issued by the first-named Pope on February 10, 1606, by the Bull 'Ex quo in Ecclesia Dei multa.'

degrades (the priest), effectively and from his heart, and with all insistence, intercede with the secular judge for that miserable castaway, that he will limit his sentence against the degraded man to something short of danger of death or mutilation, saying: 'Sir Justice, we beg of you with all the affection we can, that for the love of God, and from feelings of piety and pity, and through the intervention of our prayers, you bring no danger of death or mutilation on this most miserable person.']

A pontiff, gentlemen, thought it obligatory to implore mercy [229] for a wretched priest or friar who had been abandoned to the secular arm by reason of his misdeeds. It is also held incumbent on a bishop to conjure the judge with all possible insistence, and that, too (which is the most important), when the culprit has dishonoured religion, and profaned its sacred character most disgracefully. Yet the Lord Bishop of San Thome does not think it sufficient to consign the poor Capuchin fathers to the secular arm, men who have left father, mother, country, relations, and friends, to labour within God's vineyard and win souls to Jesus Christ. He cannot bring against them the minutest fault, for they seek nothing but the doing of good to all the world; and they have no other enemies than those who ought to be their protectors; instead of desiring vengeance, they pray God for those who persecute them. And his lordship goes on to direct that they be treated with all severity—'Com todo o rigor'!

The truth is, gentlemen, that the matter is beyond my strength, and I am overcome by the effort of avoiding words that might give offence to someone; and certainly my senses leave me when I merely reflect upon proceedings of this sort. Why should the Lord Bishop of San Thome, a prince of the Church, who ought to cherish as the pupil of his eye the reputation of all those placed under his jurisdiction, be unable to write a letter to the Reverend Father Esprit without such an outburst of anger over the matter? 'I will write,' says the Lord Bishop, 'for the satisfaction of you gentlemen to the Reverend Father Spirito, but I have already written him a letter wherein I exhorted him to peace. This letter, when brought to him, he threw contemptuously upon the ground, and declined to receive it. You gentlemen ought not to wish me to expose myself to his further anger and rudeness.'

XLVIII. Huntsman with CHITAH

Vol. IV *To face page 286*

Gentlemen, even were what is here imputed to the Reverend Father Esprit as true as it is most false, ought not the Lord Bishop of San Thome, a prince of the Church [230], to follow on such an occasion the admirable advice of the Council of Trent?[1] Tllud primum eos admonendos censet, ut se Pastores non per-cussores esse meminerint atque ita praeesse sibi subditis oportare, ut non in eis dominentur sed illos tamquam filios et fratres diligant.' [The Council thinks it meet that the bishops be first of all admonished to bear in mind that they are pastors and not *strikers* (Titus i. 7), and that they ought so to preside over those subject to them as not to *lord it over them* (Luke xxii. 25), but to love them as sons and brethren.] Even had the Reverend Father Esprit been wanting in respect towards his Lordship, and had also thrown the bishop's letter on the ground in anger (a thing he is incapable of doing), still, the Lord Bishop of San Thome ought to display greater love, and nourish more tenderness for all priests and friars, more even than a father could have to his own sons. He ought to have written a second letter to the Reverend Father Esprit, or, at the least, if he declined to do him that honour and afford him that consolation, he should have directed his vicar-general, or someone else he might depute, to declare to him (Esprit) his intentions. He need not have blackened the poor Capuchin fathers before your tribunal; he need not have taken away their reputation; he need not have loaded them with the grossest calumny that ever was heard of.

Gentlemen, I claim here your whole attention, because this affair touches us to the very quick, and we are so wounded by it that it is necessary for the whole world to be informed of it. On November 3, 1706, at about five or six o'clock in the evening, the Reverend Fathers De la Breuille and Turpe,[2] both

1. 'Canones et Decreta,' edition 1845, p. 62, Sessio XIII., cap. i., 'De Reform atione'; Waterworth, p. 84.
2. The incident is given, with some graphic details, by Father Thomas in his letter of 1733 (Norbert, 'Mémoires Historiques,' ii. 301). Dominique Turpin, born February 2, 1672, became a novice 1693; went to India 1700; died at Pondicherry July 2, 1740 (see Sommervogel, 'Bibliographic'). Father Turpin was still at Pondicherry on January 15, 1716 (Norbert, i. 392), and a letter of his, dated 1718, is in 'Lettres Edifiantes.' The name of Charles de la Breuille appears in Norbert, i. 392, and elsewhere. Mauricet, the alleged writer of the letter, appears in Father Thomas's 'Lettre Apologétique' of 1733 as 'Frdre Morisef (Norbert, 'Mémoires Historiques,' 1747, ii. 301).

Jesuits, presented a letter to the Reverend Father Esprit of Tours[1] Superior of the Pondicherry Capuchins. The address was in French, in the handwriting of Father Mauricet (Moriset), also a Jesuit; the letter was sealed with the seal of the Reverend Father Tachard. The last named has testified that the letter was from him, a fact that many of you gentlemen have graciously signified to us in the shape of affidavits. Afterwards the Lord Bishop of San Thome, who, according to *jus*, natural and divine, was bound to sift the matter to the very foundation before pronouncing upon it, wrote to your Council that the Reverend Father Esprit had thrown contemptuously on the ground a letter written to him by his Lordship. 'I will write to the Reverend Father Friar [231] Spirito to satisfy you gentlemen, but there was a letter I wrote exhorting him to make peace and be quiet; taking it, he threw it to the ground with contempt, and declined to receive it. Thus you gentlemen ought not to desire me to expose myself to his further anger and rudeness.'

O God! how is it possible for a prince of the Church to write like this? If the Lord Bishop of San Thome wished to honour the Reverend Father Esprit by writing to him, could he not have written direct, as done previously, without forwarding his letter to the reverend Jesuit father? Or if his Lordship decided to send it to them, could he not seal it with his own seal, and write the address in Portuguese, as is his habit when he writes any letter that is in his mother-tongue, instead of in a foreign language? Or if he objected to observing any restraint in regard to the Capuchin fathers because they do not deserve any respect from him, ought not the Reverend Father Esprit to have been told that this pretended letter (which apparently possessed the horse of Pacolet,194 since it traversed in two days and a half more miles

Claude Moriset was born at Paris January 20, 1667, and entered the novitiate September 8, 1690, as Frere Coadjutor. He left for India before 1691, and died at Pondicherry January 13, 1742. He assisted the priests in their astronomical observations (see C. Sommervogel, s.v.).

1. 194. Pacolet, a legendary person, who possessed an enchanted wooden horse capable of going a thousand leagues in a minute (Bescherelle Ainé, 'Nouvelle Dictionnaire Nationale,' 1887, iii. 731). But in our French text, Codex No. CXXXV., for 73*a*, the words are 'chapeau' (hat) 'de paccolete,' instead of 'chevau' (horse).

than could be covered in six days by the best foot-runner employed by your Company) came from Monsignor, and that under the outer covering was a letter his Lordship had written, instead of saying, as they did, that it was from the Reverend Father Tachard?

Without a doubt, gentlemen, the Lord Bishop ought to have thus acted. But the Reverend Father Tachard meant to take the Capuchin fathers unawares. They are not so skilful as he is in such work, and it was not necessary to say that this letter was from Monsignor. It was quite sufficient to present it to the Reverend Father Esprit as coming from the Reverend Father Tachard, and assert it to be his, when the only object was to enable him (Tachard) to write to his Lordship that the Reverend Father Esprit had thrown a letter written by his Lordship on the ground with anger and contempt [232]. Gentlemen, who has ever seen an act like this? How could the Reverend Father Tachard, whose conscience ought to be more tender than yours, he being a regular cleric while you are not, dare all this in order to extort a Pastoral, which cannot shield him from the censures of the Church. Such a thing would not have been done by you for all the riches in the world.

But since you may not, perhaps, know, gentlemen, the motive of the calumny with which they assail us, I will expose it to you in a few words. The Reverend Father Tachard, and all the reverend Jesuit fathers of Pondicherry, perceived that the decrees had been published, and that, because we had published them, we were probably in possession of Monsignor's permission, as is most fully the truth, these being the words that his Lordship appended to the petition of the Reverend Father Michel Ange, which I never tire of repeating as our justification: 'I did not give permission to your Reverence, neither in thought, much less in words; all I said to you was that you might publish the decrees, as you could publish other orders in your church, without my permission and without anyone preventing you.'

Those Reverend fathers (the Jesuits) knew not what to do to prevent the bad effects, and said to themselves: 'Here are the decrees published without an express Pastoral from My Lord Bishop. Nothing else appears possible, so let us write meanwhile to the Reverend Father Esprit of Tours, who has published the said decrees. Under present circumstances he will decline to take the letter in question, if we omit on it the designation he is entitled to. When that has happened we can write to his Lordship that the said Reverend Father Esprit has thrown on the ground with contempt and anger a letter written to him by Monsignor.' Gentlemen, these words of Ps. lxiii. might with a clear conscience be applied to the reverend Jesuit fathers: 'Scrutai sunt iniquitates' [They have searched after iniquities (verse 7)],[1] and then might well be added: 'defecerunt scrutantes scrutinio' [they have failed in their search (verse 7)]. For it is most certain [233] that, having invented this calumny, they said: 'Who is there who will ever find us out? No one.' 'Illi dixerunt quis nos videbit.' (They have said, Who shall see us?] But they have deceived themselves, because their work was of too gross a kind for the calumny they affixed to us not to be discovered: 'defecerunt scrutantes scrutationis consilia mala.'

And in effect, who was it that could have written to the Lord Bishop of San Thome that the Reverend Father Esprit had thrown on the ground with disrespect a letter written to him by his Lordship? You gentlemen could hardly have done it, since you are incapable of inventing so enormous a calumny. Again, the Capuchin fathers could not have been the persons, for, besides there being no hint of such a thing, to do it would have been too much to their disadvantage. Now, if neither the one nor the other of the above could have done it, as must be admitted, it follows by necessity that it was the reverend Jesuit fathers. For, to sum up, the Lord Bishop of San Thome not having the gift of prophesy, he could not know what never had happened. Yet his Lordship launched his Pastoral and founded it upon this calumny. The reverend Jesuit fathers, who invented it, know thoroughly well that it is not in the power of the Lord Bishop to put them in possession of the cure of the Malabaris. Because, as it runs in the decrees of the Sacred Congregation: 'Ulam sub quovis pratextu aut authoritate exercere absque expressa licentia ejusdem Sacra Congregationis sub poena privationis officii, privilegii et facultatis ipso facto incurrenda non obstantibus quibuscumque.'[2] At present they enjoy the fruit of their iniquity.

After all this, shall I not believe what I hear everywhere as to the conduct of the reverend Jesuit fathers? After all this,

1. In the Authorized Version it is Ps. lxiv. 6. Mr. Philipps points out that in the Vulgate Ps. ix. and x. are made into one (Ps. ix.).
2. See *ante*, fol. 200, for the text of this decree of January 11, 1656.

shall I continue to wear myself out in trying to persuade myself that they are not [234] the authors of all that was done by the Lord Patriarch some two years ago? After all this, can I say that there is passion and exaggeration in the eight volumes of the 'Morale Practique [des Jesuites]'?[1]

Gentlemen, he who is capable of inventing such a calumny, and employing so many kinds of stratagem to justify it, is capable of anything. If it had been private persons who had committed this fault I would suspend judgment, but the culprits being a bishop, who is a former Jesuit Provincial, and the whole body of regular clerics in a Jesuit community, there is ground for my believing, and that not without good reason, that these are the maxims prevailing throughout that Society.

Gentlemen, when God decided to punish Pharaoh, as the Scripture tells us, he hardened the heart of that unhappy prince —'Induravit cor Pharaonis' (Exod. vii. 22, and viii. 32). I know not, gentlemen, if God, who hates iniquity, means to punish the reverend Jesuit fathers. But of this I feel assured: that hearts must be very hard which act as they do. For, finally, there is no mental reservation here that can absolve them from the guilt of such a calumny, still less any which could authorize their doing these things. I do not speak solely of their usurpation of our cure over the Malabaris, but also of their conduct in regard to the said cure, which they carry on in the accustomed manner in spite of the censures fulminated in the decrees.

However, this is an affair which, please God, will be examined into at the court of Rome, and I do not wish to enlarge farther upon it. All I will say in passing is that the following words of Ps. cxiii.[2] are applicable to the reverend Jesuit fathers:

1. La Morale Pratique des Jésuites représentée en Plusieurs Histoircs arrivées dans Toutes les Parties du Monde,' 8 vols., 18mo., published between 1684 and 1695. The work was inspired by the Jansenists, and the authors to whom it was attributed are S. J. de Coislin du Cambout de Pontchateau (the Abbé de Pontchâteau, 1648-90), Nicolas Perrault (Doctor of Theology), Antoine Arnauld (1612-94), Pierre Nicole (1625-95), and Varet. The 'Biographic Universelle,' under 'A. Arnauld' 'vol. ii., p. 510), passes the judgment that there is exaggeration, but that the documents themselves have never been challenged even by the Jesuits.
2. Ps. cxv. 5, 6 of the Authorized Version.

'Oculos habent et non videbunt, aures habent et non audient.' For, of a truth, it would be necessary to have lost one's brains to [235] imagine that acts done so openly and so maliciously should not be known everywhere, above all at the court of Rome, where causes are gone into closely, where they weigh them in the scales of justice and with the weights of the sanctuary. Can they persuade themselves that nothing will be said to them when their disobedience to the Holy See is known? Do they consider they did well to extort a Pastoral by pretexts and the use of calumny? Do they think that his Holiness will approve the decision of the Lord Patriarch, which was given after he was told that this mission had applied to the Holy See, which was pronounced without the consent of the parties, which was not promulgated until two years afterwards? Do they believe that the Lord Bishop of San Thome will be approved at Rome when his Holiness and the Sacred Congregation learn that his Lordship has acted formally against their orders? Can they persuade themselves that my lord, after having written such a fulminating letter as that sent to your Council, will be absolved and acquitted by merely saying he had been misled? Do they believe that he will not be cross-questioned as to why he was misled, why he sent the letter referred to, and how he came to know what he has imputed to the Capuchin fathers? If they believe all that, then 'oculos habent et non videbunt, aures habent et non audient.'

Decide now, gendemen, how far we are guilty and have deserved to be treated as scandalous persons—'The Reverend Fra Spirito came out with a despairing and scandalous resolution.' Decide how far we are culprits, that we should be branded as liars—'Without order of His Holiness or mine, as they falsely allege.' Decide in what we have sinned, that we should be [236] dealt with as disobedient persons—'I have not given permission to your Reverence, neither in thought, still less in words.' Decide how far we are of evil mind, that we should be called over-bold—'Nor was the Pastoral issued to hinder the decrees, but to repress the temerity with which the Reverend Father Spirito,' etc. Decide how far we have been violent and hasty, that we should be dismissed as madmen—'But as he has had a letter exhorting him to peace and quietness, which he took and threw on the ground with contempt, not troubling himself to accept it, you, gentlemen, ought not to wish me to expose myself further to his anger and rudeness.' Decide, gentlemen, what offence we have committed, that we should be called seditious, that we should be delivered to the secular arm with an order to deal with us most severely—'It concerns you, gentlemen, to keep the peace and uphold my jurisdiction in the form in which I have stated it, and force the Capuchin fathers by full severity to desist.' Decide how dishonourable and to be avoided must be that habit we wear, one for which the Supreme Pontiffs have themselves shown the respect they have felt by conceding indulgences to those who out of devotion kiss it; since it suffices to say: 'God deliver me from the hood of the Capuchin fathers'—words heard to fall from the mouth of the Lord Bishop himself by the gentlemen Cesar and Khwajah Ivanos, Armenians.[1] Now, if we be thus treated without any fault, what would it be, gentlemen, if we had been guilty? I leave it to you to decide, and instead ask [237] you the favour of becoming witnesses of the truth and replying to the questions which I take the liberty of putting to you. For you know during a long time past, not only the good reputation gained by the Capuchins in France, but equally the manner in which they have always borne themselves, be it at Madras, at Surat, or at Pondicherry, since they have been at those places.

If the reverend Jesuit fathers had procured against us such decrees as we have against them, could they have conducted themselves with more moderation than we have displayed? If the reverend Jesuit fathers had been our forerunners in Pondicherry, and were in possession of the cure of the Malabaris, would the Capuchin fathers have tried to take it from the reverend Jesuit fathers, as these latter have not only desired to take, but have effectually taken it from the Capuchin fathers? Had the Capuchin fathers been menaced by the Sacred Congregation with the censures of the Church, would they have resisted as the reverend Jesuit fathers are resisting? If the reverend Jesuit fathers had been involved in such a contest as we have been for approximately two years, and had they wished to send a religious to the court of Rome, there to explain their conduct, would the Capuchin fathers have employed every

1. Farther on, upon fol. 269, these two gentlemen are called Avanes and Cesare Luigi Melique.

device to prevent his journey, as the reverend Jesuit fathers did in respect of the Reverend Father Eusebius of Bourges? If any Capuchin of Madras had gone to Pondicherry, and had at once gone to visit the reverend Jesuit fathers, and the reverend Jesuit fathers had come to the Capuchins to see them, would the Capuchin fathers ever have [238] replied, 'We do not want to speak to him'? This is what was done by Father Dolu at Madras not a very long time ago. Finally, if the reverend Jesuit fathers had obtained a decision from Rome as we have done, would they have submitted to the Lord Bishop of San Thome when be annulled what had been ordained by the Sacred Congregation, to whom his Lordship ought to submit just as much as we? I know not, gentlemen, what you may think, but for my part I am quite certain that regulars who resist his Holiness and the Sacred Congregation face to face could have equally resisted a single bishop.

On the contrary, we obey blindly, however many valid reasons we might have for declining to do so, and this, moreover, in spite of their persecuting us, calumniating us, menacing us, consigning us to the secular arm. Alas! where, then, is the crime of the Capuchin fathers, that they are dealt with so unworthily? I know not, gentlemen, unless it be their simplicity, sincerity, and too great kindness of heart. If we were less humble, less good-tempered, less obedient, justice might, perhaps, have been done to us. But God forbid that we should purchase the right to get back our mission at a price so ruinous! Rather lose a thousand cures and a thousand lives, if we had them, than at any time to do the least thing unworthy of our ministry and our vows. God, who sees the depths of our hearts, and who sees that we work good (Rom. viii. 27), will espouse our cause, as has always happened unto this day by the working of His paternal bounty. We shall see what will come to pass through His divine grace. It will come in the course of time [239], and may happen in two years or thereabouts.

We were, as you know, gentlemen, defamed in these regions. While his Holiness laboured hard to restore us to the possession of the Malabari cure, they (the Jesuits) wanted to deprive us of the Madras mission, just as the reverend Jesuit fathers had designed with the Malabari (Tamil) charge in Pondicherry. At a time when his Holiness was making over to the Capuchins the new missions to Ethiopia and to Tibet,[1] they (the Jesuits) tried to tear to pieces our reputation at Pondicherry and at Madras, hurling thunderbolts at our heads, and placarding notices in all the public squares and on the doors of the churches. But at Rome the Sacred Congregation and two cardinals did us the honour of writing to us, setting forth the gifts that they had graciously forwarded to us, just as if their letters were not enough to convince and persuade us of their goodwill, in addition to the assignment to us of so many new charges. So true is it that those whose only trust is in the Lord, and not in men, can never perish: 'Beati qui confidunt in Domino' (Ps. xxx., cxxiv. and cxxvii.).[2]

We close this letter, gentlemen, by praying God to pardon the reverend Jesuit fathers and the Lord Bishop of San Thome for all the steps they have taken against us. If we have taken the liberty of addressing this manifesto to you, we most earnestly beg you to believe that it was not to besmirch them, but entirely for our own justification from the calumnies that were published about us. Moreover, before the said tribunal [the Pondicherry Council], along with our conduct the good reputation of our whole order would be exposed to censure and might be blackened by malicious tongues, if we did not present our defence on the heads [240] under which we are accused.

Be not scandalized, gentlemen, if the Capuchin fathers have been unable to endure the sufferings caused them without this cry of pain. For there are some things that must be borne heroically, and others which must necessarily be repudiated. The Saviour of our souls, who is our example, who took flesh in order to the salvation of men through His own agony, has not omitted a justification of Himself, nor to make complaint on certain occasions. When they said to. Him (John viii. 48), 'Daemonium habes?' He replied, 'Daemonium non habeo' (verse

1. Father Thomas, Capuchin, in his narrative of 1733, suggests that the appointment of François Marie of Tours, Capuchin, to the Tibet Mission was due to a Jesuit intrigue, as they wanted the Father removed from Rome, where he was pushing the Capuchins' Pondicherry claim too vigorously (Norbert, 'Mémoires Historiques,' 1747, ii. 298).
2. These words are not in the three Psalms named, though in the Vulgate Ps. cxxiv. begins: "Qui confidunt in Domino." I suppose the writer means that if we read these three Psalms we shall find his ideas' (W.R.P.).

49). When Judas betrayed Him into the hands of His enemies, He asked them: 'Amice, ad quid venisti?' (Matt. xxvi. 50). When Malchus smote Him with such indignity and such cruelty, He said to him: 'Si male locutus sum, testimonium perhibe de malo: si [autem] bene, locutus sum quid me cædis?' (John xviii. 23). [If I have spoken evil, bear witness of the evil: but if well, why smitest thou Me?]

If I have made use of rather strong and pungent expressions, and if you cannot pardon me for feeling resentment, glance for a moment at the outrageous manner in which we have been dealt with, and notice whether, in expressing myself in such terms, I have done so without just cause. Furthermore, I wish the Jesuits no evil, since God forbids my doing so any my own feelings also. I advise others to pardon their enemies while I remain their, as I am your [friend], *et cetera*.

Gentlemen

As it is said in Holy Scripture, one abyss produces another: 'Abyssus abyssum invocat' (Vulgate, Ps. xli. 8) [A.V., xlii. 7: 'Deep calleth unto deep']. Thus, after we have been so unjustly calumniated and persecuted by the reverend Jesuit fathers and the Lord [241] Bishop of San Thome, we have little room for hoping to be able for long at a time to enjoy our original quiet. It seems impossible for us to be left a month in peace where there are any reverend Jesuit fathers. In fact, hardly had we begun to comfort ourselves after our past struggles, when about nine or ten days ago we heard that the Reverend Father Esprit of Tours, Capuchin Apostolic Missionary and Superior at Pondicherry, had been declared by the Lord Bishop of San Thome to be excommunicated. The way in which we have learnt this it will not be out of place to tell you, gentlemen, to show to you conspicuously what is the nature of the reverend Jesuit fathers, and the spirit animating all the members of that saintly and illustrious Society.

The Reverend Fathers Tachard and Dolu,[1] both Jesuits, being fervently resolved to see us ruined and deprived of reputa-

1. Charles Frarnois Dolu (really Dolfs or Dolfus), an Alsatian, born 1651; went to India 1688; curé of Pondicherry 1699; returned to France 1710; died January 6, 1740 (Sommervogel, 'Bibliographies s.v. Dolu). For G. Tachard, see note 77, Vol. IV., Part V., fol. 100.

tion in the hearts of all laymen, unexpectedly wrote to Madras informing everybody of this fine piece of news. The Reverend Father Dolu wrote to a person in holy orders that the Reverend Father Esprit was excommunicated; and the Reverend Father Tachard wrote to Monsieur Guety,[1] not, it is true, quite so coarsely, but in other phrases which, in spite of their being a little more polite, are none the less pungent. Here they are; listen to them, I pray of you. 'The Reverend Father Esprit has started from Pondicherry, and is transferring himself to San Thome. It does not suit me to have to impart to you this sad news. All I will say is, that it would be very appropriate to apply to this friar the medical axiom: "Magna mala extremis carent remediis." ' That is as much as to say that for great ills you want great remedies.

Admire, gentlemen, the prudence of the reverend fathers, and reflect on the height to which passion can rise when the persons [242] concerned once lose their heads. If the Reverend Father Tachard and the Reverend Father Dolu itched so much to see us defamed, neglected, deprived of reputation, as much at Madras as at Pondicherry, could they not have found some other course for doing it without writing the good news to persons in holy orders, without writing in terms so insulting, without causing so grave a scandal in a town where for one Christian there are a thousand heathen? The reverend Jesuit fathers state in letters to Europe that they never convert idolaters in less than thousands. Judge what fruits they can gather in countries where they employ such fine methods of bringing men to our holy faith.

Gentlemen, to speak the truth, if these reverend fathers had any—I will not say virtue, but the smallest dose of religion and of concern for their eternal salvation, would they ever act contrary to those two great precepts which call on us to love God above all things and our neighbour as ourself? 'Diliges dominum Deum tuum ex toto corde tuo et proximum tuum sicut te ipsum' (Lev. xix. 18; Rom. xiii. 9: Gal. v. 14; Jas. ii. 8; Matt, xxii, 37, 39; Mark xii. 33). No, without a doubt, gentlemen, they would not. Still, as we have already seen what are their maxims, you can judge equally the purity of their intentions.

---

1. This Monsieur Guelly or Guety at San Thome has been named before in Part IV., fols. 70 and 188, and will appear again in Part V., fols. 242, 244, 261, 284.

After we knew from Monsieur Chardin and Monsieur Guety[1] that the Reverend Father Esprit of Tours had been declared excommunicated, we had the confirmation thereof the next day from the Reverend Father Esprit himself, who had travelled post to Madras to justify himself in the presence of the Lord Bishop of San Thome in regard to what had been imputed to him, and to hear from the mouth of his Lordship the cause of his excommunication, and why he had attached the notice to the door of the church [243] of the reverend Jesuit fathers, while neither he nor any one of us was told the reason.

No one doubted, whether at Pondicherry or at Madras, that the Reverend Father Esprit of Tours, Capuchin, must be the winner in his dispute, and would return in triumph after he should have better informed the Lord Bishop of all that had passed at Pondicherry. But we, who know by experience what is the nature of the reverend Jesuit fathers, were already informed by persons of integrity that those fathers had plotted our ruin. Therefore we did not share the opinion above referred to, nor in this were we deceived. For you will see, gentlemen, something that perhaps was never seen before, something that it will be hard to credit in Europe, it being hardly credible on the spot where the thing happened. Yet this is so admittedly true that if I were in the throes of death, on the point of yielding an account to God of all the actions of my life, and if it were required of me to say whether in all I have written there is any falsehood or exaggeration, I could withdraw nothing without denying the truth.

If after the oath I have taken to speak the truth, and after the protest now made of rather diminishing than exaggerating events, any man still blames the Capuchins (as I know of a certainty some do, who are the cause of my issuing this manifesto), he would need to be worse than a Turk, a Hindu, or an idolater. Indeed, it is not possible, gentlemen, for a Turk to learn what I am about to recount without having some [244] little compassion

1. Daniel Chardin, brother of Sir John Chardin, the traveller, was a free merchant, who by this time (1706) has been about twenty years at Madras. He died there on September 7, 1709 (see Mrs. Penny, 'Fort St. George,' p. 191). For Guety, see Part IV., fol. 188, and Part V., fols. 241, 244, 261, 284.

for us and doing us justice. Here I give, gentlemen, word for word, how the affair occurred, so far as I am able to recollect.

Beholding the miserable condition to which the Reverend Father Esprit of Tours had been reduced by being declared excommunicated, and the injury done to our mission by the removal of a friar who can use the Portuguese, Malabari, and Arab languages perfectly, and has, in addition, been twenty-five years a missionary without causing any scandal or doing the slightest thing unworthy of his ministry, we resolved that we would go to the Lord Bishop of San Thome, praying him with all possible insistence that he would be good enough to remove the excommunication fulminated by his Most Illustrious Lordship against the person of the Reverend Father Esprit, and taking with us a written petition in case he should decline to listen to our spoken arguments.

We had only just arrived at the house of Monsieur Guety,[1] where we had gone to rest after the fatigues of the journey, when we found a copy of the declaration that the reverend Jesuit fathers had published and subsequently affixed to the door of their churches, adding a prohibition to the Capuchin fathers against putting their foot within the house of the Lord Bishop. It was as if the Capuchin fathers were worse than those criminals who are condemned without being told the reason; even they, however, have never been denied a hearing [245] when they have prayed their judges to grant them one, as we shall go into farther on, in its proper place.

I wish to give you first a copy of the declaration, in order that everybody may know that the reverend Jesuit fathers do not confine themselves to warfare against idols, but the zeal with which they are filled is so great and so burning, that they would like not only to destroy the Capuchin fathers, but, if they could, render their memory odious to all men. Here is the copy of the declaration[2] fulminated against the Reverend Father Esprit of Tours, apostolic missionary and Superior of the Capuchins at Pondicherry, simply for having published the decrees of the

1. See also Part IV., fol. 188, and Part V., fols. 241, 242, 261, 284.
2. The original in Codex No. CXXXV. is in Portuguese. This declaration is printed, with slight variations, but to the same general effect, in Norbert, 'Mémoires Utiles, 1742, p. 233.

Sacred Congregation; for having said that the reverend Jesuit fathers are not the legal pastors of the Malabaris at Pondicherry; for having reduced to writing the names of the Malabar gods in order to acquaint the Sacred Congregation with the number of Christians living there;[1] finally, for having cited the reverend Jesuit fathers to the court of Rome, upon our discovering that they were acting contrary to the decrees given in favour of the Capuchin fathers.

BISHOP'S DECLARATION

Dom Gaspar Affoneo, by the grace of God and of the Holy Apostolic See Bishop of the city of San Thome of Mailapur, and of the Council of his Majesty, *et cetera*. To all [246] those who shall see this our letter declaratory, salutation and peace for ever in our Lord Jesus Christ, who is the true healer of all men and their salvation.

We make known that it is fitting to and incumbent upon our pastoral office to defend conscientiously our jurisdiction as Ordinary; and since Father Fra Esprit of Tours, Capuchin, has infringed it by publishing, without authority for so doing, certain decrees which the Sacred Congregation sent for presentation to us; also by proclaiming to the people on All Saints' Day that the fathers of the Society of Jesus were not the parochial priests of the Malabaris, over whom the cure and jurisdiction as parish priests had been given by us to the aforesaid Reverend Fathers under the authority conferred on us by the Sacred Canons and by the decrees of the Sacred Council of Trent, permitting us to found parishes, or divide those already founded, whenever we may judge it necessary for the welfare and instruction of our flock: we sent an admonishment full of gentleness to the reverend Capuchin fathers, to the end that they might desist and await a decision from Rome, and that if they did not desist we should take proceedings against them. Seeing, then, the Father Fra Esprit of Tours declined to desist, but after issuing the three canonical

1. 'Dei' (gods) must be used here in the sense of 'castes.' The enumeration, dated November 6, 1706, is printed in Norbert, 'Mémoires Utiles,' 1742, p. 225. The total of Tamil Christians is given as 1,122 persons, young and old. Their castes were Gambadi, Vollaren, and Pariahs. The first may be meant for *Shembadava*, or fishermen, and the second for the *Vellaula*, or agriculturist caste ('Madras Manual of Administration,' iii. 510, 968).

monitions has cited anew, without any authority of a judge, or of the Sacred Congregation, the Reverend Father Guy Tachard of Pondicherry and those subject to him to appear in Rome:

We declare the said Father Fra Esprit of Tours, Capuchin Superior of Pondicherry, to have incurred the excommunication in the Bull 'In Cæna,'[1] fulminated against those who interfere with and perturb a bishop's ordinary jurisdiction [247]; and we denounce the said father by public excommunication, as accursed at the hands of God Omnipotent, of the holy Apostles St. Peter and St. Paul, and of all the saints in the quire celestial. We separate the said excommunicated person from the communion of the faithful, and furthermore, under the same penalty of the greater excommunication, by the very act incurred, we ordain that no one give him water, fire, or other necessary, nor favour or aid him in anything where not required for the well-being of his eternal salvation, and in which we may have commanded to the contrary. In order that it may come to the notice of everyone, and that none may allege ignorance, we ordain that these presents be sent to all places, where they shall be published by any priest to whom they may be consigned, under the same penalty, in the churches and the most public places in Pondicherry, and after publication they shall be fixed on the door of the church of the reverend fathers of the Society of Jesus, whence they may not be removed, under the same penalty of excommunication, without our express permission. We notify, also, to the persons to whom may belong obedience to these presents, that they shall thus observe them, preserve them, and obtain their complete carrying out and preservation.

Given in San Thome under our sign and seal on the 27th November, 1706. I, Father Simon di Loyola, writer of the Episcopal and Ecclesiastical Office, have written this.

SEAL

Signed) DOM GASPAR AFFONÇO, BISHOP OF MELLIAPUR.

(Signed) SIMON DI LOYOLA.[2]

1. The Bull 'In Cæna Domini' was first issued in 1536 by Pope Paul III. (1534-49) (see note 190. Vol. III., Part IV., fol. 129).
2. This man has already been mentioned in Part TV., fol. 188, as taking part in the procession at San Thome which was broken up by the Mahomedans on September 24, 1704.

[248] Gentlemen, I have already shown you in my preceding letter what powers the Sacred Council of Trent and the Sacred Canons confer on the Lord Bishop of San Thome. By your giving tliis a little consideration, you will see that His Most Illustrious Lordship has acted formally against the said decrees. I have also caused you to see in many passages that it was not without authority that we have published the decrees referred to. For the Lord Bishop gave the permission orally to the Reverend Father Michel Ange, and confirmed it in writing when we begged his Lordship to witness to the truth.

I have shown, in addition, that we are not perturbers, nor capable of taking away the jurisdiction of our Lord Bishops, knowing, as we do thoroughly well, by the grace of God, the veneration and respect that we ought to render to their holy persons. So true is this that, when we notified the said decrees of the Sacred Congregation to the Reverend Father Tachard, Jesuit, under the orders of my Lord Bishop of San Thome, although he presented to us a finding and decision of the Most Illustrious and Most Reverend Lord Patriarch, promulgated at a time when our case was in the hands of the said Sacred Congregation, we said nothing. That decision was issued without our knowledge, and not notified to us for a period of two years. Finally, his Lordship himself caused it to be written to us, and he said it also with his own mouth [249] that all the things done by the Lord Primate of Goa had been approved at the court of Rome, and all those done by the Lord Patriarch disapproved.

Up to the present time, gentlemen, it seems to me that we have never been disrespectful to the Lord Bishop of San Thome, nor have we done the slightest possible act for which we could be reproved, much less anything for which we could be declared accursed and doubly accursed of God, *et cetera*. Now consider, for the rest, I beseech you, the way in which we bore ourselves when we learnt from the mouth of his Lordship that all the things done by the Lord Patriarch had been disallowed at the court of Rome; and finding that the decision given by his Excellency (the Patriarch) against us could no longer be any obstacle to the execution of the decrees, as the reverend Jesuit fathers had always pretended it was, Father Michel Ange paid a visit to the Lord Bishop, and prayed him to put into execution the decrees of the "Sacred Congregation. He then found out that the bishop was in search of other reasons for dispensing with so doing. Therefore the next morning the father put in the annexed petition:[1]

'Father Fra Laurent says that, for helping him to obtain justice, it is necessary that the decrees of the Sacred Congregation "de Propaganda Fide," issued about the Malabari parishioners of Pondicherry, should be published in Pondicherry, the question being in litigation, in order that he may establish at Rome the diligence that he has employed. To this what your Most Illustrious Lordship advanced when I presented my last request is no obstacle. Your Lordship said that the Sacred Congregation could not send missionaries to India without the consent of His Most Serene Majesty the King of Portugal. But your Lordship has already recognised His Most Christian Majesty [the King of France] as the patron of this cure [250] by sending to him this dispute for a decision, as is plain from his letter. Therefore I urge on your Lordship that you be pleased to allow kindly the publication in Pondicherry of the decrees of the Sacred Congregation "de Propaganda Fide," the same having been laid before your Lordship, and by your order notified in legal form to the reverend fathers of the Society of Jesus at Pondicherry. In case of refusal, petitioner hereby records a protest as proof of the diligence he has exercised in calling for the publication of the said decrees—"Pro qua gratia Deus," ' *et cetera.*

This petition placed his Lordship in a position of great embarrassment, owing to certain expressions which you will have observed in it, which are, however, the very ones used by his Lordship himself. He therefore replied that he could not pass an order on the above petition without being attacked by either the court of Portugal or the court of Rome; but we might publish the decrees in our church at Pondicherry. Father Michel Ange then retorted: 'Can we, then, publish the decrees in our church?' And his Lordship answered: 'Yes, you can; who can hinder?'

If after such a permission his Lordship writes that the decrees were published without his leave and authority, finally inserting this statement in his Pastoral and Declaration, what do you think we can do when a bishop denies what he has said?

1. In Codex No. CXXXV. the petition is in Portuguese. It is printed in Norbert, 'Mémoires Utiles,' 1742, p. 185, in practically the same terms. From the affidavit appended to it there, it would seem that N. Manucci was present when the petition was handed in.

Meanwhile, Father Michel Ange, reading in the pastoral of Monsignor what he could not believe when first told, wrote to his Lordship the following letter:

LETTER OF THE REVEREND FATHER MICHEL ANGE 'MOST ILLUSTRIOUS AND MOST REVEREND LORD BISHOP,

'Your Most Illustrious Lordship will recollect that on September 28[1] last a petition was presented to you in the name of Father Fra Laurent, wherein you were begged to give him permission for the publication in the church at Pondicherry of the decrees of the Sacred Congregation, which permission [251] your Lordship declined to give in writing, but only orally, saying we might read them out in our church; and I repeated your Lordship's words, "They may then be read?" Your Most Illustrious Lordship said to me: "Who can hinder?" These are the very words heard twice from your mouth, and on which I relied. Since then Your Illustrious Lordship has forwarded a Pastoral which has been promulgated. This act has been done by your Lordship, I suppose, because you have repented of the oral permission that you gave me. Supposing, then, this to be correct, let your Lordship inscribe some order upon my last petition, which will enable me to carry out the wishes of your Lordship and obey them completely. As I see now that your Lordship means to prevent the carrying out of the said decrees by the issue of the said Pastoral, I have obeyed as was incumbent on me. But in order to seek for justice I have had a copy taken, and to obtain this justice I put in with this a petition, with a view to its being made over to me properly authenticated.'

REPLY OF THE LORD BISHOP TO THE LETTER OF THE REVEREND FATHER MICHEL ANGE

'Reverend Father,[2]

'I have not given permission to your Reverence, not even in thought, much less in words. All I said to you was that you could publish the decrees on your own authority, as you could publish any other sort of order in your church, just as you thought fit, without my leave and without anyone hindering you;

1. The letter in Codex No. CXXXV. is in Portuguese. This incident on September 28, 1706, is again referred to in Part V., fol. 262.
2. The original in Codex No. CXXXV. is in Portuguese.

I did not, however, issue the Pastoral to hinder the decrees of the Sacred Congregation, but to suppress the boldness with [252] which the Reverend Father Fra Esprit declared in his church on All Saints' Day [November 1, 1706] that the reverend Jesuit fathers of the society were not the parochial priests of the Malabaris, the whole of whom were his parishioners, thereby encroaching on our jurisdiction, and acting against what I had ordered in virtue of the jurisdiction possessed by me as bishop, and conferred on me by the Sacred Canons and the decrees of the Sacred Council of Trent, in regard to the erecting and dividing parishes by following what I might think best for the welfare of my flock. The demand, as it is not founded on truths falls of itself to the ground . . ., ' *et cetera*.

Gentlemen, having already replied at length to this letter of the Lord Bishop in the previous letter which I did myself the honour of writing to you, I will say no more than merely pray you to observe if any permission could be given more authentic than the one above recorded. Yet his Lordship has written to your Council, and also said in his Pastoral, that we have published the decrees without his permission, and makes use of this assertion to take away our mission to the Malabaris, and to fulminate his anathemas against the Reverend Father Esprit.

To speak the truth, gentlemen, do hot all these things cry aloud for vengeance in the presence of God? The French themselves, who know the innocent and irreproachable life of the said Reverend Father Fra Esprit, flee from him as if he were a wild beast. Should they not rather blush with shame, and at least spare us the fatigues, the afflictions, the sadness, to which we are daily subjected by them? Yet it is thus that they act against a poor friar who suffers persecution in the cause of justice—a humble man, if ever there has been one in this world.

[253] To see the Reverend Father Esprit declared excommunicated by a Portuguese bishop, whose nation is at this time warring and contesting with France, does not afflict us, knowing most thoroughly that they hate to the very death the French nation. To see attached to the doors of the reverend Jesuit fathers a declaration against the Reverend Father Esprit, wherein he is pronounced accursed, and doubly accursed of God Omni-

potent, of the Apostles St. Peter and St. Paul, and of all the other saints in the quire celestial, in spite of its cutting us to the quick, does not surprise us, because we have known the reverend Jesuit fathers for many a day, and we are aware by full evidence that they are our sworn enemies. But to see French gentlemen allow the reverend Capuchin fathers, who for over thirty years have had charge of their consciences, to be tyrannized over, outraged, and persecuted, without lifting a finger to help them; that, seeing what we suffer—seeing, finally, their own pastor ex-communicated, and knowing his innocence, they leave him exposed to the fury of his enemies, and take no steps to find out what sin he has committed—alas! gentlemen, this is the thing which pierces us to the heart, which so pains us, that if God did not uphold us by His grace we should have succumbed inevitably under so great a burden. What boots it to live under the flag of France, in a city having a supreme Council, in the midst of men who know quite well that our Invincible Monarch lias taken us under his singular protection and safeguard; who know perfectly the orders [254] they have received from his Majesty and the Royal Company to succour and protect us as often as necessary; who recently discovered the false devices through which we were damaged by the reverend Jesuit fathers; who have seen the oppressive way in which Monsignor has behaved to us several times; who know sufficiently well that we have not done a single thing unworthy of our ministry? In the teeth of all this, can you leave us in abandonment—nay, throw the blame upon us Capuchins? Not to resent these things we should need to be more than human, and not mere men.

Who has ever beheld so many excommunications, so many interdicts, so many suspensions, against the poor Capuchin fathers? The Reverend Father Michel Ange of Bourges, Superior at Madras, after twenty years and more of service in these regions, where he has gained the love of all the people by an exemplary life, suspended from divine duties ! Father René of Angoulesme, after being in the mission fifteen years, and without the commission of anything for which he could be reproved, also suspended like the first-named! The Reverend Father Eusebius of Bourges, after twelve years in India, where he had reaped a great harvest, suspended, interdicted, and excommunicated! The Reverend Father Esprit of Tours, Superior of Pondicherry, after twenty-five years of mission work, in which he has sweated blood and water, declared accursed, doubly accursed of God Omnipotent, of the Apostles St. Peter and St. Paul [255], and of all the other saints in the quire celestial! Should you desire to know the reason why the first three were so treated, it was because they did not appear at Pondicherry, owing to the English gentlemen having retained them by force at Madras; and the last one, for having published decrees of the Sacred Congregation, and having cited his opposing party before the courts at Rome.

Gentlemen, I ask you, can any other crimes than the above be laid to our charge? I trow not. If you have anything to reproach us with of which we are ignorant, kindly oblige us by stating it; even publish it clearly in the face of heaven and of earth: we give you free license. But if you know us innocent, then have for us the same consideration that you have for the reverend Jesuit fathers, and when they take our business in hand, do not pay more deference to Portuguese or Savoyard[1] prelates than to those of France. For, to sum up, it is a barbarous thing that Father Laurent of Angoulesme, Vice-Provincial in India, for having published in our church a provisional order about our cure issued by the Lord Bishop in his favour, should find himself forthwith summoned to appear before your Council and called upon to state by what authority he had acted; while the reverend Jesuit fathers, who have published in their church an excommunication launched against the Reverend Father Esprit by the self-same bishop, have not been cited, like Father Laurent of Angoulesme, to file any answer. Nay, on the contrary, it would seem that they have received your plaudits, while we are derided. It is a cruel measure that a patriarch from Savoy, and a bishop from Portugal—the latter country at this moment at war with France—should discharge their weapons at us poor Capuchin fathers; but when a bishop of France [256] —that is, monsignor of Tiripoli[2]—tries to justify us and prove

1. Cardinal Charles Maillard de Tournon, Patriarch of Antioch, Papal Legate to India and China, was a Savoyard, while the Bishop of San Thome was a Portuguese.
2. This must be meant for Marin Labbé, Bishop of Tilopolis and Coadjutor in Cochin China. He was at Pondicherry in February, 1705 (see note 33, Vol.

us not guilty, it should become necessary for a captain and a whole company to be put in motion before allowing a passage to a humble Capuchin father on his way to see his Holiness and report to him his whole conduct, to be followed by chastisement in case of his meriting it.

Gentlemen, if we were invoking your aid in an unjust cause, it would be open to you to deny it to us; but since we ask you only reasonable things, listen at least to our arguments, and, after having heard and thoroughly considered them, if we are guilty, punish us; but if we are innocent, for God's sake do us justice. Here, then, are the great crimes we have committed; examine into them well, I implore you. Observe the want of justice that has been shown to us, the calumnies against us in the letter written by Monsignor to your Council, in which his Lordship begs you to proceed against us with all possible severity. The same is the case with the petition that the Reverend Father Tachard presented to Monsieur de Flacourt, judge at Pondicherry, in the hope of hindering the decrees. Having be held, I say, conduct in direct opposition to the maxims of the Gospels, and so little agreeing with the ordinances of the Supreme Pontilf, we have cited the reverend Jesuit fathers to Rome for using violence to us and refusing to do us justice. This is the great crime we have committed, gentlemen. I know no other whatever, although his Lordship, in his Declaration, may allege [257] that he acted in consequence of our having published certain decrees—that it was not until we had done so that he sent a Pastoral to the reverend Jesuit fathers as our punishment. But we have not taken any step, not even the slightest, since the issue of the said Pastoral, beyond the citation to Rome of the Reverend Father Tachard. Even if we were to be punished for having published the decrees and summoned the reverend Jesuit fathers, who has ever before heard of a case where a friar was anathematized and excommunicated for reasons of that sort? I cannot believe that since the world became a world up to this very day there ever happened a case of this sort, for the thing appears an impossibility. In fact, if such a thing were likely to happen, it would be much better for the Sacred Congrega-

IV., Part V., fol. 37). The allusion to hindering a Capuchin from sailing to Europe must be meant to refer, I think, to Father Eusebius.

tion to issue no decrees; and if it is allowable to excommunicate a friar when he summons his opposite party to Rome, the only thing left for the Lord Bishop of San Thome to do is to remove all the missionaries who are dependent upon him and replace them by Jesuit fathers.

But supposing, gentlemen, what cannot be admitted—that is, that the Lord Bishop could excommunicate for publishing the decrees of the Sacred Congregation and citing an opponent to Rome; how, even then, can his Lordship excommunicate or declare excommunicated a friar of the Order of St. Francis in face ot the Bulls, Decrees, and Privileges conceded to friars of that Order? Here is the Brief of Martin V.,[1] which states in express terms that no ordinary or prelate can deliver a sentence of excommunication, suspension, or interdict, nor openly promulgate such against the said friars: 'Ordinarii et prælati alii, sive quævis alia [258] persona generaliter, vel specialiter, aut communiter aut divisim, non possunt quavis authoritate ex-communicationis, suspensionis, et interdicti sententias pro-mulgare.' [Neither ordinaries nor other prelates, or other persons whatsoever, acting either generally or specially, or in common or singly, are authorized in any way to publish sentences of excommunication, suspension, and interdict.]

These words are to be read in the book entitled 'Monumenta Oidinum,' under the name of Eugenius IV.[2] There is also what Clement IV.[3] says: 'Concessit fratribus minoribus ne ab aliquo legato, nisi de Latere Sedis Apostolicæ misso, vel delegato, vel subdelegato authoritate litterarum Sedis prædictæ, possint excommunicari suspendi vel interdici nisi litteræ ipsae plenam et expressam de ordine praefato et indulto hujusmodi facerent mentionem.' [He granted to the Friars Minor that no legate, except a legate commissioned *de latere* of the Apostolic See, and no delegate or sub-delegate, by virtue of letters of the aforesaid See, should have the power of excommunication, suspension, or interdict over them, unless the

1. Martin V. (Otho Colonna), elected in 1417; died 1431.
2. Eugenius IV. (Gabriele Condolmero), elected Pope 1431; died in 1447. The work intended seems to be 'Monumenta Ordinis Minorum' (In civitate Salmantina, Impensis Joannis de Porras, 1511), but the letter of Martin V. cannot be found in it.
3. Clement IV. (Guido Fulcodi), elected February. 1265; died in 1268. The Bull is 'Exigentibus Vestræ Devotionis Meritis . . .' dated July 17 in the first year of his pontificate (1265) (see 'Monumenta Ordinis Minorum,' 1511, fol. 29, verso).

letters themselves made full and explicit mention of these powers concerning the aforesaid Order enjoying this indulgence.]

The same thing has been laid down by Sixtus IV.[1]: 'Ne locorum diocesani vel alii ordinarii vel alii quicumque in personas aut [et] loca fratrum minorum contra privilegia[2] exemptionis sibi quamcumque jurisdictionem *aut* superioritatem vindicare praesumant, et dislricte inhibuit ne quispiam absque Sedis Apostolicæ speciali *concessione aut* auctoritate, in personas, domos, et loca dicti Ordinis Minorum[3] (ut pote prorsus exempta) aliquas[4] censuras vel sententias, specialiter vel generaliter audeat promulgare.'[5] [That the local diocesans or other ordinaries, or any others whosoever, should not presume to arrogate to themselves any kind of jurisdiction or lordship over the persons or estates (lit. 'places') of the Friars Minor contrary to their privileges of exemption; and he strictly enjoined that no one without the special permission or authority of the Apostolic. See should dare to publish, either specially or generally, any censures or sentences against the persons, houses, and estates of the said order of Minor Friars, seeing that they are entirely exempt.]

Further, let us admit, gentlemen, that the Lord Bishop of San Thome possessed the power of excommunicating, or declar-

---

1. Sixtus IV. (Francesco della Rovere), elected August 9, 1471; died in 1484 ('Bullarium,' i. 393, 'Regiminis Universalis Ecclesiæ,' dated September 1, 1474, Section IX.). A marginal note says reference must be made to the Council of Trent's direction (Session XIV., cap. vii.) ordering otherwise; also see declaration of Clement VIII. (1592-1605) in Constitutione XXXIX., 'Suscepti' (*ibid.*, vol. iii., p. 59), dated March 7, 1596. There are some variants found in the 'Bullarium' printed text; these are chiefly verbal and unimportant. The rest are given in footnotes. The Bull of Sixtus IV. is also found in 'Bullarum Diplomatum et Privilegiorum Sanctorum Romanorum Pontificum Taurinensis Edito' (August Taurinorum, 1860), vol. v., p. 220, with the date of August 31, 1474.
2. Variant, insert [ejusdem dementis praedecessoris in fine literarum prædictorum ordinum].
3. Variant, insert [fratrum].
4. Insert [aliquam excommunication is suspensions et interdicti].
5. Variant, insert fquo modo libet].

ing excommunicated, the friars of the Order of St. Francis, notwithstanding the Privileges and Bulls of Martin V., Eugenius IV., Clement IV., and Sixtus IV.; still, his Lordship could not exercise this power without having called upon the friar to put in an appearance, without having taken legal steps against him, without having heard the case, without having found him guilty [259] on untainted evidence. My Lord Bishop took the deposition of the reverend Jesuit fathers, who are our adversaries, who would like to see us lost without hope of recovery. Upon these depositions (at the very time, too, when his Lordship had discovered the foulest calumny ever uttered), without any other foundation or process, without summoning the Reverend Father Esprit, and without passing sentence, my lord declares him accursed, and doubly accursed of God Omnipotent, the Apostles St. Peter and St. Paul, and all the other saints in the quire celestial. He prohibits, under penalty of the greater excommunication, all inter-course with him; and directs that he be not given water, fire, *et cetera*. He orders this wonderful Declaration to be affixed to the door of the church of the reverend fathers of the Society of Jesus, and that, too, in the sight of the heathen and of the Christians who have been but lately born into the faith. Gentlemen, does not this seem to you a fine sort of zeal for the glory of God? Does it not seem to you a fine observance of the Church's rules? Does it not seem to you a curiously judicious course of action? Does it not strike you as an excommunication launched in the very nick of time? Is not this a splendid device for rendering us odious to every lover of justice? But who is aware that Monsignor and the reverend Jesuit fathers have followed rides which are directly opposed to the prescriptions of the Church? We find their pretended excommunication to be null and void, as even you can see, gentlemen, from the following words: 'Judex declarans aliquem excommunicatum vel incidisse in excommunicationem'—[If a judge declares anyone excommunicated or fallen [260] under excommunication, although he has not been cited to appear, the declaration is absolutely null and without any effect] —'ipso jure sine citatione illius, qui declarandus est, declaratio est nulla: ' Glossa in Clementina 'Præsenti' in versu 'Constiterit' 'De Censibus,' and in the Clementine Constitutions, second vers.,[1]

1. For the first passage, see 'Corpus Juris Canonici' (ed. Æ. L. Richter and Æ. Friedberg), 4 to, 1839, pars ii., column 1091, clementinarum' ('dementis

'De pœnis,' and Navar. 'Con.' 4 et 9, nunc 4, 'De Sententia Excommunicationis.'[1]

You cannot deny, gentlemen, that we fall under this rule, and I can never believe that you can approve those who act entirely contrary to the above ordinance of the Church. Yet this is what the Lord Bishop and also the reverend Jesuit fathers have done, for where is the citation issued to the Reverend Father Esprit of lours? You know very well, gentlemen, that he was never cited. Where are the proceedings that ought to have been held in the case against him? Where are the depositions of the witnesses to be found? Where is the official record of the case? No one has seen it, and they decline to show it in spite of an express demand for its inspection. Apparently they desire so passionately to see us lost and defamed in reputation that they have not complied with either the one or the other

---

Papæ V. Constitutiones'), liber iii., titulus xiii., 'De Censibus, Actionibus, et Procurationibus,' caput iii., commencing 'Praesenti constitutione jubemus.' The word 'constiterit' is in line 7 of the paragraph. For the 'Gloss,' which is quoted in the text, see Joannes Andraae, canonist, 'Liber Decretalium D. Bonifacii Papæ VIII. dementis Papæ V. Constitutiones,' vol. ii., (1584). It was written in 1326, and is called 'Glossa Ordinaria' (Wetzer and Welte, French edition, iv. 433, under 'Clementines'). The other reference to the 'Clementinarum' seems to be to liber v., titulus viii., 'De Pœnis,' caput ii., same edition of 'Corpus,' column 1106.

1. Martin Azpilcueta, called Navarrus, born 1493; died June 21, 1587. In his time he was the most eminent doctor in Canon Law. His works appeared at Rome in 3 vols. (1599 and subsequent editions). The work referred to in the text may be 'Consiliorum seu Responsorum,' in five books, on the order of the Decretals (editions in 1591, 1594, 1597, etc.). There is a compendium of Navarrus's writings by Jacobus Castellanis (Venice, 1598) (H. Hurter, 'Nomenclator,' i. 124). It is also possible that the reference is to his 'Relectiones duæ in cap. "Si quando" et in cap. "Cum Contingat. de Rescriptis" ' (Romæ, Ex Officina Jacobi Tornerii et Jacobi Berichiæ, 1585). One passage on p. 154 is on the necessity of citation, § 3 ('Citatio iure naturali facienda, et earn nec princeps tollit'), in the chapter 'Octava Caussa Nullitatis,' part of the 'Relectio in cap. "Cum Contingat." ' It would be interesting to know if this Navarrus is identical with the writer of whose work the Emperor Akbar possessed two copies (see E. D. Maclagan's article on 'Jesuit Missions to Akbar' in the *Journal of the Asiatic Society of Bengal*, vol. lxv., part i., 1896, p. 68, quoting Father Pinheiro's letter from Lahor of September 3, 1595. Mr. Maclagan proposes to identify that Navarrus with Juan Aspidueta, S.J. (died 1555).

of the above conditions, and as an inevitable consequence of their having sinned against principles, their so-called excommunication falls rather upon them than upon the Reverend Father Esprit of Tours.

Let us farther assume, gentlemen, since I do not wish merely to prove the innocence of the Reverend Father Esprit, but also to display to the whole world the estimable conduct of our adversaries—let us assume, I say, that the Lord Bishop of San Thome had the power of excommunicating or declaring excommunicated the friars of St. Francis. Let us also assume that his Lordship had permission to act without any rules or formalities. Let us assume plainly that the Reverend Father Esprit was really excommunicated, the which he most decidedly is not; yet even then who has ever heard it said [261] that a judge could forbid a culprit to appear before him, when he has come for the express purpose of expounding to him his arguments, and submitting himself to punishment if it is decided that he has earned it? Nobody, I could never believe, gentlemen, that you would be so cruel that you would deny an audience to an innocent though calumniated man, who had come a distance of thirty leagues to demand from you as a favour that you would kindly listen to his arguments, and after hearing them, pass such orders as you pleased. Yet this was what Monsignor has done; he sent his secretary to Monsieur Guety's house, praying him to tell us not to go to his palace. If you decline to believe a statement which does not seem credible, Monsieur Guety,[1] is present at San Thome: write to him if you like, and see whether what I say is true or false.

Although the Lord Bishop had caused this prohibition against us to be issued, nevertheless, after reflection over a mode of action as extraordinary as it is unjust, we determined to go and see his Lordship, and as an auspicious opening to the excellent feast of St. Thomas the Apostle of India [December 21], meant to urge him, to conjure him, with all tenderness and good feeling, to be graciously pleased to listen to the arguments of the Reverend Father Esprit; we also intended to present a petition in case of refusal. Hardly had we entered when we were asked what we wanted, and what we had come for. Immediately we answered

1. For Guety, see also Part IV., fol. 188, and Part V., fols. 241, 242, 244, 284.

that we had come to congratulate his Lordship upon the feast-day. When he learnt that the Reverend Father Esprit was with us, he sent word that we could come in, with the exception of the Reverend Father Esprit. We went in then, but in a sad mood, having had such a [262] compliment as we had hardly expected from a bishop. After having congratulated his Lordship on the festival, he asked us how we were. Our Reverend Father Guardian and Vice-Provincial in India replied:[1] 'Monsignor, we are all well, through God's grace, but most deeply afflicted and pained at seeing the Reverend Father Esprit in the very pitiable state to which your Lordship has reduced him; in if as an effect of your fatherly goodness you would deign to remedy it, we should express the greatest possible gratitude.'

To these words Monsignor made answer: 'He has been the cause of it, not I.' 'But what has he done,' said our Reverend Father Guardian, 'since neither he nor we know yet the reason?' 'He has published the decrees of the Sacred Congregation without my permission' (this is not true, gentlemen, as you must have ascertained from many passages), 'and has, besides, cited the Reverend Father Tachard to the courts at Rome.' 'Then, my lord,' replied the Reverend Father Guardian, 'your Lordship has declared Father Esprit to be excommunicated because he has published the decrees themselves with your permission, and because he has cited the reverend Jesuit Fathers, who are acting in direct opposition to the decrees?' 'I gave no sort of permission,' then replied Monsignor. Thereupon, falling upon my knees and craving leave to speak, I asked him in the hearing of two Jesuits, the old curé, the secretary, and of a reverend Cordelier father (that is to say, a Franciscan): 'Your Lordship has not, then, given permission to the Reverend Father Esprit, or, to speak more strictly, to Father Michel Ange, on the eve of St. Michael,[2] for the publication of the decrees?' 'No, I have not given it to him,' replied his Lordship without hesitation [263]. 'It is quite true I said to him that he could publish the decrees of the Sacred Congregation, by virtue of their authority, in exactly the manner he could publish in his church whatever to him might seem meet, without my permission and without anyone being able to hinder him.' I had my answer ready, but I was interrupted by the

1. This would be Father Laurent (Lorenzo) of Angoulême.
2. That is, on September 28, 1706 (see ante, Part V., fol. 250).

XLVIII. Dakhin women

Reverend Father Guardian, who with all possible insistence prayed the Lord Bishop to kindly hear the Reverend Father Esprit, who had been waiting at the door for now nearly an hour.

As his Lordship persisted not only in declining to admit him, but also in prohibiting us from continuing the subject, the Reverend Father Guardian, a man who has made himself widely known in India by his virtues and other merits, flung himself on his knees, and, bathing his Lordship's feet with a torrent of tears, asked him for the love of God and of St. Thomas, whose festival was then being celebrated; by the love of Jesus Christ, whose natal day was so near at hand, to be so good as to relieve the woes of the Christian people of Pondicherry, who had been left groaning over the loss of their pastor. To get rid of the scandal growing greater day-by-day, and to satisfy us, would he kindly allow the Reverend Father Esprit to enter his presence, would he listen to his arguments? But we observed that the greater the pressure applied the less the bishop seemed to feel for us, and the more the father humiliated himself the more furious against us his Lordship grew. A posture which would have softened the hardest heart raised no hope of advancing [264] our cause in the slightest degree with Monsignor. Our Guardian, therefore, put in our petition, which proved clearly that the Reverend Father Esprit had not become liable to excommunication, and that, even had he become so liable, the Bishop could not excommunicate or declare excommunicated any friar of the order of St. Francis, as he thereby infringed our Privileges, Bulls, and Decrees obtained from four Supreme Pontiffs. Further, it follows that, even could he excommunicate, the act would be null and void for want of compliance with the rules of the Canon Law and the formalities that must be observed.

His Lordship took the petition, and noticing that he had read no more than two or three lines, I went down on my knees again and said to him: 'Monsignor, by the love of God, read it all, from beginning to end.' Then he ordered me to rise, and said to me he knew within a word or two all that it contained; that he would take upon his own head the responsibility about the said privileges; and that he was fully cognisant of the respect and veneration due to the Supreme Pontiffs. Nevertheless, seeing that the Lord Bishop would not even now do us the slightest justice,' I took upon myself the liberty of saying to him: 'Monsignor, what good does it do us for you to take upon your head the responsibility for our privileges, or for you to cherish such respect and veneration for the Supreme Pontiffs, when your Lordship acts to the precise contrary, and is more stubborn than ever was known before? You not only refuse to absolve the Reverend Father Esprit from an excommunication to which he is not liable, but still farther you refuse him permission to present himself before you' [265J.

'If the Reverend Father Esprit has not incurred excommunication,' replied his Lordship, 'what is your object, then, in asking me to set it aside?' 'We call for that,' added I forthwith, 'not because he has become liable to it, for he is as much excommunicated as I am, but to avoid scandal, which must without fail arise it the Reverend Father Esprit, who has been declared accursed and doubly accursed of God, *et cetera*, should say Holy Mass before the publication of another declaration setting aside the former one. In addition to this, the simple folk do not judge by reality, but only by appearances, by which they are misled. Without considering whether the said reverend father is excommunicated or not, it is open to them to believe that he is a malefactor, for they are unable to persuade themselves that a bishop, whom here they venerate like the Pope is venerated at Rome, could treat a friar so unworthily without his having merited it. Moreover, as we clearly comprehend that no limit will be placed on what is done to us, we have just reason to fear that, having declared the Reverend Father Esprit out of rule, you will equally launch an interdict against our church, if he should celebrate publicly Holy Mass without your Lordship's leave.'

At these words the Lord Bishop of San Thome said that if the Reverend Father Esprit were to be allowed in, it was necessary beforehand for him to admit three things, to be reduced to writing. The first was that he must confess himself to be guilty; the second, [266] that, having confessed his fault, he must humbly ask pardon; and the third, he must promise he will no longer claim the cure of the Malabaris. We could not accept these conditions, which absolved Monsignor from his acts and threw the blame on the Capuchins. They also deprived us of all hope of a re-entry on our original mission. Shortly afterwards we took our leave. We suddenly perceived what had led to this declaration, and what, if only a little attention is paid, will clearly explain the maxims followed by the reverend Jesuit fathers.

These reverend fathers desire to be masters wherever they are, and to gain their designs make use of falsehood as if it were truth; they regulate their consciences by their ambitions, and follow no other rule than what suits their interests. We see this in their falsely alleging His Most Christian Majesty's order; in their having written to France and to Rome that there were thirty thousand Christians[1] where there were only two thousand; in their having produced a decree two years after it had been pronounced; in their having disobeyed in formal terms the Sacred Congregation; in the fact that the authorities they have quoted in the Pastoral are more against them than against us, as you will perceive in the course of time; in their having recourse to the secular arm to impede the execution of the decrees; in their spreading the calumny about the Reverend Father Esprit; in their making us over to your hands [267] with a precise direction to chastise us with all possible rigour. Looking to all the above things, I say, and foreseeing the consequences (for what has been approved at Pondicherry will not remain unpunished at Rome), they have behaved almost identically as did the Scribes and Pharisees who assembled and took counsel to betray Jesus: 'Collegerunt pontifices et pharisæi concilium, ut Jesum dokv tenerent' (Matt. xxvi. 3, 4, and John xi. 47).[2]

As a matter of fact, after having plotted the destruction of the Reverend Father Esprit, the person who caused them the greatest umbrage, they sent off as quick as they could the Reverend Father de la Breuille to San Thome, where, for three days on end, there were four Jesuits and some other friars not particularly well-intentioned towards us examining into the best means of succeeding in their pernicious enterprises. The vicar-general, who was present at their last meeting, finding there had been such a precipitate excommunication of the Reverend Father Esprit, asked the reasons. After having reflected over them in a judicial spirit, he said such an act could not be done without injustice, and if they carried it out they would be forced one day to repent it. But perceiving what little account they made of his arguments, and that they had sworn our ruin, he shut the door behind him

1. This assertion occurs in the 'Mémoire' of the Jesuits of 1703, to be found at the Archives Nationales, K 1,374, Document No. 52, '. . . les Malabares, dont il y a ordinairement plus de vingt à trente mille à Pondicherry . . .'
2. 'This is not an exact quotation, but a combination' (W.R.P.).

in a rage and fled. Never again did he appear in the midst of such a saintly assembly.

Gentlemen, it is hardly to be presumed that, in a case of injustice which cries aloud for vengeance in the presence of God and before men, there should be no one who would take our cause in hand. But as the reverend Jesuit fathers were in search of any method of covering up their evil deeds against us, they thought it better to sacrifice a [268] poor friar to their anger than to see a whole order dishonoured by the perverse behaviour of seven or eight individuals: 'Expedit ut unus moriatur homo pro populo, et non tota gens pereat (Vulgate, John xi. 49). As, however, man proposes and God disposes, they were deceived. For they had imagined that the Reverend Father Esprit would subscribe to anything and everything they wished, in order to be relieved from the so-called excommunication of which they had procured the issue against him. But the Reverend Father Esprit foresaw most clearly the consequences that would have arisen if he had subscribed to the propositions made to him. In addition to the witness of his conscience, which in this affair in no way stung him, he knew by full evidence that all they had done was intended solely to force him into returning to his province. Because the reverend Jesuit fathers hold it as an axiom that, when they cannot effect their designs by acting justly, they must persecute so vigorously that, no longer able to endure the persecution, such an one may be obliged to withdraw and escape by flight. The Reverend Father Esprit, I say, knowing all these things, held it much better to decide on a return to Europe, there to petition the courts at Rome, than to subscribe such ridiculous propositions.

Since we were now forced to return to our hospice at Madras without having been able to make any impression on the mind of my lord, we consulted together as to the best course to adopt on this occasion. After we had thoroughly deliberated, we saw that our opponents were our judges; that there was no hope whatever [269] of obtaining justice from men who did not even know what justice was; and we resolved to make an appeal to the Holy See. Our appeal was drawn up on the 23rd December, 1706, in the presence of Messieurs Cesar Louis Melique and Khwajah Joannes, Armenian,[1] whom we had for this end prayed to

1. Mr. Philipps thinks that 'Melique'—that is 'Malik'—is a title of respect, just as 'Khwajah' is. For the other name, besides Joannes

accompany us, not only to act as witnesses to our petition of appeal, but chiefly to let the whole world see that, when the Capuchin fathers were driven to such an extreme necessity, it was because we had been persecuted to the very last point and there was no other possible resource left.

In fact, before delivering our petition of appeal to his Lordship, we opened the conversation with the usual compliments, and after a somewhat prolonged conversation on indifferent subjects, our Reverend Father Guardian—that is, custodian and vice provincial in the Indies [Laurent (Lorenzo) of Angoulême—' begged once more the Lord Bishop to be so kind as to have the goodness to adjust the affair of the Reverend Father Esprit, and not to leave him to pass the Festival of the Nativity in such a pitiable condition. His Lordship replied that the said Reverend Father Esprit declined to submit himself. Upon hearing this our Father Guardian replied at once: 'My lord, he has travelled post from Pondicherry with that object, and it is barely two days ago that he was an hour and a half in your entrance-hall awaiting the moment when he would be allowed to see your Lordship once more, and present to you his most humble supplications and pray you urgently to listen to his arguments.' 'Call you that a submission?' said my Lord Bishop. 'He must admit himself wrong; he must ask pardon for his misdoing; he must promise to cease further turbulence until some new [270] decision comes from Rome.'

'Let Monsignor permit the Reverend Father Esprit to appear before him,' replied the Reverend Father Guardian, 'and after you have heard his reasons, if you are not satisfied, you may do whatever you judge most appropriate.' We noticed then that his Lordship, instead of answering, turned his head in another direction. The more urgent we were with him the more obdurate he became. The Guardian continued and said: 'Monsignor, if the Reverend Father Esprit were at Rome, instead of being at San Thome, and he were to present himself to his Holinessto report to him on imputations made against him, and were to submit himself to punishment in case he had merited it, would

(in the French text) and Giovanni (in the Italian text), we have the forms 'Ivanos' (fol. 236) and 'Avanes' (fol. 287), which are both, as Mr. Ellis tells me, forms for John. An Armenian of the name of Avannes is prominent in the Fort St. George records of these years and may be the person intended.

his Holiness order him to go away without having granted him an audience?' The cases are not parallel,' said a Jesuit who was present. This having afforded me an opening, I said: 'A pope would not refuse an audience to the Reverend Father Esprit if he were at Rome; and my Lord Bishop, upon the depositions of the reverend Jesuit fathers, whose most iniquitous calumny, worse than any ever yet heard, has been unmasked, excommunicates the Reverend Father Esprit without any regular form of process; and then, when he presents himself at his Lordship's to lay before him the true facts, he (the bishop) desires him to confess himself in fault before he has been convicted.' Who has ever heard such a thing, gentlemen, and amongst laymen where is to be found a judge who has fallen into this error? There certainly never has been any such, and if by any chance one were found in the world, he could easily be brought to punishment.

'This reverend father,' said his Lordship quickly, without replying to my question, 'publishes certain decrees without my permission; declares publicly [271] that the reverend Jesuit fathers are no longer the legal pastors of the Malabaris at Pondicherry; goes from house to house to take down the names of the Christians, and that notwithstanding the prohibition I have issued. I shall know, however, quite well how to reduce him to order and bring him back to his duty.' 'My Lord,' said I, 'the Reverend Father Esprit has not published the decrees without your Lordship's permission, since you gave it *vivâ voce* to the Reverend Father Michel Ange, which you confirmed in writing when we asked as a favour that your Lordship should testify the truth. It was not the Reverend Father Esprit either who declared the reverend Jesuit fathers to be no longer the legitimate pastors of the Malabaris at Pondicherry, but rather it is the decrees that say so.' Here I repeated to him the whole decree of the Sacred Congregation, word for word, exactly as it stood in the original. 'Furthermore, subsequent to the Pastoral his Lordship issued, the Reverend Father Esprit has performed no function at all as curé, nor uttered the slightest word transgressing the respect he owes to your Lordship.'

'In addition, it was before the publication of the said Pastoral that the Reverend Father Esprit wrote down the names of the Malabari Christians; hence, when he did this, it was not to take away your Lordship's jurisdiction. He knew thoroughly well the obedience he owed you. It was done in order to inform the court at Rome of the number of Malabari Christians in Pondicherry. For the reverend Jesuit fathers, be it in France, be it at Rome, say there are to be found twenty to thirty thousand Christians, where we give details that show there are not even two thousand. Your Lordship yourself, did you not say to the Reverend Father Guardian, here present, that a reverend Jesuit father had baptized six thousand Christians in one day?' [272]

These words caused the company present to smile; they knew very well indeed that I was speaking the truth. But our Reverend Father Guardian, whose heart was sore, wished to urge nothing but the matter of the Reverend Father Esprit. A second time he prayed his Lordship to have pity upon the poor Capuchin Fathers, who were thrown into the utmost consternation at seeing one of their friars declared excommunicated when he was innocent and had not done anything, not even the slightest, unworthy of his vocation. All this he poured forth with such energy, and in such touching and penetrating language, that, with the exception of the reverend Jesuit fathers, who seemed pleased at our troubles, all the others present were unable to do otherwise than shed tears. But, coming to the conclusion that all his eloquence was vain, and that he could easier convert a Turk than secure the very slightest hold upon my lord's mind, the Reverend Father Guardian presented to him the following petition of appeal.

PETITION IN APPEAL OF THE REVEREND FATHER ESPRIT OF TOURS TO THE COURT AT ROME.[1]

A quodam decreto,[2] *seu* declaratoria lata ab Illustrissimo et Reverendissimo D.º, D.º Alphonso Meliapurepsi Episcopo contra Patrem Spiritum Turonensem Capucinum Missionis Pudicheriensis, nec non ejusdem Ordinis Religiosorum Missionariorum in ea commorantium[3] Superiorem, in qua ipsum declarat incidisse in excommunicationem Bullae Tin Caena Domini,' privatque communione fidelium[4] et timens dictus Pater magis aggravari in posterum, judicem superiorem, cui de

1. The petition is printed in Norbert, 'Mémoires,' 1742, p. 236 *et seq.* Additions from that text are inserted in the footnotes, and any words omitted by Norbert I print in italics.
2. Variant, insert [super].
3. Query, read 'Choromandalum.'
4. Variant, insert [ecclesiastical.]

jure competit, in his scriptis [273] provocat, et appellat, et de nullitate dicit, petens Apostolos[1] sæpè sæpius, *sæpissime, instant er, instantius, instantissime*; salvâ semper et intactâ reverentiâ debita[2] Prœlato *lllustrissimo* et Reverendissimo Meliapurensi Episcopo quam vel minimum lædere nullo modo intendit appellans, sed solummodo se ipsum à gravamine liberare: tenebatur namque lllusIrissimus *ac* Reverendissimus Meliapurensi Episcopus contra dictum appellantem procedere juxta formam juris præscriptara in Capite 'Qualiter et quando de accusatione et denunciatione' in 'Decretalium'[3] et observare sacras sanctiones in dicto capite express as, quibus non servatis quidquid contra *dictum* appellantem intentatum fuit absque formâ ibidem præscriptâ cassum et irritunr[4] dibet reputari. Et ideo ab iis omnibus provocat *et* appellat, et de nullitate dicit, ut supra, et à non admissione praesentic appellations, *vel à denegatione Apostolorum, aut a quocumque actu alio in spretum hujus appellationis* in posterum forsan facienda (quod non credit) iterum provocat et appellat et de nullitate dicit non solum semel, sed bis, et ter, *et* toties quoties opus fuerit, ita ut sit semper ultimus *in appellatione et* in appellando et protestando[5] de attentatis *et attentandis* non solum *isto, sed, omne alio meliori modo.*

Datum Madraspatam sub die 23 mensis Decembris, 1706.

FRATER SPIRITUS TURONENSIS,
Cap^s Miss^us Apost^us.

[Father Esprit of Tours, a Capuchin of the Pondicherry mission, and also Superior of the Religious of that order, the missionaries dwelling there, in these presents (lit., 'writings') earnestly appeals against and proclaims the nullity of a certain decree or declaratory sentence passed by the Most Illustrious and Most Reverend Lord Alphonso, Bishop of Meliapur, in which the father is declared to have fallen into the excommunication of the

1. *Petens Apostolos.*—'The *Apostoli* are the letters by which the judge who has passed sentence sends the case to the appellate judge' (Todeschi, 'Manuel du Droit canonique,' p. 169, chapter on 'Manner of Appealing: Application for the *Apostoli*') (W. R. P.).
2. Variant, insert [praedicto].
3. Variant, insert [in Sexto].
4. Variant, insert [esset].
5. Variant, insert [protestatur].

Bull 'In Cæna Domini,' and to be excluded from the communion of the faithful.

The said father, fearing that worse will befall him hereafter, appeals to and invokes the superior judge, who is legally competent to entertain the appeal, and he maintains the nullity of the sentence, seeking the *Apostoli* (the leave of the Court of First Instance to appeal) over and over and over again, earnestly, very earnestly, most earnestly, preserving always intact the reverence due to the most Illustrious and Reverend Prelate, the Bishop of Meliapur, which he has no intention of lessening, but merely desirous to free himself from the weight of the accusation. For the Most Illustrious and Reverend Bishop of Meliapur was bound to proceed against the said appellant, according to the form of law laid down in the chapter of the Decretals, 'Qualiter et Quando de Accusat,' (lit., How and When concerning Accusations and Denunciations), and to observe the sacred sanctions laid down in the said chapter. And as these conditions have not been observed, whatever proceedings were taken against the said appellant without the prescribed form ought to be considered null and void. And therefore from all these proceedings he appeals, protests, and maintains their nullity, as above: and against the [possible] non-admission of the present appeal, or denial of letters of appeal (*Apostoli*), or anything which may hereafter, perhaps, be done by anyone in despite of this appeal, he again protests, appeals, and declares null, and that not only once or twice or thrice, but as often as occasion should arise: so that he may always be the last [*i.e.*, 'be always to the fore'] with his appeal, and in appealing and protesting not only in this, but in any other better method, against the things attempted, or which may be attempted, against him.

Given at Madras on the 23rd day of December, 1706.

FRIAR ESPRIT OF TOURS, *et cetera*.]

The Lord Bishop, after having refused many times to receive it, at last, by dint of supplications, was made to read the above petition of appeal; and the Reverend Father Guardian then praying him to be so good as to verify it, he wrote on the margin the following words: 'We have replied to the request here made—S. Thome, 23 December, the Bishop of Meliapur.'[1] Gentlemen,

1. Printed in Norbert, 'Mémoires Utiles,' 1742, p. 238. In Codex No. CXXXV. these words are in Portuguese.

you [274], who have unbounded understanding, just read, please, the petition in appeal and the reply to it. Consider, I conjure you, what connection there can be between the one and the other; since it is a white answer to a black question. The same peculiarity is found in all the documents we hold. Therefore judge now if it is necessary to lay any great stress on the unworthy way in which we are treated; and from this you can gather, gentlemen, if the Capuchin fathers occasionally moan, whether they do so without cause or meaning.

When we had in our hands the petition of appeal which his Lordship had so admirably justified, the Reverend Father Guardian, after a minute or two's conversation, rose to take leave of the Lord Bishop. I, however, before I rose, said; 'My Lord, if I had known what I do at this moment, I should certainly never have come to a country where they behave so well to poor missionaries—men who have abandoned father, mother, relations, and friends; who have suffered so many dangers, and have come from such far-off countries in the hope of gaining some souls to Jesus Christ; who have been on their feet for twenty-five to thirty years, like the Reverend Father Esprit, and thoroughly wearied themselves from morning to night, without an hour of quiet on any one day: only to have had perhaps the discomfiture, such as this reverend father has had, of seeing affixed to the doors of the churches an excommunication or declaration against myself, whereby I was declared accursed, and doubly accursed of God Omnipotent, of the Apostles St. Peter and St. Paul, and of all the other saints in the quire celestial; at the very time, too, when your priests, who lead [275], for the most part, idle and scandalous lives, are treated by you with the greatest softness—yes, there have been men to be found among them, and are yet to be found daily, who have fallen into such disorders that propriety forbids my stating them; men who have caused public scandal in many places; who trade openly; who in drunkenness have lain down in the middle of Madras streets in the sight of the heathen and of the English gentlemen; there have been some among them, I say, who have gone to your Lordship's very door, arms in hand, and, unable to obtain the execution of what they had premeditated, have abused you up-hill and down-dale without the slightest correction being applied to them. But the poor Capuchin fathers! who have shown to your Lordship nothing but respect; who rush hither and thither from morning to night to gain even one soul to Jesus Christ; who cannot be accused of the minutest fault in their lives and habits; who seek to do good to all men; who have never given an opening for anybody to complain—these fathers receive from you nothing but inhuman treatment! Of a truth, my Lord, we feel this acutely enough, nor can I conceive how a bishop, who ought to follow the dictates of equity more than anyone else in the world, can leave the transgressor in impunity and chastise the innocent.' As I was finishing what I had to say his Lordship turned his back on me, whence I was aware that there was nothing more to be done. Therefore, making a sign to the gentlemen who had come with us, we withdrew at once.

The Reverend Father Esprit and the Reverend Father Michel Ange had supposed that the Lord Bishop would have adjusted the dispute so happily as to render it unnecessary to present the above-referred-to petition of appeal [276]; for they had been assured that his Lordship meant to quiet things down. Now they found there was no other course open than to secure the attestation of the papers they held, and to call the fourth time for the *Apostoli*[1] in the process of the Reverend Father Esprit.

After having put in order all the papers, ready for the attestation of his Lordship, the Reverend Father Michel Ange started the next morning for San Thome. On arriving at the palace of Monsignor, he asked for leave to speak to him; the answer he received was that if he was come on a visit he could enter, but if he came on business he could just go back to Madras. Although he thought this a most surprising and extraordinary procedure, yet, not wishing to give any incitement to his Lordship for farther hurting us, what he had done already being more than we could bear—for an excommunication is a most insupportable thing—the Reverend Father Michel Ange said that he only came to see his Lordship, and put off speaking of business till the next morning. He then went again, taking the Reverend Father Esprit, so that the Capuchins might not be accused of declining to submit themselves to the Lord Bishop.

When his Lordship learnt that the Reverend Father Michel Ange was at his door with the Reverend Father Esprit, he sent word to the former that he was free to enter. The message given to Father Esprit was that he must wait at the door. This order

1. For *Apostoli*, see note 235 to fol. 273.

he obeyed with all possible patience without a murmur. He made no complaint whatever of the bad treatment to which he had been subjected up to that time.

Having greeted Monsignor and presented congratulations on the Festival of the Nativity, the Reverend Father Michel Ange, after a little [277] conversation lasting half an hour, finding his Lordship in a fairly good humour, asked him why he had declared the Reverend Father Esprit to be excommunicated—was it because the said father was the *curé*, or was it because he had published the decrees without permission? His Lordship answered at once that he had done so for both reasons. Upon hearing this the Reverend Father Michel Ange showed him the Bull of Pius V.,[1] which not only disapproved of excommunications launched so inconsiderately, but, in addition, showed the nullity of the Pastoral that his Lordship had sent to the Reverend Jesuit fathers with the object of placing them a second time in possession of our mission to the Malabaris. Here are the very words of the Bull: 'Et insuper ne in locis illarum partium' (that is, in India, of which the Bull is speaking), 'in quibus sunt religiosorum monasteria qui animarum curam exercent, aliquid per praedictos episcopos inno-vetur, eadem authoritate et tenore statuimus et ordinamus, ac quidquid secus super his à quocumque quavis authoritate scienter vel ignoranter attentari contigerit, irritum et inane decernimus.' [And, moreover, by the same authority and to the same purport, we decree and ordain that in places in India where there are monasteries of religious who exercise a cure of souls, no innovation be made by the said bishops, and whatever may chance to be attempted by any person, whosoever and whatever his authority and whether he act with or without knowledge, contrary to this order, in respect of those religious, we decree to be null and vain.]

'As regards the second reason—that of having published the decrees without permission,' said the Reverend Father Michel Ange, 'have you not, my Lord, given me permission, orally and in writing, to have them published in our church at Pondicherry?' 'No,' replied his Lordship. 'Let us suppose that you did not give it to me,' said the Reverend Father Michel Ange—'a matter that will be seen to in due time and place—have I not presented the

1. Pius V. (Michele Ghislieri), elected in 1566; died in 1572. 'Pius' in the text is probably a mistake for 'Paul V.' (1605-21), in whose pontificate the See of San Thome of Meliapur was erected.

decrees to your Lordship, and have you not written on the margin of the said decrees: "The Reverend Father Guy Tachard has seen this petition and also the decrees of the Sacred Congregation,"[1] *et cetera*?' [278]. 'That is true,' said his Lordship. 'Then, surely,' retorted the Reverend Father Michel Ange, 'that sufficed without other permission, not only for publishing the decrees, but equally for performing the functions of our mission to the Malabaris, for which purpose the decrees were issued. This is so, since the Sacred Congregation "de Propaganda Fide" issued a decree of September 19, 1630, where they say in so many words that it is sufficient for patents to be presented to the bishop to allow of the functions being performed, permission or no permission: "Sacra Congregatio censuit missionaries quibuscumque sufficere, quod suas Patentes suae missionis ostendant, ut illis ostensis, sive obtenta sive non obtenta licentia, libere et licite suum officium et munus exercere valeant."' [The Sacred Congregation has ruled that it is sufficient for the missionaries of every sort to show their patent letters of their own mission, and that, after showing them, they are empowered to exercise their office and duties, whether permission be obtained or no.]

Having heard these words, the Lord Bishop grew a little angry and wanted to leave the place. But the Reverend Father Michel Ange has the gift of gaining hearts by sweet and obliging manners.

'My Lord,' said he to him, 'listen to my arguments, I conjure you; reflect well whether they are correct or not.'

'Speak, then,' said Monsignor to him. 'Perhaps you say,' then resumed the Reverend Father Michel Ange, 'that the Reverend Father Esprit has incurred excommunication under the Bull "In Cæna Domini," through having published the decrees?'

'No,' answered his Lordship.

'It was perhaps for having summoned the Reverend Father Tachard to the courts at Rome?'

'Not in the least, although it was possible to have found something to object to,' retorted the Lord Bishop.[2]

1. In Codex No. CXXXV. these words are in Portuguese.
2. There is a break of continuity here in Zanetti, codex No. XLV. (Italian translation), as the conclusion of the interview is not given. I have restored the omitted passage from the original French in Codex No. CXXXV., fols. 82*a*, 82 *b*,and 83*a*, 83*b*.

[82*a*] 'But one does not incur excommunication for that,' replied Father Michel Ange. 'How is it, then, that your Lordship has stated in the Declaration that Father Esprit has incurred excommunication under the Bull "In cæna Domini" by reason of having published certain decrees without your permission, and for having cited Father Tachard to appear at the court of Rome?' 'Oh! I do not want any of your arguing,' said the Lord Bishop.

Seeing that his Lordship contradicted himself, and was not willing to reply to his question, Father Michel Ange said to him with a smile:

'If the Reverend Father Esprit has not incurred excommunication by publishing the decree, nor by citing the Reverend Father Tachard to Rome, why, then, has your Lordship declared him excommunicated, ordering, in addition, that your Declaration should be posted on the door of the Jesuit' church?'

'Oh! he (Esprit) said that the reverend Jesuit fathers were not the parish priests of the Malabaris at Pondicherry—there's the reason, since you want to know.'

Upon this Father Michel Ange said that this single reason should have been stated in the Declaration, and not the two others. He followed this up by praying his Lordship to tell him this. If a man menaced a priest with violence, saying he would beat him or even slay him, did he incur excommunication under the Bull 'In Cæna Domini' or not? The Lord Bishop answered at once that it was not enough to threaten, that there must be an overt act. This was so, because the Bull said: 'Si quis percuserit clericum anathema sit.' After hearing these words Father Michel Ange said to him: 'Then Father Esprit has not incurred excommunication, for, besides the fact that he has not opened his mouth since the Pastoral, of itself a severe enough punishment for us, even had he spoken after the issue of the Pastoral it was impossible for him, until he had done some overt act, to become liable to excommunication. The use of words only is not a sufficient ground for excommunication; acts are necessary. Where, then, are the acts as a curé performed by Father Esprit after the publication of your Pastoral? Has he married, baptized, buried, any Malabari? No one can assert this, much less prove it.'

It is true that the reverend Jesuit fathers, who are so benevolently inclined towards us that they would rejoice to see us destroyed root and branch, caused an infant to be carried into our church. They wanted to see if the Reverend Father Esprit would confer on it Holy Baptism. But the said father perceived at once that it was a snare laid for him by his enemies, and all that they wanted was something they could lay hold of against us. He sent back the infant forthwith to the reverend Jesuit fathers, although they would have much preferred to see it baptized than to get it again unbaptized.

'What do you call that, Monsignor?' said Father Michel Ange to him.

'Oh! I have already told you I want none of your arguments.'

'I have one more, if it please you, for the love of God,' replied the Reverend Father Michel Ange.

'What is it, then?' asked the Lord Bishop.

'Here it is,' said Father Michel Ange: 'let us suppose that a person has brought a suit before a divisional court (*presidial*), and there loses his case. He then appeals to the *Parlement*, empowered to decide in the last instance. If that *Parlement* decides in his favour, can the divisional court, subordinate to that *Parlement*, revive the suit, and once more decide it against the appellant suitor, in spite of the *Parlement* being in no manner under its control?'

'No,' says Monsignor.

'Now, here I have you, my Lord,' replied the Reverend Father Michel Ange, 'and this will demonstrate to the entire world that you had no power to excommunicate the Reverend Father Esprit; still less could you restore the reverend Jesuit fathers to the possession of our cure of the Malabaris, as you have done by a special Pastoral.'

'Let us see a little how that is,' said the Lord Bishop.

'Were we, or were we not, eight years ago the *curés* of the Malabaris?' retortd Father Michel Ange. 'Did not your Lordship himself, five or six months before you took away that cure and gave it to the reverend Jesuit fathers, issue to us an executive order (*provision*) to that effect?'

'Yes,' replied Monsignor.

'As the reverend Jesuit fathers were then making every effort to withdraw the said cure from us, did not your Lordship say to me repeatedly that I was to resist them firmly, and that you would never consent to such a piece of injustice?'

'That is true,' replied Monsignor.

'Then the reverend Jesuit fathers falsely alleged an order of his Majesty (Louis XIV.), as we afterwards ascertained; and upon the solicitation of the late Chevalier Martin, did not your Lordship issue an executive order about the cure in favour of the reverend Jesuit fathers?'

'Again that is quite true,' [82*b*] replied Monsignor; 'but I did not know that the order of the prince was falsely alleged.'

'Of that I am quite persuaded,' said Father Michel Ange; 'nevertheless, as your Lordship, when you discovered the falsity of the reverend Jesuit fathers' allegation, did not restore us to our ancient mission, we had recourse in appeal to the King of France for the temporalities, and to his Holiness, together with the Sacred Congregation, in regard to the spiritual charge. Thus his Holiness and the aforesaid Sacred Congregation upon perusal of our appeal, cited to appear before them the Very Reverend Father the Procurator-General of the Society of Jesus and the Very Reverend Father the Procurator of the Capuchins. After listening to the arguments on both sides, decrees were issued in favour of the Capuchin fathers, which they directed to be presented to your Lordship: "Dentur decreta episcopo Meliapurensis." This we did, my Lord; yet after you had approved them and recognised them as genuine, when we promulgated them in our church with your special permission, your Lordship issued a second Pastoral in favour of the reverend Jesuit fathers, who are the very persons against whom the decrees were issued. This is to act directly in the teeth of the Sacred Congregation's decrees. You have also excommunicated the Reverend Father Esprit. Can such a thing be done, my Lord, I ask you? and is it permissible for a bishop to meddle with a case, and attempt to decide it after judgment has been given by the Sacred Congregation?'

'You did not appeal to the Holy See or to the Sacred Congregation about this cure?' said the Lord Bishop.

'We have not appealed!' replied Father Michel Ange. 'Why is it, then, that the Sacred Congregation has sent these decrees, if it is not in connection with our appeal? If your Lordship is in doubt, here is the petition of the Reverend Father François Marie of Tours, laid by him in person before the Sacred Congregation."

[Father François Marie's petition of March 26, 1703, is omitted, as it has been already given in full on fol. 218, Part V.]

'If after that your Lordship still doubts whether we have appealed to the Sacred Congregation, I produce the protest of the reverend Capuchin fathers against the acts of the reverend Jesuit fathers. This protest was notified to them in legal form and in the presence of witnesses. Its terms are as follows:

"The Capuchin fathers of the province of Touraine, who for thirty-five years or thereabouts have been in possession of the cure of Pondicherry, as well in regard to the French gentlemen as to the natives of the country styled Malabaris, having been informed that the reverend Jesuit fathers, at the request of Monsieur the General Martin, and to their (the Capuchins') prejudice, have obtained from the Lord Bishop of San Thome an executive order (*provision*) in regard to the cure of the said Malabaris at Pondicherry, the said Capuchin fathers, with reference to the order granted them by the said prelate in regard to the cure of the said Pondicherry, dated July 12, 1699, protest by this present document against the said executive order issued by my Lord of San Thome, and appeal therefrom to the Holy See and to the Sacred Congregation, to whom is confided all matters touching the business of bishops and regular clergy with regard to the spiritual question, and as regards the temporalities to the Most Christian king, under whose protection and safeguard they have the honour to dwell," *et cetera*.

'Have you any doubts left, my Lord, that we did appeal on this matter to the Holy See and to the Sacred Congregation? Do you still doubt whether the decrees of the aforesaid Sacred Congregation were addressed to our Lordship for the object of replacing the Capuchins in possession of their ancient cure [83a] of the Malabaris? If you have no doubts under either head, why, then, insert in your Pastoral that the Sacred Congregation sends you certain decrees accompanied by no farther orders. Must I play the schoolmaster to a bishop? Are not the orders by themselves sufficient to justify their execution? Must they write: "We order you to put into execution to the very letter what is recorded in the said decree"? I am in astonishment that your Lordship allows the Capuchins to be at Pondicherry and Madras, for it is not said in the orders you undertook to obey: "We direct the Lord Bishop of San Thome to allow Capuchins to work in his diocese."

'But I am assuming what cannot be—I mean that it should be requisite to have an order from Rome before putting into execution Bulls and Decrees received from Rome. Whence is it, then, that your Lordship has declared the Reverend Father Esprit to be excommunicated, while you have not carried out the order of the Sacred Congregation? I cannot see what reason there can be for doing the one and not the other. For, after all, if the decrees of the Sacred Congregation themselves are not enough to secure their execution, but require a separate order from the same Sacred Congregation for that purpose, it follows of necessity that when a priest or religious infringes on the jurisdiction of a bishop (a thing Father Esprit has never done), there must come a second order from Rome declaring him ex-communicated. The reason is obvious. In the Bull "In Cæna Domini" it is provided that those who act contrary to the jurisdiction of bishops shall be held excommunicated; but it is also laid down in the decrees of the Sacred Congregation, which have been produced before your Lordship, that no person may on any pretext or show of authority whatsoever remove a cure from the religious of one Order and give it to those of another without previous reference to the aforesaid Sacred Congregation, the penalty for disobedience being "subpoena privationis officii, privilegii, et facultatis, ipso facto incurrenda, et cetera." '

'Furthermore, my Lord, do me the favour of clearing up a doubt I entertain—that is, if a person who interferes in a bishop's jurisdiction is to be excommunicated, why is not the same penalty incurred by those who interfere in the jurisdiction of the Sacred Congregation? It is a point, Monsignor, that I am very desirous of having settled.'

Upon hearing such just reasoning, and such a very embarrassing question, the bishop said he declined to argue. The Reverend Father Michel Ange saw that nothing would serve to convince the Lord Bishop of the injustice that his Lordship had committed in regard to us, and that no impression could be made on his mind by reasoning. He therefore, for the last time, begged Monsignor to restore Father Esprit to his previous status. We would then await a fresh decision from Rome; while, should his Lordship fear that we might hereafter stir again in the matter, he (Michel Ange) would bring all the papers we possessed and burn them in the bishop's presence.

It seems to me, gentlemen, that it is impossible to speak fairer, and that the Capuchins have gone far beyond what they could be called upon to do. Every body knows, both at Pondicherry and at Madras, that we gave no occasion for treating us in such an unworthy manner. If any scandal has arisen, it has been caused by the reverend Jesuit fathers, whose only object is to make themselves redoubtable. The fault is not that of the poor Capuchin fathers, who would glory in their humiliation so long as religion did not thereby suffer.

However, the Lord Bishop was not mollified by Father Michel Ange's proposal. What he would have liked, for the contentment of the reverend Jesuit fathers and the humiliation of the Capuchins, was that Father Esprit should bare his back to be scourged by one of the bishop's priests until he was flayed.

This was what they did some two years ago to the Confraternity of the Holy Rosary, some of the sufferers being over eighty years of age. Then all of them were excommunicated, somewhat in the style practised with the said Father Esprit. Such conduct was not only lamentable and dishonourable to religion, but quite sufficient to turn the best cause in the world into the worst.

Thus Father Michel Ange and Father Esprit were forced to return to Madras without having been able to gain in the slightest degree on the mind of Monsignor, having only rendered him more unfeeling towards us. What say, you, gentlemen, of the course taken by the Capuchin fathers compared with the line of action adopted by the Lord Bishop, as well as by the reverend Jesuit fathers? Have we been guilty of anything unjust or not conformable to right reason? On their side have they in the slightest point been other than unjust, or acted otherwise than in direct opposition to the precepts of the Gospel?

No; I cannot conceive our doing more to make our case a good one, or their doing more to make theirs a bad one. In effect, [83*b*] gentlemen—for, although our cause from the very first was the best in the world—for what is more natural than a demand for justice against violence, for a restoration to our rights after gaining our case?—no one can make us the reproach, still less prove against us, that we have said or done the least thing to disturb the minds of the Lord Bishop and the reverend Jesuit fathers; and that, too, in the face of the cruelest and most harassing treatment that it is possible to conceive. For, after all, I should prefer a great deal to die on the gallows than to find myself publicly excommunicated, damned, and doubly damned of God Omnipotent, of the Apostles St. Peter and St. Paul, and of all the other saints in the quire celestial.

It is not the same thing, gentlemen, with the reverend Jesuit fathers, although their case was a bad one from the very first, since they began by capturing our cure through a false allegation. Besides their frontal resistance to his Holiness and to the Sacred Congregation; besides their untrue assertion that the Capuchin fathers had attempted to infringe the jurisdiction of a bishop; besides their obtaining the excommunication of the Reverend Father Esprit, in contravention of our privileges, and without the observance of any form of law, we can produce in due time and place over twenty documents where we have been spoken of so unworthily that, if such papers, emanating from Capuchins and derogatory to Jesuits, were in their possession, one single paper out of them would be enough to destroy us poor Capuchin fathers for ever. But we have no protectors, unless it be a just God who knows our innocence.

Gentlemen, nothing beyond a mere perusal of what I have written in this manifesto is required to free the Capuchin fathers from all blame. The only blame which can be imputed to them is to have so deeply suffered without uttering any complaint. But perhaps you have not noticed the way in which Monsignor's Pastoral, as well as his Declaration, is drawn up; I proceed, therefore, to point out to you that there is no less of contradiction in the one and in the other, not to call it malice or ignorance, than there is in all the rest that you have read up to this point. I begin with the Declaration, wherein I pray you to consider three things inserted by his Lordship. The first one is the three monitions put into the Pastoral; the second regards the gentleness with which his Lordship, as he says, has always treated us; and the third refers to the proceedings to be taken against us if we should contravene the aforesaid Pastoral.

As to the three monitions, they are inserted in one document. Added to this is the fact that the short interval specified did not permit of the Pondicherry Capuchins informing their Guardian and Vice-Provincial then actually at Madras. To write to and receive a reply from that place requires eight days. Now, we have never done the slightest act contravening the said Pastoral, and if our enemies accuse us of such an act, let them prove it. It will then be demonstrated, in due time and place, that nothing can be more untrue. For we are not so devoid of friends at Pondicherry that we cannot find fifteen or so persons, men of the highest position and zealous for justice, who will sign attestations to the contrary. It is true that we have cited the reverend Jesuit fathers to Rome; this has not been done singly by Father Esprit, but by all of us, by all of the Capuchins belonging to Pondicherry and Madras. For have we not all signed upon the citation? Thus, if excommunication is incurred under the Bull 'In Cæna Domini,' by citing an opposite party to appear before the courts in Rome, the Lord Bishop must declare us all excommunicated like Father Esprit. He is no more at fault than we are, and we are as guilty as he is.

You may wish to know, gentlemen, why the reverend Jesuit fathers and the Lord Bishop have decided to make this difference, and have singled out Father Esprit from the rest; why they have made him feel the effect of the threats with which they intimidate everybody opposed to their violences, saying that they will bring ruin on them. It is because the said Father Esprit has always boldly faced them in things which he considered necessary to the welfare of Christianity and the honour of our religion; because he succeeded in having a church built at Pondicherry, much to their umbrage; because they thought they could drive him away to Rome or to his province, after a public declaration of excommunication. In that case the building would be left incomplete. It is also because he knows the Portuguese, Malabari, and Arabic languages to perfection; and they imagined that when he had quitted Pondicherry we should no longer be capable of carrying on the mission. By this means they would be able to insinuate themselves into the cure of the French gentlemen and the Portuguese, as they have already done into that of the Malabaris. There you have, gentlemen, their reasons for selecting the Reverend Father Esprit rather than the other Capuchins at Pondicherry and Madras.

Most assuredly there are no other reasons; but perhaps they will assert [278, resumed] that it is for having said that the reverend Jesuit fathers are not the legitimate pastors of the Malabaris at Pondicherry. That, however, gentlemen, we have not said, however much they believe that we did say it. Still, outside the fact that they accuse us of this falsely, I go farther, and say that, had we even made use of the words, they are insufficient to bring down on us an excommunication. For it is a condition precedent that we proceed [279] to overt acts, as I have already indicated above.

As regards the gentleness with which his Lordship claims to have always treated us, I have already, gentlemen, in a passage near the end of the first manifesto that I did myself the honour of sending to you, called your attention to the fact that the Lord Bishop has designated us as scandalous persons, liars, disobeyers, over-bold, and madmen. Again, every inhabitant of Pondicherry knows as well as you do that his Lordship has made us over to the secular arm; not only so, but has further directed that we be dealt with all possible severity. Therefore, to the end that all may know the unworthy manner in which the Capuchins are handled—men who have no enemies in India except the reverend Jesuit fathers—I wish to give you a demonstration of the great 'gentleness' the Capuchin fathers have always enjoyed from the Lord Bishop, as he states in his Pastoral and in his Declaration.

The wife of Signor Manucci, a Venetian by origin, a man who has become sufficiently known in Europe by his writings, when on her death-bed made a bequest to the Lord Bishop of San Thome of two hundred *pagodas*. After her death the said Signor Manucci, having become extremely ill pleased with the part taken by his Lordship, showed reluctance in making up his mind to execute the bequest. Hearing this, the Reverend Father Michel Ange of Bourges, Superior of the Capuchins at Madras, begged him for the love of God to send this money to Monsignor, and added that he was conscientiously under an obligation to do so. Signor Manucci made excuses, saying he had not the cash to meet it. The Reverend Father Michel Ange promised he would get some one to lend him the money, so that he might pay the legacy. Signor [280] Manucci said he did not want to increase his indebtedness, which was already quite heavy enough. After this time, the Lord Bishop, upon the deposition of one of our enemies, took steps to sue the Reverend Father Michel Ange. He asserted that it was he who had forbidden him (Manucci) to pay; and without fail he (the

Bishop) would have brought the suit, as many persons worthy of belief asseverate, had not the clerk of Signor Manucci, then in San Thome on some business, offered to swear upon the Holy Gospels that the whole thing was absolutely false. Here you have, gentlemen, his excessive 'tenderness.'

A reverend father, an Armenian by race, belonging to the Order of St. Dominic, died at Madras after living there a whole year.[1] He received the last sacraments at the hands of the Capuchin fathers who dwell in that town. After the death of the said father, the Superior of the reverend Dominican fathers was written to at San Thome, advising him that a friar of his order had died. This was at eight o'clock in the morning. He was requested to write at once whether he meant the defunct to be buried in our church or in his. We waited for an answer up to six o'clock in the evening, though we could have had the answer by midday. Therefore, finding no one came, and the corpse beginning to be offensive owing to the great heat, we went to the spot in order to bury the said body in our church. After we had chanted the 'Libera,' a jacobin,[2] who had concealed himself in a shop so as not to be seen, in order to affront us threw himself on the body, saying he wanted to inter it at [281] San Thome. The Reverend Father Michel Ange, and all the other priests and friars taking part in the funeral, said to him: 'Reverend father, this is not the way to behave before a thousand heathen here assembled; we wrote to you, and it seems to me you ought to have replied without falling into these excessive ways. Besides, when you come to remove the body of a deceased person, it is necessary to come in the proper vestments with surplice and stole, not in a palanquin and with a cap like an Englishman's on your head. We are going to take the body to our church, and chant the office for the dead. After that is done we shall make it over into your hands, and we in person will follow it as far as San Thome.' The reverend father Dominican began to shout, just as a blind man does who has lost his stick, and then, like a man in despair, started to run to San Thome to report to the bishop. The latter learnt from the

1. This Dominican died at Madras on December 6, 1703 (see Part IV., fol. 165, and Part V., fol. 69).
2. 'Jacobin'—that is, a Dominican (*note by Senhor Cardeira*). The *Libera* is the last responsory in solemn Matins for the dead; also said or sung at funerals.

reports of his own priests that the Capuchin fathers had behaved with all possible prudence. If there had been anything wrong it had not proceeded from them, since they had themselves carried the body to their church against their will. Yet he (the bishop) did not fail to send the Capuchin fathers a very sharp letter, conveying an order that they must send the body. This is what we did, without hesitating a single moment. Here you have, gentlemen, the great 'tenderness' displayed to the Capuchin fathers, who better deserved to be praised than to be blamed, as they are day after day.

Gentlemen, I should write a big book if I attempted to narrate to you all the injustice done to us, without telling you the bitter things the Lord Bishop has made us swallow on thousands of occasions [282]. However, I will produce to you no more than two of his letters, collated copies of which are in my possession. You have only to pay very slight attention and you will see, gentlemen, that we could not be dealt with more harshly and more cruelly than we have been dealt with by his Lordship. The first is the letter which Monsignor wrote to your Council, which I wish once more to lay before you in writing, although the original is in your hands, because I hope by God's grace that this manifesto will appear in Europe also, and not only at Pondicherry. The second letter is the reply to the Reverend Father Guardian, who had begged his Lordship to be good enough to clear the Reverend Father Esprit of the calumny imposed on him by the reverend fathers of the Society of Jesus.

Copy of the letter of the lord bishop of san thome written to the supreme council of pondicherry against the reverend father esprit of tours, capuchin and apostolic missionary in the east indies.[1]

Most noble lord councillors,

The Reverend Father Esprit came out with a resolution, most unexpected and scandalous, upon no other basis than that

1. The copy of this letter, printed in Norbert, 'Mémoires Utiles.' 1742, p. 22, bears the same date and relates to the same subject, but the wording differs. The printed version says nothing about Father Esprit's throwing down the Bishop's letter. Manucci's text, coming from a contemporary present on the spot, is more likely to be correct. In Codex No. CXXXV, it is given in the original Portuguese.

of his many letters—that is, his great learning. He ought to have awaited the decision from France, where this affair had been sent; but he took it upon himself to act as judge about the decrees of the Sacred Congregation, which he declares have reference to the division of the parishes made by us, confiding the cure of the Malabari natives to the reverend Jesuit fathers. If your lordships will glance at the decrees, you will see they say nothing about the parishes of Pondicherry. I have sent forth a Pastoral through which I declare once more that the reverend fathers of the society are the parish priests of the Malabaris. [283] Furthermore, the said Malabaris appertain in no way to the reverend Capuchin fathers, neither by order of his Holiness nor by mine, as they falsely allege It is your duty, my lords, and it belongs to you to maintain peace and uphold my jurisdiction, according to the manner in which I have exercised it, by forcing the reverend Capuchin fathers by every severity to cease disturbance, and not to introduce any innovation until a decision comes from Rome or France. Thus I call upon your lordships with the greatest insistence to see to the quiet of this Christian community. If by any chance the Reverend Father Fra Esprit comes out with some new resolve, your lordships will know that the whole is null and of no effect, because he has neither authority nor power. Although he is a vicar with judicial powers, he has not thereby any such jurisdiction, nor do I mean to concede to him any such. To satisfy your lordships I will write to the Reverend Father Fra Esprit, but there was another letter I wrote to him exhorting him to peace and quiet. This he took and threw on the ground with contempt, and declined to receive it. Thus your lordships ought not to desire that I should expose myself to his anger and rudeness. God have you in His keeping.

San Thome, November 10, 1706,

Your lordships' most faithful servant and friend,

THE BISHOP OF MELIAPUR.

Truly, gentlemen, does not the gentleness seem very great that was displayed to us on the part of the Lord Bishop of San Thome? Nor has his Lordship better foundation for saying in his declaration that he has dealt with the Reverend Father Esprit with all the gentleness [284] imaginable. It would not be possible to treat a friar more basely, particularly when acting on a calumny so manifest. You will know from the second letter.

which is a reply to the petition of the Reverend Father Guardian of the Capuchins, handed in after the receipt of the preceding letter—you will know, I say, with what gentleness the Lord Bishop treats us, at the very time when he claims to be indemnifying us for a calumy uttered against us. When he is confessing he was mistaken, he writes the above letter to the Pondicherry Council, and cannot avoid using the most degrading language in so doing. Here it is, gentlemen; read it with care and diligence.

Reply of the lord bishop of san thome to a letter of the reverend father guardian of the capuchins upon the matters dealt with in the preceding letter.[1]

Most reverend father fra lorenzo,

I have written to the Reverend Father Fra Esprit, and to the gentlemen of the Pondicherry Council. But as your Reverence does not believe it—on the contrary, you say I am mistaken on this subject—I sent to get back the letters, which were already in the hands of Monsieur Guety. I showed your Reverence's petition to the Reveiend Father Carlo de Labros.[2] He says when he made over the letter to the Reverend Father Esprit he told him it was from the Reverend Father Tachard, and not from the Lord Bishop; that the superscription on the letter was in French; that it was in the handwriting of a brother (*fratello*) of the Society; he did not tell the Reverend Father Esprit that under the outer covering was a letter from the Lord Bishop; the seal on the letter was that of the Reverend Father Tachard, and not that of the Lord Bishop; but he (de Labros) could not swear these things in a legal proceeding without the leave of his superior, and even if he obtained it, he would not swear, as it was not necessary; that your Reverence could think [285] and suspect what you liked; that your suspicions could not be proof of the falsity that your Reverence wished to impute to the members of the Society of Jesus. I owe, however, infinite

1. In Codex No. CXXXV. the original is in Portuguese.
2. No one of the name of C. de Labros can be traced. It was Charles de 1 Breuille and Domenic Turpin, Jesuits, who carried the letter to Father Esprit on November 3, 1706 (see *ante*, Part V., fol. 230, and Father Thomas's narrative of 1733, Norbert, 'Memoires', 1747, ii. 301). Monsieur Guety has been already mentioned in Part IV., fol. 188, and Part V., fols. 241, 242, 244, 261.

Women of Hindustan

Vol. IV *To face page 340*

thanks to your Reverence for saying that by appealing to the gentlemen of the Council, in the hope that they might compel your Reverence by every severity to remain quiet until the arrival of a finding from Europe, I have consigned your Reverence to the secular arm. Such a thing your Reverence could only say when an ecclesiastical judge has recourse to the secular courts, as frequently happens. But the evil-disposed mind of your Reverence, either directly or by some twist, must needs always interpret words in their worst sense. The two petitions are returned to your Reverence, since the Reverend Father de Labros dclines to be sworn to the interrogatory sent by your Reverence along with the petition. May God keep your Reverence.

San Thome, November 26, 1706,

Of your Reverence the most humble servant,
THE BISHOP OF MEUAPUR.

This is the exceeding tenderness that we have received from the Lord Bishop of San Thome, At the very time his Lordship confesses his mistake, and replies in conformity to the demands of the Reverend Father Guardian, he will not make use of an opening to declare our innocence, and he thereby shows to all the world the maxims which are acted upon by the reverend Jesuit fathers. The least he could have done was not to inveigh against us and say that we [286] wanted to fix a falsehood on the reverend Jesuit fathers; that we were carried away by a spirit of malignance; that we always put the worst construction upon his best-meant acts. But, gentlemen, his Lordship, while confessing he has been misled, denies (can we credit it?) that this happened owing to the calumny uttered against us by the reverend Jesuit fathers. If they were not its inventors, how, possibly, could his Lordship have been able to assert a thing which never happened? And why has he written to your Council a letter the most outrageous, the most pungent, that could ever have been written? Still farther, gentlemen, the Lord Bishop writes to you asking you to treat us with all possible severity; he accuses the Reverend Father Esprit of having thrown one of his letters on the ground, refusing to take it. This being untrue, as you will have already seen, he tells you besides that he does not wish to expose himself to the rage and rudeness of the said Reverend Father. When we ask his Lordship to testify to the truth, while on one hand he acquits us, on the other he endeavours to make us out greater culprits than he had ever done before. While you are considering this we pray you to tell us, please, the way in which you would have interpreted this precious letter, which is in your possession, had his Lordship written it as an accusation against you, instead, as he did, writing it against the poor Capuchins.

[287] Before discussing the methods which ought to be adopted against us in case of disobedience, I beg you to bestow your attention on the first three lines of the said letter, where his Lordship accuses us of refusing credence to his words. He granted permission to the Reverend Father Michel Ange for the publication of the decrees in our church at Pondicherry, and after we had published them he wrote in his Pastoral that we had acted without his permission. After that, how can we place reliance upon what he says? Messieurs Cesare and Khwajah Ovanes presented a petition to his Lordship on behalf of the Father Guardian of the Capuchins. After he had accepted it and promised to those gentlemen that he would send it on after comparison, three days afterwards he returned it unauthenticated. Now, how can you expect us to believe in what he promises to do? You will find it too much for you, perhaps, to believe that a bishop can be false to his word. Here, then, is the affidavit given to us by the above-named gentlemen, Cesare and Khwajah Ovanes.[1] 'We, the undersigned, certify that, seeing we were told by the Very Reverend Father Frey Laurent of Angoulesine how the Most Illustrious Lord Bishop of Meliapur would not listen to any representations about his petitions, he (Fatner Laurent) asked us to take the above petition and present it; whence we did present the same on November 24, 1706, and the said Most Illustrious Bishop accepted it. But upon his being requested by us to pass an order on it, he declined to do so then, telling us that he would send us the petition after the order had been passed, and we might rely [288] upon his word. In spite of all these promises, two days afterwards—that is, on the 26th of

1. For these men, see notes 199 to fol. 236 and 230 to fol. 269. They also appear in Norbert, 'Mémoires Utiles,' 1742, p. 187, as signatories to a declaration of January 10, 1707, stating that on September 28, 1706, the Bishop gave Father Michel Ange verbal permission to publish the Decrees of the Sacred Congregation. In Norbert they appear as Louis Melluc, Loja Ourianes (meant for 'Coja Ouvanes'?), and Joseph Cesarini. Manucci himself is the fourth witness to this affidavit. The original in Codex No. CXXXV. is here in Portuguese.

the said month—he sent it to us without any order endorsed on it.'

The Reverend Father Michel Ange presented a petition to his Lordship wishing to know from his own mouth the reason for which he had taken from us the cure of the Malabaris and given it to the reverend Jesuit fathers.[1] He replied that it was done on the initiative of the general, Monsieur Martin, who told him that thus His Most Christian Majesty wished and had ordained. Here is his answer to the question of the Reverend Father Michel Ange:

'In compliance with the order above referred to of the Most Illustrious and Most Reverend Lord Dom Gaspar Alfonso, Bishop of the city of San Thome of Meliapur, I declare that by order of the said Lord Bishop was published the executive order (*provision*) mentioned in the petition of the Reverend Father Francesco Henriques Dolu of the Society of Jesus, declaring the said reverend Jesuit father to be the parish priest of the Malabar Christians dwelling in Pondicherry. This was done at the instiga-

1. In this paragraph the writer goes back suddenly to the original ejectment of the Capuchins from the spiritual charge of the native Christians of Pondicherry. This took place in 1699. Before the restoration of Pondicherry, the Bishop sanctioned the Capuchins holding the cure by his (Portuguese) order of December 12, 1698 (Norbert, p. 105). Letters Patent to Father Jacques of Bourges as Vicar-General were issued on December 13, and he was sworn in as *cure* on December 14, 1698 (*ibid.*, pp. 110, 114). Then, on June 10, 1699, the same Bishop granted the same cure to Father Dolu, Jesuit (*ibid.*, p. 121), following this act, on July 12, 1699, by a letter of regret to Father Michel Ange. Capuchin (ibid., p. 122), in which he said his hand had been forced by Governor François Martin, who alleged the express orders of Louis XIV. Official declarations to the same effect were drawn up on July 15, 1699 (*ibid.*, pp. 124-126). A protest was prepared on July 23, 1699, and signed by Fathers Fra Michel Ange of Bourges, Espŕit of Tours, and René of Angoulême, Capuchins. The two latter Fathers notified it to the Jesuits at Pondicherry on July 23, 1699, and to Governor Martin on the same date. Again, on December 23, 1700, and January 19, 1701, some difficulties having arisen about the Pariahs, the Bishop expresses the repugnance with which he had made the change in the cure (ibid., pp. 136, 141). The Capuchins petitioned Louis XIV. on March 12, 1701, and on the same day his Secretary of State wrote to Governor Martin denying the issue of any order by the King for the transference of the cure from the Capuchins to the Jesuits (*ibid.*, p. 148). Then came the appeal to Rome and the decree in favour of the Capuchins, dated May 15, 1703, over the Promulgation of which this dispute of 1706 broke out.

tion and on the petition of Monsieur Martin, [Director] General of the Royal Company of France, who wrote to the Lord Bishop, as appears from his letter, because it was so desired and directed by the Most Christian King, his sovereign lord. This is what I know, and it is true. The above was signed by me on July 15, 1699.'[1]

Can anything, gentlemen, be more precise? In spite of that, however, when we showed to his Lordship that the king had never given any order of the sort, that His Most Christian Majesty had never even had such a thought, he (the bishop) [289] says that he did not transfer the cure for that reason; on the contrary, he has no recollection of Monsieur Martin ever having written to him to the effect that such was the will and order of His Most Christian Majesty: 'I do not recollect that Monsieur Martin wrote to me that it was the order of the most Christian King.'[2] Taking all this into consideration, who would, gentlemen, be able to confide in the word of Monsignor?

When the Reverend Father Michel Ange saw there was no more hope of being allowed to re-enter on our mission to the Malabaris, since Monsieur Martin alleged the king's order, and the Lord Bishop submitted to that order, which he had never at any time received, he wrote to his Lordship asking if he would resent the Capuchins seeking to enforce their rights elsewhere. His Lordship then wrote him the answer which follows:[3]

'MOST REVEREND MIGUEL ANJO,

'The letter of the Lord Director [Governor] (?François Martin) is very short. In it he complains that it should be necessary to write to me so many times to prove his sincerity in

---

1. In Codex No. CXXXV. this document is in Portuguese. On July 15, 1699, Father Michel Ange asked the Bishop for a formal declaration that he had transferred the cure to Father Dolu, Jesuit. The Bishop directed the reverend secretary of the Bishop's chamber to draw up a declaration, and the document in the text was then prepared by Alexo Baretto, the secretary, and sealed with the episcopal seal (Norbert, 'Mémoires Utiles? 1742, pp. 125, 126).
2. The Bishop's words are reproduced in Portuguese in Codex No. CXXXV.
3. Norbert, 'Mémoires,' p. 122, No. 9, gives French and Italian translations; the original Portuguese is given in Codex No. CXXXV. The date was July 12, 1699. There are some slight discrepancies between Norbert's translation and that by Cardeira in Codex No. XLV.

the matter on which he wrote to me. He begs me not to believe anyone who asserts the contrary. I sent him the *provision* (executive order) for the fathers of the Society. A rumour was current that the Malabaris were furious and did not want it sent, but I saw that that would only confirm the Lord Director in his want of confidence. Your Reverence must now do what you think advisable for your negotiations and for getting justice, as to which I cannot feel any grievance myself.'

[290] After that answer, gentlemen, written with his own hand, although the decrees have now arrived in our favour, his Lordship treats the Reverend Father Michel Ange in the most haughty manner. Seeing this attitude, the reverend father wrote asking to be informed whether he had given authority that he might sue for his rights wherever he pleased, without his Lordship being in any way offended. Monsignor replied in a single phrase: 'I do not recollect your Reverence asking for a "bene placito" in order to seek your rights in whatever tribunal you could obtain them.' Gentlemen, how can you expect us to trust the words of the Lord Bishop?

His Most Illustrious Lordship knows very well indeed that taking without cause the cure over the Malabaris out of the hands of the Capuchin fathers, and making it over to the reverend Jesuit fathers, was the greatest possible of unjust acts. The very least he could do was to abstain from writing a letter to the Reverend Father Esprit of Tours, Capuchin, with the idea of persuading him that all was done much against his (the bishop's) will. Here are the very words of the letter the bishop honoured him with:

'MOST REVEREND FATHER FRA SPIRITO,

'Foreseeing occasion for discord, which may arise in the division of these two churches, I had great repugnance to separating them, as my desire was all along that they should form one only, which would be assigned to your Reverence. . .,' *et cetera.*

In spite of that, however, after writing those words, and after receiving the decrees from Rome which restored us to the cure taken from us by [291] his Lordship against his will, he having had the greatest difficulty in making up his mind to it, we are surprised to find he makes no attempt to put the said decrees into execution. Nay, when we ask him to remember what he told us so often with his own lips and has so plainly written—namely, that he had done violence to his own feelings in taking the cure of the Malabaris away from the Capuchin fathers, and giving it to the reverend Jesuit fathers—he replies now quite to the contrary of what he wrote at first. He now says: 'I know not what change it is that your Reverence says you find in me in regard to your Reverences; still, as I am now so old,[1] I do not recollect what I said to your Reverence about making the transfer in opposition to my natural inclination.' Having regard to all this, how is it possible for his Lordship to complain if we have not relied upon his words, when to-day he writes one thing and to-morrow the contrary?

Gentlemen, hitherto I have put restraint upon myself not to disclose to the public the doings of the Lord Bishop; but since he accuses us of having no confidence in him; since, in addition, he treats us in a manner the most unworthy that has ever yet been seen; since you yourselves allow a Portuguese bishop to excommunicate without cause your very pastor and make no attempt to apply any remedy, I wish to demonstrate that these are maxims of the reverend Jesuit fathers, because the Lord Bishop is a Jesuit, and is controlled by Jesuits, French and Portuguese.

As for the legal proceedings that were to be instituted against the Reverend Father Fra Esprit in case of disobedience [292] after the publication of the Lord Bishop's Pastoral, up to this very day we have seen no sign of them. We have demanded them and redemanded them over and over again, as you can see in our notice of appeal, but without our ever having them set in motion. Gentlemen, in order that you may have no doubts, and to show you what rules of justice are followed against us, I will enter here the last petition we have presented to his Lordship, calling for the proceedings taken against Father Esprit, and asking to have all the letters in our hands attested and certified; after that, you will find the reply to the said petition, which is within a trifle as fair and just as that given by his Lordship to our notice of appeal.

1. As the Bishop was born in 1626, he was at this time eighty years of age. The passage is in Portuguese in Codex No. CXXXV.

Petition of the reverend father laurent of angoulesme, vice-provincial of the capuchins in the east indies, presented to the lord bishop of san thome by the reverend father michel ange of bourges.

Most illustrious and most reverend the bishop of meliapur,— The Reverend Father Fra Laurent of Angoulesme, Guardian of the Capuchin friars, missionaries in this East India, states that he has appealed from a Declaration of Your Most Illustrious Lordship launched against the Reverend Father Fra Esprit of Tours to the effect that he has incurred excommunication; and that, having several times asked for the Apostoli,[1] his request was refused; and since it will be necessary for the suppliant to have attested copies of the orders passed against the Reverend Father, also attestations to the copies herewith submitted, with a view to their presentation to he competent tribunal, where he hopes to be listened to and restored to his rights [293]; he hereby prays Your Most Illustrious Lordship to be pleased to order the Notary of your Chancery to thoroughly compare the copies with the originals and attest them, certifying the signatures and attestations, so that they may be admitted as good evidence and equal to the originals.

REPLY OF THE LORD BISHOP OF SAN THOME TO THE SAID PETITION.

Until the Reverend Father Fra Spirito submits himself to the Declaration wherein he was declared to have incurred excommunication, he cannot be heard in law.

San Thome, December 29, 1706.

THE BISHOP OF MELIAPUR.

Receiving a reply which adjusted, itself so well to his request, the Reverend Father Michel Ange said: 'My Lord, I do not claim that you should give audience to the Reverend Father Esprit, nor that you release him from the excommunication, because he has already appealed to his Holiness, and to him alone does he mean to have recourse. I am only asking you to give me the record of the Reverend Father Esprit's case, and to attest the papers which I have in my hands. "Well, then," said his Lordship, "I have no other reply to give you than what I have given."

1. *Apostoli*, see note 235 to folio 273. The whole of this petition, and the reply to it, are in Portuguese in Codex No. CXXXV.

"Very well," replied the Reverend Father Michel Ange, "although your reply be irrelevant to my demand, it will still serve as a proof in the Roman courts that I have asked you for the record of the Reverend Father Esprit's case, and have also prayed you to attest my papers.

What say you, gentlemen, of all this that you have heard up to this point? Does it not look to you a very fine way of behaving? O God! who has ever heard such things? What person can there ever be who, reading a manifesto thus full of injustice, contradictions, and cruelty to the Capuchin fathers, will not conceive [294] a holy hatred for the bishop and a few regulars who, in order not to have to succumb in a wretchedly bad affair, heap iniquity upon iniquity. If this matter had fallen into the hands of the reverend Jacobin fathers (that is, the Dominicans), or even of the reverend Cordelier fathers (that is, the Franciscans), and it had been vigorously worked, you would then have known how little would be enough to completely destroy the reverend Jesuit fathers. I leave to the reader's consideration, if he will read attentively all that I have written, whether I exaggerate, and I beg him at the same time to reflect whether or not Monsignor has done the exact contrary of what he has reduced to writing in his Declaration, having declared the Reverend Father Esprit of Tours excommunicated before his having done any act contrary to the Pastoral, and condemned him without having cited him to appear. The bishop has used against him (Esprit) nothing but harsh measures, and has drawn up no record. The same can be said almost exactly of the Pastoral published by his Lordship in favour of the reverend Jesuit fathers. Because, just as the Jesuits could not have obtained the Pastoral otherwise than by calumniating the Reverend Father Esprit, equally his Lordship only gave it at a time when he believed the calumny to be true. For he could not have imagined that religions were capable of committing such an impious act in the execution of their designs. Even if it were not by reason of the calumny that his Lordship sent out the said Pastoral, I assert that there is no less contradiction in that document than in the Declaration, since the Bull of Clement X. and the Instruction of the Sacred Congregation, both of them issued to the Vicars Apostolic of the Indies,[1] which are quoted by his Lordship to

1. Mr. Philipps says that at this time (1706) there were two vicariates in India proper: (I) that of Malabar, erected December, 1659; and (2) that of

prove that he had power to do all he has done, are quoted out of place. In making use of them for the commission [295] of an injustice, he not only makes an abusive use of sacred things, but dishonours equally the court of Rome and the Sacred Congregation, who have never asserted that their authority could be invoked unless in things which were true and not false. It is in regard to a falsity, however, that the Lord Bishop and the reverend Jesuit fathers make use of these authorities. This I will demonstrate to you so plainly that there will be left no one who could have a doubt, even the very slightest.

I begin with the Bull of Clement X.,[1] of which these are the precise words, which I have taken from the Pastoral of his Lordship; its opening words are 'Decet Romanum Pontificem' [It behoves the Pope of Rome]. The words which follow are these:

'Cum autem prae multitudine neophytorum in una Provincia aut Civitate, vel praenimia earum amplitudine, unus aut alter qui eis praesunt missionarii non sufficiunt, si aliqui suppetunt sacerdotes Seculares aut Religiosi licet alterius ordinis, quorum tamen subsidium nec illi quaerant, nec oblatum recipiant, tunc habito duntaxat respectu ad Christianorum necessitatem, possint ac debeant Vicarii Apostolici praedicti operarios multiplicare, Parochias dividere, aliaque eiusmodi facere iuxta præscripta à Sacris Canonibus et Concilii Tridentini decretis.

'Datum Romae apud Sanctam Mariam sub annulo Piscatoris die 23 Decembris milesimi sexcentesimi septuagesimi tertii, Pontificatus nostri anno quarto.' [But when, on account of the multitude of neophytes in one Province or town, or because the size of the town or district is excessive, the one or two presiding missionaries are found insufficient for the work, and other priests are available, whether secular or religious, no matter of what order, even should the missionaries in charge neither ask for additional help from outside, not accept it when offered, yet it is the duty of the aforesaid Vicars Apostolic, and they are empowered, regarding only necessities of the Christians, to multiply the number of labourers, to divide the parishes, and to

---

Great Mogul (including the Gulkandah and Bijapur kingdoms), erected about 1660.

1. Clement X. (Emilio Altieri), elected 1670, at the age of eighty; died 1676. The words quoted are § 12 of the Bull (see 'Bullarum Diplomaticum et Privilegiorum editio Taurinensis' [Augustæ Taurinorum, 1869], vol. xviii., p. 449).

do anything of the kind which the case demands, according to the directions prescribed by the Sacred Canons and by the decrees of the Council of Trent.

Given at St. Mary's at Rome under the ring of the fisherman on the 23rd day of December, 1673, in the fourth year of our Pontificate.]

Gentlemen, nothing more terrifies poor people, who cannot judge except by appearances, than hearing some great Papal Bull in Latin cited, as to which they understand and can conceive nothing. These names of 'Bull' and of 'Clement X.' have I know not what of awful about them which carries terror into the heart. Since it is impossible to pay too much respect [296] and show too much submission to what the Holy See has ordered, the ignorant fear to take any action which might, in however small a degree, wound so sacred a tribunal. Would to God that the reverend Jesuit fathers who have concocted this Pastoral were of the same mind [as the lowly], and did not employ for the benefit of their insatiable ambition what is most holy and most sacred in the Christian religion.

Gentlemen, mark well what says the Bull, and then see whether the reverend Jesuit fathers who have quoted it in their Pastoral make use of its appropriately or not. Here is the passage in French:[1] 'Quand dans une ville ou dans une province, il y a une si grande multitude de Chrestiens ou que leur etendue est si considerable que les missionaires qui enont le soin ne puisse[nt] pas y suffire, s'il y a d'autres Prestres Seculiers ou Religieux d'un autre Ordre qui puisse[nt] les ayder a faire leur[s] functions, si ils ne cherchent pas leurs secours ou qu'ils le refusent quand on leur offre, alors les Vicaires Apostoliques voyant que c'est une necessity peuvent et doivent mesmes multiplier les ouvrie[r]s, diviser les Paroisses,' *et cetera*.

Now I ask you, gentlemen, since you live in Pondicherry, if there are in it more than one thousand four hundred Christians, including the French gentlemen, the *topasses* (persons of mixed blood), and the Malabaris (Tamils); I do not believe there can be more, and I look on it as rathef an exaggeration than an underestimate. Again I ask you, and entreat you for the love of God to tell me, if in the whole territory of Pondicherry and its dependen-

1. See the Latin and English versions of this passage already given on fol. 212.

ties there is more than an area four leagues in circumference. Excepting Ariancupam,[1] where there may be some forty Malaban Christians and as many Frenchmen, and where one of our fathers is stationed to minister to them, is there any other place where [297] a single Christian could be found? Gentlemen, you are incapable of asserting the contrary, for I am persuaded your consciences are much more timid than those of the reverend Jesuit fathers.

Lastly, I ask you once more, and beg of you to tell me this, too, gentlemen: During the time when the Capuchin fathers were the pastors of the French gentlemen, the *topasses* and the Malabaris, has any man been known to die without receiving the sacraments? Have not, throughout that period, the functions of zealous missionaries been fulfilled? When the Lord Bishop judged it well to send us any priest or friar to aid us in the mission, have we refused to receive him? This no one can affirm, much less prove. If, then, there are four of us Capuchin friars, all in priest's orders,[2] without referring to the catechists, and the Reverend Father Esprit, who has been sacrificed to their (the Jesuit') passion, stationed at a place where at the outside there are only one thousand four hundred Christians, why do they quote a Bull which puts them in the wrong and justifies us?

If, then, we cannot be accused of letting any man die without the sacraments; if it cannot be proved that we have not carried out the duties of our mission; if it cannot be said that we have refused to receive priests or friars, when his Lordship has offered us any (although by God's grace we have never been reduced to that extremity), whence arises it that his Lordship and the reverend Jesuit fathers have robbed us of our mission and refuse to give it back, even after orders from the Sacred Congregation, especially when the Bull of Clement X. prescribes 'quorum tamen subsidium nec illi quærant nec oblatum recipiant' as the only condition required and necessary for the [298] division of a parish.

From this you will see, gentlemen, that the reverend Jesuit fathers and the Lord Bishop not only make a wrong use of the Bulls of the Supreme Pontiffs, which they quote at the wrong

1. A village, on the sea-coast, three miles south of Pondicherry.
2. Part of the Jesuit case was that there were never more than two Capuchins at Pondicherry, and that there were 20,000 to 30,000 Malabar Christians there (see Father Tachard's defence, Archives Nationals, K 1,374, No. 52).

time, but, furthermore, wish to dishonour the Capuchin fathers by trying to make them pass for men of such limited zeal that four friars present at Pondicherry are unable to do what is so completely carried out by one village curé in France. No, gentlemen, nothing but their passion for display, and the jealously with which they look on those who think more of God's interests than men's, could make them act in this manner. I know no other cause. The reason I have for so thinking is this: if his Lordship had no other aim than the pure glory of God, and no other motive than to set up an improved mode of working where there are not over fourteen hundred Christians, then his Lordship would not have left the Reverend Father Bacchet (Bouchet)"[1] all by himself in a mission where there were over thirty thousand, and that for a period of seven or eight years; nor would he leave at this present moment Sadrasta (Sadras) and Puliacat,[2] where there are large numbers of Christians, without sending one single priest to take charge, while his Lordship has fifteen or so of them at San Thome with nothing to do except to play the bully and ruffler from morning to night.

You have just seen, gentlemen, how the Lord Bishop, or, rather, the reverend Jesuit fathers, who have fabricated the said Pastoral, make a wrong use of the Supreme Pontiff's authority, and attempt to discredit the poor Capuchin fathers. Observe now a still more unworthy item in the second quotation. It is from a recommendation made by the Sacred Congregation to Vicars Apostolic for suspending the execution [299] of what it has ordered, when they know as an absolute certainty that they are unable to execute those orders without creating a scandal, tumult, or disturbance of men's minds. Here are the very words, which I have taken out of the Pastoral itself. I pray you to weigh them well; for if you do that, gentlemen, you will see that it is without any reason that they alleged this authority of the Sacred Congregation. Nor could they raise a suggestion more harmful to the

1. Jean Venant Bouchet, born April 12, 1655; entered the novitiate, in the Aquitaine province, October 1, 1670; started for Madura about 1688, became Superior of that mission, and died March 13, 1732. There are several of his letters in 'Lettres Edifiantes,' and a protest of January 15, 1716, in Norbert, Lisbon edition of 1766, i. 390 (C. Sommer-vogel, 'Bibliographic,' i., column 1864).
2. Sadras, forty miles south, and Puliacat, twenty-four miles north, of Madras ('Madras Manual of Administration,' iii. 671, 775).

Capuchin fathers than this attempt to make the court at Rome believe that a tumult and a sedition would have arisen among the Christians, if they (the Capuchins) had obtained possession of their former mission to the Malabaris. 'Si in exsequendis Sacra Congregationis mandatis tarn magnat vobis difficultates occurrent, ut sine tumultu non possint acceptari, omnino cavete ea invitis prabere, et ob eorum inobedientiam dissensiones serere, mentes alienare, animos exacerbare, verum indulgendo tempori et neophytorum infirmitati compatiendo, mandata in prasens omittere satius erit; ad Sacram Congregationem omnino sinceritate summa prascribatis eaque quid sit agendum rescripserit.' [If you should meet with such great difficulties in carrying out the orders of the Sacred Congregation that you find they cannot be executed without creating a tumult, take great heed not to thrust them on unwilling persons, and thus, through their non-obedience, sow dissensions, alienate minds, and embitter souls; but, for the indulgence of the time, and in compassion for the weakness of the neophytes, it will be better to let the orders of the Sacred Congregation stand over a while. Write to the Sacred Congregation with the utmost frankness, and it will write back what is to be done.]

Gentlemen, since this matter is one of the greatest consequence to us, and you are under obligation in conscience to testify to the truth, tell us whether you foresee any difficulty in replacing the Capuchin fathers in possession of their cure of the Malabaris, as directed by the Sacred Congregation? Tell us, also, if any tumult or sedition would have occurred by taking out of the hands of the reverend Jesuit fathers a mission forcibly taken by them from the Capuchin fathers. Tell us, once more, whether the Capuchin fathers, who are as well known in Pondicherry as in France, are capable of causing turbulence and of [300] irritating men's minds? Tell us, lastly, when it became known at Pondicherry that decrees had come from Rome in favour of the Capuchin fathers, was there one single Malabar Christian who showed any displeasure, even the slightest? But what am I saying, gentlemen? Was there even one who did not rejoice? Was there ever known such a day of joy to the Malabar Christians as that Feast of all the Saints? Since on that day, when we published the decrees of the Sacred Congregation, no other disturbance of minds was to be seen than that suddenly our church was crammed with people, while that of the reverend Jesuit fathers became a desert: if, then, in the course of these proceedings there has broken out any disorder or tumult among the said Malabar Christians, it can only have been because they were not allowed to perform their heathen ceremonies as sanctioned by the reverend Jesuit fathers.

After having stated all this, I leave it to you to think what will be said at Rome when it is seen that the Lord Bishop and the reverend Jesuit fathers so lead astray the court of Rome that they want it to be believed there are thirty to forty thousand Christians where there are not even two thousand. We leave it to you to think what will be said by the Sacred Congregation when it knows that none of the reasons requiring the suspension of the decrees were to be feared or anticipated. Far from that, the rarest benefit that could have accrued to the Malabar Christians of Pondicherry would have been the restoration of that mission into the hands of the Capuchin fathers. Nothing in condemnation of the Capuchins was ever reported to Rome, nor was any Patriarch deputed, as had to be done about the reverend Jesuit fathers.

[301] But what will they say at Rome, gentlemen, when they see that a superior, a friar of twenty-five years' missionary work, has been declared excommunicated and accursed, and doubly accursed of God Omnipotent, *et cetera*, and that, too, in a city where there are fifty thousand idolaters. Will not this strike them as an excellent way to attract men to our Holy Faith, and a lofty example of virtue for the instruction of those who have already embraced that faith? Is this, gentlemen, the scandal, the sedition, and the tumult from which they ought to flee? Is this the disturbance which they have implanted in the minds of Christian converts, who rejoiced at returning to the sheepfold of their legitimate pastor, and [now] begin to vacillate in the religion they have professed, on seeing such bad treatment of a friar who by his efforts had gained them over to Jesus Christ. Yet this friar had never been guilty of the slightest act unworthy of his calling. What will they not say at Rome when they learn that the Reverend Father Esprit has been declared excommunicated for having published the decrees of the Sacred Congregation and citing there the reverend Jesuit fathers for acting directly contrary to those decrees? What will they not say at Rome when they hear that the reverend Jesuit fathers have had recourse

to the secular arm, and have laid a petition before Monsieur de Flacourt, judge of Pondicherry, to stop the execution of the said decrees? What will they not say at Rome when they see that the Reverend Father Esprit had gone post-haste from Pondicherry to Madras to appear before Monsignor, and that his Lordship would not grant him even one audience? What will not be said at Rome when they are aware of the repeated submissions made by these Capuchins [302], a thousand times in excess of what I have recorded in this manifesto, and on the other side such inflexibility displayed by the Lord Bishop and by the reverend Jesuit fathers? What will they not say at Rome when they see the petitions of the Capuchins and the wise answers of my Lord Bishop of San Thome? What will they not say at Rome when they find so many contradictions, so many perversions of words, as those I have shown you, and so many errors committed by a prelate, who ought never to allow himself to transgress—at any rate, in what regards the rendering of justice to those entitled to it? I have, however, two documents in my possession in which his Lordship says, in one, 'I have made a mistake;' in the other, 'The error was mine.' What will not be said at Rome when they see the truculent letter which the Lord Bishop has written to your Council, conceived in such excellent terms and sent so exactly at the right moment? What will they not say at Rome when an infamous calumny comes to be unmasked and they read a Pastoral issued in favour of the Jesuits, who are the authors of that very calumny? Finally, what will they not says at Rome on finding that his Lordship is not content with disobedience to the decrees of the Sacred Congregation, when they could have been carried out to the joy and with the universal consent of all the people, but he (the Bishop) must needs send out also a Pastoral in favour of those against whom the decrees are directed, and adds to it the excommunication of the Reverend Father Esprit, who has never done the slightest act in contravention of that Pastoral.

Father Fra Esprit, according to Monsignor, has said that the reverend Jesuit fathers are not the legitimate pastors of the Malabar Christians at Pondicherry, therefore it is necessary to declare him excommunicated. Behold the mighty crime he committed, which drew upon him a declaration that he was accursed, and doubly accursed under the maledictions [303] of God Omnipotent, of the Apostles St. Peter and St. Paul, and of all the other saints in the quire celestial, *et cetera*. But, let alone the fact that he never said anything of the sort after the publication of the Pastoral issued by the Lord Bishop of San Thome, let us suppose that he had said it but without following it by any overt act—I mean by that, performing any function arising out of the cure—he cannot incur any excommunication, as I have already demonstrated in two places. For if, in this country, excommunication is so cheap that a friar can be excommunicated for having said that the reverend Jesuit fathers, having robbed us of our poor mission, and having declined to obey the orders from Rome, were not the legitimate pastors of the Malabaris in Pondicherry, there is nothing left for them but to excommunicate me too, and hang the order on the doors of their church, because I have said the same thing many times, and I repeat it once more, that they are not, and never have been, the legitimate pastors of the Malabari Christians at Pondicherry.

My reasons for this assertion are that, besides encroaching upon our mission without first informing the Sacred Congregation, they have, moreover, entered on it under false allegations and by devious routes. The true shepherd, said Christ, ought to enter by the door, 'qui intrat per ostium pastor est ovium' (Vulgate, Gospel of St. John, x. 2); and he who does not enter into the fold by the door, but by another place, is a thief and a robber: 'Amen, amen, dico vobis qui non intrat per ostium in ovile, sed ascendit aliunde, ille fur est et latro' (*loc. cit.*, x. 1). How, then, have the reverend Jesuit fathers intruded themselves into our mission? Perhaps they did so by order of the said Sacred Congregation, to whom alone belongs the sanctioning of missions, whether [304] generally or in particular instances. No; for no sooner did it become known that the reverend Jesuit fathers had taken possession of our mission to the Malabaris of Pondicherry than it (the Sacred Congregation) has ordered them to make it over again to us. Perhaps it was because the Capuchin fathers had occasioned some scandal, or had not looked after those Malabaris efficiently enough. You know the fact, gentlemen, and all the other Christians who live at Pondicherry will bear witness not simply as to our lives and conduct, but will also confess (and of this I can boast without any display of pride) that never did that mission flourish like it did when in our hands. Perhaps it was because the Capuchins were not enough for the administration of the sacraments to fourteen hundred Christians living in Pondicherry. On that head there is not much to say, for, although the reverend Jesuit fathers desire to exhibit us as persons or scant zeal for the glory of God, and incapable of taking over again our former mission without some great outbreak and sedition among the Malabar Christians, I assert that three of our fathers, among whom I have the honour to be reckoned, hold the cure at Madras of over fifteen thousand Christians, French, Portuguese, and Malabaris, without anybody being able to complain not only of their behaviour, but of their ever having left any person to die without administration of the Sacraments, or of their ever having left any person uninstructed each in his own tongue. A convincing proof of the truth of this is that the Lord Bishop and the reverend Jesuit fathers, who are so kindly intentioned towards us that without any cause they declare to be excommunicated one of our friars, would without fail [305] have proclaimed our fault in the sight of heaven and of earth had we fallen short in any particular, or neglected to perform exactly all the functions of our ministry. Perhaps it was by order of His Most Christian Majesty that they made themselves masters of the poor Capuchins' mission. Certainly they have said so, gentlemen, and on the strength of their word the Lord Bishop of San Thome has issued a *provision* for the cure to our prejudice; but that assertion was false and a lie, deserving of public castigation, since, upon our causing a petition to be presented to our Invincible Monarch by means of the Reverend Father Seraphin of Paris, Capuchin, and preacher in ordinary to his Majesty,[1] his said Majesty replied that he had no recollection of having ever given such orders. If you find it difficult to believe a thing which does not seem credible, read the following words, and you will see that nothing can be more certain or more true:

'The king[2] having ordered me to enquire into the difference which has arisen between the Capuchins and the Jesuits with

1. For the Père Seraphin's account of his interview with Louis XIV., see his letter of June 13, 1701 (Norbert, 'Mémoires Utiles,' 1742, p. 157).
2. Norbert, 'Mémoires Utiles,' 1742, p. 148, where the date is given as 1701. The writer was the Count de Pontchartrain and the addressee the Governor of Pondicherry. The last sentence does not appear in full in our text. Louis Phélypeaux, Count of Pontchartrain (1643-1727), was Chancellor from 1699.

regard to the cure of Pondicherry, and make a report thereon to him, his Majesty, from the statements and accounts I have given him, learnt that the Lord Bishop of San Thome had asserted, from inspection of a document produced before him by the reverend Jesuit fathers, that the provisional orders given to Father Dolu, Jesuit, making him *cure* of the Malabaris, were conceded at your instance and at your request, and that you [Governor Martin] had written to him that such was the will of his Majesty. His Majesty does not remember ever having given any such order.

'(Signed) PONTCHARTRAIN.

'VERSAILLES,
'March 12, 1702.'

[306] Gentlemen, as I do not wish to prove anything beyond the animus with which the reverend Jesuit fathers act (which thing is in no way unusual), I pass over in silence the rest of the letter, and go on to tell you that they have possessed themselves of our cure without our having caused any scandal, without our having failed in our obligations, without it being possible to say that the Capuchin fathers were not sufficient for the administration of the sacraments, without having first informed the Sacred Congregation, which has reserved to itself the authority of arranging for missions and making changes in them when it thinks fit; to sum up, without any valid reason, solely upon a piece of deceit already exposed, and upon a fictitious order of His Most Christian Majesty. They are, therefore, thieves and robbers, as says the Saviour of our souls: 'Amen, amen, dico vobis qui non intrat per ostium in ovile ovium, sed ascendit aliunde, ille fur est et latro.' Now, the thief comes for nothing else but to rob, ruin, and slay: 'Fur non venit nisi ut furetur et machet et perdat' (John x. 10).

Thus you should not wonder, gentlemen, if the Malabari Christians, who had about them nothing of the heathen when under the guidance of their legitimate shepherd, have become more heathen than Christian after falling under the rule of thieves and robbers. You who are on the spot see every day the poor Christians smearing themselves over like masqueraders.[1] Some

1. *Note by Cardeira.*—An allusion to those heathen rites that the Jesuit Fathers allow to all Christian converts. The author has spoken of these in his Part IV., fols. 63-76.

cover their bodies with heathen marks, others cover their foreheads with cows' ashes. These carry their dead to burial with the sound of trumpets and of drums; those carry them to the grave on a species of throne, as done by the Hindus, and decline to put them in a bier, as all Christians ought to do. The men wear jewels in their ears [307] representing the attributes of the false gods; the women hang *talis*[1] on their necks with a cross on one side and the head of an idol upon the other. These ornaments are blessed by the reverend Jesuit fathers, and in their church they cause them to be put by the bridegroom upon the bride. One caste is separated from another in church; and the wretched Pariahs[2] receive the most Holy Sacrament at the door, while the other castes are admitted to the Holy Table.

You, I say, who live in these places, and know more of these things than I could tell you, I need not seek to make you read what was written and sent to Rome by Monsignor de Toumon, Patriarch of Antioch and Legate a Latere;[3] nor what the Reverend Father François Marie of Tours sent in to the Holy Inquisition. This last is the sole cause of our being so basely treated in these regions. All I will say to you, gentlemen, is that the reverend Jesuit fathers mislead the poor populace by saying these things are done to gain more souls to Jesus Christ; whereas we have at Madras ten times more Malabari Christians than those found in Pondicherry. Although they [the Madras Christians] wear talis with two crosses, one on one, the other on the other side; although they are all seated in church indiscriminately, just as in France; although they all communicate at the same table; although we inter their dead like any other Christians; yet we have ten times more Malabari Christians at Madras than the

1. *Note by Cardeira.*—'A tali is almost the same as what we call a medal' (see note 65, Vol. III., Part III., fol. 122).
2. 'Pariahs are Christianized Hindus, who live partly as Hindus and partly as Christians' (*Note by Cardeira*). [This definition is absurd. Pariahs are Pariahs, whether heathen or Christian (W. R. P.).] As to these observances, compare the wording of Father Esprit's (Spirito's) letter of September 15, 1706, to Father Timothée de la Fléche (Norbert, 'Mémoires Utiles,' 1742, p. 223).
3. *Note by Cardeira.*—Monsignor de Toumon, Cardinal, was he who was sent by the Holy See to put an end to the many disorders permitted by the missionaries among their converts. The author wrote about this Prelate in Part IV., fols. 165-175.

reverend Jesuit fathers have at Pondicherry. We should have had a hundred times more were it not for the reverend Jesuit fathers. Because I say, as in the presence of God, and were I in the last agony of death I should say the same thing, if we have not greater number of Christians, if we cannot free those we have from some remaining superstitions, it arises from nothing else than their asking us if we are heretics, since the Capuchins teach in one way and the reverend [308] Jesuit fathers in another.

There is, however, one extraordinary thing which you have not perhaps noticed. It is that all the rules of justice have for us a contrary application; our opponents violate them, they transgress them, they act to the direct contrary of what is therein ordained. Indeed, there is a precept about rendering to Caesar what is Cæsar's: 'Reddite quae sunt Caesaris Caesari (Matt, xxii. 21). There is a precept telling us to love God with all our heart, and our neighbour as ourself: 'Diliges Dominum Deum tuum ex toto corde tuo et proximum tuum sicut te ipsum' (Deut. vi. 5).[1] There is a precept forbidding the use of lying for obtaining success in one's designs and undertakings: 'Mendacium fugies' (Exod. xxiii. 1, 7). There is a precept which; enjoins doing justice to him who is entitled to it: 'Facite justitiam coram Deo' (Lev. xix.)[2] There is a precept telling you to obey your superiors: 'Obedite praepositis vestris' (Heb. xii. 17).[3] There is a precept against robbing another man of his goods: 'Non furtum facies' (Exod. xx. 15), and in St. Matt. x. 19, 'ne fureres.' There is a precept against speaking ill of the poor: 'Pauperem noli calumniare' (Lev. xix. 13); and there is a curse pronounced by God against those by reason of whom scandal arises: 'Necesse est ut veniant scandala; verumtamen vae homini illi per quem scandalum venit' (Vulgate, Matt. xvii. 17).

I do not think, gentlemen, you can doubt that the cure of the Pondicherry Malabaris was ours until about eight or nine years ago; neither can you doubt that the reverend Jesuit fathers became masters unjustly of our cure, since you have been ocular witnesses of these facts. You ought not to doubt that the said reverend Jesuit fathers have spoken a very considerable untruth,

1. Only part of this, up to 'corde tuo,' is in Deuteronomy; but the whole is in Matt. xxii. 37, 39, though not continuously (W.R.P.).
2. This quotation cannot be found in Lev. xix.
3. The Vulgate is 'Non facies calumniam proximo tuo' (W.R.P.).

having falsely alleged the order of his [309] Majesty, as we have already demonstrated, and you can also gather from this manifesto. You ought not to doubt that the same fathers have imposed on us the most infamous of all calumnies, since you have recognised this yourselves, and many of your number have testified thereto on our behalf. You ought not to doubt, finally that the reverend Jesuit fathers have disobeyed his Holiness and the Sacred Congregation; that they have not been willing to return goods which do not belong to them; that they have written to Madras; that they have gone from house to house hoping to render us hateful to all the Christians; that they have made us over to the secular arm; that they have directed us to be treated with all possible severity; that hey have presented a petition to Monsieur de Flacourt, judge of Pondicherry, to stop the execution of the decrees; that they inflict on us daily some fresh mortification; that they have been the cause of all the trouble which has arisen in Pondicherry and Madras through their having unjustly taken from us our cure, through their open resistance to his Holiness and the Sacred Congregation—in short, through their having declared as excommunicated a superior who has been a missionary five-and-twenty years without one action unworthy of that calling.

Nevertheless, the Lord Bishop of San Thome, although he knew that he ought to render to Cæsar what is Cæsar's—'Reddite quae sunt Cæsaris Cæsari'—instead of giving back the disputed cure to the Capuchins, made it over once more to the reverend Jesuit Fathers under an expressly issued Pastoral. Although his Lordship knew as an absolute certainty [310] that it is necessary to obey superiors:—'Filii obedite præpositis vestris'—in order to disculpate himself and place in safety the reverend Jesuit fathers, quotes in his Pastoral two great authorities, from which it is to be inferred that there are ten times more Christians in Pondicherry than there really are, and that the decrees of the Sacred Congregation could not have been executed without raising tumult and sedition. This is in the highest degree untrue, since we have certificates on both heads signed by more than five-and- twenty persons of the best position at Pondicherry.

Although the Lord Bishop knew there is a precept that we should love God above all things, and our neighbour as ourself—'Diliges Dominum Deum teum ex toto corde tuo, et proximum sicut te ipsum'—notwithstanding this, in place of suppressing the audacity of the reverend Jesuit fathers, who decry us everywhere as if we were so much false coin, he suffers and allows them to go from house to house, to write to persons in holy orders, to come even as far as Madras to tell everybody that all we Capuchins, whether at Pondicherry or at Madras, are excommunicated and must not be spoken to, but must rather be shunned like the plague.

Although the Lord Bishop knew there was a precept against calumniating anyone—'Pauperem noli calumniare'—and for the punishment of calumny whenever discovered—'Anima quæ pec- caverit, et contempto Domino, negaverit proximo suo depositum, quod fidei ejus creditum servaverit, vel vi aliquid extorserit, aut calumniam fecerit, sive rem perditam invenerit, et inficians insuper peieraverit, et quodlibet aliud ex pluribus fecerit, in quibus solent peccare homines, convicta delicti, reddet omnia, quæ per fraudem [311] voluit obtinere, integra, et quintam insuper partem domino, cui damnum intuleraf (Lev. vi. 2-5). [(2) If a soul sin and commit a trespass against the Lord, and lie unto his neighbour in that which was delivered him to keep, or in fellowship, or in a thing taken away by violence, or hath deceived his neighbour; (3) Or have found that which was lost, and lieth concerning it, and sweareth falsely; in any of all these that a man doeth, sinning therein; (4) Then it shall be, because he hath sinned, and is guilty, that he shall restore that which he took violently away, or the thing which he hath deceitfully gotten, or that which was delivered to him to keep, or the lost thing which he found, (5) Or all that about which he hath sworn falsely; he shall even restore it in the principal, and shall add the fifth part more thereto, and give it unto him to whom it appertaineth, in the day of his trespass offering' (Authorized Version)]—his Lordship, in place of punishing the reverend Jesuit fathers who had raised the calumny, and instead of justifying the poor Capuchin fathers who are innocent, sends the latter a Pastoral founded on that very calumny. He himself derides us, and makes a joke of us, when, after admitting he had made a mistake, he describes us as moved by an evil spirit, always interpreting his best intentions in the worst sense. This he says after having made us over to the secular arm, after having ordered that we should be punished with all possible severity, after having written to your Council that he declined to expose himself to the rudeness and anger of the reverend Father Esprit.

Although the Lord Bishop of San Thome knew exceedingly well that lying is prohibited—'Mendacium fugies'—that robbery is not allowed—'Non furtum facies'—and that before God we are under an obligation to do justice to those seeking it— 'Facite justitiam coram Deo'—instead of casting forth the reverend Jesuit fathers from our mission which they had robbed us of, and that by a lie they told in alleging the order of His Most Christian Majesty, a thing that had never entered that monarch's thoughts, his Lordship gives them new authority and walks in their footsteps. He declares we have published the decrees without his order, after he had given it us by word of mouth and in writing. He informs many secular persons that his word may be relied on, yet he afterwards goes from it. First he wrote to the Reverend Father Michel Ange that he had given our mission to the reverend Jesuit fathers solely at the instance of the [Director-] General Martin, who had assured him that such was the intention of his Majesty [312]. Now he writes that he has no recollection of ever having said this, we having demonstrated to him that the order of his Majesty had been falsely alleged. Again he wrote to the said father [Michel Ange] that he could prosecute his rights wherever he liked, that he (the Bishop) could not complain of that. Then, when his Holiness and the Sacred Congregation have given judgment in our favour, he writes that he does not remember having ever said the above words. He wrote to the Reverend Father Esprit of Tours that he had only taken away the cure most reluctantly and against his own inclination; yet, in spite of a favourable opening for restoring the said father to his former cure, he writes now the exact contrary, and adds that he is very old and he does not remember having said that he acted against his own inclination, when he took the mission from the Capuchin fathers and gave it to the reverend Jesuit fathers.

Finally, the Lord Bishop, although he knows that Jesus Christ has said that scandals must come, but woe to that man. through whom the scandal cometh—'Necesse est ut veniant scandala; verumtamen vae homini illi per quern scandalum venit'— in spite of this, instead of suppressing the scandal that the reverend Jesuit fathers have caused in these regions—by seizing from us such a flourishing mission without why or wherefore; by non-obedience to the orders of the Sacred Congregation, which commands that we be replaced in possession of our cure under penalty of privation of offices, privileges, and faculties conceded to missionaries; after we had published those decrees of the said Sacred Congregation with his own (the Bishop's) permission, although such consent was not an absolute necessity; after finding that all [313] the poor Malabari Christians shouted for joy at seeing themselves once more under their first pastor, and that our church was crowded with people, while, on the contrary, that of the reverend Jesuit fathers was deserted—his Lordship created anew a still greater scandal than before by sending forth a Pastoral to the reverend Jesuit fathers, and excommunicating a poor friar who had never done any act in opposition to the said Pastoral.

'Quis audivit unquam tale? et quis vidit huic simile?' (Vulgate, Isa. lxvi. 8). Gentlemen, who has ever heard such a thing? who has ever seen procedure like this? Of a truth, I remain in wonderment; nor can I conceive how persons so intelligent as you are, who have yourselves perceived more passion, more injustice, more deceit in the reverend Jesuit fathers than I have been able to include in these two manifestoes of mine, could shun the Reverend Father Esprit and leave him in the sad condition to which he has been reduced by passion alone and not by any crime of his. Gentlemen, I know perfectly well that you dread the reverend Jesuit fathers, that you fear them more than you do us humble Capuchins, for you know that Capuchin fathers are not capable of bearing malice, not even to those who try to make them hateful to all the world, while on the contrary the Jesuit fathers intimidate by their menaces all those who endeavour to oppose, either their perfidious injustice or their insatiable ambition. Allowing for all that, gentlemen (although I know this to be the sole reason which drives you to it, if you will permit me to say so), yet our too great goodness of heart ought not to be the cause of our not receiving justice. Your office compels you to enter equally into the interests of the one side as of the other [314]. Because the reverend Jesuit fathers use at every turn such emphatic words as, 'The king shall hear of it,' 'We shall inform the court,' 'What will his Majesty say when he hears of this?' it is not necessary to imagine that they have such complete hold over the minds of princes. Besides, the King of

France thinks less of the Jesuits at Pondicherry than you do. I will say more: even did his Most Christian Majesty prefer them to all his other subjects, his sense of equity equalling his greatness of heart, he could never approve what is unjust or blame what ought to be praised.

To believe the contrary, gentlemen, would be an attempt to tarnish the reputation of a prince who is more jealous of doing justice than he is of his own might, who would hold it preferable to lose his title of Louis the Great than that of Louis the Just.

Furthermore, religious who seek nothing beyond inspiring terror and making themselves feared; who have no other answer to give you beyond, 'You will ruin yourselves,' or else, 'We shall destroy you;' who follow no other rules in their acts than those directly opposed to the maxims of Christianity—these men, I tell you, instead of being feared and dreaded, deserve to be despised and held things of naught. Nor can this last result fail to come to pass, if not now, then at some future time. For, let them take what measures they please to exalt themselves and display themselves before the world, it is absolutely inevitable that the Divine oracles must be fulfilled: 'He who humbles himself shall be exalted, and he who exalts himself shall be brought low' (Matt, xxiii. 12, Lev. xiv. and xv.)[1]—'Qui se humiliat exaltabitur, et qui [315] se exaltat humiliabitur.'

Gentlemen, I am unwilling to state anything to you that I cannot prove; at the same time I am anxious to impress on you so acutely all that I tell you that no possibility of doubt may remain. Thus, although I have written more than was required to show that the reverend Jesuit fathers act to the direct contrary of Jesus Christ's ordinances given in the Holy Gospels, the very least I can do is to bring under your consideration two portions of Holy Scripture which in all good faith can be applied to the reverend Jesuit fathers.

Here is the first passage: 'Learn of Me, who am meek and lowly of heart'—'Discite à me quia mitis sum et humilis corde' (Matt. xi. 29). This is the second one: 'Behold, I send you like lambs in the midst of wolves: be therefore wise as serpents, and harmless as doves (Matt. x. 16, Luke x. 3)—'Ecce ego mitto vos

1. 'Leviticus' must be a copyist's mistake for 'Lucas.' 'Quia omnis se exaltat humiliabitur: et qui se humiliat exaltabitur' (Luke xiv. 16 and xviii. 14), the same in both places (W.R.P.).

sicut oves in medio luporum. Estote ergo prudentes sicut serpentes et simplices sicut columbæ.' Gentlemen, where is the tenderness of the reverend Jesuit fathers? Oh! had I only the spirit of prophecy to divine what they are thinking in their minds, and the eyes of Argus to behold their external acts, then, by God, I could tell you a fine story indeed! All the same, although I possess neither the one nor the other, yet, without alluding to a thousand anecdotes I have heard, I desire to bring forward only what we know by experience—what you know as well as we do— that is, that they have taken from us our cure of the Malabaris, as everyone knows, and they have falsely alleged the orders of his Majesty, as is a most indisputable truth.

The Lord Bishop, after having given an executive order (*provision*) for the cure in favour of the reverend Jesuit fathers, to the detriment of the Capuchin fathers, writes to us that we may seek our rights wherever seems to us [316] best, that he could in no manner complain. This you have seen already in this manifesto. We brought an appeal before the Holy See and the Sacred Congregation, as you can see in our notice of appeal. His Holiness and the Sacred Congregation have sent out here decrees in our favour; that of this fact you have no doubt I may take as certain. We presented those decrees to the Lord Bishop, as proved by the words written on the margin of the petition from the Capuchin fathers. We notified them to the Reverend Father Tachard by order of Monsignor in the presence of two of you, gentlemen, and you have attested the fact.[1]

The Reverend Father Tachard resisted us by a decision of the Lord Patriarch given without our knowledge, and produced now two years after it had been given in favour of the reverend Jesuit fathers. This you know as absolute fact. Yet that decision was the most unjust in the world, not only from not having been drawn up according to juridical rules, but also from being passed at the very time that our appeal was in the hands of his Holiness and the Sacred Congregation. Still, we obeyed it blindly; that is an asseveration nobody can deny.

Then, hearing from the mouth of the Lord Bishop that all the things done by the Lord Primate of Goa had been approved

1. See the attestation of March 12, 1706, signed by De Flacourt and d'Hardancourt of the Pondicherry Council (Norbert, 'Mémoires Utiles,' 1742, p. 189).

at the Court of Rome, and, on the contrary, all that the Lord Patriarch had done was disapproved by his Holiness and the Sacred Congregation, we presented a petition to his Lordship for leave to publish our decrees. If you have any doubt, you can see the petition we presented, which has been already inserted in full. His Lordship said to the Reverend Father Michel Ange that he could not grant us that permission in writing, for reasons known to him, but we could [317] publish them in our church at Pondicherry. Then, after having said the contrary to this in his Pastoral, he has now confirmed in writing what he had said only viva-voce. This I have pointed out in many places of my first and second manifestoes.

After getting this permission, we published the decrees on All Saints' Day of the year 1706, and all the Christians were frantic with joy, as is seen from many affidavits signed by more than thirty of the best-placed Frenchmen in Pondicherry. The Lord Bishop then accepted a calumny against us originated by the reverend Jesuit fathers, and on this foundation his Lordship issued a Pastoral in favour of the reverend fathers just named. We have done no act opposed to the said Pastoral, which fact will be seen at Rome from the affidavits we have forwarded. All we did was to cite there the reverend Jesuit fathers for having acted contrary to the decrees of the Sacred Congregation.

Could we have done otherwise without falling into the same defect into which the reverend Jesuit fathers have fallen in paying such little heed to the above-named orders of the Sacred Congregation? However, after our line of action was taken, in which, as I believe, there is nothing to condemn, Monsignor, who is a Jesuit, styled us rash and scandalous persons, liars, disobeyers of orders, and madmen. He also asserted that we always interpreted his best intentions the reverse way, that we turned everything into evil, that we were carried away by an evil spirit, that he prayed God to deliver him from the Capuchins' hood. Just as if all these pleasing epithets applied to us by his Lordship did not sufficiently express the hatred he bore us, he issued a Declaration against Reverend Father Esprit, whereby he was declared to be publicly excommunicated accursed, and doubly accursed [318] by the arm of God Omnipotent, of the Apostles St. Peter and St. Paul, and of all the other saints in the quire celestial. He was deprived of the communion of the faithful, who were ordered, under the same penalty of the greater excommunication, not to supply him with fire or water, cetera. He prohibits the father being spoken to, orders that the said Declaration he affixed at the door of the right reverend Jesuit fathers' [church], from which no one can remove it without exposing himself to the same excommunication. When this poor father leaves Pondicherry for San Thome, there to give an account of his conduct, his Lordship's heart is so hardened that he refuses him an audience; he has the callousness to see our reverend father custodian prostrate at his feet, with eyes brimful of tears, unable to utter anything except through sighs and sobbing; and yet he was not softened by a sight which would have converted a Turk and melted a heart of bronze. Where, then, gentlemen, do we find the gentleness that the Saviour of our souls desires us to leare from him? I answer: Everywhere, except among the reverend Jesuit fathers!

But not only does Jesus Christ require us to learn gentleness from Him, but He also enjoins on us to be humble in heart: 'Discite a me, quia mitis sum et humilis corde.' Now, where is the humility of heart of the reverend Jesuit fathers? Perhaps it is found in their personality, in their words, in their business dealings, in their talk, their modes of work, in the smaller openings that present themselves for practising it. Were I to answer 'Yes,' you would not believe me, gentlemen, and you would be right; for, briefly, everybody knows too well that they aim at lording it everywhere: they must act the great man

wherever [319] they find themselves. They must know all that goes on within families. To hear them talk, they are such oracles that they command the very essence of knowledge; such stern moralists, such Catos, that they engross all wisdom par excellence; such Aristotles in philosophy, such Saint Thomases in theology, such Saint Peters, that they disdain to convert the heathen in less than thousands at a time. Engage them in conversation, and they will soon begin to glorify themselves; for then, unable to put restraint on their tongues, they assume the pontiff, affect the magnifico, and expatiate on nothing but their own talents.

In the sight of people who know them not they display the intensity of a zeal which leads them to the ends of the earth; then they exalt the reverend fathers' De la Chaise and Bour-

LI. Camel Litter

daloue.[1] From time to time they let drop discreetly the illustrious names of dukes, princes, kings, and sovereigns under their spiritual direction. On this intimacy they pretend to be able to found the fortunes of those who favour them, or the inevitable ruin of those honest men who refuse to take in hand their interests at the peril of their own souls.

If you speak to them of the reverend fathers of the Jacobins, Carthusians, Benedictines, Camaldolese,[2] or the Trappists, et cetera, and say a word or two in their praise, they reply to you with a certain air of depreciation: 'Those reverend fathers are certainly good sort of men, virtuous and worthy of their calling, but... ' When you beg them to attend at some ceremony they make a thousand protests, asking to be left in the lowliest place; but should you forget to give them the chief place, if they do not show their resentment, they seize the first pretext and soon withdraw. I know this sort of thing from experience, having observed it on many an occasion. Tell me, gentlemen, whether I exaggerate when I say that the reverend Jesuit fathers follow the precepts of this world, and not those of Jesus Christ, which apply more to them than even to you; 'Discite à me, quia mitis sum et humilis corde.'

[Folio 320 of the text is blank.]

NOTE ON EVENTS CONNECTED WITH FATHER ESPRIT, AFTER 1707

[It remains, in conclusion, to say a word or two about the subsequent course of the dispute and the ultimate fate of the Reverend Father Esprit. First of all, action was taken by the Capuchins at Goa, and the Archbishop Primate set aside the excommunication. Next the Guardian, Father Laurent, and the other four Capuchins at Pondicherry submitted a joint petition to the Pope dated January 26, 1707; on January 21, 1709, the Sacred Congregation upheld its decree of 1703, and also absolved

1. François de la Chaise d'Aix, a French Jesuit (1642-1709; from 1675 he was confessor of Louis XIV. Louis Bourdaloue, Jesuit, the famous preacher (1632-1704); preacher at Court from 1669 to 1689.
2. *Camaldolesi*, or, in French, *Camaldule*, 'religieux d'un ordre monastique fondè à la fin du xme siècle par Saint Romuald, l'habit est blanc, et la règle celle de Saint Bernard. *Stymologie*: Camaldoli, locality de la Toscane, où l'ordre dut d'abord établi' ((*littré* 'Dictionnaire'). [Pope Gregory XVI. (1831-46), a Camaldolese friar, was the re-establisher of the Jesuit missions in India (W.R.P.)].

Father Esprit from excommunication. Apparently Father Esprit proceeded to Europe to urge his suit in person, travelling by way of Arabia and Persia. He was back again in Pondicherry in February, 1711. During his first term of government (July, 1708, to October, 1713) Monsieur Hebert was strongly anti-Jesuit in feeling, and there was a calm; but in his second term, from February, 1715, to 1718, he was as strongly the other way. At this time the Pere le Tellier, S. J., confessor of Louis XIV., obtained the issue of three *lettres-de-cachet* (dated February 9, 1715) against Bishop Visdelou, S.J., Father Esprit, guardian at Pondicherry, and Father Thomas, guardian at Madras. The governor was afraid to lay hands on a bishop, and a plot to lure Father Thomas from Madras was a failure. Esprit received warning, and although then over sixty, set out on foot, hoping to find a refuge under the English flag at Madras. He was captured, brought back, and sent on board ship. This arrest must have been shortly after January 17, 1716, as Father Esprit was still in Pondicherry on that date. France was reached after the death of Louis XIV, (which occurred on September 1, 1715), and the Regent took a different view of things. By his order the Cardinal de Noailles investigated the case, and Father Esprit was acquitted of blame. After a stay of six or seven months in Europe, permission to return to India was given on December 8, 1716, and in August, 1717, Father Esprit arrived at Pondicherry, where he was received with every demonstration of joy. At length, in 1738, the venerable man died at the age of eighty-four years, being still Superior of the Capuchins and parish priest of the French. Apparently the native parish was never recovered from the Jesuits, in spite of the Decrees from Rome.

AUTHORITIES

Norbert, 'Mémoires Utiles,' 1742, 42, 243-265, 269, 283. *Ibid.*, 'Mémoires Histoiiques,' 1747, i. 269-273, 313, 393 (note), 420, 424; ii. 106, 311, 339-342, 348, 349]

NOTE ON FATHER NORBERT, CAPUCHIN, AND HIS WRITINGS

[Since, in connection with these disputes between the Jesuits and Capuchins, I haves quoted largely from the books of Father Norbert, Capuchin, some words of justification of that much-maligned missionary seem to be called for, especially when a scholar like the late A. C. Burnell makes no scruple of calling him a 'rascally old Capuchin' ('Hobson Jobson,' 2nd edition, 473).

The only 'rascality' I can discover in him is that he made himself extremely disagreeable to the Jesuits. Undoubtedly he was a strenuous pamphleteer, and, provoked by persecution, as time went on he became more bitter and more violent in his expressions. But the documents he prints are, I am persuaded, quite authentic, and worthy of admission as evidence. My greatest complaint against him is his overwhelming prolixity, and I also agree with his spiteful biographer, Chevrier, that he wrote in Walloon rather than in French.

Pierre Parisot was born at Bar-le-Duc, in Lorraine, on March 8, 1697. After attending a Jesuit school he became a Capuchin novice on April 13, 1716. In 1734 he proceeded to Rome, and became Procurator-General of the 'Missions Etrangeres.' About 1736 he was sent to India to the Pondichery mission, where he took an active part at the side of Claude Visdelou, Bishop of Claudiopolis, in the still continuing dispute between the Jesuits and his own order. After the death of Visdelou in 1739, he returned to Europe to represent the Capuchin case and was well received by Benedict XIV. The Jesuits were roused to action. Norbert was alarmed, and removed to Lucca, where he found a protector, and brought out his book 'Memoires Utiles . . .' (1742).

From that time he remained more or less a wanderer. From Lucca he went to Venice, from Venice to Holland by sea. Thence he moved to London, and finally was employed at Lisbon by the Marquis Pombal, then engaged in his campaign against the Jesuit order. A final edition of Norbert's second book 'Mémoires Historiques,' was brought out there in the year 1766 in eight volumes, quarto. In 1759, with the Pope's consent, Norbert had resigned his monastic orders, and thenceforth was known as the Abbé Curel Platel (or perhaps that was his real family name). He returned to Lorraine, and died there in poverty on July 7, 1769 ('Biographie Universelle,' Michaud, Paris, 1822, vol. xxxi., p. 360, article by W[eis]s).

The attack made on Norbert's morals by T. H. Chevrier, alias 'Le Colporteur' (born at Nancy, 1720; died 1762), in his 'La Vic du Fameux Pere Norbert, ex-Capuchin ...' (London, 1762), is mere silly backbiting, and is rendered still less worth notice when contrasted with the praise he had already lavished on his victim in a previous work ('Memoires des Hommes Ulustres de Lorraine,' ii. 83). The charge made by the Jesuits that Norbert falsified a document at Pondicherry I hold to be quite groundless. On the other hand, some of his charges against them are trivial, and a few are not proven; but the remainder of them are abundantly proved, and could hardly be seriously disputed. I am speaking solely of the facts as facts, and not of the interpretations put upon them by controversialists.

In my opinion, the Jesuit concession to caste distinctions in Christian worship was their gravest mistake, for the recognition of any such differences strikes at the root of Christianity conceived as a religion for all men, and not only for some chosen race of peculiar people. Surely in the sight of God all Christians are equal? Another prominent point which strikes one in these disputes is the excessive reluctance of the Jesuit order to bow to authority, although implicit obedience is one of their fundamental doctrines. From 1699 to 1744, for five-and-forty years, they struggled with the Popes, and tried their best to get their own way. Perhaps their most sensible defence is that put forward by a modern writer, the Reverend Father Auguste Jean, S.J., in 'Le Madure, l'Ancienne et la Nouvelle Mission' (Brussels, Société de St. Augustin, 1894, 2 vols.), i. 209: 'Nous nous soumettons a sa' (the Church's) 'decision d'esprit et de coeur. Nous regardons cette decision comme definitive: elle ne laisse plus place a la discussion. Rome a parlé il suffit.' He holds that up to 1744 the Pope's approval of Cardinal de Toumon's decree was provisional, and left it open for the Jesuits to refuse to obey it while prosecuting their appeals.

Strange to say, this question of recognising castes is, I am told, still under discussion in the non-Catholic missions of Southern India. In Northern India the missions seem to have ignored caste after conversion; in the South it has been different.

The Abbé J. A. Dubois, though not a Jesuit, upheld caste Christianity as a merely civil or social distinction; Bishop Heber seems to have been of much the same opinion ('Narrative of a Journey,' 4th edition, 1829, 3 vols., iii. 444; 'Life,' 2 vols., 4to., 1830, ii. 221, 399). Swartz and the Lutheran missionaries had tolerated caste and divided the Pariahs from the Sudras at public worship; but the younger school of clergy were actively opposed to any such concessions. Even the Bishop calls the high caste demand for a separate cup for the sacrament an 'abominable claim.' Daniel Wilson, Bishop of Calcutta and Metropolitan of India, would allow of no compromise, and denounced all such concessions as inadmissible ('Life of the Right Rev. D. Wilson,' by Josiah Bateman, 2 vols., 1860, i. 392, 424, 437; ii. 218). I believe that in the South of India the question is still one that provokes controversy.]

[339] ANOTHER DETACHED LEAF TRANSLATED FROM THE PORTUGUESE BY COMMANDATORE ANDREA CARDEIRA, P.P.[1]

With this I bring to an end Part V., and if time allows me, and I should come across anything worthy of record, I will go

1. Andrea Cardeira was, like his father Stefano, Public Professor of Law in the University of Padua; he died in 1721. I here follow the order of Codex No. CXXXV. (the original text in Portuguese) instead of that of Codex No. XLV. (the Italian translation). The following passage seems intended for the conclusion of Part V., and thus ought to precede instead of follow the loose leaves in French, which are bound up in Codex No. CXXXV.

on with a Sixth Part, hoping thereby to complete the satisfaction of the inquiring reader. Let us now turn and say something of the old and wily king, Aurangzeb. We find him, then, with his army not far from the fortress of Ahmadnagar, of which we have spoken before (V. 202), feeble and old, full of disillusions, and near to the day of his death. On February 7, 1707, he fell ill, and on no day was he able to appear in public audience.[1] His absence raised a tumult in the camp, the shops were closed, supplies grew dear, and many other disorders arose.

The chief *wazir*, Asad Khan, worked hard among both the nobles and the smaller men to keep them quiet, and did all that was possible to show the royal person to the populace, as he had done on other occasions. But the king's weakness was so complete that this had become impossible. Meanwhile the king, being somewhat afraid of A'zam Tara, ordered him not to come to audience without being sent for. But Prince Kam Bakhsh went frequently to see his father. He perceived the king's malady was mortal, and petitioned his Majesty before he died to give him liberty to depart as promised. Otherwise it was quite certain that he would lose his life. Then the king ordered him to surround the royal tent with his guards, and to this direction effect was given at once.

A'zam Tara refused to endure this; he imagined that Prince Kam Bakhsh was trying to take possession. Forthwith he sent some of his own troops to chase away the guards round the royal tent and take their place. In this affair some force was used on both sides, and some men were killed—twelve on Kam Bakhsh's side and eight on A'zam Tara's. Hearing the great uproar, the king asked what was the matter. Asad Khan, who was always present during the king's sickness [340], told him the whole story. Then the king ordered him to go at once at the head of a number of eunuchs and suppress the tumult. By other orders Aurangzeb directed Prince A'zam Tara to leave the army; he was appointed lord over Aarangabad, Burhanpur, Barar, *et cetera*, as far as the Narbada river. An order was issued to Prince Kam Bakhsh making him lord over the provinces of

1. Compare with this account the statements previously made on fol. 202 and the notes there.

Bijapur and Gulkandah. A letter was delievered to him addressed to the governor of the former place, ordering the delivery of the fortress.[1]

The prudent *wazir* so adjusted matters that both princes quitted the army. A'zam Tara marched very slowly and the Prince Kam Bakhsh in haste, being anxious to take possession of the fortress of Bijapur. Four days after the above disturbance, the king being still in the same state—nay, in the agonies of death—the *wazir*, being a partisan of A'zam Tara, sent that prince a message telling him to return in all possible haste. When he arrived the king was already dead, having died on the Friday. This was one day before the arrival of A'zam Tara, which took place on March 4 [1707], an hour after noon.[2]

Aware that he was near the hour of death, the king had ordered and eagerly pressed the *wazir*, Asad Khan, to unlock the treasury and pay the soldiers all that was due to them. If he neglected this direction, he would have to give answer for it in the presence of God, and in the meanwhile his conscience would hurt him. Thus the *wazir*, with the consent of the new king, A'zam Tara, carried out the order.

When the old king found himself in this helpless condition, he said just before he died: 'I die happy, for at least the world will be able to say that I have employed every effort to destroy the enemies of the Mahomedan faith.' At this time there were many friends of Shah 'Alam who attempted to get the king before he died to nominate that son as his successor. But his answer was that he made him (Shah 'Alam) King of Hindustan, which he had already made over to him; but as to his reigning there or elsewhere, that was in the hands of God alone.

At the time the king died a whirlwind arose, so fierce that it blew down all the tents standing in the encampment. [341] Many persons were killed, being choked by the dust, and also

1. Kam Bakhsh left for the south on February 17, 1707, N.S., and Azam Shah marched northwards on February 22, 1707, N.S. (Mirza Muhammad's Tazkirah,' and Bhim Sen's 'Tarikh-i-dilkusha', fol. 158a; both writers were present in the imperial camp).
2. This makes Aurangzeb's death take place on March 3, 1707, N.S., which corresponds to the official date of the 28th Zul,l Qa'dah, 1118 H. On fol. 322 Manucci puts it on March 4, and the sentence here might be construed to mean the same—*viz.*, the 4th. Khafi Khan, ii. 566, places A'zam Shah's arrival on the second night after Aurangzeb's death.

animals. The day became so dark that men ran into each other, being unable to see where they were going; villages were destroyed, and trees overthrown. This whirlwind lasted up to six o'clock in the evening.

The chief *wazir*, the principal officials at the court, and the generals went out to meet A'zam Tara, and escorted him to the royal tents. For several days before taking his seat on the throne he directed everybody to appear at court in rich and handsome robes.

On March 15 [1707J A'zam Tara decided to take his seat on the throne.[1] This day was fixed by the astrologers when they came to see him. On beholding the throne afar off, A'zam Tara stopped, and raising his hands and eyes to heaven, prayed God to grant him favour and confer on him understanding to govern with strict justice, and gain the victory over his enemies. He appeared clad in rich vestments adorned with precious stones. His prayer finished, he sat on the throne at ten o'clock, and remained seated until midday. He ordered new money to be coined, one-twelfth part larger than the pieces current, and of the small change he ordered two coins to be made into one. Thus nowadays one rupee is worth thirty-two pieces of copper. Upon the new coin were impressed the words:

'Secadzad der Jaan badablout iaè.
Patxa mamalek Azamxa'
(Sikkah zad dar jahan ba daulat wa jah
Padshah-i-mamalik-i-A'zam Shah).

which means 'Struck. . . . . .' [the rest is wanting].[2]

[342] Omitted fols. 342-345, account of events following the Battle of Jajau in June, 1707, which has already been taken from Part IV. (Codex XLIV., fol. 241).

END OF THE FIFTH PART OF THE STORIA DEL MOGOL OF SIGNOR NICCOLO MANUCCI, VENEZIANO

1. On fol. 322 the date given is the 19th, but March 15 seems correct (see note to above folio on page 377, Vol. IV.).
2. See British Museum Catalogue, 162, 163, 371. and Plate XX. 'Coin was struck in the world with fortune and dignity by the Emperor of the Kingdoms, A'zam Shah.'

DETACHED LEAVES

TRANSLATED FROM THE FRENCH INTO ITALIAN BY THE CAVALIERE ANDREA CARDEIRA, PUBLIC PROFESSOR.

[321] The emperor of the Mogul country, called Aurangzeb, has exerted himself to the utmost during twenty-six years to destroy his enemy Shiva Ji [the Mahrattahs] without having been able to do him any damage. When this king was encamped near a town in the Dakhin realms called Sholapur, he fell ill. This was on February 14 of the year 1707.[1]

There were then present at court two princes, one named A'zam Tara, his second-born, approaching the age of sixty; the other prince was younger, his name Kam Bakhsh, upon whom the king lavished all his affection.[2] Finding himself reduced to such a state of weakness, Aurangzeb ordered him [Kam Bakhsh] to surround the royal tent with guards; he feared a sudden attack by A'zam Tara. But the latter heard of the order beforehand, and being much irritated by it, sent some troops to disperse the guards that the prince, his younger brother, had posted. This began a dispute between them, opening the way to a conflict in which many were slain on both sides. On the emperor becoming acquainted with this act, he sent to the spot Asad Khan, the grand *wazir*, to adjust the quarrel between the princes in the best way he found possible. He told him to inform A'zam Tara that if he would withdraw from the army he would give him the provinces of Aurangabad, Burhanpur, Barar, *et cetera*. The

1. There is some repetition here of the preceding narrative, but, as the events are important, I retain the whole as it stands. The mention of Sholapur is a mistake, the imperial camp having been since January 31, 1706, at Ahmadnagar, some 200 miles away. The date, February 14 (N.S.), is eleven days in advance of the then English reckoning.
2. A'zam Shah, having been born on the 12th Sha'ban, 1063 H. (July 9, 1653). was fifty-five lunar years, three months, sixteen days, or fifty-three solar years, seven months, twenty-four days, of age. Kam Bakhsh, the Benjamin of the family, had reached forty-one lunar years, two months, eighteen days, or thirty-nine solar years, eleven months, twenty-seven days.

prince obeyed, and marched away by short stages and encamped his division only eight leagues from the royal quarters. There he resolved to await the news of the emperor's death.

Prince Kam Bakhsh remained in attendance on the king. Seeing his father's death was near, this son supplicated that while his father still remained alive he would grant to him (Kam Bakhsh) entire liberty to go, for he feared that after his father's death his throat would be cut [322] by his enemies. The king granted his prayer, and also placed in his hands a letter addressed to the Viceroy of Bijapur, containing an injunction to permit his youngest son to make himself master of that kingdom.

Then the prince (Kam Bakhsh) hastened his departure, and four days after he had started—namely, on March 4 [1707][1]—the king died two hours after midday. At that very moment there arose a whirlwind which overturned all the tents in the camp, knocked down elephants, camels, *et cetera*, uprooted trees, even those of prodigious size; in short, a very large number of persons were killed, and the effects extended also into the adjacent villages, the tempest lasting until the evening.

As soon as he heard this news A'zam Tara made all haste to return to court, seized all the treasure, and with great vigour reduced everyone to obedience. The king's body was lifted and laid in a palanquin for removal to the city of Aurangabad, there to be interred in the sepulchre that he had caused to be prepared in his lifetime not far from a large reservoir.[2]

When he found himself absolute master, A'zam Tara, in order to capture the affection of those serving, raised the pay of the officials and soldiers. On the 19th of the same month [March, 1707] he was crowned as king.[3] Then he prepared for an immediate march towards the city of Ágrah in order to obtain recognition as emperor. Shah 'Alam, the first-born son of the

1. The recorded date is the 28th Zu,l Qa'dah, 1118 H., which I make out as equivalent to March 3, 1707, N.S. Kam Bakhsh left the camp on the 14th Zu,l Qa'dah, 1118 H. (February 17, 1707).
2. Aurangzeb's tomb lies about fourteen miles north-west of Aurangabad; the place is called Rauzah or Khuldabad (Syed Hossain and C. Willmott, 'Historical Sketch of Nizam's Dominions,' ii. 714).
3. This enthronement took place on the 10th Zu,l Hijjah, 1118 H. (March 15, 1707) (see Khafi Khan, ii. 566). On fol. 341 Manucci himself flays it was on March 15, and not on March 19. For the inscription on the new coin, see the folio just named.

late king, who was at this time close to the Indus river, as soon as he heard of the king's death began a march in all haste, taking his family with him and a strong force. On arrival at Agrah he occupied the city, and was acclaimed by all the people.

Having heard that A'zam Tara was advancing against him, Shah 'Alam wrote him a letter [323] in most courteous terms, intimating that it was their bounden duty to live in peace and amity with each other during the few remaining days of their mortal journey. Both of them were sufficiently advanced in years and he (A'zam Tara) ought to content himself with the provinces that the emperor, their father, had given him. As for himself, he had not the least intention of interfering with him; on the other hand, he claimed to be left undisturbed with what territory he had already.

A'zam Tara was very little satisfied with this suggestion, and answered that he meant to be emperor and uncontrolled master, for which purpose he was marching against him (Shah 'Alam). To this Shah 'Alam replied that he might come if he liked; he would find his nephews ready to receive him, and give him a good account of themselves.[1]

A'zam Tara continued his march, and the two armies met on the very plain where Aurangzeb gave battle to his elder brother Dara. It was close to a stream which is called Schaba (? Chambal), or Dolpur (Dholpur), a distance of twenty leagues from Agrah towards the south. The battle began on June 19 of the same year [1707] by small skirmishes.[2] The next day the fighting was more vigorous, and it grew still more intense towards evening. Two princes, Bedar Bakht, and Beelem Tabach (? Wala Jah), both sons of A'zam Tara, and also a grandson of Shah 'Alam, fell in this action.[3]

Late in the morning of the 21st [June, 1707], A'zam Tara, still

---

1. The correspondence will be found in the 'Jangnamah' of Danishmand Khan, 'Ali, and in other Persian works.
2. The battle began to the north of Jajau, a place about twenty miles south of Agrah, and about thirty miles north of Dholpur, on the 18th Rabi', 1119 H. (June 18, 1707, N.S.) (see Danishmand Khan's 'Jangnamah,' and Kam Raj's ' 'Ibratnamah,' fol. 23).
3. According to the histories, the second prince killed was Wala Jah. I cannot identify Manucci's name for him, nor find any mention of a grandson of Shah 'Alain's being slain. A'zam Shah was shot dead, and did not 'commit suicide.'

very indignant, although he saw he was enveloped by the enemy, did not hesitate to recommence the battle. Great courage was displayed on both sides, and the fight lasted until the evening. The story is told that one hundred and eighty thousand horsemen lay dead, without speaking of the infantry or of the elephants. The people for seven leagues round could recognise what was going on from the dust, the smell of powder, the smoke, and the sparks [324], which rose into the air. It may be asserted that there never was fought in India so memorable a battle. Discerning that he was beaten, and anxious not to fall alive into the hands of the enemy, A'zam Tara plunged a poignard into his breast, and died on the field of battle. Shah 'Alam remained victor. He decided no longer to observe the promises he had made to the Hindu princes who had served him well at this conjuncture. On the contrary, he moved against them with the hostile intention of occupying their territories.

The other prince, Kam Bakhsh, learnt the above news at Bijapur, where he had already sufficiently established his authority. Therefore he quitted that place and made himself master of Gulkandah. He made the governor thereof a prisoner, and caused him to be trodden to death under the feet of an elephant along with twenty-three other officials. He took their women and children, and confiscated their wealth, besides ill-treating the inhabitants and robbing them of any money they possessed. This series of confiscations added greatly to his power, and this again inspired him with the idea of becoming emperor. He thought he could put himself into a state to resist Shah 'Alam, his eldest brother.[1]

When he (Shah 'Alam) was informed of Kam Bakhsh's projects, he made the best peace he could with the Hindu princes, and then began his march early in February, 1708. At the beginning of June he found himself on the Gulkandah frontier, close to a town called Bidar.[2] His whole family accompanied him.

1. On the date of his father's death, Kam Bakhsh had only reached Parendah, seventy or eighty miles from Ahmadnagar (Khafi Khan, ii. 569; Elliot and Dowson, vii. 389). Compare Khafi Khan, ii. 608, for Kam Bakhsh's mad doings.
2. Shah 'Alam's start from Agrah took place on November 12, 1707 (Khafi Khan, ii. 605, and Danishmand Khan, 'Bahadur Shah-namah'). In February, 1708, Shah 'Alam, now become Bahadur Shah,

His army consisted of one hundred and twenty thousand horsemen and two hundred thousand infantry. But the heavy rains having caused the rivers to overflow their banks, he was constrained to stop where he was. Prince Kam Bakhsh left Gulkandah and encamped with his army two leagues from that place. His position was at the foot of a hill, and here he prepared to give battle.

Shah 'Alam wrote to the principal officers in his (Kam Bakhsh's) army, hoping to induce them to desert and join him. By [325] this means he induced many to come over. In the following August, when the rain had ceased, Shah 'Alam sent an envoy to the prince his brother, escorted by one hundred horsemen, and through this agent he made him an offer of three presents. The first was a Quran, to signify the real peace and amity in which he wished to live with him, his own aspirations being towards rest and quiet. The second was a bowl full of gold and silver money; this was meant as a hint that he (Kam Bakhsh) ought to prefer to live quietly at the city of Bijapur, busying himself in the extension of his authority for twelve leagues around it, and avail himself of the permission to coin money in the emperor's name, though still paying him tribute. The third gift was a scimitar, as a sign that, if he refused the other two presents and the offers made through them, but accepted the scimitar instead, war would be declared against him.

The prince decided to rely on the last-named course, and, refusing the two other presents, accepted the scimitar, and announced that he wanted to become emperor and govern in his own name alone. When Shah 'Alam learnt this resolve he began to march, and, by short marches, moved to a territory lying at the edge of the Gulkandah kingdom. It is called Kouir (Kohir);[1] and here he halted.

Meanwhile he set apart a large division from his army, numbering thirty thousand horsemen and fifty thousand infantry, which he placed under the command of his son, Sultan Mu'izz-

---

was in the neighbourhood of Ajmer. He crossed the Narbada on May 17, and he reached Zafarabad Bidar on November 5, 1708.

1. Kohir or Koyer, a town in the Bidar district of the Nizam's territories, fifty-five miles west-north-west of Haidarabad, lat. 17° 38', long. 77° 46' (see map in Syed Hosain's and C. Willmott's 'Sketch,' vol. ii., and Thornton's 'Gazetteer,' 529).

ud-din, with whom was joined General Zu,lfiqar Khan and many other officers of repute. Their orders were to march forward by short stages and locate the position of the prince Kam Bakhsh.

During the interval Shah 'Alam wrote several letters to his brother, praying him not to go to war, but content himself with what he had already, and not run the risk of being killed, like his other brother had been, by putting [326] his fortunes to the doubtful issue of a battle. But Kam Bakhsh turned a deaf ear to this advice, and was firm in wishing to fight.

While this discussion was going on his army was shrinking daily through the numerous desertions of men who espoused the cause of Shah 'Alam. Thus he found himself reduced to a force of four thousand horsemen and eight thousand infantry. This condition of things forced him to retreat on Gulkandah, where he entrenched himself.

The news of his retirement occasioned so great an uproar in that city that he was forced to quit it again and withdraw a distance of three leagues, near a large market town called Daubipench.[1] It is situated on an eminence; and here a few weak entrenchments were constructed.

Sultan Mu'izz-ud-din began his movement, and, ascertaining that his opponent was quite weak, he offered battle on January 15, 1709.[2] The combat was bloody; the horsemen preferred being cut to pieces to surrendering; the infantry made a little resistance under cover of their slight entrenchments. This constrained Prince Mu'izz-ud-din to assault their position with his elephants. They were entirely defeated.

Recognising that he was defeated, Kam Bakhsh withdrew at the head of some of his most faithful servants to a small

1. Major Wolsley Haig, First assistant Resident, has been kind enough to make a search for this place. All his efforts have failed—the place does not seem to exist any longer—and thus it is impossible to rectify the spelling, which may be meant for Dhobi-pet, Dube-pet, or Daribah-pet. But the distorian Danishmand Khan, 'Ali, says this last stand was made at Talab Mir Jumlah. This tank is under the eastern wall of Haidarabad city; but in 1709 there was no wall, and at that period there may have been a Dhobi-pet (washermen's quarter) adjoining the tank. The place is seven miles from Gulkandah as the crow flies, and might well be called three leagues by road.
2. According to the historians, the battle was fought on the 3rd Zu,l Qa'dah, 1120 H. (January 13, 1709, N.S.).

eminence, where he was surrounded. Refusing to surrender, he was mortally wounded by an arrow. He was carried to the prince's (Shah 'Alam's) palace, and the next morning he died. One of his sons, two daughters, his wives, and his whole family, were taken to the palace.

This action was decisive, and gave the crown to Shah 'Alam, and thus rendered him uncontrolled possessor of the Mogul empire. We received this news at Pondicherry on Thursday, January 31, 1709, and it was confirmed by a number of persons from the army who arrived here on February 2 of the same year.

[327] Prince Shah 'Alam has gone off with his army in the direction of Aurangabad.[1] The people who gave me this news were sent me by Ode Khan (?), and they told me he was the man who wounded Prince Kam Bakhsh with an arrow from his bow.

[328] OTHER PAPERS TRANSLATED FROM THE FRENCH BY COMMENDATORE ANDREA CARDEIRA, PUBLIC PROFESSOR.

[Omitted, fols. 328-334, last letter of Aurangzeb to Prince Akbar, and Prince Akbar's answer, having been already given in Part V., fols. 39-50].

[335] OTHER DETACHED LEAVES TRANSLATED FTOM THE PORTUGUESE BY THE ABOVE NAMED.

[Omitted, fols. 335-337, story of the Spanish priest D. Giovanni di Guevara, who came from Manila to Tranquebar, it having been already given in Part. IV., fol. 243*b*.]

[Omitted, fols. 337, 338, story of a Madura Christian family sold at Tranquebar as slaves, it being already given in Part IV., fol. 244.]

[NOTE FROM THE ITALIAN OF CAVALIERE CARDEIRA.

Pages not numbered, without opening sentence or conclusion, inserted in the manuscript at the beginning of part v. Immediately after the letter.][2]

1. Shah 'Alam, Bahadur Shah, reached Aurangabad on June 19, 1709.
2. These passages do not appear in Codex No. CXXXV. as it now exists; they are only found in MS. (Zanetti) No. XLV.

. . . according to the quality of those who receive it. The Christian artillerymen, as also the surgeons, are paid in the same way. All the said soldiers, captains, and generals, whatever their birth or position, are obliged to furnish sureties. Without this they will not be taken into the service. The thing is universal, and no one can complain. Nor is there any ground for complaint, the same rule being observed in the case of princes of the blood royal.

When a trooper's horse dies, he is obliged on the same day to produce the piece of the hide bearing the brand before the officials who are told off for that duty. These men grant the trooper seven days' time for buying another horse. If he fails to buy one within the time his pay is reduced.

The *Bakhshi,* who is the commissary-general of the cavalry, holds reviews of all the cavalry stationed at court twice a year, at which times he examines and passes the horses. If he sees an old horse, or one unfit to gallop, or vicious, he gives the trooper an order at once to buy another within a fixed number of days. All over the kingdom are officials with the same name of *Bakhshi,* who are continuously employed on the same duty.

When his Majesty orders that any general with his regiment, or any captain with his company, should be sent on the march anywhere, it is necessary for that officer to appear on the river bank within sight of the palace windows and parade the whole of his cavalry and infantry. Three days after the inspection he must begin his march.

The soldiers are extremely careful, when passed thus in review, to appear with their full equipment, and to have their arms in the best order, for otherwise they would be discharged on the instant. Usually captains and generals keep in their stables one or two hundred horses, which are used both for show and service. On the day appointed for a parade they mount their servants on these horses; these men are also enrolled as soldiers. But only the true income and pay are received from the prince; and the officers have no other profit from these extra men beyond appearing at the head of some well-clad and excellent horsemen on the day fixed for the parade.

There are throughout the realm officials who look after what I have spoken of. However, those who are distant from the court do not conduct themselves either as loyal subjects or good administrators. They make a profit from the gifts and grants offered to them, and therefore neglect what they ought to do as a matter of duty and obligation. Thus men who ought to maintain, for example, fifty horses or so, do not keep in their stable more than four or eight. What is worse, they entertain not a single soldier, though the neglect is good for their purse. Some of these (? the horses) are marked with brands as above referred to.

Throughout the world the vice is rampant of being ambitious for the acquisition of wealth. But in no part of the world is this so much the case as in the Mogul Empire and the rest of India. There our Italian proverb applies: 'The big fish eat the little ones.' Particularly is it true at the court and in the army of the Mogul, where the captains and generals observe no fixed rules in paying their soldiers, conforming neither to the rank they have granted them nor to the men's merit. The rank the soldiers receive is high in name, but as for the pay, it is never more than half what the rank indicates.

The soldiers accept anything and everything, being forced by necessity; for if they cannot obtain military service, they have no means of living. Speaking generally, all these soldiers are badly paid and ill-satisfied, for what should be given them in eight months they do not receive in a year. What is worst of all, they are never paid the exact amount due, but little by little. Then they always have to take in the course of a year's service two months' pay in second-hand goods. In many cases they are kept two and three years in arrears. This forces the soldiers to borrow money at interest from the traders in the camp; these lend it with the consent of the men's own captains and generals, with whom they then . . .

[The paper ends with this uncompleted sentence.]

END OF VOL. IV.

ADDITIONAL NOTES AND EMENDATIONS

Page 2, paragraph 2: *Complaints against the Jesuits.*—The Capuchin case will be found set out in a small volume of eighty-five pages now in the Archives Nationales, K. 1374, document No. 54. The title-page is 'Questions proposées à la Sacrée Congrégation de la Propagande sur les Cérémonies payennes yue certains Missionaires permettent aux Chrétiens Malabarcs dans les Indes Orientates,' par le R. P. François Marie de Tours, Capuchin, Missionairc aux Indes Orientates (A liège, chez Guillaume Schuppen, rue des Maures, proche la Grande Eglise, M. DCC. IV.). At the foot of the title-page in an eighteenth-century hand are the words: 'Pàru a Paris vers la my-Scptember, 1704.'

Page 4: *Addition to my note on the Patriarch.*—A contemporary account of the Patriarch's acts in China is printed in 'O Chronista de Tissuary,' edited by J.H. da Cun'na Rivara (1866), i., p. 44. The Patriarch arrived at Macao from the Philippines on April 4, 1705, and left Canton for Pekin, September 9, 1705. Sigotti, the surgeon, died at Pekin, December 12. The dispute in China is dealt with by the Rev. R. C. Jenkins, The Jesuits in China' (1894). He takes an unexpectedly favourable view of the Jesuit motives and aims, and lays the burden of the Patriarch's fate on Pope Clement XI. The faults laid to the Pope's charge are: (1) his choice of a young and inexperienced though saintly legate, a man quite ignorant of China, of feeble constitution, and of a somewhat testy temper; (2) his failure, from considerations due to European politics, to put the requisite pressure on the King of Portugal to procure the Patriarch's release.

Page 57, paragraph 1: *Surat.*—The troubles recommenced in July, 1704, under Najabat Khan. Another new governor arrived in July, 1705. See Kaepplin, 533, 534.

Page 60, note 56: *Date of riot.*—The mistake is mine and not Manucci's. September 24, Old Style, corresponds to October 5, New Style, which was moreover, a Sunday.

Page 61, line 20: *Guety.*—There was a Frenchman of the same name, a clockmakcr, in the service of the Emperor of China at this period. See 'Memoric Storiche,' viii., pp. 92-103. He may have been a relation of the Guety at San Thome.

Page 93, line 16: *Cutting off their noses.*—By the kindness of Mr. Williams, Resident, and Mr. J. Rennie, Assistant Resident, in Maisur, I have obtained the following information from the Archadogical officer of that State. In Kanarese works of the seventeenth century there are frequent references to cutting off the nose of an opponent in battle. See *A pratimavira-Charita*, pp. 38, 144, 147; *Chika-deva-raya-bamsavali*, pp. 15, 49, 50, 62, 64, 67. There is a tradition that when Randulha Khan, a Bijapur general, was repulsed from before Srirangapatam, all his men had their noses cut off. I have since found the practice described in a Fort St. George resolution of January, 1679, even to the cutting instrument,

Manucci's 'half-moon of iron' (Wheeler, 'Madras,' i., p. 204). The upper lip was removed along with the nose.

Page 93, line 18: So *active*:—The Archaeological officer is inclined to think that the allusion is to the Bedars, a very active and agile tribe, the members of which used to conceal themselves in the forests and harass travellers on the roads. J. H. Grose, 'A Voyage to the East Indies' (edition 1766), p. 247, speaks about the singular methods of the Maisur troops, and their 'particular dexterity in cutting off noses.' In the Maisur campaign of 1659 against Madura, 'under direct orders of the Raja of Maisur, the invaders had cut off the noses of all their prisoners, and sent them in sacks to Srirangapatam as glorious trophies' (J. H. Nelson, 'Madura,' part iii., p. 139). This campaign was known as 'The Hunt for Noses.' Shortly afterwards a counter-invasion of Maisur was undertaken by Kumara Murtee, younger brother of Tirumala of Madura. This effort was crowned with complete success; the King of Maisur was captured, his nose was cut off, and it was sent to Madura ('Madras District Gazetteers—Trichinopoly', 1907, vol. i., p. 55). An author who wrote sixty years ago, Muhammad Rafi', ''Akhbarat-ul-Hind,' British Museum, Oriental MS., No. 1,726, fol. 522b, declares that to the south of Chinapatan (Madras) was a kingdom once ruled over by Kanti Ram, where an ancient temple exists to whose idol the most acceptable offering is one of men's noses. Hired servants are employed to collect them by attacking travellers. Haidar Nayak (of Maisur) was the Rani's ally, and adopted the cutting of noses as a regular punishment, the mutilated culprits being formed into a regiment by themselves.

Page 98 last line: *Captured English vessel.*—Bouynot arrived at Pondicherry from Calicut January 17, 1705, after taking an English brigantine, which he released in exchange for a draft on Madras for 3,000 *pagodas*. See Kaepplin, 512.

Page 137, note 10: *G. Pelle.*—I am indebted to Monsieur P. Kaeppeln ('Agrege d'Histoire,' Paris) for the following notes from his forthcoming 'La Compagnie des Indes orientales ct François Martin, 1664-1719.' G. Pellé reached Surat as an under-merchant, October 15, 1681, on the President, which had left Port Louis on March 26 in the company of the Blanc Pignon. He left Surat with F. Martin and A. Deslandes on the *St. Louis*, May 1686. After arrival at Pondicherry he was promoted to merchant, and sent to Bengal in August, 1686, where he was placed under Deltor; he and Regnault both sailed in the *St. Joseph*. In 1701, after A. Deslandes. had left Chandarnagar, he became member of Council, and one of the principal men there. He died at Chandarnagar on March 7, 1703.

Page 139, noie 12: *Deslandes.*—Probably we ought to read 'Dulivier' in place of 'Deslandes.'

Page 143, note 18: *The game of pallone.*—'This bat is as noteworthy as the ball. A wooden cylinder, about 8 inches long and 6 inches in diameter, with an outer array of inserted wooden spikes, and an interior cross-grip shaped to the player's hand—such is the arm-piece or *bracciale* (article on 'Pallone, the National Game of Italy,' by J. F. Mather, jun., in the *Century Magazine* for August, 1907, p. 607). The bracciale is figured on p. 611.

Page 144, line 20: *Prostitution* of wives and *daughters.*—Captain Robert Knox, in his 'Ceylon,' edition 1681, p. 92 (or edition, 1817, p. 186), bears out this statement.

Page 150, note 30: *Boissieux.*—J. B. de Boissieux was Military Commandant at Pondicherry from February, 1701, to February, 1709. See Kaepplin, 550, 611.

Page 157, note 33: d' Hardancourt.—C. d' Hardancourt took chare at Chandarnagar in March, 1711, and died there on November 28, 1717 (Kaepplin, 636, 639).

Page 168, line 3 from foot: *Nicolao Rodriguez.*—On pp. 144 and 146, ante, he was styled 'Joao.' See also p. 247 for a 'Brother Nicolo Rodriguez,' who is possibly the same man.

Page 185, note 58: *Begam Jani.*—She died of cancer in the breast from which she had suffered for two years ('Ma,asir-i-'Alamgiri,' p. 494).

Page 185, line 26: *Sipihr Shukoh.*—Sipihr Shukoh, son of Dara Shukoh, and son-in-law of 'Alamgir, died 14 Rabi' II., 1120 H., July 2, 1708, at Dihli, aged sixty-seven (lunar) years ('Tarikh-i-Muhammadi,' 1120 II.).

Page 195, line 19, and note 69: *Mirza Arjanj.*—For a proposed identification, see additional note to Vol. I., p. 312.

Page 1%, line 5 from foot: Chulia.—For a good account of these men, see T. Bowrey, pp. 256, 257.

Page 198, line 12: *Pegu fireworks.*—Captain Hamilton, ('New Account,' 1744, ii., p. 55), who saw these 'rockets,' gives a better description. The carcass, made of a large hollowed tree, was filled with gunpowder and bound round with green buffalo-hide thongs; the tail, sometimes 120 feet long, was a large bamboo. The whole was attached to the branch of a high tree, from which it was discharged.

Page 202, note 78: *Flacourt.*—There were three Flacourts in the French Company's service. The father came to India among the first arrivals, and retired to Europe in 1684, leaving his two sons, Charles and Francois, behind. I am indebted to Dr. Kaepplin for this information. F. de Flacourt was sent from Pondicherry to Bengal, and left the service in 1711 (Kaepplin, p. 636).

Page 204, note 80, second sentence.—Read 'just outside the old Black Town.' See correction to Introduction, p. lxiv. (Additional notes and emendations, Vol. 1).

Page 212, line 4: *They buried the blood.*—'It is a common rule that royal blood may not be shed upon the ground, nor in bleeding should it be allowed to fall' (J. G. Frazer, 'Golden Bough,' second edition, i., p. 354).

Page 218, note 91: *Bouynot.*—His name crops up in 1713 and 1715 as the captor in the China Seas of an English vessel, which he sold at Manila. On its coming to Madras, the original owners claimed it (C. R. Wilson, 'Early Annals,' ii., part i., pp. xlvii, 230, October 10, 1715). This officer is also mentioned several times in the French archives between

1705 and 1715. He died in India about 1714, just as an inquiry into his conduct was commencing. See Kacppiin, 599, 600, 609, 610.

Page 225, paragraphs 1 and 2: *French envoy to Daud Khan.*—Marlin says a Brahman was sent towards the end of 1705, but he does not give his name. Daud Khan had demanded, m July, 1705, the restoration of the *Phenix* to the Dutch and a payment of 100,000 rupees as fine for building a fort without leave (Kaepplin, p. 517).

Page 230, line 20: *A'zam Tara.*—In the description opposite his portrait in O.D. 45, Reserve, there is the following character of this prince: 'It is he whom Aurangzeb caused to be arrested because he suspected him of an intention of taking flight to Bengal. . . . This prince is by nature very choleric, a debauchee, rough and discourteous to everybody, also avaricious.'

Page 242. last line: *tattoo marks.*—Tor a full account of Burmese tattooing, see John Nisbet, 'Burma' (1901). Captain Hamilton, 'New Account' (1744), ii. 48, says the tattooing was conhned to the Burmans.

Page 247, line 15: *Rodriguez* — Perhaps tins is the Rodriguez twice mentioned already, iv, pp. 144, 168.

Pago 248, line 6: *Hindu Rao.*—f or other evidence of his connection with Penukonda, see *ante*, p. 235. note 115, at end.

Page 250, last line: *Fra* Ivo.—Father Ives (or Yves) was for a time pro-vicar at Surat, but was deposed in 1695 in favour of a Jesuit. He died before 1700 (See Archives Nationales, K 1,374, Document No. 43).

Page 256, note 146, at end.—Dr. Ross informs me that he has now presented the manuscript to the India Office Library (January, 1908).

Page 307, note 214: *Eusebius.*—Father Tachard and the other Jesuits prevented François Martin from appointing Father Eusebius chaplain of the *Saint Louis*, but he was allowed to proceed as a passenger. See Kacppiin, 557.

LIST OF AUTHORITIES QUOTED OR REFERRED TO

'Abd-ul-Hamid, Lahori, 'Badshahnamah' ('Bibliotheca Indica'), 2 vols., Calcutta, 1867. 1868.

'Abdullah-bin Yusuf 'Ali, Indian Civil Service, 'Monograph on Silk Fabrics,' Allahabad, 1900.

Abu,l Fazl, 'Allam i, 'Akbarnamah,' translated by H. Beveridge ('Bibliotheca, Indica'), Calcutta, 1897 (in progress).

Abu,l Fazl, 'Allami, 'A,in-i-Akbari,' translated by H. Blochmann and H. S. Jarrett ('Bibliotheca Indica'), 3 vols., 8vo., Calcutta, 1873, 1891, 1894.

Agrah, Archæological Society of, Transactions, 1874-78, 8vo., Agra, 1874-78.

'Agra Catholic Calendar and Directory for 1907,' 'Notes on Jesuit Missions,' by Father Félix, Capuchin, Simla, 1907.

'Ahkam-i-'Alamgiri,' Persian MS., Irvine Collection, No. 252.

Ahmed Khan. Syud, 'Asar-oos-sunnadced,' 8vo., Delhi, 1854.

Airy, O., 'Charles II.,' 1904.

Allen, Grant, 'Evolution of the Idea of God,' 8vo., 1897.

Ahvis, C., article by (see *Orientalist*).

Anand Ram, Mukhlis, 'Chamanistan,' Lakhnau, litho., 1294 H. (1877).

Anderson, John, 'Mandalay to Momien,' 8vo., 1876.

Andrcae, Joannes, 'Conslitutiones dementis Pape Quintiuna,' folio, Venice, 1479.

Andrcae, Joannes, 'Liber Decrctaium folio, 1584.

Angles, Joseph, Valentinus, 'Flores Theologicarum Questionum in Quartum Librum "Sententiarum" Collecti,' 8vo., Leyden, 1587.

O Anglo Lusitano, Bombay, June 2, 1887.

Annuaire Dominicaine for September, 1906.

'Annuario do Arcebispado de Goa,' Nova Goa, 1885.

Anquetil Dupcrron, A. H., 'Essay on Tanjor Rajahs' in 'Recherches sur rinde' (sec Bernouilli).

Anquetil Dupcrron, A. H., 'Zendavesta,' 3 vols, 4to., Paris, 1781.

'Arabian Nights,' translated by R. F. Burton (edition L. C. Smithers), 12 vols., 8vo., 1894-97.

Arvieux, Le Chevalier Laurent d', 'Mémoires,' edited by J. B. Labat, 6 vols., 12mo., Paris, 1735.

'Asiatic Researches,' 4to., Calcutta, 1799.

Asiatic Society of Bengal. Journal of, vol. lxxiii., 1904.

Atkinson, E. T., 'Himalayan Districts of the North-Western Provinces of India,' 3 vols. (vols. x.-xii. of 'Gazetteer of North-Western Provinces'), Allahabad, 1882-86.

Baciardo, Gerolamo, 'Nuova Enciclopedia Italiana,' Torino, 1887.

Baden-Powell, B. H., 'Handbook of the Manufactures and Arts of the Punjab,' Lahor, 1872.

Badger, G. P., translator, 'Imams and Seyyids of Oman,' Hakluyt Society, vol. xliv., 1871.

Bail, Louis, 'Summa Conciliorum Omnium,' 2 vols., folio, Paris, 1701.

Baldæus, P., 'Naauwkeurige Beschryvinge van Malabar en Choromandel,' folio, Amsterdam, 1672.

Baldaius, P., 'Coromandel' in Churchill's 'Voyages,' vol. iii., 1745.

Ball, V., article in *Journal of Asiatic Society of Bengal*, vol. 1., 1881.

Ball, V., editor, Tavernier's Travels in India,' 2 vols., 1889.

Barbosa, Duarte, 'A Description of the Coasts of East Africa and Malabar,' edited by Hon. E. I. Stanley, Hakluyt Society, 1866.

Barenton, Pére Hilaire de, 'Les Capucins de la France,' 8vo., 1903.

Baronius, Cesare, Cardinal, 'Annales Ecclesiastici,' 12 vol., folio, Venice, 1602.

Barr, Lieutenant W., 'Kabul and the Punjab in 1839,' 1844.

Barretto, Francesco (see Cardim, A. F.).

Barros, João de, and D. de Couto, 'Decadas da Asia,' 24 vols., 12mo., Lisbon, 1778-88.

Batavia, 'Dagh Register gehouden int Casteel Batavia,' edited by J. A. van der Chijs and others, 24 vols., 1887-1907.

Bateman, Josiah, 'Life of the Right Rev. D. Wilson,' 2 vols., 1860.

Baulez, M. J., 'Vingt ans dans l'lnde,' 1886.

Baumer, S., translated by R. Biron, 'Histoire du Breviaire,' 2 vol., 8vo., Paris, 1905.

Bayley, Sir E. C., 'History of Gujarat,' 8vo., 1886.

Beale, T. W., 'Miftah-ut-tawarikh,' folio, litho., Lucknow, 1867.

Beale, T. W., 'An Oriental Biographical Dictionary,' edited by H. G. Keene, second edition, 1894.

Bell, Richard, 'Travels,' British Museum, Sloane MSS., No. 811.

Bellarmino, Roberto F. R., Cardinal, 'Disputationes de Controversy Christianæ fidei adversus Hæreticos,' 4 vols., Rome, 1832-38, or Venice, 1599.

Bernier, Francois, 'Histoire de la dernidre Revolution dcs Etats du Grand Mogol,' Paris, 1670, 1674.

Bernier, F., 'Travels,' edited by A. Constable, 8vo., 1891.

Bernouilli, Johann, 'Beschreibung von Hindustan,' 3 vols., 4to., 1785-88.

Bernouilli, J., 'Description de 1'Inde,' 3 vols., 4to., 1786-88.

Berruycr, I. J., 'L'Histoire du Peuple de Dieu,' 18 vols., 8vo., Paris. 1753-54.

Bertrand, J., S. J., 'Mission du Madure,' 4 vols., 8vo., Paris, 1847-54.

Bescherelle, L. N., 'Nouveau Dictionnaire Nationale,' 4 vols., 4to., Paris, 1887.

Beschi, C. J., 'Dictionary of Common Tamil.'

Beveridge, H., (see Abu,I Fazl, 'Allami).

Bhim Sen, 'Nuskbah-i-dilkusha,' British Museum, Oriental MS., No. 23.

'Bibliotheca Meermanniana sive Catalogus ...,' 4 vols., 1824.

'Bibliothèque de l'Ecole des Chartes,' Paris, 1888, vol. xlix.

'Biographic Universelle,' Michaud, 52 vols., 1811-28; Supplément, 33 vols., 1832-62; new edition, 45 vols., 1854-65.

Birch, W. de G., translator, 'Commentaries of the Great Alfonso Dalboquerque,' 4 vols., Hakluyt Society, 1875, 1884.

Birdwood, Sir George, 'Catalogue of the Economic Products of the Presidency of Bombay,' Bombay, 1864.

Bleeck, A. H., 'Avesta,' translated from Spiegel, 8 vo., 1864.

Blochet, E., article in *Gazette des Beaux Arts*, Paris, 1897.

Blochet, E., Tnventaire et Description des Miniatures des MSS. Orientaux dans la Bibliothèque Nationale à Paris,' 1900.

Blochmann, H., translator (see Abu,l Fazl, 'Allami).

Bocarro, Antonio, 'Decada 13 da Historia da India,' Academia Reale das Sciencias de Lisboa, 4to, Lisbon, 1876.

Boehmer, J. H., and Richter, Æ. L., 'Corpus Juris Canonici,' 4to., Leipzig, 1839.

'Bombay Gazetteer': 'Gazetteer of the Bombay Presidency,' 25 vols., Bombay, 1877-86.

Borghesi, G., 'Litlera Scripta da Pondicerri,' translated by G. M. de' Crescimbeni, Rome, 1705.

Boverio, or Boverius, Z., 'Annalium ...,' Lugduni, 2 vols., folio, 1632-39.

Bowrey, Thomas, 'Countries round the Bay of Bengal,' edited by Sir R. C. Temple. Hakluyt Society, Series II., vol. xii., 1905.

Bowring, L. B., 'Haidar Ali and Tipu Sultan' ('Rulers of India' Series), Oxford, 1893.

Bras de Sa (see de Sa).

British Museum, Egerton MSS., No. 1,971.

British Museum, Sloane MSS., No. 811.

British Museum, 'Catalogue of Coins of the Mogul Emperors,' by S. Lane Poole, 1892.

Brown, H. S., 'Handbook to the Ports on the Coast of India,' 'Mangalore, 1897.

Browne, Sir Thomas, 'Works,' edited by S. Wilkin, 4 vols., 1835-36.

Brunus, Conradus, 'Opera Tria Nunc Primum Edita,' folio, Moguntiæ, 1548.

Bullarium—'Magnum Bullarium Romanum,' 19 vols., folio, 1720-58.

'Bullarum Diplomatum et Privilegiorum Sanctorum Romanorum Pontificum Taurinensis Editio,' 4 to.; Turin, 1857, etc.

Burckhardt, J. L., 'Travels in Nubia,' 4to, 1822.

Burgess, James, 'Rock Temples of Elura,' 1897.

Burnes, A., 'Travels in Bokhara,' 3 vols., second edition, 1835.

Burton, R. F., translator, 'Thousand Nights and One Night' (edition Smithers), 12 vols., 8 vo., 1894-97.

Calcutta Review, vol. liii., 1871, quoted by A. Constable.

Caldwell, R., 'The Tinnevelly Shanars,' Madras, 1849.

Caldwell, R., 'Comparative Grammar of the Dravidian Languages,' 1875.

Campbell, Walter, 'My Indian Journal,' 1864.

Campbell, J. M., articles in *Indian Antiquary*, vols., xxix. and xxx.

Capellan, Girolamo Alessandro, 'II campodoglio Venete,' MS. in Biblioteca Nazionale di San Marco at Venice.

Cardim, Antonio Francesco, 'Relation de ce que s'est passé au Japon... au Malabar ...,' 12mo., Paris, 1645-46, translated from the Italian of F. Barretto, S.J.

Carmichael Smyth, W., editor, 'Lata,if-i-Hindi,' 1840.

Carr, M. W., 'Descriptive and Historical Papers relating to the Seven Pagodas,' Madras, 1869.

Carré, —, 'Voyage des Indes Orientales,' 2 vols., 12mo., Paris, 1699.

Carte MSS., vol. cxxx., Bodleian Library, Oxford.

Casanova de Seingalt, J., 'Memoires,' quoted from C. Whibley.

Castellanis, Jacobus, 'Compendium' of Navarrus, Venice, 1598.

Castonnet des Fosses, H., 'L'Inde Français au XVIIIme Siècle,' Paris, no year.

Castonnet des Fosses, H., 'La Boulaye le Gouz, sa Vie et ses Voyages,' 8vo., Angers, 1891.

Castrensis, Franciscus (F. de Castro), 'Constitutes Synodaes do Bispado da Guarda,' 1621, or folio, 1759.

'Catalogus Vicariorum Apostolicarum ... Bombayensi,' third edition, Bombay, 1883.

Catrou, François, 'Histoire G6nerale de l'Empire du Mogol,' 4to., Paris, 1715 (for other editions, see Introduction, xxv.).

'Census of India,' 1901, vol. i.—'India,' part i., Calcutta, 1903.

Cerreto, Stanislao Melchiorrus de (see Waddingius).

Cerri, Urbano, 'Etat present de l'Eglisc Romaine,' Amsterdam, 1716, quoted by Müllbauer, and an English translation of 1715.

'Ceylon Literary Register,' vol. iv., 1889(7).

Ceylon, 'Glossary of Names and Terms in Singhalese and English,' folio, Colombo, 1865.

Challes, Robert, 'Journal d'un Voyage, 1690-91,' 3 vols., Rouen, 1721.

Chance, J. F., M.A., article in *English Historical Review*, vol. xi., 1896.

Chandon, L. M., and Dclandine, F. A., 'Dictionnaire Univcrsel,' 20 vols., 8vo., Paris, 1810-12.

Chardin, Sir John, 'Travels into Persia,' folio, 1691.

Chassagne, A. dc la, and Lcf6vre de Saint Marc, 'Vie de M. Nicolas Pavilion, Evêque d'Aleth,' 3 vols., 12mo., Saint Michel, 1738.

Chijs, J. A., van de (see Batavia).

'O Chronista di Tissuary,' Goa, 1866.

Churchill, A. and J., 'A Collection of Voyages and Travels,' 3 vols., folio, 1744-46.

Cicogna, Emanuele Antonio, 'Inscrizioni Venezianc,' Venice, 1830.

'Civiltâ Catholica, La,' eighth series, 8vo., Firenze, 1871-73.

'Clarendon State Papers in the Bodleian, Calendar of,' 3 vols., Oxford, 1869-76.

Clarke, Sir Caspar P., article in *Journal of Indian* Art, vol. vii., October, 1896.

Clement, Dom, 'Catalogus Manuscriptorum Codicum Colleggi Claromontani,' Paris, 1764.

Clough, Rev. B., 'Singhalese-English Dictionary,' Colombo, 1821.

Cóggiola, Dr. Giulio, 'Sulla nuova integrale publicazione della Storia del Mogol' (Sixth Geographical Congress of Italy, May, 1907), *Tirage à part*, Venice, 1908.

Cokayne, G. E., 'Complete Baronetage' (in progress), Exeter, 1900, etc.

Coles, W., 'Miscellaneous Collections for Cambridge,' vol. xv., British Museum MS., No. 5,816.

Constable, A., 'Hand Atlas of India,' 8vo., 1893.

Cordeiro, Luciano, 'Como se perdeu Ormuz,' Lisbon, 1896.

Coriolanus, F. (Longus). 'Breviarium Chronologicum Pontificum et Conciliorum Omnium,' 7 vols., folio, Rome, 1622, or Leyden, 1633.

Coriolanus, F. (Longus), 'Summa Conciliorum Omnium,' 2 vol., Antwerp, 1623, or Paris. 1639.

Couto, Diogo de, 'Decadas da Asia' (continuation of J. de Barros), 24 vols., 1778-88.

Craesbeeck, Paulo, 'Commentarios do Grande Capitan Ruy Freyre de Andrade,' Lisbon, 1647.

Crente,' Goa, 1887.

Crescimbeni, G. M. (see Borghesi, G.).

Cristofori, F., 'Storia dei Cardinali,' 4to., Rome, 1888.

Crooke, W., 'Tribes and Castes of the North-Western Provinces,' 4 vols., Calcutta, 1896.

Crooke, W., 'Popular Religion and Folk lore of Northern India,' second edition, 2 vols., 1896.

Crook, W., 'Things Indian,' 1906.

Cultru, Prosper, 'Dupleix,' Paris, 1901.

Cunha, J. Gerson da, 'Antiquities of Bassein' (*Journal of Royal Asiatic Society*, Bombay Branch), Bombay, 1874.

Cunha, J. G. da, 'Notes on the History and Antiquities of Chaul and Bassein,' Bombay, 1876.

da Cunha Rivara, J. H., 'Ensaio Historico da Lingua Concani,' 4 to., Nova Goa, 1858.

Dalgado, Monscnhor Sebastião Rodolpho, 'Dialecto Inclo-Pcrtuguese de Goa,' reprint from 'Revista Lusitania,' vol. vi., Porto, 1890.

Dalgado, Monscnhor S. R., 'Dialecto Indo-Portuguêse de Ceylão,' Lisboa, 1900.

Dalton, Colonel, article in *Journal of Asiatic Society of Bengal*, vol. xliii., 1874.

Dalton, Charles, F.R.G.S., 'English Army Lists and Commission Registers, 1661-85,' 1892.

al Damiri, 'Hayat-ul-hayawan,' 2 vols., Bulak, 1868.

Daniell, T. and W., 'Oriental Scenery,' 4 vols., 1795-1807.

Danishmand Khan, A'li, 'Bahadur Shah-namah,' Persian MS., Jones Collection, India Office, No. 10.

Danishmand Khan, 'Ali, 'Jangnamah,' litho, 1297 H. (1880).

Danvers, F. C., 'Portuguese in India,' 2 vols., 8vo., 1894.

Delisle, L., 'Le Cabinet des MSS. de la Bibliothèque Imperiale,' folio, Paris, 1868.

Dellon, C., 'Histoire de I'Inquisition de Goa,' Amsterdam, 1737; first edition is of 1688 (?).
Dellon, C., 'Voyage to the East Indies,' 1698.
Desalles, Adrien, 'Histoire Générale des Antilles,' 5 vol., Paris, 1847-48.
Deslandes, André Daulier, 'Les Beautés de la Perse,' Paris, 1673.
Deslandes, A. F. Boureau, 'Remarques Historiques ... d'un Cosmopolite,' 8vo., 1731.
Deslandes, A. F. Boureau, 'Histoire de Constance, Premier Ministre du Roi de Siam,' 12mo., 1756.
Devi Prasad, Kayath, 'Raja Birbar ka jiwan-charitra,' Dilli, S. 1952 (1895).
'Dictionary of National Biography,' 63 vols., 1885-1900.
Dijk, L. C. D. van, 'Tes Jaren uit het leven van Wemmer van Berchem,' Amsterdam, 1858.
Donovan, Jeremiah, D. D., 'Catechism of the Council of Trent,' 1854.
Dorville, Albertus (see Grueber, J.).
Dow, Alexander, 'History of Hindustan,' 3 vols., 8vo., 1803.
Dowson, John, 'Classical Dictionary of Hindu Mythology,' 1879.
Drake, H. H., 'Hundred of Blackheath' (see Hasted, Edward).
Drew, F., 'Jummoo and Kashmir,' 1875.
Dubois, G., 'Henri de Pardaillan de Gondrin, Archcveque de Sens, 1646-74,' 8vo., Alençon, 1902.
Dubois, Jean Antoine, 'Hindu Manners...,' translated by H. K. Beauchamp, 2 vols., 8vo., Oxford, 1897.
Dubois, Abbé J. A., 'The People of India,' translated from the French, Madras reprint, 1879.
Dubois, J. P. I., 'Vies des Gouvemeurs Généraux,' 4to., La Haye, 1763.
Duchesne, Abbe Louis, 'Christian Worship,' translated by M. L. McClure, London, 1903.
Du Jarric, Pierre, S.J., 'Historic des choses plus memorables advenues tant ez Indes...,' 3 vols., Bordeaux, 1608, 1610, 1614.
Durandus, Gulielmus, Bishop of Mende, 'Rationale Divinorum Ofliciorum,' folio, 1459.
Durandus a S. Porciano, Gulielmus, 'In Sentential Theologicae Petri Lombardi Commentariorum,' Leyden, 1566.
Du Tertre, Dominican, 'Histoire Générale des Ant-Isles,' 4 vols., 4to., 1671.
Dutt, U. C., 'Materia Medica of the Hindus,' Calcutta, 1877.
Earle, J. C., 'Manual of the Lives of the Popes,' London, 1866.
Elliot, H. M., and Dowson, John, 'History of India,' 8 vols., 8vo., 1867-77.
Elliott, Sir Walter, articles on China Pagoda in *Indian Antiquary*, vol. vii., 1878; vol. xv., 1886.
Elphinstone, Mountstuart, 'History of India,' fourth edition, 8vo., 1857.
'Ensaios sobre a Estatistica das possessoes Portuguezas no ultra mar,' ii. serie, 8vo., Lisbon, 1862.
Erskine, W., 'History of India (Baber and Humayun),' 2 vols., 1854.
Esquer, A., 'Essai sur les Castes dans l'Inde,' 8vo., Pondicherry, 1870.
Eusebius, 'Enchiridion,' Rome, 1734.

Eymerich, Nicholas, 'Directorium lnquisitorum,' edited by Francisco Pefia, folio, Venice, 1595.

Fanshawe, H. C. 'Delhi, Past and Present,' 1902.

Fanthorne, J. F., 'Reminiscences of Agra,' second edition, Calcutta, 1895,

Faria y Souza, M. de, 'Asia Portuguesa,' 3 vols., 4to., 1666-75.

Faria y Souza, M. de, 'Portuguese Asia,' translated by J. Stevens, 3 vols., 8vo., 1695.

Farid-ud-din 'Attar, 'Tadhkiratu'l-Awliya,' edited by R. A. Nicholson, 1905.

Fatinelli, G. J., 'Relazione del Viaggio dall' lsola de Teneriff,' 4to., Rome, 1704.

Fausboll, V., 'The Jataka,' edited by, 6 vols., 1896.

Ferguson, D. W., 'Captain Robert Knox,' 8vo., 1896-97.

Fergusson, J., 'Picturesque Illustrations of Ancient Architecture in Hindustan,' London, 1847.

Fergusson, J., 'History of Indian and Eastern Architecture,' 1876.

Flechia, Giovanni (see Marmocchi, F. C.).

Fonseca, J. N. da, 'Historical and Archaeological Sketch of Goa,' 8vo., Bombay, 1878.

Formaleoni, V., 'Compendio della Storia Generale dei Viaggi, opera di M. de la Harpe,' 16 vols. Venice, 1782.

Forrest, G. W., 'Selections from State Papers, Bombay Home Series,' 2 vols., Bombay, 1887.

'Fort St. Gorge Press List of Ancient (MS.) Records,' No. 7 (for 1700-04).

'Fort St. George' (see also India Office).

Forteguerri Nicoló, 'Memoric intorno alle Missione' MS., quoted by Müllbauer.

Foscarini, Doge Marco Nicolo, 'Della Litteratura Veneziana,' Venice, 1854.

Foster, W., B.A., 'The Embassy of Sir Thomas Roe, 1615-19' Hakluyt Society, Series II., 42), 2 vols., 1899.

Foster, W., 'Founding of Fort St. George,' 8vo., 1902.

Foster, W., 'English Factories in India, 1622-23,' 8vo., 1908.

Francklin, W., 'The Reign of Shah Aulum,' 4to., 1798.

Franco, Antonio, S.J., 'Synopsis Annalium Soc. Jesu in Lusitania, 1542-1725,' folio, 1726.

François Marie de Tours, Capucin, 'Questions proposes à la Sacree Congregation de la Propagande. . .,' 85 pp., Liège, 1704 (in Arch. Nat., K. 1,374, No. 54).

Frazer, J. G., Golden Bough,' second edition, 3 vols., 1900.

Fryer, John. 'New Account of East India,' folio, 1698.

Fryer, Dr. John, 'Travels in India' (reprint), 1873.

Fullarton, publisher, 'Gazetteer of the World,' 7 vols., Edinburgh, 1850-56.

Gait, E. A., 'History of Assam,' Calcutta, 1906.

Gardiner, S. R., 'History of Commonwealth,' 3 vols., 1894-1901.

Garrett, John, 'Classical Dictionary of India,' Madras, 1871, 1873.

Geographical Journal, vol. x., 1897.

Gerini, Colonel G. E., in *Journal of Royal Asiatic Society* for 1904.

'Gesta Romanorum,' 2 vols., 1824.

Ghulam Husain, Salim, 'Riyaz-us-salatin' ('Bibliotheca Indica'), Calcutta, 1890.
Ghulam Husain, Salim, 'Riyaz-us-salatin,' translated by Maulavi Abdus Salam M.A. ('Bibliotheca Indica'), Calcutta, 1904.
Ghulam Sarwar, Lahori, 'Khazinat-ul-asfiya,' 2 vols., Kanhpur, 1312 H. (1894).
Gladwin, F., 'Alfaz Udwiyeb,' of Nooreddeen Shcerazy, translated by, 4to., Calcutta, 1793.
Goa, 'Archivo da Relacao de Goa,' edited by Jose Ignacio de Abranches Garcia, Nova Goa, 1872.
Godefroy, Frédéric, 'Dictionnaire de FAncienne Langue Francaise, 9 vols., 1881-98.
Grant-Duff, James, 'History of the Mahrattas' (Bombay reprint), 8vo., Bombay, 1873.
Grose, J. FI., 'A Voyage to the East Indies,' 2 vols., 1766.
Grueber, J., and Dorvillc, A., 'Voyage a la Chine' in M. Thevenot's 'Relations,' folio, Paris, 1663-72.
Guilhermy, Elesban de, S.J., 'Ménologe de la Compagnic de Jésus, Assistance de Portugal,' 2 vols., 4to., Poitiers, 1867-68.
Hadji Khan, M.R.A.S., 'With the Pilgrims to Mecca,' 8vo., 1903.
Hague (MS.), Dutch Archives at, 1659, 1688, 1689, 1690.
Hague (MS), Dutch Colonial Archives, 1705, 1706, 1707.
Hague (MS.), Kolonial Archief, Dicl 1412.
Hague (MS.), Kolonial Archief, Extracten uit de Generals Rcsolutien van Gouverneur-Général en Rade,' Batavia, 1693.
Hamilton, A., 'A New Account of the East Indies,' 2 vols., 1727 or 1748.
Hamy, Alfred, 'Documents pour servir . . . 1540-1773, Paris, 1892.
Harcourt, A., 'Guide to Delhi,' second edition, Meerut, 1870.
'Harleian Miscellany,' vol. i., 4to, 1808.
Harwood, Thomas, 'Alumni Etonenses,' 4to., 1797.
Hasted, Edward, 'History of Kent'; new edition, 'Hundred of Blackheath,' by H. H. Drake, large folio, 1886.
Havart, D., 'Op en Ondergang van Cormandel,' 4to., Amsterdam, 1693.
Hayat Khan, 'Hai,at-i-Afghani,' translated by H. Priestley, Bengal Civil Service, Lahor, 1874.
Haye, J. B. de la, 'Journal du Voyage des Grandes Indes,' 12mo., 1697.
Hazart, Cornelius, S.J., Kercklycke Historic van de Geheele Werelt,' 4 vols., folio, Antwerpe, 1677.
Heber, Bishop R., 'Narrative of a Journey,' fourth edition, 1829.
Hebcr, Mrs. 'Life of Bishop Heber,' 2 vols., 4to., 1830.
Heeres, J. E., 'Corpus Diplomaticum Neerlando-Indicum.' part i. (1596-1650), the Hague, 1907.
Hefele, C. J. von, 'History of the Councils of the Church,' English translation, 5 vols., 1871-96.
Helyot, Pierre, 'Histoire des Ordres Monastiques,' 4to., 1714-19.
d'Herbelot, Barthélémy, 'Bibliothéque Orientale,' folio, 1697.
Herbert, Sir Thomas, Bart., 'Some Years' Travels into Divers Parts,' fourth edition, folio, 1677.

Herklots, G. A., translator, 'Qanoon-e-Islam,' by Jaffur Shurreef, second edition, Madras, 1863.
Hodgson, B. H., 'Essays on Language ... of Nepal,' 1874.
Hossain, Sycd, and Willmott, C., 'Historical and Descriptive Sketch of the Nizam's Dominions,' 2 vols., Bombay, 1884.
Hughes, T. P., 'Dictionary of Islam,' second edition, 1896.
Hume, Martin, 'Spanish Influence on English Literature,' 1905.
Hunter, W. W., 'History of British India,' 2 vols., 1899, 1906.
Huonder, H., S.J., 'Deutsche Jesuiten Missionäre des 17 und 18 Jahrhunderts,' Freiburg, 1899.
Hurgronje, C. Snouck, 'Bilder aus Mekka,' 4to., Leiden, 1889.
Hurter, H., 'Nomenclator Literarius Recentioris Theologiæ Cathol.', 3 vols., 8vo., Œniponte, 1892-95; and vol. iv., 1896.
Ibbetson, D. J. C., 'Panjab Ethnography,' 4to., Calcutta, 1883.
Ibn-el-Beithar, 'Traite des Simples,' translated by N. L. Leclerc, 'Notices et Extraits,' Paris, vols. xxiii., xxv.
al Idrisi, 'Nuzhat-ul-mushtak' (Elliot and Dovvson, i. 92).
'Imperial Gazetteer of Tndia,' 14 vols., 1885-87.
Indian Antiquary, articles by K. Raghunathji on 'Bombay Beggars,' vols. ix-xi., 1880-82.
Indian Antiquary, articles by Sir Walter Elliott, vol. vii., 1878; vol. xv., 1886.
Indian Antiquary for 1890, article by E. Rehatsek.
Indian Antiquary, Bombay, vols. xxix., xxx.
Indian Art, Journal of, article by Sir C. P. Clarke, vol. vii., 1896.
Indian Magazine, May 1903.
India Office (MS.), 'Original Correspondence,' Nos. 2,200, 2,228, 2,238, 2,246, 2,426, 2,455, 2,508, 2,525, 2,534; 3,157, 3,163, 3,185; 3,203; 3.213, 5,658; 5,698; 5,881; 5,886, 6,685; 6,737, 6,790; 6,836; 6,919, and vol. lii.
India Office (MS.), 'Court Book,' vol. xxxviii.
India Office (MS.), 'Factory Records, Miscellaneous.'
India Office (MS.), 'Bombay Letter Book,' No. 12, 1703.
India Office (MS.), 'Calcutta Factory Records,' 1690, 1698, 1699, 1700.
India Office (MS.), 'Fort St. George Letter Books,' vols. ix., x.
India Office (MS.), 'Fort St. George Public Dispatches,' vol. xi.
India Office (MS.), 'Fort St. George Records,' vol. xiv.
India Office (MS.), 'Fort St. George Public Consultations,' vol. xxviii.
India Office (MS.), 'Fort St. George Public Consultations,' Range 239, vol. lxxxiii, 1706.
India Office (MS.), 'Fort St. George Factory Records,' vols. xiii., xxxv., Nos. 20, 30.
India Office (MS.), 'Wills Proved in Mayor's Court, Madras,' vol. lx.
India Office (MS.), 'Hugh Factory Records.'
India Office (MS.), 'Masulipatam Records.'
India Office (MS.), 'Surat Factory Records,' vol. xiii.
India Office (see also 'Fort St. George').

India Office (MS.), transcripts of Portuguese documents, 'Books of the Monsoons' (translations), vol. xvii.

India Office (MS.), transcripts of Portuguese documents, 'Noticias da India' (translations), vols. i., ii.

Ishar Das, Nagar, 'Fatuhat-i-'Alamgiri,' British Museum, Additional MS., No. 23,884.

Jag Jivan Das. 'Muntakhab-ut-tawarikh,' British Museum, Additional MS., No. 26,253.

Jagor, F., 'Travels in the Philippines,' English edition, 1875.

Jahanara Begam, 'Munis-ul-arwah'; C. Rieu, 'Catalogue of Persian MS. in British Museum,' p. 3576.

Jahangir, the Emperor, 'Tuzuk-i-Jahangiri' (Sayyid Ahmad's edition, Aligarh, 1864. or British Museum, Additional MS., No. 26,215).

James, M. R., 'Catalogue of King's College MSS.,' 1895.

de Jancigny, A. P. Dubois, and Raymond, L. A. Xavier, 'Inde' in TUnivcrs Pitloresque,' Paris, 1845.

Jarrett, Colonel (see Abu,l Fazl, 'Allami).

Jayakar, Lieutenant-Colonel, translator, 'Hayat-ul-hayawan,' vol. i., 1906.

Jenkins, R. C., 'The Jesuits in China,' London, 1894.

Jesuits, 'Annual Letter of 1668 from Agrah,' British Museum, Additional MS., No. 8,954.

Jesuits, 'Annual Letter from the Mogor for 1670-78,' British Museum, Additional MS., No. 9,855.

Jesuits, 'La Morale Pratique des Jésuites . ..,' 8 vols., 18mo., 1684-95.

Jesuits, 'Lettres Edifiantes et Curieuses,' 26 vol., 1780-83.

Jesuits, 'Lettres Edifiantes et Curieuses,' edited by M. L. Aime Martin ('Panth6on Litteraire'), 1840.

Joanne, P., 'Dictionnaire Géographique de la France,' folio, Paris, 1888-1905.

Joret, C., 'J. B. Tavernier, Baron d'Aubonne,' 1886.

Jourdain, Isambert, Decrusy, and Taillandier, 'Recueil Général des Anciennes Lois Francaises,' 29 vols., 8vo., Paris, 1822-77.

Jourdain, John, 'Journal, 1608-17,' edited by W. Foster, B.A., Hakluyt Society, 1905.

Justi, Ferdinand, 'Iranisches Namenbuch,' 4to., Freiburg, 1895.

Kaeppelin, Dr. P., Agrégé d'Histoirc, Paris, 'La Compagnie des Indes et Francis Martin, 1664-1719,' Paris, 1908.

Kam Raj, ' 'Ibratnamah,' India Office Library, MS. No. 1,534 (Ethe, 'Catalogue,' p. 146).

Kamwar Khan, 'Tazkirat-us-salatin-i-Chaghatae,' Irvine MS.

Karkaria, R. P., 'The Death of Akbar,' in *Journal of Royal Asiatic Society, Bombay Branch*, vol. xxii., 1906.

Keene, H. G., 'Handbook to Delhi,' Calcutta, 1874.

Keene, H. G., 'Turks in India,' 1879.

Keene, H. G. (see also Beale, T. W.)

Keith Johnston, A., 'General Dictionary of Geography,' 1877.

Kennedy, Lieutenant-Colonel Vans, 'Hindu Mythology,' 4to., 1831.

Kewal Ram, 'Tazkirat-ul-umara,' British Museum, Additional MS., No. 16,703.

Khafi Khan, 'Muntakhab-ul-lubab' ('Bibliotheca Indica'), 8vo., 2 vols., Calcutta, 1874.

'Khatut-i-Shiva Ji,' Royal Asiatic Society's Persian MS., No. 71.

Khushhal Chand, 'Nadir-uz-zamani,' British Museum, Oriental MS., No. 3,288.

Kielmansegg, Erich, Graf, editor, 'Briefe des Herzogs Ernst August zu Braunschweig an Johann Franz Diedrich von Wendt.' 8vo., 1902.

Kircher, A., 'China Illustrata,' Amsterdam, 1667, and French translation, 1670.

Knox, Robert, 'Historical Relation of Ceylon,' folio, 1681.

Kripa Ram, *Diwan*, 'Gulabnamah,' Srinagar (Kashmir), 1875.

Kunos, Dr. Ignaz., 'Sheikh Suleiman Efendi's Chagatae-Osmanli Wörterbuch,' Buda-Pest, 1902.

de Läet, Joannes, 'De Imperio Magni Mogolis sive India Vera,' 1631.

Langlès, L. M., 'Monuments Anciens et Modernes de l'Hindustan,,' 2 vols., folio, Paris, 1821.

La Croze, M. V., 'Histoire du Christianisme des Indes,' 2 vols., 1758.

La Loubere, Simon de, 'Royaume de Siam,' 2 vols., Paris, 1691.

Lane-Poole, Stanley, 'Mohammadan Dynasties,' 8vo., 1894.

Lane-Poole, S., 'Aurangzib' ('Rulers of India' Series), 1893.

Lane-Poole, S., article on Sir W. Norris in 'Dictionary of National Biography..'

Lane-Poole, S., 'Coins of Moghul Emperors in British Museum,' 1892.

Launay, Abbè Adrien, 'Histoire des Missions de l'lnde (Société des Missions Etrangères),' 2 vols., Paris, 1903.

Layman, Paul, S.J. (work not defined).

Lecky, W. E. H., 'History of England in the Eighteenth Century,' 8 vols., 1878-90.

Leclerc, N. L., translator (see Ibn-el-Beithar).

Le Gouz, François de la Boullaye, 'Les Voyages et Observations,' Paris, 1653.

Legrenzi, Angelo, 'II Pellegrino nell' Asia,' Venice, 1705.

Lessing, G. E., 'Nathan der Weise,' Berlin, 1888.

Linschoten, Jan Huygen van, 'Voyage to East Indies,' Hakluyt Society, vols. lxx., Ixxi., 1885.

Lipscomb, George, 'History of Buckingham,' 4 vols., 4to., 1831-47.

Litta, Count Pompeo, 'Famiglie Celebri Italiane,' 10 vols., large folio, Milano, 1819-72.

Littre, Emile, 'Dictionnaire de la Langue Francaise,' 9 parts, 4to., 1863-92.

Lloriente, Juan Antonio, 'Histoire Critique de l'Inquisition d'Espagne,' translated by Alexis Pellier, 4 vols., Paris, 1818.

Lobo, Jeronymo, 'A Voyage to Abyssinia,' from the French of Le Grand, by S. Johnson, 8vo., 1735.

Lockyer, C., 'Account of Trade in India,' 1711.

Longman and Co., publishers, 'Gazetteer of the World,' 8vo., 1895.

Lopes, David, 'Historia dos Portugueses no Malabar,' 8vo., 1898.
Louvet, L. E., 'La Cochin Chine Religieuse,' 2 vols., Paris, 1885.
Lucas, C. P., 'Historical Geography of the Colonies,' vol. ii., 1888.
Lucino, Fra Luigi Maria, Dominican, 'Esame e Difesa del Decreto publicato ... da Monsignor Carlo T. di Tournon ...,' 4to., Venice, 1729.
Luillier, le Sieur, 'Nouveau Voyage aux Grandes Indes,' 16mo., Rotterdam, 1726.
Lyon, C. J., 'Personal History of King Charles II.,' 8vo., 1851.
McCrindle, J. W., 'Ancient India as Described in Classical Literature,' 1901.
Macdonell, A. A., 'History of Sanskrit Literature,' 8vo., 1900.
Mackenzie, G. T., Madras C.S., 'Christianity in Travancore' (in vol. ii., 'Travancore State Manual,' by V. N, Aiyar, B.A.), Trivandrum, 1906.
Maclagan, E. D., 'Jesuit Missions to Akbar,' *Journal of Asiatic Society of Bengal*, vol. lxv., 1896.
Maddison, A. B., 'Lincolnshire Pedigrees,' Harleian Society, vols. 1., li., 1902-1903.
Madras (MS.), 'Fort St. David Factory Records,' vol. i., 1698.
'Madias District Gazetteers—Trichinopoly,' 1907.
'Madras Catholic Directory' for 1867, 1878, 1906, 1907, Madras.
Maffci, G. P., author, edited by C. Cocquelincs, 'Degli Annali di Gregorio XIII.,' 2 vols., Rome, 1742.
MatTeius, J. P., Jesuit, 'Historiarum Indicarum,' Libri XVT., 1589.
Magakh-Theophileants, M., 'Biographical Dictionary of Eminent Men' (in Armenian), Venice, 1839.
Maha Narayan, editor, 'Lata, if-ul-Akbar,' Dihli, 1876.
'Mahavarnsa,' part ii., chaps, xxxix-c., translated by L. C. Wijesinha, Mudaliyar, Colomb, 1889.
S. Mahomed Latif, 'History of Lahore,' 8vo., Lahore, 1892.
S. Mahomed Latif, article on Shah Dulah in *Journal of Royal Asiatic Society*, 1896.
Mamye-Clairac, L. A. de la, 'Histoire de Perse,' 3 vols., Paris, 1750.
Martgclius, 'Bibliotheca Pharmaceutica-Medica,' Coloniae, 1703.
Mannque, Sebastian, 'Itincrario de las Missiones que hizo el padre Fray S.M.,' Roma, 1649.
'Manu,' translated by G. Bubler (see 'Sacred Books of the East,' vol. xxv., Oxford, 1882).
'Manual of the Administration of the Madras Presidency,' 3 vols., folio, Madras, 1885-93.
Margry, Pierre, article on Francois Martin, 'Biographie Universelle,' new edition, vol. xxvii.
Margry, Pierre 'Relations et Mémoires inedits . . . tirés des Archives du Ministdre des Colonies,' Paris, 1867.
Marmocchi, F. C., and Flechia, G., 'Storie delle Indie Orientali,' 2 vols., 4to., Torino, 1862.
Marre, Aristide, 'Grammaire Tagalog,' 8vo., 47 pp., Leiden, 1902.

Martial, 'M. Val. Martialis Epigrammata,' edited by W. M. Lindsay.
Martial, 'Epigrams of Martial translated into English Prose,' Bohn's edition, 1897.
Martin, le Chevalier François, 'Mémoires,' 1664-96 (MS. in Archives Nationales, Paris, Serie T,* 1169).
Martyres, Barth, dos, 'O Catechismo,' small 4to., Lisboa, 1610.
Marucci, Jean, S.J., 'Relation de ce que 'est passe dans les Indes Orientales . . .,' Paris, 1651.
Mason, Rev. F., 'Burmah,' Rangoon, 1860.
Mateer, Rev. S., 'Land of Charity,' 1871.
Mateer, Rev. S., 'Native Life in Travancore,' 1883.
Mater, Andre, 'L'Lglise Catholique: sa Constitution, son Administration 18mo., Paris, 1906.
Mather, J. F., junior, 'Pallone, the National Game of Italy' (*Century Magazine*, August, 1907).
Maurice, T., 'Indian Antiquities,' 7 vols., 1800.
'Médailles sur les Principaux Evénements du Régne de Louis le Grand,' folio, Paris, 1701.
'Memorie Storiche dell' Ementissimo Cardinale di Toumon,' 8 vols., Venice, 1761-62.
Mercurius Politicus for 1655.
Michael is, H., 'A New Dictionary (Portuguese and English),' 2 vols., 1905.
Migne, 'Dictionnaire de Bibliographic Catholique,' Paris, 1867 (vol. xli. of 'Encyclopedic Théologique,' Series HI.).
Miles, Colonel, in 'Selections from Records of Government of India,' Calcutta, 1885.
Mir Khwand, 'Habib-us-siyar,' Bombay edition, 2 vols., 1857.
'Missiones Catholicae. . . . Descriptae, anno 1901,' Rome, 1901.
Modi, Jivanji Jamshedji, 'The Parsees at the Court of Akbar.'
'Monumenta Ordinis Minorum,' Salamanca, 1511.
'Morale Pratique des Jésuites' (see 'Jesuits').
Morelli, Abbé Jacopo, 'Della pubblica Libreria di San Marco,' Venice, 1774.
Moreri, Louis, 'Le Grand Dictionnaire Historique,' new edition, 10 vols., folio, Amsterdam, 1759.
Morier, James J., 'The Adventures of Haji Baba,' 1835.
Moschini, Gianantonio, 'Della Letteratura Veneziana del Secolo XVIII ...,' 4 vols., Venice, 1806.
Muhammad, Mirza, bin Rustam, Birlas, Tazkirah,' India Office Library, MS. No. 50 (Ethé, 'Catalogue,' No. 392).
Muhammad, Mirza, bin Rustam, Birlas, 'Tarikh-i-Muhammadi,' Persian MS., Irvine Collection, and British Museum, Oriental MS., No. 1,824.
Muhammad Husain, Azad, 'Darbar-i-Akbari,' 8vo., pp. 852, Lahor, 1898.
Muhammad Kazim Khan, "Alamgimamah' ('Bibliotheca Indica'), Calcutta, 1868.
Muhammad Khalil, son of Sultan Da.ud Mirza, 'Majma'-ut-tawarikh' (E. Denison Ross M.S., now in India Office Library).

Muhammad Ma'sum, 'Fatuhat-i-'Alamgiri,' India Office Library, MS. No. 533 (Ethe, 'Catalogue,' No. 340).

Muhammad Salih, Kambu, ''Amal-i-Salih,' MS., Irvine Collection.

Muhammad Waris, 'Badshahnamah' (continuation), British Museum, Additional MS., No. 6,556.

Muhsin Fani, 'Dabistan,' translated by D. Shea and A. Troyer (Oriental Translation Fund), 3 vols.. Paris, 1843.

Muir, John, 'Original Sanskrit Texts,' 4 vols., 1858-72.

Müllbauer, Maximilian, 'Geschichte der Katholischen Missionen in Ostindien,' 8vo., Freiburg im Breisgau, 1852.

Mtiller, F. Max, 'India: What can it Teach Us?' 8vo,, 1883.

Musta'id Khan, Muhammad Saqi, 'Ma,asir-i-'Alamgiri,' ('Bibliotheca Indica'), 8vo., Calcutta, 1871.

Navarrus (Martino de Azpilcueta, called), 'Relectiones duæ .. .,' Rome, 1585.

Navarrus (Martino de Azpilcueta, called), 'Consiliorum seu Responsorum, 4to., Venice, 1591, etc.

Nazareth, C. C. de, 'Mitras Lusitanas no Oriente,' part iii., Bombay, 1888.

Neal, J. M., and Webb, B., 'The Symbolism of Churches and Church Ornaments,' Leeds, 1843.

Nelson, J. H., 'The Madura Country,' Madras, 1868.

Nicholson, R. A. (see Farid-ud-din, 'Attar).

Nilles, Nicolaus, 'Kalendarium,' 2 vols., 8vo., CEniponte, 1896-97.

Nisbet, John, Dr. Œc., 'Burma under British Rule,' 2 vols., 8vo., 1901.

Nizami, 'Khamsah,' British Museum, Oriental MS., No. 2,265.

Norbert, Father, Capuchin, 'Mémoires Utiles et Nécessaires,' 12mo., Lucque (Lucca), 1742.

Norbert, Father, Capuchin, 'Mémoires Historiques,' 3 vols., 4to., Besaneon, 1747-52.

Norbert, Father, Capuchin, 'Mémoires Historiques,' 8 vols., 4to., Lisbon, 1766.

North Indian Notes und Queries, Allahabad, November, 1893.

'Notices et Extraits,' vols. xxiii., xxv. (see Ibn-el-Beithar).

'Nouvelle Biographie Générale' (Didot), 46 vols., 1855-66.

Ogilvie, 'English Dictionary,' edited by C. Annandale, 1895.

Olearius, A., 'Reise Beschreibungen,' folio, 1696.

Oldenberg, Hermann, 'Religion des Vedas,' 1894.

Omont, Henri, 'Documents sur la Vente des Manuscrits du Collége de Clermont à Paris,' *Bulletin de la Société de l'Histoire de Paris*, 1891.

Orientalist, edited by W. Goonetilleke, 4to., Bombay, 1884 (article by C. Alwis).

Orleans, Pére P. J. d', 'Vie de Constance,' 1690.

Orme, Robert, 'Historical Fragments,' 8vo., 1782: 4to., 1805.

Orme, Robert, 'Military Transactions,' Madras reprint, 3 vols., 1861.

Ouscley, Sir Gore, 'Biographical Notices of Persian Poets' (Oriental Translation Fund), 1846.

Ovington, J., 'Voyage to Suratt,' 1696.

Padfield, J. E., 'The Hindu at Home,' Madras, 1896.

Pall Mall Magazine, September, 1905.

Paris, Archives Nationals, MS., Série T*, 1169.

Paris, Archives Nationales, MS. No. K. 1,374, Documents 34-43, 51-55.

Paris, Archives Nationales (Marine), 'Campagnes,' Registers B^4 25, B^4 26.

Paris, Bibliothéque Nationale, Cabinet des Estampes, O.D., No. 45 (*reserve*).

Paris, Bibliothèque Nationale, MS. Francais, No. 6,231, 'Mémoire sur la Compagnie des Indes Orientates.'

Paris, Bibliothèque Nationale, MS. Français, No. 8,971, note by Pilavoine on l'Abbe Guyon's 'Histoire.'

Paris, Bibliotheque Nationale, MS. Français, No. 27,462.

Paris, Bibliothèque Nationale, 'Nouveau d'Hozier,' 61, 64, MS. Francais, No. 31,286; *ibid.*, 122, MS. Francais, No. 30,351.

Paris, Bibliothèque Nationale, Nouvelles Acquisitions Francises, MSS. Nos. 9,346, 9,352.

Paris, Archives du Ministère des Colonies, Registers C^2 63-66.

Paris, Archives du Ministère des Colonies, 'Correspondance Gènèrale, C^2 II., 67-69.

Paris, Archives du Ministère des Colonies, MS. 'Etat Civil de Pondicherry, 1705.

Paris, *Gazette des Beaux Arts*, 1897, article by E. Blochet.

Paris, *Revue des Bibliothèques*, 1899, 1900, articles by E. Blochet.

Parkes, Fanny, 'Wanderings of a Pilgrim,' 2 vols., 1850.

Pavet de Courteille, A., 'Mémoires de Baber,' 2 vols., Paris, 1871.

Pavel de Courteille, A., 'Dictionnaire Turk Oriental,' 8vo., Paris, 1870.

Pavie, Théodore, 'Tarikh-i-Asham, traduit de l'Hindoustani,' Paris, 1845.

Pellier, Alexis (see Lloriente, J. A.).

Peña, Franciscus (see Eymerich, N.).

Penny, Mrs. 'Fort St. George,' 8vo., 1900.

Penny, the Rev. F., 'Church in Madras,' 1904.

d'Penta, G. F., 'Folklore in Salsette,' *Indian Antiquary*, xx., 1891.

Percival, Rev. P., 'Tamil-English Dictionary,' 8vo., Madras, 1861, or second edition, 4to, 1870.

Pererius, Benedictus, S.J., 'Commentariorum in Danielem Prophetam Libri

Sexdecim,' folio, Rome, 1587.

Pessoa, Joao Chrystomo d'Amorim, 'Obras,' Lisboa, 1887.

Pharaoh and Co., 'Gazetteer of Southern India' and 'Atlas,' Madras, 1855.

Phayre, Sir A. P., 'History of Burma,' 8vo., 1883.

Philipps, Jenkin T., 'An Account of the Religion . . . of Malabar . . . 12mo., 1717.

Phillipps, Sir Thomas, 'Catalogues Librorum Manuscriptorum . . . ab anno 1824 ad 1837' (privately printed).

Pilavoine, —, 'Notes Critiques sur l'Histoire . . . de M. l'abbé de Guyon,' Paris, Bibliothéque Nationale, MS. No. 8,971.

Platts, John T., 'Urdu, Hindi, and English Dictionary,' 8vo., 1884.

Platzweg, S. J., 'Lebensbild deutscher Jesuiten,' 1882.

Plowden, Captain T. C., translator, 'Kalid-i-Afghani,' Lahor, 1875.

'Pondicherry Dictionary, Tamil and French.'

'Pontificale Romanum Clementis VIII. ac Urbani VIII.,' Rome, 1868.

Priestly, H., Benagl Civil Service, translator (see Hayat Khan).

Pringle, A. T., 'The Diary and Consultation Book of Fort St. George,. 1682-85,' Madras, 1894-95.

Puini, Carlo, 'II Tibet' (from MS. of Ippolito Desideri, S.J., 1715-21), Rome, 1904.

Purshoram Vishram Mawjee, 'Shiva Ji's Swarajya' (Bombay Branch of the Royal Asiatic Society, December 17, 1903).

Pyrard de Laval, François, 'Voyage to the East Indies,' edited by A. Gray and H. C. P. Bell (Hakluyt Society), 2 vols., 8vo., 1887-90.

Rabbath, A., S.J., 'Documents Inedits,' vol. i., Paris, 1907.

Raghunathji, K., 'Bombay Beggars' in *Indian Antiquary*, vols. ix.-xi., Bombay, 1880-82.

Raphael du Mans, Capuchin, 'Estat de la Perse en 1660,' edited by C. Schefer, Paris, 1890.

Raulinus (J. F. Raulin), 'Historia Ecclesiæ Malabaricae' (quoted by Mullbauer), 4to., Rome, 1745.

Raverty, H. G., 'Notes on Afghanistan,' 4 parts (foolscap), 1880-83.

Rawlinson, G., 'The History of Herodotus,' 4 vols., 1858-62.

Record Office, 'Calendar of State Papers (Domestic), Charles II.,' vol. xvii

Redi, Francesco 'Etimologie Italiane' in 'Opere,' Napoli, 1778.

Rehatsek, E., article in *Indian Antiquary* for 1890.

Renevier, L., 'Notice sur l'origine de la Chapelle . . . à Villenour,' Pondicherry, 1877.

Ribeiro, J., 'History of Ceilao,' translated by P. E. Pieris, part ii., Galle (no date); or French edition of J. Le Grand, Amsterdam, 1701.

Richardson, John, 'Dictionary, Persian, Arabic, and English,' edited by F. Johnson, 4to., 1829.

Richter, Æ. L., editor, 'Corpus Juris Canonici,' Leipzig, 1839.

Rieu, Charles, 'Catalogue of the Persian MSS. in the British Museum,' 3 vols. and Supplement, 4to., 1879-95.

'Rituale Romanorum Pauli V. Pontifices Maximi jussu editum,' Mechlinr 1872.

Roe, Sir Thomas (see Foster, W.).

Roger, Abraham, 'La Porte Ouverte,' 4to., Amsterdam, 1670, or a German edition, 12mo., Ntirnberg, 1663.

Roquette, J. I., 'Dict. Portugais-français,' Paris, 1841.

Rose, Valentin, 'Die Meerman Handschriften des Sir Thomas Phillippsr (vol. i. of 'Verzeichniss der Lateinischen Handschriften,' Berlin, 1893).

Ross. Colonel E. C., 'Annals of Oman,' Calcutta, 1874.

Rottler, J. P., 'Tamil-English Dictionary,' 4to., 4 parts, Madras, 1834-41.

Royal Asiatic Society, Journal of, for 1904.

Rui Freire de Andrada, 'Commentarios' (see Craesbeeck, Paulo).

'Ruqa'at-i-'Alamgiri' ('Alamgir's letters), British Museum, Additional MS.,. No. 18,881.

'Ruqa'at-i-'Alamgiri,' India Office Library, Persian MS., No. 1,344.

de Sa, Jose Manuel Bras, 'O Apostolo das Indias S. Francisco Xavier,' 8vo., Nova Goa, 1878.

Sachau, C. E., and Ethé, H., 'Catalogue of Persian MSS. in the Bodleian Library, Oxford,' 4to., 1889.

'Sacred Books of the East,' vol. xxv. ('Manu,' translated by G. Buhler), 1886.

Sadiq Khan, 'Tarikh-i-Shahjahan,' British Museum, Oriental MS., No. 174.

San Bartolomeo, Fra Paolo da, 'Voyage to the East Indies,' translated by W. Johnston, 8vo., 1800.

Sanbenedetti, Benedetto, 'Annali dell' ordine de' Frati Minori Cappuccini,' Venice, 1643.

S. Filippo, P. Amat di, 'Studi sulla Storia della Geografia in Italia,' second edition, 2 vols., Rome, 1882.

Sainte Anne, Berthold Ignace de, Carmelite, 'Mission de Perse,' Bruxelles, 1885.

Sandeus, F. M., Ferrariensis, 'De Oflicio et Potestate Judicis Delegati,' folio, Milan? (no date, 1490?).

Sandeus, F. M. Ferrariensis, 'Consilia seu Responsa,' 4to., Venice, 1574.

Sanson, Nicolas, Map of India in 'L'Asie,' 4to., Paris, 1652.

Sarkar, Jadunath, 'India of Aurangzeb,' Calcutta 1901.

Schefer, C. (see Raphael du Mans).

Schlimmer, J. L., 'Terminologie Pharmaceutique Française-persane,' litho., Tihran, 1874.

Schmidt, Richard, 'Beiträge zur Indischen Erotik,' Leipzig, 1902.

Schouten, Wouter, 'Oost Indische Voyagie) 1676.

Schulze, A., 'Die Romanische Meerman Handschriften der Sir Thomas Phillipps,' 4to., Berlin, 1892.

Schwabe, J. J., 'Allgemeine Flistoire der Reisen,' 1747.

Schweitzer, Federico, 'Serie delle Monete . . . di Venezia,' 2 vols., 8vo., Trieste, 1852.

Scott, Eva, 'The King in Exile,' 8vo., 1905.

Scott, Jonathan, 'History of Dekkan,' 2 vols., 4to., Shrewsbury, 1794.

Sewell, R., 'A Forgotten Empire (Vijayanagar),' 1900.

Shahab-ud-din, Talish, 'Fathiyah-i-'Ibratiyah,' British Museum, Additional MS., No. 25,422.

Shahnawaz Khan, Mir Ghulam 'Ali, Azad, and 'Abd-ul-hai Khan, 'Ma,asir-ul-Umarạ' ('Bibliotheca Indica'), 3 vols., Calcutta, 1888, 1890, 1891.

Sharaf-ud-din 'Ali, 'Zafarnamah,' Persian text ('Bibliotheca Indica'), Calcutta, 1887-88.

Sharaf-ud-din 'Ali, 'Zafarnamah,' translated by Petis de la Croix, English edition, 2 vols., 1723.

Shea, D., and Troyer, A., translators, 'Dabistan' (Oriental Translation Fund), 3 vols., 1843.

Shungoonny Menon, P., 'History of Travancore,' Madras, 1878.

Sleeman, W. H., 'Rambles and Recollections,' 2 vols., 1844.

Smith, Sydney F., S.J., articles on the 'Bull of the Crusade' in the *Month*, February and March, 1904.

Smith, V. A., 'Early History of India,' 1904.

Sommervogel, Carlos, S.J., 'Bibliographic de la Compagnie de Jesus, 9 vols., 4to., 1890-1900.

Sottas, Dr. Jules, 'Histoire de la Compagnie Royale des lndes Orientales, 1664-1719,' Paris, 1905.

Sousa, Francisco de, S.J., 'Oriente Conquistado,' folio, Lisbon, 1710. de Souza, C. F., 'Estudos historico-archcologicos . . . no Oriente,' 8vo., Bombay, 1890.

Southey, R., 'Commonplace Book,' series 1 to 4, edited by J. W. Warter, 4 vols., 8vo., 1849-51.

Southey, Commander Thomas, 'Chronological History of the West Indies,' 3 vols., 1827.

Steingass, F., 'Persian-English Dictionary,' 1892.

Stephen, Carr, 'Archaeology of Dehli,' 8vo., Ludhiana, 1876.

Stevens, John, 'New Collection of Voyages and Travels' (P. Teixeira), 2 vols., 4to., 1711.

Stewart, Charles, 'History of Bengal,' 4to., 1813.

Stewart, Charles, translator, 'Tezkereh-al-Vakiat of Jauhar Aftabchi' (Oriental Translation Fund), 4to., 1832.

Stiffe, Captain A. W., article on Masqat, *Geographical Journal*, 1897.

Stoecklein, Joseph, S.J., 'Der neue Welt-bott,' 4 vols., folio, Augsburg, etc., 1728-55.

Suarez, F., S.J., 'Defensio fidei Catholicae adversus Anglicanae Seclae Errores,' 1613 ('Opera,' 25 vols., 1856-61, vol. xxiv.).

Swinton, R. B., 'An Indian Tale or Two,' Blackheath (no date).

Symson, Captain, 'Voyage to East India,' 12mo., 1715.

Tanner, Adam, S.J., 'Disputationum Theologicarum . . . Libri Quatuor,' 2 vols., Ingolstadi, 1618.

Tavernier, J. B. 'Les Six Voyages,' 1692, or 2 vols., 4to., 1676.

Tavernier, J. B., 'Recueil de plusieurs Relations,' 4t., Paris, 1679.

Tavernier, J. B., 'Travels,' English edition, folio, 1677 or 1678.

Tavernier, J. B., 'Travels in India,' edited by V. Ball, 2 vols., 8vo., 1889.

Tawney, C. H., M.A., translator, 'Katha Sarit Sagara; or Ocean of the Streams of Story,' 2 vols., Calcutta, 1884.

Teixeira, P., 'Travels,' edited by W. Sinclair and D. W. Ferguson, Hakluyt Society, 1902.

Tennent, Sir J. E., 'The Wild Elephant ... in Ceylon,' 1867.

Ter-Yovhaneants, Y. Th., 'History of New Julpha in Ispahan' (in Armenian), New Julpha, 1880.

Terry, E., 'Voyage to East India,' 1655.

Terry, E., 'Voyage to East India' (reprint of original edition of 1655), 1777.

Theal, G. M., 'Beginnings of South African History, 1902.

Thevenot, Jean de, 'Voyages,' 5 vols., 8vo., 1727.

Thevenot, Melchisedec, 'Relations de divers Voyages Curicux,' folio,. Paris, 1696.

Thevenot, Melchisedec, 'Recueil de Voyages,' 12mo., Paris, 1681.

Thomas, Edward, 'Chronicles of the Pathan Kings of Delhi,' 1871.

Thornton, Edward, 'Gazetteer of the Territories under the Government of the East India Company,' new edition, 8vo., 1862.

Thurston, E., 'Ethnographic Notes on Southern India,' Madras, 1906 Tieffentailer, Joseph, S.J. (see Bernouilli).

Tiele, P. H., 'Mémoires Bibliographiques sur les Journaux des Navigateurs Néerlandais,' 8vo., Amsterdam, 1867.

Tiepolo, Lorenzo, 'Relazione della sua Ambasciate a Luigi XIV. di Francia' (MS. in Biblioteca Nazionale di San Marco, Venice).

Tod, James, 'Annals of Rajasthan' (reprint), 2 vols., 8vo., Calcutta, 1894. Todeschi, V., 'Manuel du Droit Canonique,' Paris, 1880.

Tomaschek, Wilhelm, 'Die Topographischen Capitel des Indischen Seespiegels Mohlt,' folio, Vienna, 1897.

Tosi (or Tossi), l'Abate, 'Dell' India Orientale Descrittione,' 2 vols., Rome, 1669.

Tostatus, Alphonsus, Abulensis, 'Opera Omnia,' 27 vols., folio, Venice, 1728. Trent, Council of, 'Canones et Decreta Sacrosancti Œcumenici Concilii; Tridentini,' 8vo., Rome, 1845.

Tylor,, E. B., 'Primitive Culture,' 2 vols., 1891, and second edition, 1893. Valentijn, F., 'Oud en Nieuw Oost-Indien,' 5 vols., folio, Dordrecht, 1724. de la Valle, Pietro, 'Les Famcux Voyages,' 4 vols., 1663-64.

Vasquez, Gabriele, S.J., 'Commentarium ac Disputationum in Tertiam Partem Sancti Thomas,' Leyden, 1631.

Venice, State Archives (MS.), 'Despatches of L. Tiepolo, Ambassador to France, 1704-1708.'

Venice, State Archives, 'Senato Terra,' vol. 254, folio 39, March 26, 1707.

Venice, State Archives, Senato I., Secreta, Filza No. 203, Francia, May 1. 1705, to May 28, 1706 (Despatches Nos. 301 and 305 of L. Tiepolo, February 19 and March 5, 1706).

Venice, State Archives, Senato I., Secreta, Filza No. 204, Francia, 1706-7 (Despatch No. 338 of L. Tiepolo, June 25, 1706).

Venice, State Archives, Senato I., Secreta, Registro No. 83 (1706), folios 7, 17, 122, and 131; decrees of March 6, March 20, July 10, July 24, 1706.

Venice, State Archives, Scrittura dei RilTormatori, Filza No. 5, March 23, April 7, April 19, April 27, 1707; January 4, 1708 (letter to Cardeira); March 29, 1708.

Venice, State Archives, Scrittura dei Rifformatori, Filza No. 7, June 23, 1712 (Decree 'in Pregadi' [Senate], with report of Rifformatori and letter of Zambelli), Decree of Senate, January 19, 1713.

Vincenzo Maria, P., 'II viaggio all' Indie Orientale,' folio, Roma, 1671.

'Vishnu Purana,' translated by H. H. Wilson and edited by Fitzedward Hall, 'Works of H. H. Wilson,' vols. vi.-x., 1862-77.

Waddell, L. A., 'Buddhism of Tibet or Lamaism,' 8vo., 1895.

Waddingius (Wadding), Lucas, 'Annales Minorum . . . continuata P. F. Stanislao Melchiorras de Cerreto,' Ancona, 1844.

Wali Quli, 'Qisas-ul-khaqan,' British Museum, Additional MS., No. 7,656. Ward, Rev. W., 'View of History ... of Hindus,' fifth edition, 1 vol., Madras, 1863.

Waterworth, J., The Canons and Decrees of the Council of Trent,' London, 1848.

Watt, George, 'Dictionary of Economic Products of India,' 9 vols., 1889-93.

Weber, Albert, 'Life of Father Adam Schall von Bell, S.J..,' Schaffhausen, 1781.

Weber, Henry, 'La Compagnie Française des Indes, 1604-1875,' Paris, 1904.

Wetzer, H. J., and Welte, B., 'Kirchenlexicon,' second edition, 12 vols., Freiburg, 1882-1901, or the French translation, 'Dictionnaire Encyclopédique de la Théologie Catholique,' third edition, 26 vols., 1869-70.

Wheeler, J. T., 'Madras in the Olden Time,' 3 vols., Madras, 1861-62.

Wheeler, J. T., 'History of India,' vol. iv., 1876.

Whibley, C., article by Macmillan's Magazine, February, 1903.

Wijesinha, L. C. (see 'Mahavamsa').

Wilkins, William Joseph, 'Hindu Mythology,' second edition, 8vo., 1901.

Wilks, M., 'Historical Sketches of the South of India,' 3 vols., 4to., 1810-17.

Williams, Monier, 'Indian Wisdom,' 1875.

Williams, Monier, 'Sanskrit Dictionary,' new edition, 4to., 1899.

Williams, Monier, 'Brahmanism and Hinduism,' third edition, 1887.

Willson, Beckles, 'Ledger and Sword,' 2 vols., 1903.

Wilson, H. H., 'Glossary of Indian Judicial and Revenue Terms,' 4to., 1855.

Wilson, C. R., 'Early Annals of English in Bengal (Surman Embassy),' vol. ii., part ii. (unpublished).

Winslow, Rev. M., 'Tamil Dictionary,' 4to., Madras, 1862.

Wolfe-Murray, Colonel J., 'Dictionary of the Pathan Tribes,' Calcutta, 1899.

Yahya Khan, 'Tazkirat-ul-muluk,' India Office, MS. No. 1,147 (Ethé, No. 409).

Yule, Sir H., 'Diary of W. Hedges,' Hakluyt Society, 3 vols., 1887-89.

Yule, Sir H., 'Book of Marco Polo,' second edition, 2 vols., 1875.

Yule, Sir H., 'Book of Marco Polo,' third edition (by H. Cordier), 8vo., 1903.

Yule, H., and Burnell, H. C, 'Hobson-Jobson: a Glossary,' second edition (by W.,Crooke), 8vo., 1903.

Zachariæ, Theodor, 'Zur Indischen Witwenverbrennung' in *Zeitshrift des Vereins für Volkskunde in Berlin*, 1904, 1905.

Zachariæ, T., 'Zur Geschichtevom weisen Haikar' in *Zeitschrift des Vereins für Volkskunde in Berlin*, Heft ii., 1907.

Zanetti, Antonio Maria, 'Latina et Italica D. Marci Bibliotheca Codicum Manuscriptorum,' etc., folio, Venice, 1741.

Zeitschrift des Vereins für Volkskunde in Berlin, 1904, 1905, 1907.

Zibaldone (MS.), 'Notice on Manucci's Parentage,' Biblioteca di San Marco, Venice, Italian MSS., Class VII., No. 2,321.

Ziegenbalg, B., 'Genealogie der Malabarischen Gotter,' Madras; 1867.

Zulali of Khwansar, 'Ayaz wa Mahmud,' British Museum, Oriental MS., No. 350.

NOTE

The present edition is a verbatim reprint of the book first published in the year 1907. During this long period there has been considerable change in the art of typography and as such it has not been possible to reproduce this book keeping page to page of the original edition. Accordingly for the convenience of the readers a chart showing the page numbers of the original edition and the corresponding page numbers of the present reprinted edition is given below.

The Index portion of the book has been printed keeping all the reference page numbers of the original edition. This has been done at the request of many of our readers who have got some of the volumes in original edition. Accordingly, the readers when referring to index, arc requested to find out the corresponding page numbers and footnote numbers under reference of this edition from the following chart.

Vol. I

For v *see* v
„ vi *see* v, vi
„ vii *see* vi, vii
„ viii *see* vii, viii
„ ix *see* viii, ix
„ x *see* ix, x
„ xi *see* x, xi
„ xii *see* xi
„ xvii *see* xvii
„ xviii *see* xvii, xviii
„ xix *see* xviii, xix
„ xx, *n.* 1 *see* xix, xx, *n.* 1
„ xxi *see* xx, xxi
„ xxii *see* xxi, xxii
„ xxiii *see* xxii, xxiii
„ xxiv *see* xxiii, xiv
„ xxv *see* xxiv, xxv
„ xxvi *see* xxv, xxvi
„ xxvii *see* xxvi, xxvii
„ xxviii, *n.* 1 *see* xxvii, xxviii, *n.* 2
„ xxix, *n.* 1, 2 *see* xxviii, xxix, *n.* 3, 4
„ xxx *see* xxix, xxx
„ xxxi *see* xxx, xxxi
„ xxxii, *n.* 1, 2 *see* xxxi, xxxii, *n.* 5, 6
„ xxxiii, *n.* 1 *see* xxxii, xxxiii, *n.* 7
„ xxxiv, *n.* 1, 2 *see* xxxiii, xxxiv, *n.* 8, 9
„ xxxv *see* xxxiv, xxxv
„ xxxvi, *n.* 1, 2, 3 *see* xxxv, xxxvi, *n.* 10,,12

For xxxvii, *n.* 1 *see* xxxvi, xxxvii, *n.* 13
„ xxxviii *see* xxxvii, xxxviii
„ xxxix, *n.* 1 *see* xxxviii, xxxix, *n.* 14
„ xl *see* xxxix, xl
„ xli *see* xl, xli
„ xlii *see* xli, xlii
„ xliii *see* xlii
„ xliv *see* xlii, xliii
„ xlv *see* xliii, xliv
„ xlvi, it. 1 *see* xliv, xlv, *n.* 15
„ xlvii *see* xlv, xlvi
„ xlviii, *n.* 1 *see*. xlvi. xlvii, *n.* 16
„ xlix *see* xlvii, xlviii
„ 1 *see* xlviii, xlix
„ li *see* xlix, 1
„ lii *see* 1, li
„ liii *see* li, lii
„ liv *see* lii, liii
„ lv *see* liii, liv
„ lvi *see* liv, lv
„ lvii, rt. 1, 2 *see* lv, lvi, it. 17, 18
„ lviii *see* lvi, lvii
„ lix *see* lvii, lviii
„ lx, *n.* 1 *see* lviii, lix, it. 19
„ lxi, rt. 1 *see* lix, lx, *n.* 20
„ lxii, rt. 1 *see* lx, lxi, *n.* 21
„ lxiii, it. 1 *see* lxi, lxii, rt. 22
„ llxiv *see* lxii, lxiii
„ lxv, *n.* 1 *see* lxiii, lxiv. *n.* 23

For 92 *see* 91, 92
,, 93 *see* 93
,, 94 *see* 93, 94
,, 95, *n.* 1, 2 *see* 94, 95, *n.* 1, 2
,, 96, *n.* 1, 2 *see* 95, 96, *n.* 3, 4
,, 97, *n.* 1 *see* 97, *n.* 1
,, 98, *n.* 1, 2 *see* 97, 98, *n.* 2, 3
,, 99 *see* 98, 99
,, 100 *see* 99, 100
,, 101, *n.* 1 *see* 100, 101, *n.* 4
,, 102, *n.* 1 *see* 101, 102, *n.* 5
,, 103 *see* 102, 103
,, 104 *see* 103, 104
,, 105, *n.* 1 *see* 104, 105, *n.* 6
,, 106, *n.* 1 *see* 105, 106, *n.* 7
,, 107 *see* 106, 107
,, 108, *n.* 1 *see* 107, 108, *n.* 8
,, 109, *n.* 1, 2 *see* 108, 109, *n.* 9, 10
,, 110, *n.* 1 *see* 109, 110, *n.* 11
,, 111, *n.* 1 *see* 110, 111, *n.* 12
,, 112 *see* 111, 112 113 *see* 112
,, 114, *n.* 1 *see* 113, *n.* 13
,, 115, *n.* 1 *see* 113, 114, it. 14
,, 116 *see* 114, 115
,, 117, *n.* 1. 2, 3 *see* 115, 116, *n.* 15, 16, 17
,, 118, *n.* 1 *see* 116,117, *n.* 18
,, 119, *n.* 1 *see* 117,118, 11. 19
,, 120, *n.* 1 *see* 118.119, 11. 20
,, 121, *n.* 1 *see* 119,120, 11. 21
,, 122 *see* 120, 121
,, 123 *see* 121, 122
,, 124, *n.* 1 *see* 122, 123, *n.* 22
,, 125 *see* 123, 124
,, 126 *see* 124. 125
,, 127 *see* 125, 126
,, 128 *see* 126
,, 129 *see* 126, 127
,, 130, *n.* 1 *see* 127, 128, *n.* 23
,, 131, *n.* 1 *see* 128, 129, *n.* 24
,, 132, *n.* 1 *see* 129, 130, *n.* 25
,, 133 *see* 130, 131
,, 134 *see* 131, 132
,, 135 *see* 132, 133
,, 136 *see* 133, 134
,, 137 *see* 134, 135
,, 138, *n.* 1 *see* 135, 136, *n.* 26
,, 139 *see* 136, 137
,, 140 *see* 137
,, 141, *n.* 1 *see* 137, 138. *n.* 27
,, 142. *n.* 1, 2, 3 *see* 138, 139, ii. 28. 29, 30
,, 143, *n.* 1 *see* 139, 140. *n.* 31
,, 144 *see* 140, 141
,, 145 *see* 141, 142
,, 146 *see* 142, 143

For 147 *see* 143, 144
,, 148 *see* 144, 145
,, 149, *n.* 1 *see* 145, 146, *n.* 32
,, 150 *see* 146, 147
,, 151, *n.* 1 *see* 147, 148, *n.* 33
,, 152, *n.* 1, 2 *see* 148, 149. *n.* 34, 35
,, 153. *n.* 1, 2, 3 *see* 149, 150, *n.* 36, 37, 38
,, 154, *n.* 1, 2 *see* 150, 151, *n.* 39, 40
,, 155 *see* 151
,, 156 *see* 151, 152
,, 157 *see* 152, 153
,, 158 *see* 153, 154
,, 159, *n.* 1 *see* 154, 155, *n.* 41
,, 160 *see* 155, 156
,, 161, *n.* 1 *see* 156, 157, *n.* 42
,, 162 *see* 157, 158
,, 163 *see* 158, 159
,, 164, *n.* 1 *see* 159. 160, *n.* 43
,, 165 *see* 160, 161
,, 166 *see* 161
,, 167, *n.* 1 *see* 161, 162, *n.* 44
,, 168, *n.* 1 *see* 162. 163, *n.* 45
,, 169, *n.* 1, 2 *see* 163, 164, *n.* 46, 47
,, 170 *see* 164, 165
,, 171 *n.* 1 *see* 165, 166, *n.* 48
,, 172 *n.* 1 *see* 166, 167, *n.* 49
,, 173 *see* 167, 168
,, 174 *see* 168, 169
,, 175, *n.* 1 *see* 169, 170, *n.* 50
,, 176, *n.* 1 *see* 170, 171, *n.* 51
,, 177, *n.* 1 *see* 171. 172, *n.* 52
,, 178, *n.* 1, 2 *see* 172. 173, *n.* 53. 54.
,, 179, *n.* 1 *see* 173, *n.* 55
,, 180, *n.* 1 *see* 174, *n.* 56
,, 181, *n.* 1 *see* 174, 175, *n.* 57
,, 182, *n.* 1 *see* 175, 176, *n.* 58
,, 183, *n.* 1 *see* 176, 177, *n.* 59
,, 184 *see* 177, 178
,, 185. *n.* 1, 2 *see* 178, 179, *n.* 60, 61
,, 186 *see* 179, 180
,, 187 *see* 180, 181
,, 188 *see* 181, 182
,, 189 *see* 182, 183
,, 190 *see* 183, 184
,, 191, *n.* 1 *see* 184, 185, *n.* 62
,, 192. *n.* 1 *see* 185,186, *n.* 63
,, 193. *n.* 1, 2 *see* 186, 187, *n.* 64. 65
,, 194. *n.* 1 *see* 187. 188. *n.* 66
,, 190. *n.* 1 *see* 188, 189. *n.* 67
,, 196. *n* 1 *see* 189, 190. *n.* 68
,, 197 *see* 190

Vol. II

For 190, *n.* 1, 2 *see* 177, 178, *n.* 198-99
„ 191, *n.* 1 *see* 178, 179, *n.* 200
„ 192, *n.* 1 *see* 179, 180, *n.* 201
„ 193, *n.* 1 *see* 180, 181, *n.* 202
„ 194, *n.* 1 *see* 181, *n.* 203
„ 195, *n.* 1 *see* 181, 182, *n.* 204
„ 196, *n.* 1, 2 *see* 182, 183, *n.* 205-6
„ 197, *n.* 1. 2 *see* 183, 184, *n.* 207-8
„ 198 *see* 184, 185
„ 199, *n.* 1, 2 *see* 185, 186, *n.* 209-10
„ 200, *n.* 1 *see* 186, 187, *n.* 211
„ 201 *see* 187, 188
„ 202, *n.* 1, 2 *see* 188, 189, *n.* 212-13
„ 203, *n.* 1, 2 *see* 189, 190, *n.* 214-15
„ 204, *n.* 1, 2 *see* 190, 191, *n.* 216-217
„ 205, *n.* 1, 2 *see* 191, 192, *n.* 218-19
„ 206 *see* 192, 193
„ 207, *n.* 1-4 *see* 193, 194, *n.* 220-23
„ 208 *see* 194, 195
„ 209 *see* 195, 196
„ 210, *n.* 1, 2 *see* 196, 197, *n.* 224-25
„ 211 *see* 197, 198
„ 212 *see* 198, 199
„ 213 *see* 199
„ 214, *n.* 1 *see* 200, *n.* 226
„ 215 *see* 200, 201
„ 216, *n.* 1 *see* 201, 202, *n.* 227
„ 217 *see* 202, 203
„ 218 *n.* 1 *see* 203, 204, *n.* 228
„ 219 *see* 204, 205
„ 220 *see* 205, 206
„ 221, *n.* 1, 2 *see* 206, 207, *n.* 229-30
„ 222, *n.* 1-3 *see* 207, 208, *n.* 231-33
„ 223 *see* 208, 209
„ 224, *n.* 1 *see* 209, 210, *n.* 234
„ 225, *n.* 1 *see* 210, 211, *n.* 235
„ 226, *n.* 1, 2 *see* 211, 212, *n.* 236-37
„ 227, *n.* 1, 2 *see* 212, 213, *n.* 238-39
„ 228, *n.* 1-3 *see* 213, 214, *n.* 240-42
„ 229, *n.* 1 *see* 214. 215, *n.* 243
„ 230, *n.* 1 *see* 215. 216, *n.* 244
„ 231, *n.* 1-3 *see* 216, 217, *n.* 245-47

For 232, *n.* 1, 2 *see* 217, 218, *n.* 248-49
„ 233, *n.* 1-3 *see* 218, 219, *n.* 250-52
„ 234, *n.* 1, 2 *see* 219, 220, *n.* 253-54
„ 235, *n.* 1 *see* 220, *n.* 255
„ 236, *n.* 1 *see* 220, 221, *n.* 256
„ 237, *n.* 1 *see* 221, 222, *n.* 257
„ 238, *n.* 1 *see* 222, 223, *n.* 258
„ 239, *n.* 1-3 *see* 223, 224, *n.* 259-61
„ 240, *n.* 1 *see* 224, 225, *n.* 262
„ 241, *n.* 1 *see* 225, 226, *n.* 263
„ 242 *see* 226, 227
„ 243, *n.* 1 *see* 227, 228, *n.* 264
„ 244, *n.* 1, 2 *see* 228, 229, *n.* 265-66
„ 245 *see* 229, 230
„ 246, *n.* 1 *see* 230, 231, *n.* 267
„ 247, *n.* 1 *see* 231, 232, *n.* 268
„ 248, *n.* 1 *see* 232, 233, *n.* 269
„ 249, *n.* 1 *see* 233, 234, *n.* 270
„ 250 *see* 234, 235
„ 251, *n.* 1, 2 *see* 235, 236, *n.* 271-72
„ 252, *n.* 1 *see* 236, 237, *n.* 273
„ 253, *n.* 1 *see* 237, 238, *n.* 274
„ 254, *n.* 1, 2 *see* 238, 239, *n.* 275-76
„ 255, *n.* 1 *see* 239, *n.* 277
„ 256, *n.* 1 *see* 239, 240, *n.* 278
„ 257, *n.* 1, 2 *see* 240, 241, *n.* 279-80
„ 258 *see* 241, 242
„ 259, *n.* 1 *see* 242, 243, *n.* 281
„ 260, *n.* 1, 2 *see* 243, 244, *n.* 282-83
„ 261, *n.* 1 *see* 244, 245, *n.* 284
„ 262, *n.* 1 *see* 245, 246, *n.* 285
„ 263, *n.* 1-4 *see* 246, 247, *n.* 286-89
„ 264 *see* 247, 248
„ 265, *n.* 1 *see* 248, 249, *n.* 290
„ 266, *n.* 1, 2 *see* 249, 250, *n.* 291-92
„ 267, *n.* 1 *see* 250, 251, *n.* 293
„ 268 *see* 251, 252
„ 269, *n.* 1, 2 *see* 252, 253, *n.* 294-95
„ 270, *n.* 1, 2 *see* 253, 254, *n.* 296-97
„ 271 *see* 254, 255
„ 272 *see* 255
„ 273 *see* 255, 256
„ 274, *n.* 1, 2 *see* 256, 257, *n.* 298-99

Vol. III.

For 281, *n*. 1-5 *see* 267, 268, *n*. 26-30
,, 282, *n*. 1 *see* 268, 269, *n*. 31
,, 283 *see* 269
,, 284, *n*. 1-3 *see* 269, 270, *n*. 32-34
,, 285, *n*. 1 *see* 210 , 271, 272, *n*. 35
,, 286 *see* 212
,, 287, *n*. 1 *see* 212, 273, *n*. 36
,, 288, *n*. 1, 2 *see* 273, 274, *n*. 37, 38
,, 289 *see* 274, 275
,, 290 *see* 275, 276
,, 291, *n*. 1 *see* 276, 277, *n*. 39
,, 292 *see* 111, 278
,, 293, *n*. 1 *see* 278, 279, *n*. 40
,, 294, *n*. 1 *see* 279, 280, *n*. 41
,, 295, *n*. 1 *see* 280, 281, *n*. 42
,, 296, *n*. 1 *see* 281, 282, *n*. 43
,, 297 *see* 282, 283
,, 298, *n*. 1 *see* 283, 284, *n*. 44
,, 299, *n*. 1 *see* 284, 285, *n*. 45
,, 300, *n*. 1, 2 *see* 285, 286, *n*. 46, 47
,, 301 *see* 286 287
,, 302, *n*. 1 *see* 287, 288, *n*. 48
,, 303, *n*. 1, 2 *see* 288, 289, *n*. 49, 50
,, 304, *n*. 1 *see* 289, *n*. 51
,, 305 *see* 289, 290
,, 306, *n*. 1 *see* 290, 291, *n*. 52
,, 307, *n*. 1, 2 *see* 291, 292, *n*. 53, 54
,, 308, *n*. 1 *see* 292, 293, *n*. 55
,, 309 *see* 293, 294
,, 310 *see* 294, 295
,, 311, *n*. 1 *see* 295, 296, *n*. 56
,, 312 *see* 296, 297
,, 313 *see* 297, 298
,, 314 *see* 298, 299
,, 315, *n*. 1 *see* 299, 300, *n*. 57
,, 316, *n*. 1 *see* 300, 301, *n*. 58
,, 317, *n*. 1 *see* 301, 302, *n*. 59
,, 318 *see* 302, 303
,, 319, *n*. 1 *see* 303, 304, *n*. 60
,, 320, *n*. 1 *see* 304. *n*. 61
,, 321. *n*. 1-3 *see* 304. 305. *n* 62-64
,, 322 *see* 305, 306
,, 323 *see* 306, 307
,, 324 *see* 306, 308
,, 325, *n*. 1-4 *see* 308, 309, *n*. 65-68
,, 326, *see*. 309, 310
,, 327 *see* 310, 311
,, 328 *see* 311, 312

For 329, *n* l, 2 *see* 312, 313, *n*. 69, 70
,, 330 *see* 313, 314
,, 331, *n*. 1-3 *see* 314, 315, *n*. 71-73
,, 332, *n*. 1, 2 *see* 315, 316, *n*. 74, 75
,, 333, *n*. 1-3 *see* 316, 317, *n*. 76-78
,, 334 *see* 317, 318
,, 335, *n*. 1 *see* 318, 319, *n*. 79
,, 336, *n*. 1, 2 *see* 319, 320, *n*. 80, 81
,, 337, *n*. 1 *see* 320, 321, *n*. 82
,, 338, *n*. 1-3 *see* 321, 322, *n*. 83-85
,, 339, *n*. 1 *see* 322, 323, *n*. 86
,, 340, *n*. 1,2 *see* 323, 324, *n*. 87, 88
,, 341, *n*. 1, 2 *see* 324, 325, *n*. 89, 90
,, 342, *n*. 1 *see* 325, 326, *n*. 91
,, 343, *n*. 1, 2 *see* 326, 327, *n*. 92, 93
,, 344, *n*. 1-3 *see* 327, *n*. 94-96
,, 345, *n*. 1 *see* ' 328, *n*. 97
,, 346, *n*. 1, 2 *see* 328, 329, *n*. 98, 99
,, 347, *n*. 1-5 *see* 329, 330, *n*. 100-04
,, 348, *n*. 1-6 *see* 330, 331, *n*. 105-10
,, 349 *see* 331, 332
,, 350 *see* 332, 333
,, 351, *n*. 1-6 *see* 333, 334, *n*. 111-16
,, 352 *see* 334, 335
,, 353, *n*. 1-3 *see* 335, 336, *n*. 117-19
,, 354, *n*. 1, 2 *see* 336, 337, *n*. 120-21
,, 355, *n*. 1 *see* 337, 338, *n*. 122
,, 356, *n*. 1, 2 *see* 338, 339, *n*. 123-24
,, 357, *n*. 1, 2 *see* 339 , 340, *n*. 125-26
,, 358 *see* 340, 341
,, 359 *see* 341, 342 343.
,, 360, *n*. 1 *see* 342, *n*. 127
,, 361 *see* 343, 344
,, 362 *see* 344, 345
,, 363 *see* 345, 346
,, 364 *n*. 1 *see* 346, 347, *n*. 128
,, 365 *see* 347, 348
,, 46 346, 348 347, *n*. 128
,, 366, *n*. 1 *see* 348, 349. *n*. 129
,, 367, *n*. 1-2 *see* 349, *n*. 130-31
,, 368, *n*. 1, 2 *see* 349, 350, 351, *n*. 132-33

For 467, *n.* 1 *see* 444, 445, *n.* 221
,, 468, *n.* 1, 2 *see* 445, 446, *n.* 222-23
,, 469, *n.* 1 *see* 446, 447, *n.* 224
,, 470 *see* 447
,, 471, *n.* 1 *see* 447, 448, *n.* 225
,, 472 *see* 448, 449
,, 473 *see* 449, 450
,, 474, *n.* 1 *see* 450, 451, *n.* 226
,, 475, *n.* 1 *see* 451, 452, *n.* 227
,, 476, *n.* 1 *see* 452, 453, *n.* 228
,, 477 *see* 453, 454
,, 478 *see* 454, 455
,, 479, *n.* 1 *see* 455, 456, *n.* 229
,, 480, *n.* 1-3 *see* 456, 457, *n.* 230-32
,, 481 *see* 457, 458
,, 482, *n.* 1 *see* 458, 459, *n.* 233
,, 483, *n.* 1, 2 *see* 459, 460, *n.* 234-35
,, 484, *n.* 1 *see* 460, 461, *n.* 236
,, 485, *n.* 1-3 *see* 461, *n.* 237-39
,, 486, *n.* 1, 2 *see* 462, *n.* 240-41
,, 487, *n.* 1 *see* 462, 463, *n.* 242
,, 488, *n.* 1 *see* 463, 464, *n.* 243
,, 489, *n.* 1 *see* 464, 465, *n.* 244
,, 490 *see* 465, 466
,, 491, *n.* 1, 2 *see* 466, 467, *n.* 245-46
For 492, *n.* 1, 2 *see* 467, 468, *n.* 247-48
,, 493, *n.* 1, 2 *see* 468, 469, *n.* 249-50
,, 494 *see* 469, 470
,, 495 *see* 470, 471
,, 496 *see* 471, 472
,, 497, *n.* 1, 2 *see* 472, 473, *n.* 251-52
,, 498, *n.* 1, 2 *see* 473, 474, *n.* 253-54
,, 499, *n.* 1 *see* 474, 475, *n.* ' 255
,, 500, *n.* 1, 2 *see* 475, 476, *n.* 256-57
,, 501, *n.* 1 *see* 476, 477, *n.* 258
,, 502, *n.* 1 *see* 477, 478, *n.* 259
,, 503, *n.* 1, 2 *see* 478, 479, *n.* 260-61
,, 504, *n.* 1-3 *see* 479, 480, *n.* 262-64
,, 505 *see* 480
,, 506, *n.* 1 *see* 480, 481, *n.* 265
,, 507, *n.* 1 *see* 481, 482, *n.* 266
,, 508, *n.* 1, 2 *see* 482, 483, *n.* 267-68
,, 509, *n.* 1, 2 *see* 483, 484, *n.* 269-70

Vol. IV.

For 1, *n.* 1 *see* 1, *n.* 1
,, 2 *see* 1, 2
,, 3 *see* 2, 3, 4
,, 4, *n.* 1 *see* 4, 5, *n.* 2
,, 5, *n.* I, 2 *see* 5, *n.* 3, 4
,, 6, *n.* 1 *see* 5, 6, *n.* 5
,, 7 *see* 6, 7
,, 8, *n.* 1 *see* 7, 8, *n.* 6
,, 9 *see* 8, 9
,, 10 *see* 9, 10
,, 11, *n.* 1 *see* 10, 11, *n.* 7
,, 12 *see* 11, 12
,, 13 *see* 12, 13
,, 14 *see* 13, 14
,, 15, *n.* 1 *see* 14, 15, *n.* 8
,, 16, *n.* 1 *see* 15, 16, *n.* 9
,, 17, *n.* 1, 2 *see* 16, 17, *n.* 10, 11
,, 18 *see* 17, 18
,, 19 *see* 18
,, 20, *n.* 1, 2 *see* 18, 19, *n.* 12, 13
,, 21, *n.* 1 *see* 19, 20, *n.* 14
,, 22, *n.* 1 *see* 20, 21, *n.* 15
,, 23 *see* 21, 22
For 24 *see* 22, 23
,, 25, *n.* 1 *see* 23, 24, *n.* 16
,, 26, *n.* 1, 2 *see* 24, 25, *n.* 17, 18
,, 27, *n.* 1, 2 *see* 25, 26, *n.* 19, 20
,, 28, *n.* 1 *see* 26, 27, *n.* 21
,, 29, *n.* 1, 2 *see* 27, 28, *n.* 22, 23
,, 30 *see* 28, 29
,, 31, *n.* 1 *see* 29, *n.* 24
,, 32 *see* 30
,, 33, *n.* 1, 2 *see* 30, 31, *n.* 25, 26
,, 34, *n.* 1 *see* 31, 32, *n.* 27
,, 35, *n.* 1 *see* 32, 33, *n.* 28
,, 36 *see* 33, 34
,, 37 *see* 34, 35
,, 38, *n.* 1 *see* 35, 36, *n.* 29
,, 39, *n.* 1 *see* 36, 37, *n.* 30
,, 40, *n.* 1 *see* 37, 38, *n.* 31
,, 41 *see* 38, 39
,, 42 *see* 39, 40
,, 43, *n.* 1, 2 *see* 40, 41, *n.* 32, 33

INDEX